T0396534

International Trade, Capital Flows and Economic Development

68

World Scientific
Studies in
International
Economics

International Trade, Capital Flows and Economic Development

Editors

Francisco L. Rivera-Batiz
Columbia University, USA

Luis A. Rivera-Batiz
University of Puerto Rico, USA

World Scientific

NEW JERSEY · LONDON · SINGAPORE · BEIJING · SHANGHAI · HONG KONG · TAIPEI · CHENNAI · TOKYO

Published by

World Scientific Publishing Co. Pte. Ltd.

5 Toh Tuck Link, Singapore 596224

USA office: 27 Warren Street, Suite 401-402, Hackensack, NJ 07601

UK office: 57 Shelton Street, Covent Garden, London WC2H 9HE

Library of Congress Cataloging-in-Publication Data
Names: Rivera-Batiz, Francisco L., author. | Rivera-Batiz, Luis, author.
Title: International trade, capital flows and economic development / Francisco L. Rivera-Batiz
    (Columbia University, USA), Luis A. Rivera-Batiz (University of Puerto Rico, USA).
Description: Hackensack, New Jersey : World Scientific Publishing Co. Pte. Ltd., [2018] |
    Series: World Scientific studies in international economics ; volume 68 |
    Includes bibliographical references.
Identifiers: LCCN 2018000482 | ISBN 9789813209381 (hardcover)
Subjects: LCSH: International trade. | Capital movements. | Investments, Foreign. |
    Income distribution--Social aspects.
Classification: LCC HF1379 .R578 2018 | DDC 330--dc23
LC record available at https://lccn.loc.gov/2018000482

British Library Cataloguing-in-Publication Data
A catalogue record for this book is available from the British Library.

For any available supplementary material, please visit
http://www.worldscientific.com/worldscibooks/10.1142/10431#t=suppl

Desk Editor: Jiang Yulin

Typeset by Stallion Press
Email: enquiries@stallionpress.com

Printed in Singapore

In memory of Luis

Contents

About the Authors

Luis A. Rivera-Batiz   Francisco L. Rivera-Batiz

Francisco L. Rivera-Batiz is a professor emeritus of economics and education at Columbia University where he remains teaching at the School of International and Public Affairs. At Columbia, he has had professorial appointments in the Economics Department, the School of International and Public Affairs and at Teachers College, and has been the Director of the Program in Economic Policy Management, the Latino Studies Program, and the Institute for Urban and Minority Education. Rivera-Batiz has also held teaching or research appointments at the University of Chicago, Harvard University, Indiana University at Bloomington, the University of Pennsylvania, Rutgers University in New Brunswick, and the University of Wisconsin at Madison.

Francisco has written and published extensively on topics relating to international economics, regional science, growth, labor migration and the economics of education. His articles have been published in leading academic journals such as *The American Economic Review*, *International Economic Review*, *Journal of Development Economics*, *The Quarterly Journal of Economics*, *The Journal of Population Economics*, and *Regional Science and Urban Economics*. His books include *The Political Economy of the East Asian Crisis and Its Aftermath: Tigers in Distress*, co-edited with Arvid Lukauskas (Edward Elgar, 2001), *Island Paradox: Puerto Rico in the 1990s*, co-authored with Carlos Santiago (Russell Sage Foundation, 1996), *International Finance and Open Economy Macroeconomics*, co-authored with Luis Rivera-Batiz (Prentice Hall, 1993), and *U.S. Immigration Policy Reform in the 1980s: A Preliminary Assessment*, co-edited with Selig L. Sechzer and Ira N. Gang (Praeger, 1991). He is currently Editor-in-Chief of the *World Scientific Encyclopedia of International Economics and Global Trade*.

Born in Puerto Rico, Francisco obtained his Bachelor's degree in Economics *with Distinction* from Cornell University in 1975 and a Ph.D. in Economics from the Massachusetts Institute of Technology in 1979.

Luis A. Rivera-Batiz was, at the time of his death, a professor and director of the Center for Business Research at the Graduate School of Business Administration at the University of Puerto Rico in Rio Piedras. He had previously held teaching positions at the University of California at San Diego, the University of Florida at Gainesville, McGill University in Montreal and the Universitat Pompeu Fabra in Barcelona. He was a research associate at the Centre for Research on Employment and Economic Fluctuations at the Université du Québec à Montréal, the Financial Research Centre at McGill University, the Center for Financial Economics Research at the Universitat Pompeu Fabra in Barcelona, and the Center for Economic Policy Research (CEPR) in London. He was a consultant at the Inter-American Development Bank and the International Monetary Fund.

Luis published extensively on topics relating to international trade and finance, economic growth, macroeconomics, and regional economics. His articles were published in prestigious academic journals such as *The American Economic Review, European Economic Review, Journal of Development Economics, The Quarterly Journal of Economics,* and *Regional Science and Urban Economics.* His books include *International Trade Analysis: Theory, Strategies, and Evidence,* co-authored with Maria-Angels Oliva (Oxford: Oxford University Press, 2003), and *International Finance and Open Economy Macroeconomics,* co-authored with Francisco L. Rivera-Batiz (Prentice Hall, 1993).

Born in Puerto Rico, Luis obtained his Bachelor's degree in Economics *Magna cum Laude* from the University of Puerto Rico in Rio Piedras, and an M.A. and Ph.D. in Economics from the University of Chicago.

Acknowledgements

This volume contains a selection of the research papers written by my brother, Luis, and I over a period of several decades. Luis died suddenly on April 14, 2006 at the early age of 56. The papers included here bear the fruit of a close partnership forged over many years of collaboration. In these acknowledgements I speak on Luis' behalf.

We want to thank first of all our professors in the fields of international trade, economic development, and macroeconomics at the University of Chicago, Cornell University and the Massachusetts Institute of Technology, from whom the papers published in this volume owe a great intellectual debt. These include Jagdish N. Bhagwati, Rudiger Dornbusch, Richard S. Eckaus, Jacob A. Frenkel, Milton Friedman, Arnold Harberger, Harry G. Johnson, Charles P. Kindleberger, Arthur B. Laffer, Robert E. Lucas, Jr., Rachel McCulloch, Paul A. Samuelson, Robert M. Solow, Lance Taylor and Jaroslav Vanek.

Some of the papers in this collection have had the benefit of collaboration with several colleagues. We particularly thank Paul M. Romer, who served as dissertation committee Chair, co-author and mentor for Luis, and Maria-Angels Oliva, with whom Luis had a long and productive relationship. We also wish to thank our other co-authors, Carlos M. Asilis, the late Luca Barbone and Danyang Xie for their invaluable intellectual contributions to this work. Luis' daughter, Nadia Rivera-Nieves, was an inspiration for the completion of this volume and gracefully gave her permission to use Luis' publications. We are very grateful to Melisa Morales for her efficient research assistance, without whom this project would have never been completed.

We would finally like to express our appreciation to the original publishers of the following articles for their permission to reprint them.

Chapter 1. Economic Integration and Endogenous Growth (co-authored by Luis A. Rivera-Batiz and Paul M. Romer) was originally published in *The Quarterly Journal of Economics*, Vol. 106, No. 2, May 1991, 531–555; and Economic Integration and Endogenous Growth: An Addendum (co-authored by Luis A. Rivera-Batiz and Paul M. Romer) was originally published in *The Quarterly Journal of Economics*, Vol. 109, No. 1. February 1994, 307–308.

Chapter 2. International Trade with Endogenous Technological Change (co-authored by Luis A. Rivera-Batiz and Paul M. Romer) was originally published in *European Economic Review*, Vol. 35, No. 4, May 1991, 971–1004.

Chapter 3. GATT, Trade and Growth (co-authored by Luis A. Rivera-Batiz and Danyang Xie) was originally published in *American Economic Review*, Vol. 82, No. 2, May 1992, 422–427.

Chapter 4. Integration among Unequals (co-authored by Luis A. Rivera-Batiz and Danyang Xie) was originally published in *Regional Science and Urban Economics*, Vol. 23, No. 3, July 1993, 337–354.

Chapter 5. The Economics of Technological Progress and Endogenous Growth in Open Economies (authored by Francisco L. Rivera-Batiz) was originally published in Georg Koopmann and Hans-Eckart Scharrer, eds., *The Economics of High Technology Competition and Cooperation in Global Markets*, Nomos Verlagsgesellschaft, Baden-Baden, Germany, 1996, 31–62.

Chapter 6. Increasing Returns, Monopolistic Competition, and Agglomeration Economies in Consumption and Production (authored by Francisco L. Rivera-Batiz) was originally published in *Regional Science and Urban Economics*, Vol. 18, No. 1, February 1988, 125–153.

Chapter 7. Geography, Trade Patterns, and Economic Policy (co-authored by Carlos M. Asilis and Luis A. Rivera-Batiz) was originally published in *Working Paper No. WP/94/16*, International Monetary Fund, Washington D.C., February 1994.

Chapter 8. Democracy, Governance, and Economic Growth: Theory and Evidence (authored by Francisco L. Rivera-Batiz) was originally published in *Review of Development Economics*, Vol. 6, No. 2, June 2002, 225–247.

Chapter 9. Political Institutions, Capital Flows, and Developing Country Growth: An Empirical Investigation (co-authored by Maria-Angels Oliva and Luis A. Rivera-Batiz), *Review of Development Economics*, Vol. 6, No. 2, June 2002, 248–262.

Chapter 10. International Financial Liberalization, Corruption, and Economic Growth (authored by Francisco L. Rivera-Batiz) was originally published in *Review of International Economics*, Vol. 9, No. 4, November 2001, 727–737.

Chapter 11. The East Asian Crisis and the Anatomy of Emerging Market Disease (authored by Francisco L. Rivera-Batiz) was originally published in Arvid J. Lukauskas and Francisco L. Rivera-Batiz, eds., *The Political Economy of the East Asian Crisis: Tigers in Distress*, Edward Elgar Publishers, Cheltenham, U.K., 2001, 31–73.

Chapter 12. Foreign Ownership, Non-Traded Goods and the Effects of Terms of Trade Changes on National Welfare (authored by Francisco L. Rivera-Batiz) was originally published in *Economics Letters*, Vol. 20, No. 4, July 1986, 367–371.

Chapter 13. Foreign Capital and the Contractionary Impact of Currency Devaluation, with an Application to Jamaica (co-authored by Luca Barbone and Francisco L. Rivera-Batiz) was originally published in *Journal of Development Economics*, Vol. 26, No. 1, June 1987, 1–15.

Chapter 14. The Effects of Direct Foreign Investment in the Presence of Increasing Returns due to Specialization (co-authored by Francisco L. Rivera-Batiz and Luis A. Rivera-Batiz) was originally published in

Journal of Development Economics, Vol. 34, No. 1, November 1990, 287–307.

Chapter 15. Europe 1992, and the Liberalization of Direct Investment Flows: Services versus Manufacturing (co-authored by Francisco L. Rivera-Batiz and Luis A. Rivera-Batiz) was originally published in *International Economic Journal*, Vol. 6, No. 1, Spring 1992, 45–57.

Francisco L. Rivera-Batiz

New York City

February 2018

List of Tables

List of Figures

Introduction

The rapid growth of international trade and capital flows in the last 30 years has been at the core of world economic affairs. Indeed, the expansion of trade has been unique by historical standards. The sum of the absolute value of exports and imports of goods and services as a percentage of Gross Domestic Product (GDP), a simple but popular index of trade, has grown from 36 percent in 1986 to 56 percent in 2016 for the world. In some countries, the increase has been even more dramatic. In China, for instance, the index grew from 12 percent to 37 percent between 1986 and 2016 and for Thailand, the rise has been from 54 to 123 percent.

Capital flows have also risen in the last few decades. Net foreign direct investment in developing countries, in particular, grew from $182 billion in 2000 to $543 billion in 2015, measured in constant 2015 U.S. dollars. But although the trend in the growth of capital flows has been positive, they also have become more volatile. For example, in 1997 the net flow of capital to developing countries was equal to $453 billion but this dropped to $229 billion by 2002, rising to $1,350 in 2007, declining to $743 billion in 2009, recovering to $1,466 billion in 2013, and then contracting sharply to $379 billion in 2015, with all measured in constant 2015 U.S. dollars.

This book contains a collection of articles examining the effects of increased international trade and capital flows on global economic affairs. It is a timely topic, as — at the time of writing — there is widespread skepticism and even resentment about the effects of globalization, as reflected in the divorce of the United Kingdom from the European Union (BREXIT), the election of Donald Trump in the United States (on a platform that proposed border taxes and renegotiating free trade treaties), and growing restrictions on capital flows in a number of countries. What are the mechanisms through which international trade and capital flows affect an economy? What are the costs and benefits of economic integration and the liberalization of trade and investment flows? These are some of the questions that the papers in this volume seek to answer. As will be seen, the answers are nuanced. Both the theory and evidence indicate that the elimination of restrictions on trade and investment can potentially have a positive and possibly transformative effect on the economic welfare and growth of nations, but the impacts can be complex and in the absence of the appropriate environment — policy and otherwise — they can be negative and sometimes catastrophic.

Part 1: International Trade, Technological Change and Economic Growth

Both the Ricardian and the more modern Hecksher–Ohlin–Vanek approaches to international trade theory suggest that the opening of an economy to world trade provides an overall gain in the economic welfare of the liberalizing country. The greater specialization of the economy — according to its comparative advantage — makes it relatively more productive, resulting in a real income gain. This is, however, only a short-run gain. It starts after the trade liberalization occurs and it gradually ends as the economy adjusts to the incentives provided by integration into the world trading system. There are no long-run growth effects of trade in these classical and neoclassical frameworks.

Despite the theoretical lagoon, there is substantial evidence showing that — under the appropriate conditions — trade can be a significant stimulant for growth. The empirical research by Jeffrey Sachs, Andrew Warner, Sebastian Edwards, Ann Harrison, Gordon Hanson, David Dollar, Aart Kraay, Romain Wacziarg and Karen Horn, among others, use both cross-sectional and panel data to show that (1) countries that are more open to trade tend to have higher rates of economic growth, holding other things constant, and (2) economic growth after the period of trade liberalization is on average substantially higher than that prevailing before the liberalization.

The chapters in this part of the volume examine the mechanisms through which the economic integration of a country into world markets can influence long-run economic growth. They form part of a literature that was the first in adopting models of increasing returns to scale, input specialization, and imperfect competition to study the dynamic effects of increased trade.

Chapters 1 and 2 present theoretical models showing the mechanisms through which economic integration and trade liberalization can accelerate economic growth. These chapters extend the scope of traditional theory by adding how trade in ideas — in addition to trade in goods — affects long-run growth. In a world of ever close electronic and telecommunications links, in which knowledge is increasingly transmitted worldwide, this analysis of the gains from such trade is especially relevant.

Chapter 1 analyzes the effects of integration in the case of economies or regions that have identical demand and supply characteristics. This is precisely the case for which traditional trade theory suggests trade should have very little impact, if any: in countries or regions that are identical to each other in terms of factor endowments and technology, there is no relative comparative advantage for countries to specialize on and be able to benefit from liberalization.

In the approach followed by Chapter 1, based on Paul Romer's theory of endogenous technological change, innovation — in the form of new capital goods — is generated through new knowledge and ideas that are produced by the economy's research and development sector. In this environment, when a closed economy integrates to others, the increased flow of goods and ideas may provide a stimulus to domestic and foreign research and development (R&D) sectors, thus accelerating innovation and economic growth. The paper presents different models of the economy's innovation production function and how they affect the analysis of how integration affects growth. Without integration, isolated R&D sectors may in fact reproduce the efforts in other countries, at great expense due to the fixed costs involved in these activities. Under integration this redundancy can be eliminated, making both the domestic and foreign technological change sectors more efficient, leading to greater global growth.

In a comment on the economic integration and endogenous growth models presented in Chapter 1, Michael B. Devereux and Beverly J. Lapham show that the positive impact of trade is not just related to the expansion of world knowledge brought about by trade in ideas but also to the expansion of trade in goods. As the addendum to Chapter 1 describes, Devereux and Lapham consider two economies that have different initial stocks of knowledge. In this case, trade produces worldwide growth gains associated with the greater country specialization of the two countries in producing goods or ideas.

Chapter 2 extends the analysis in Chapter 1 by providing a more comprehensive framework to examine the consequences of international trade in a dynamic context. In contrast to the results obtained in Chapter 1, the discussion in this chapter shows that the impact of trade on long-run growth may be ambiguous. The chapter first identifies two positive effects of trade, which are labeled the integration and redundancy effects, both of which unambiguously increase worldwide growth rates. The integration effect is linked to the increasing returns allowed by the larger market obtained through economic integration. The redundancy effect is linked to the fixed costs involved in innovation. Closed/isolated economies double those fixed costs when they independently seek to create new designs that may have already been created abroad. With trade liberalization, the fixed costs only need to be incurred once, as existing ideas — whether embedded in designs or products — are freely imported from abroad.

But a third effect of trade is identified in this chapter, the allocation effect, which can either increase or decrease the rate of growth. This third effect is based on the interplay between two sectors of the economy: the research and development sector that produces the new ideas that make continued growth possible, and the manufacturing sector that makes use of these ideas and produces capital and consumption goods using inputs that include physical capital, human capital, and labor. The allocation effect of trade emerges because of the various possible inter-sectoral changes generated by trade in economies that have disparate factor endowments. When these economies liberalize, each country reallocates resources toward the sector in which it has a comparative advantage, but if this reallocation reduces the size of the research and development sector it will cause a drop in innovation efforts and reduce economic growth. As emphasized by the classical and neoclassical theories of trade, these allocation effects will be larger when the differences in the endowments or technologies of the trading partners are more substantial.

The relative significance of the allocation, integration and redundancy effects determines whether growth rises or declines with increased trade. In the model presented in Chapter 1, the integration and redundancy effects of trade were emphasized and trade therefore unambiguously raised long-run growth. But Chapter 2 develops models where the allocation effects can overwhelm the integration and allocation effects. Growth can therefore slow down when trade restrictions are eliminated.

Chapter 3 examines the effects of trade liberalization obtained through the General Agreement on Tariffs and Trade (GATT). The GATT was the major force behind the multilateral trade liberalization efforts of the world since 1947. It functioned through rounds of multilateral negotiations whose purpose was to reduce or eliminate tariffs, quotas and other barriers to trade among participating nations. The GATT ended with the Uruguay Round of negotiations, which gave rise to the creation of the World Trade Organization in 1995.

Chapter 3 examines how the trade liberalization activities of the GATT–WTO can enable greater economic growth worldwide. As in the previous two chapters, Chapter 3 adopts an endogenous technological change framework. But in contrast to Chapters 1 and 2, the model used in this chapter examines the effects of trade liberalization among countries that are asymmetric, that is, that have different factor endowments and, more specifically, different supplies of human capital. Liberalization can involve trade in goods or trade in ideas.

The chapter looks first at the impact of trade in goods but without any trade in ideas. With asymmetric countries, the chapter shows that integration in this case generates an allocation effect that shifts resources toward manufacturing in the high-human-capital country and reduces its growth rate compared with autarky. In other words, integration in goods (without knowledge diffusion) restricts growth in the high-growth regions and speeds it up in the low-growth regions.

The case of no diffusion of technology just described can be interpreted as a situation in which patents are unenforceable outside a country's borders. As local inventors protect their ideas through secrecy, they avoid their international diffusion. The opposite situation, with full diffusion of technology across borders, can occur if there is an internationally enforced patent system. This can emerge through a GATT–WTO-type multilateral agreement. Patents then allow inventors to receive a profit and enhances the incentives for the international transmission of knowledge. The multilateral agreement promotes innovation and leads to faster worldwide growth.

Suppose now that full diffusion of technology has been achieved. What would be the growth effects of trade liberalization in goods, such as in the form of the reciprocal, multilateral reductions in tariffs that GATT initiated? For the case of two asymmetric countries, the relation between tariff rates and economic growth is not monotonic. There is a critical rate τ^* below which lower tariffs lead to faster growth but above which increases in tariffs speed up growth. The chapter shows that this critical rate τ^* increases with the number of countries engaging in the reciprocal reduction of trade restrictions. This suggests that multilateral negotiations for reductions in trade barriers are more likely to speed up growth than are bilateral or regional agreements.

Chapter 4 continues the analysis of the effects of economic integration but provides greater detail about the policies that accompany the trade liberalization. When nations get together to form larger economic units, they can seek to integrate their goods and services markets, capital flows, labor migration and/or the flow of technology. For instance, through their Europe 1992 initiative, the European Union started a process of closer integration toward a single internal market, seeking to establish free trade in goods and capital, and allowing free migration. On the other hand, the North American Free Trade Agreement (NAFTA) that came into force in 1994 sought to integrate goods and capital markets, but not the labor markets. Integration can also seek to cover the diffusion of technology and knowledge, through policies dealing with patents and intellectual property.

Chapter 4 adopts a two-country model that considers two distinct situations. In one case, two countries that are already hubs of innovation but of unequal size are integrated. The other case involves highly asymmetric countries in the sense that one of the countries does not initially count with the human–capital endowments needed to support a research sector. The first case can be interpreted as involving integration between industrialized, innovating countries, the second refers to North–South integration initiatives.

When two innovating countries integrate, the analysis in this chapter shows that integration through trade in goods alone results in a reduced growth rate for the initially faster-growing country and an increased growth rate for the slower-growing nation. But this result is shown to be affected by the extent to which the economic liberalization allows trade in knowledge. Once the door is opened for diffusion of technology, integration is growth-enhancing for both innovating countries. The growth effects of trade become more complex when one of the countries is not innovating under pre-integration conditions. The conclusions vary depending on whether the liberalization allows free trade in knowledge in addition to trade in goods, and whether free labor migration is part of the integration initiative. Despite the diversity of outcomes under the various types of liberalization, the chapter provides some experimental simulations showing that integration can have substantially positive growth effects.

Chapter 5 analyzes additional mechanisms through which trade can impact technological change. Firstly, the chapter develops a theoretical model of trade where increased competition between domestic and foreign produces induces firms to invest more in research and development, which stimulates innovation and economic growth. This is an idea that the economist Michael E. Porter at the Harvard Business School has studied through a variety of case studies. In his book, *The Competitive Advantage of Nations*, he concludes: "Competitive advantage emerges from pressure, challenge and adversity, rarely from an easy life. Pressure and adversity are powerful motivators for change and innovation... Complacency and an inward focus often explain why nations lose competitive advantage. Lack of pressure and challenge means that firms fail to look constantly for and interpret new buyer needs, new technologies, and new processes... Protection, in its various forms, insulates domestic firms from the pressure of international competition."

Chapter 5 incorporates this idea in a theoretical framework where two identical economies producing a variety of products in a market characterized by monopolistic competition and increasing returns symmetrically open up their markets to international trade. This approach was first developed by Paul Krugman in his analysis of intra-industry trade, but his paper did not consider the pro-competitive effect modeled in this chapter. Since both countries have the same number and type of consumers, equal factor endowments and identical technology, when the two economies trade, intra-industry trade will emerge, doubling the number of competitors domestic firms face. Chapter 5 focuses on the fact that, with a greater set of competitors in the now global market, there is more rivalry and this is reflected in a reduced price markup above marginal cost as well as with an incentive for each firm to increase its research and development expenditures, which raises technological change and growth worldwide.

Secondly, Chapter 5 recognizes that although international trade can greatly increase the local stock of information available in an economy, the extent to which such knowledge can be gainfully utilized and steered into productive new inventions depends on a variety of supporting factors. In previous chapters, the importance of the economy's endowments of human capital have been emphasized. Chapter 5 focuses instead on the role played by the country's national innovation system. A national system of innovation is the network of institutions that support the initiation, modification and diffusion of new technologies. More specifically, a national innovation system includes the wide array of specialized services that support innovation, from the firms that help design and engineer prototypes of new products to the entrepreneurs that market and distribute the finished product. The state of development of a country's national innovation system is essential in making technological change an engine of growth. If the sector is not well-developed, even though new knowledge may be flowing into the economy at a fast rate, the output of new products will lag because of the inability of the local innovators to take advantage of the new ideas and design new products and capital goods based on them. Within this context, the effects of trade on growth can be severely limited if the national innovation system is not well-developed and cannot utilize effectively the new information and knowledge in the production of new ideas.

Part 2: Trade, Increasing Returns and Economic Geography

Throughout history, urban areas — from the ancient city states of Venice and Genoa to the modern urban hubs in Hong Kong and New York City — have been at the center of international trade and growth. The papers in this section of the volume seek to explain the forces determining the geographical distribution of economic activity and the gains obtained by urban agglomeration. They form part of a set of papers that were the first to adopt models of increasing returns to scale, imperfect competition and product diversity in explaining regional and urban economics. This new economic geography literature includes the work of Masahisa Fujita, Vernon Henderson, and Paul Krugman, among others.

Chapter 6 provides an integrated view of two sets of forces providing economic advantages to cities: agglomeration economies in production and consumption. Agglomeration economies in production involve forces that make an increased agglomeration of firms more productive. The chapter focuses specifically on the role played by business or producer services — from accounting and tax law professionals to design and advertising firms — in allowing final goods firms to be more productive. The theoretical model conceptualizes the producer services sector as supplying an array of specialized, differentiated intermediate inputs within a market structure of Chamberlinian monopolistic competition. As cities grow, two forces enter into play. On the one hand, the conventional effect of an increase in the labor force is to reduce the city's wage rate due to diminishing returns. However, an increase in the size of the urban population augments the size of the industrial sector and it shifts upwards the demand for producer services. The latter leads to an expansion in the variety of such services. With a wider diversity of service firms available, the industrial sector can obtain more specialized services and its productivity is therefore enhanced. This productivity increase is then embodied into higher wage rates. The net impact of an increased population on the equilibrium wage rate in the city is related to the relative importance of the "diminishing returns" and the "increased productivity or linkage externality" effects just discussed.

Chapter 6 also analyzes the nature of urban agglomeration economies in consumption, which involves mechanisms through which the increased agglomeration of consumers in cities raises individual economic welfare or utility. The chapter recognizes that one of the key advantages of larger urban areas to consumers is the wider array of specialized consumer services — from restaurants and theatres to doctors and hair stylists — that are not found elsewhere and that make the standard of living of urbanites higher. Modeling consumer services within a market structure of monopolistic competition, the model in this chapter utilizes a Dixit–Stiglitz utility function in which consumers assign value to product diversity. As people migrate to urban areas, two forces enter into play. On the one hand, the conventional effect of an increase in urban populations is to raise the cost of housing, which reduces the real income of urbanites. However, a growing urban population also augments the demand for consumer services, resulting in an increased diversity of those services. The latter leads to an increase in the utility consumers derive from urban areas. The net impact of increased city population on the utility derived by urban residents is related to the relative importance of the "increased cost of housing" and the "increased local product diversity" effects just discussed. Chapter 6 shows how the various agglomeration economies, combined with the effects of congestion and diminishing returns, work in determining equilibrium city size.

Chapter 7 constructs a theory of interregional location and trade. In this framework, location is treated as an endogenous variable by firms, consumers and perfectly mobile workers. The model determines the potential range of locations of industrial centers in a country and the associated land and labor use patterns. Space plays a central role in location and trading decisions through transportation costs, access to markets, and distance from industrial centers that are assumed to generate pollution as an agglomeration of firms occurs. Interregional trade patterns emerge by the interaction between a manufacturing region that imports agricultural goods and an agricultural region that imports manufactured goods from the industrial center.

The theory developed in Chapter 7 goes beyond traditional trade theory — even the ones discussed in earlier chapters — because in this framework factor endowments are endogenous. Both trade and the location of factors of production are determined within a general equilibrium model that focuses instead on how the distribution of land, transportation costs and negative agglomeration externalities (such as pollution) lead to various possible outcomes of regional production, migration and trade. It provides a discussion of how the complex interaction of agglomeration economies and diseconomies can lead to the uneven regional distribution of economic activity.

The analysis in the chapter integrates previous research obtained by so-called gravity models of trade by showing the mechanisms though which increased distance may affect trade. Although the previous literature on gravity models have focused on the negative impact of distance on trade because of transportation costs, Chapter 7 suggests that the relationship is more complex and there are cases where distance may increase trade. More specifically, in cases in which population concentrates far from the center, trade will increase with distance. The point is not taken to imply that by itself higher transportation costs tend to be beneficial to trade. But any detrimental role of greater distance on trade from an industrial center because of higher transportation costs can be offset by other factors, such as the costs of congestion and environmental pollution, which disperse production away from agglomerated centers and in favor of decentralized production centers, or land productivity differentials that may favor distant agricultural production and export regions.

Chapter 7 also shows how technological change — and therefore economic growth — is affected by changes in transportation costs. Improvements in transportation efficiency emerge as a force in innovation that has not been examined in the literature. Because the gains from creating new goods are related to market size, lower transportation costs tend to expand markets and provide incentives for innovation. This effect helps to explain how innovation feeds upon itself and how historical declines in transport costs have led to a second round of related innovation.

Part 3: Public Sector Governance, Capital Flows and Economic Growth

A country's public sector institutions determine and oversee the framework within which the economy functions. As such, the quality of a country's public sector governance is bound to be essential in determining the level and growth of GDP. The chapters in this part of the volume examine various aspects of how public sector governance affects economic growth. They form part of a literature that first analyzed — both at the theory level and through empirical evidence — the role played by the public sector in influencing a country's growth. It includes the work of Daron Acemoglu, Robert Barro, James Robinson, and Dani Rodrik, among others.

Chapter 8 provides theory and evidence on one of the most controversial questions in the field of economic development: Is democracy associated with greater economic growth? Do increased political and civil rights lead to improved standards of living, compared with more authoritarian regimes? The debate on this issue has raged for centuries and continues to the present. On the one hand, a number of authors have noted that in polarized political systems, democratic institutions may lead to policy gridlock, preventing the major decisions that are required in the development process. Among those voicing this view is the late prime minister of Singapore, Lee Kuan Yew, who argued that Singaporean growth — one of the most remarkable over the last 40 years — would not have occurred without the stringent restrictions on political and civil rights under his regime. Some have also noted the successful experience of China in undertaking market reforms. At the same time, others — such as the economist Daron Acemoglu and the historian James Robinson — have argued that the rent-extraction policies generally adopted by authoritarian regimes on its population are ultimately a powerful inhibitor of long-run growth.

Chapter 8 provides a theoretical and empirical analysis of how democracy affects long-run growth. The chapter shows that the connections are more complex than they look at a first glance. Its conclusion is that democracy can effectively stimulate economic growth but only if it improves the quality of governance of the public sector in a country. In order to establish the links between improved governance and growth, the chapter carries out both theoretical and empirical analysis. The theoretical model develops a general-equilibrium, endogenous growth model showing how improvements in the quality of the public sector institutions in a country — such as a reduction in corruption — can raise growth. In this model, higher quality of a country's governance institutions makes domestic innovative activity more profitable, inducing greater technological change and growth.

The chapter then examines the empirical connection between quality of governance and economic growth using a multivariate linear regression analysis of the determinants of average growth in real GDP per capita between 1960 and 1990 in a cross-section of 59 countries. To measure the quality of governance, the chapter utilizes an index constructed by Robert Hall and Charles Jones in 1999 in which the quality of government institutions is based on a comprehensive evaluation of each country's government institutions regarding: (1) law and order, (2) bureaucratic quality, (3) corruption, (4) risk of expropriation, (5) government repudiation of contracts, and (6) the degree of openness of the economy to international trade. The empirical analysis of the connection between improved quality of public sector governance, as measured, and growth of GDP per capita shows a positive and statistically significant coefficient at conventional levels of confidence, holding equal other determinants of growth.

But is democracy associated with greater economic growth? The empirical work in Chapter 8 adds democracy as one of the variables explaining growth. To measure the strength of democratic institutions the chapter utilizes the Freedom House index of political rights. The empirical work in Chapter 8 shows that democracy is a statistically significant factor affecting total factor productivity and growth of GDP per capita between 1960 and 1990, but that the relationship is mediated by the quality of governance. Democracy influences growth mainly through its strong positive effects on the quality of governance. But once a measure of the quality of governance in a country is introduced into the growth regression equations, democracy ceases to be a statistically significant influence on growth. It suggests that if a country has an authoritarian regime which also has high-quality public sector governance, it will grow essentially as fast as the democratic country with the same quality of governance.

Of course, the question remains: do democracies promote improved public sector governance? The empirical work in Chapter 8 does show that, in the long run, democracies have a strong, positive and statistically significant association with improved quality of governance. One would expect this to be the case. After all, by definition, democracies allow populations to peacefully and regularly oust inept, inefficient, and corrupt government administrations, while allowing people to keep more efficient, successful regimes, thus tending to make the quality of governance on average higher in the long run. Authoritarian regimes may randomly provide high-quality governance, but if they do not, they can be changed only by force, which may take years or decades longer than under democratic institutions.

Chapter 9 carries out a multivariate empirical analysis of the effects of the degree of democratic development, the rule of law, and alternative forms of capital flows on the growth of real GDP per capita between 1970 and 1994 in a cross-section of developing countries. In terms of capital flows, the empirical work carried out in this chapter shows that, holding other things constant, foreign direct investment (FDI) has a positive, strong and statistically significant connection to economic growth. In fact, the estimated growth effect of FDI is found to be several times higher than the growth effect of domestic fixed investment. By contrast, the empirical analysis does not find support for the notion that non-FDI capital flows exert significant positive growth effects or improve the explanatory power of growth regressions. This general finding is robust to different econometric methods and applies to a large sample of developing countries as well as to various subsamples including those encompassing African and Latin American countries. The research also finds that a greater degree of democracy and an improved rule of law can exert indirect growth effects through other variables. For instance, the analysis offers evidence that the rule of law influences growth indirectly by encouraging FDI.

The evidence provided in Chapter 9 is consistent with the view that developing countries might do well to promote FDI. The findings are also useful for the assessment of the controversy concerning the growth consequences of capital flows and capital account liberalization. On one side, the major international institutions — such as the International Monetary Fund and the World Bank — have supported the view that capital account liberalization has strong positive growth effects. On the other side, economists such as Dani Rodrik, Jeffrey Sachs and Joseph Stiglitz, among others, claim that the growth effects of capital flows and their liberalization are not necessarily positive and could even be negative. The empirical evidence in this chapter shows that the strength of the growth effects of capital flows depends on the type of flow considered: FDI appears to have strong positive effects but no such evidence emerges for non-FDI capital flows.

The globalization of capital markets has led to a substantial increase in the trend of capital flowing into emerging markets. But many developing nations also face substantial capital outflows. According to the estimates of Global Financial Integrity, capital flight from developing countries grew from US$769 billion in 2004 to over US$1,000 billion in 2013. In sub-Saharan Africa, the estimates suggest that the cumulative outflows of capital have made the region a net creditor to the rest of the world. A significant share of the capital outflows represents undocumented transactions flowing through offshore financial centers.

Chapter 10 presents a theoretical framework showing how capital flight may be stimulated by the liberalization of a developing country's international financial transactions. It then studies the effects of the capital outflows on the long-run growth of the economy. A general-equilibrium, endogenous growth model is constructed in which corruption forms a part of the country's economic environment. Corruption is assumed to act as a tax on the firms and entrepreneurs innovating, designing, and producing new goods in the economy. This reduces the economy's rate of technological change and lowers the domestic rate of return to capital.

In this context, the chapter shows that the impact of international financial liberalization on long-run growth can be either positive or negative. A drop in growth is obtained when the level of corruption is high enough to cause domestic rates of return to capital before liberalization to drop below those in the rest of the world. Opening the capital account in this case generates capital flight, which causes the economy's innovation sector to contract, reducing the rate of technological change and causing output growth to decline. On the other hand, if the level of corruption in the economy is sufficiently low, the capital account liberalization will act to boost the country's technological change and growth by stimulating capital inflows.

Capital flight has induced policymakers in many poor countries to introduce capital and exchange controls, to block the outflows that would result if liberalization were to occur. Chapter 10 shows, however, that this is not the first-best policy. Insofar as corruption is behind the relatively low domestic rates of return to capital, the first-best policy in this context is to intervene to reduce or eliminate corruption. Indeed, improved governance would result in a burst of growth since it would allow domestic entrepreneurs and innovators to be unbound from the chattels imposed by a corrupt regime, even in a closed economy. As bribe requests are eliminated or controlled, the returns to research and development will boom, fostering technological change. But, even more importantly, a drop in corruption allows an opening of the capital account to further benefit the domestic economy. With a drop in corruption, the developing economy's natural shortage of capital will reveal itself in high rates of return to capital, which would result in capital inflows caused by international financial liberalization. On the other hand, introducing capital account liberalization without the appropriate domestic policies in place to improve governance and control corruption may result in a magnification of domestic distortions and a decline of economic growth.

In 1997, after what had been a decade of remarkable growth, the economies of Thailand, the Philippines, Malaysia, Indonesia and South Korea all came to a sudden and grinding halt, suffering a severe crisis from which it took years to recover. What became known as the East Asian crisis was not foreseen by most observers. On the contrary, these countries had been characterized in previous years as "miracle economies" and their economic policies as exemplary. What went wrong in East Asia? What reversed the situation of countries that, just a few months earlier, had been hailed as examples of economic stability and as showcases of the way economic policies should be handled?

Chapter 11 examines the causes and consequences of the East Asian crisis. Previous research considered the role of a wide array of factors that helped precipitate the debacle, including currency overvaluation, moral hazard and excessive risk-taking among financial institutions, the growth of short-term foreign-currency debt, domestic bank fragility, speculative lending bubbles, financial panic, herd effects and contagion. Although these forces are important, this chapter argues that a focus on them has missed the fundamental, underlying economic phenomenon behind the crisis. Chapter 11 insists that the crisis is a reflection of a deeper problem facing emerging markets in general, not just East Asia. The fact is that the capital inflows that cause an investment and economic boom in these countries, and puts them in the category of emerging markets, also plants the seeds of an eventual slowdown, or a bust, that may reverse the economic progress.

Chapter 11 refers to this economic phenomenon as "emerging market disease". The term disease is utilized because the forces involved are not short term in nature but are rather long term and endemic to the development strategy followed in the countries involved. In essence, emerging markets seek to achieve high rates of economic growth through the rapid and substantial expansion of domestic investment by means of increased foreign capital flows linked to a major liberalization of international financial transactions. The flood of capital inflows associated with this strategy allows the economies to boom, providing an aura of everlasting prosperity. However, the seeds of a future slowdown or bust are being planted at the same time, through the impact of the capital influx on a set of linked economic variables. Capital inflows exert upward pressure on the value of the domestic currency and may also ignite inflation. As a result, a persistent real currency appreciation develops and eventually slows down export growth, increases imports and worsens the current account balance. This has serious consequences. A sluggish export sector will reduce output growth and undermine the confidence of investors on the future of the economy. Furthermore, a widening current account balance deficit, even if initially financed enthusiastically by foreign capital, leads to an accumulation of external debt that, at some point, raises the risk of default, whether in the public or private sector. The sustained real appreciation of the currency also means that expectations of devaluation will inevitably materialize, sooner or later. All of these developments eventually precipitate a withdrawal of funds from the country and a credit crunch that plunges the economy into recession. If the domestic banking system is fragile, and if the capital flight is aggravated by policymakers who tenaciously refuse to devaluate, the result is a crisis.

The economic forces behind emerging market disease have been known for a long time. In Latin America, the "capital inflows problem" was studied by Carlos Diaz-Alejandro and Rudiger Dornbusch. The best-known cases of the disease in this region had been in Chile (1978–82) and Mexico (1980–84 and 1990–95), but there were other examples in Argentina, Brazil and Uruguay. Some of the symptoms of emerging market disease are akin to what has been called "Dutch disease" The latter describes the case of countries where a boom based on the exploitation of natural resources leads to a disastrous de-industrialization in the rest of the economy. Dutch disease erupts as a repercussion of the massive capital that flows into an economy stimulated by the discovery and exploitation of natural resources. These inflows increase the value of domestic currency, hurting the international competitiveness of local exports and shrinking the industrial base of the economy. Countries that were expected to grow rapidly due to their natural wealth end up instead with a sluggish expansion. In emerging market disease, the influx of capital is not necessarily linked to the exploitation of natural resources but is instead associated with rising domestic investment rates, financial liberalization and an opening of the capital account.

Part 4: The Effects of Foreign Direct Investment

FDI has been a growing source of capital in developing countries. And previous chapters in this volume have provided evidence showing that FDI can have a positive effect on economic growth and allow a more stable source of capital than portfolio capital inflows. The chapters in this part of the volume contain further analysis of the consequences of FDI on the level and growth of income per capita in host countries.

Chapter 12 is part of a literature in international trade theory that first examined the role that foreign-owned factors of production have on the welfare impact of external disturbances — a literature that includes the work of Jagdish N. Bhagwati, Richard Brecher and Ronald Findlay. For instance, a deterioration in a country's terms of trade — which is usually assumed to hurt domestic residents — could actually raise national welfare if there is a differential trade pattern phenomenon, defined as a situation where the national and aggregate trade specialization patterns differ due to the foreign presence in the economy. As Bhagwati and Brecher succinctly summarize the issue (as cited in Chapter 12): "The paradoxical behavior of national welfare arises simply because the aggregate pattern of trade masks a contrary pattern of trade for the domestically-owned, national factors of production."

The model in Chapter 12 extends the theory on the effects of foreign ownership to incorporate internationally non-traded goods. It is shown that, in the presence of non-traded goods, national welfare might increase in response to a deterioration in the economy's external terms of trade even when there is no differential trade pattern phenomenon. The explanation lies in that, with non-traded goods, changes in national welfare are related not only to the external trade specialization pattern of nationals but also to their pattern of specialization on internal trade in (internationally) non-traded goods. Therefore, whether national welfare rises or declines depends on the internal trade pattern in non-traded goods between nationals and the foreign-owned inputs in the country as well as on the impact of the terms of trade disturbance on the prices of non-traded goods. If nationals are exporting non-traded goods to the foreign-owned factors inside the economy and the terms of trade deterioration raises non-traded goods prices substantially, then a terms of trade that reduces the relative prices of export goods may in effect raise national welfare even if nationals within the country are net exporters of these products. There is still, of course, a reduction in real national income associated with the negative impact of the terms of trade deterioration on the net exports of the local population, but this negative impact is more than compensated by the improvement in the internal terms of trade that nationals obtain through the rise in the relative price of non-traded goods. As net exporters of non-traded goods within the economy, nationals receive a gain in real income when the relative price of their internal exports rises.

Chapter 13 studies the effects of currency devaluation in an economy that is host to foreign capital. The chapter shows that the presence of foreign capital introduces the possibility that increases in currency values could actually reduce both Gross Domestic Product (GDP) and Gross National Product (GNP), immiserizing domestic residents. That policy measures can have unexpectedly negative effects on national welfare in the presence of foreign ownership was first discussed in the trade-theoretic literature by the work of Jagdish N. Bhagwati, Richard Brecher, Carlos Diaz-Alejandro and Ernesto Tironi, among others. That currency devaluation can have a short-run negative impact on GDP has been known for many years and received serious theoretical attention when Paul Krugman and Lance Taylor utilized a simple Keynesian model of the open economy to show that the impact effect of a devaluation is to be contractionary if the economy is initially in a trade deficit, if there are export or import tax revenues which are affected by devaluation, or if the exchange rate change redistributes income from labor to capital, which results in a reduction of aggregate demand when the marginal propensity to consume out of wages exceeds the marginal propensity to consume out of profits.

Chapter 13 shows how the presence of foreign capital in an economy can make a currency devaluation contractionary, even when the other mechanisms discussed in the literature are not present. Within a short-run framework, with rigid nominal wages, a devaluation raises the prices of home goods and redistributes income from wages to profits. Some of the increased profits, however, are repatriated, and thus leak out of domestic consumption. If the leakage is large enough, the amount of home goods consumed out of the remaining profits will not be sufficient to compensate for the contraction in demand associated with lower domestic real wages. The consequence is a decline in aggregate demand and, in a short-run Keynesian context, a contractionary effect on output. Furthermore, the impact on national product (versus its impact on domestic product) will be even more negative since the claims of foreign capital on domestic output (the foreign profits) rise with devaluation: GNP declines by more than GDP.

Chapter 13 applies its model of the effects of devaluation to the case of Jamaica, which is a substantial recipient of FDI, equal to about 17 percent of GDP in 2016. A significant portion of foreign investment in Jamaica is in the bauxite and alumina sector, which has become the biggest export sector in the country since it was first exploited in the 1950s. The computations carried out for the case of Jamaica in Chapter 13 suggest that concerns regarding the contractionary mechanisms of currency devaluation in the presence of foreign capital are well-founded. For this country, using data for 1980, the presence of foreign ownership accounts for 85 percent of the potential, short-run negative impact of currency devaluation.

The literature on the effects of FDI in host countries has traditionally emphasized the positive effects arising from the employment created by the foreign capital in situations of unemployment or underemployment. Chapter 14 focuses instead on analyzing the nature of positive externalities generated by FDI. More specifically, the chapter shows how foreign capital operates to increase the extent of the local market and raise the variety and specialization of producer service firms, enhancing their productivity and, as a consequence, also that of the nationally-owned firms using them. There is, then, a direct positive externality generated by foreign capital inflows on national welfare. These external effects, in this framework, are not pure technological externalities but are closely allied to the concept of pecuniary externalities, as developed by the late economist Tibor Scitovsky. The source of pecuniary externalities here is the divergence between price and marginal cost in the service sector and the corresponding undervaluation of capital. An inflow of an input whose private reward falls short of its marginal social value leads to a welfare gain for the receiving country.

In the model presented in Chapter 14, capital inflows generate positive effects on national welfare by means of their stimulus to entry and increased specialization in the producer services sector. The resulting increase in industrial productivity acts as an external effect on nationally-owned factors that benefit from the use of the more specialized services. But it should also be noted that, in evaluating the employment effects of direct foreign investment, one should consider not only the direct employment created in the industries generated by FDI but also the induced secondary employment generated in the service sector. Foreign investments in industries that, due to their high capital–labor ratios, generate meager direct employment effects may stimulate sufficient secondary employment in services to have stronger job-creating impact than investments in industries that use substantial amounts of direct labor but do not have extensive service linkages.

The globalization of capital flows has been the result of policy moves undertaken in a wide range of countries. Within the European Community (EC), the economic integration project known as Europe 1992 pursued the creation of a single internal market that further promoted the liberalization of FDI flows among member countries, targeting particularly the service sector, including financial services. Chapter 15 examines how FDI flowing into the service sector may affect the economy differently than capital flowing into manufacturing. The chapter models sector-specific direct foreign investment into the host country's producer services sector and compares it with FDI in manufacturing investment.

Chapter 15 develops a theoretical model showing that foreign capital flowing into a service sector characterized by specialized firms operating in a market structure of monopolistic competition generates greater specialization among these services, augmenting industrial productivity. There is, then, a direct positive externality of these capital flows on national welfare. The external effects originate here in the existence of a wedge between price and marginal cost in the service sector due to the presence of imperfect competition. This wedge is directly connected to an undervaluation of capital in the service sector. But an inflow of an input whose private rate of return falls short of its marginal social value leads to a welfare gain for the receiving country. In this case, then, capital flowing into services will raise national host-country welfare. To emphasize this point, the chapter considers a situation where foreign investment in the industrial sector does not generate the external effects just described. Capital in manufacturing is assumed to be sector-specific, homogenous and traded in a competitive market. As a consequence, there is no externality originating in industry. Capital in this sector is paid its marginal product; and a small capital inflow has no effects on national welfare: the foreigners take away from the economy (as a rate of return) as much as they contribute (through their marginal productivity). Chapter 15 thus concludes that there are major differences in the way foreign investment affects the economy depending on the external effect or externality existing in the sector into which capital moves. This result is related to the literature on linkages in economic development, as first emphasized by Albert Hirschman, suggesting that industries that have numerous forward and backward linkages with other sectors of the economy are likely to generate greater growth than industries with no such linkages.

Part 1

International Trade, Technological Change and Economic Growth

Chapter 1

Economic Integration and Endogenous Growth[*]

1.1 Introduction

Many economists believe that increased economic integration between the developed economies of the world has tended to increase the long-run rate of economic growth. If they were asked to make an intuitive prediction, they would suggest that prospects for growth would be permanently diminished if a barrier were erected that impeded the flow of all goods, ideas, and people between Asia, Europe, and North America. Yet it would be difficult for any of us to offer a rigorous model that has been (or even could be) calibrated to data and that could justify this belief.

[*]This chapter includes "Economic Integration and Endogenous Growth," which was co-authored by Luis A. Rivera-Batiz and Paul M. Romer and was originally published in *The Quarterly Journal of Economics*, Vol. 106, No. 2 (May 1991), pp. 531–555; and "Economic Integration and Endogenous Growth: An Addendum," also co-authored by Luis A. Rivera-Batiz and Paul M. Romer and was originally published in *The Quarterly Journal of Economics*, Vol. 109, No. 1, February 1994, pp. 307–308. ©1991, 1994 President and Fellows of Harvard University and the Massachusetts Institute of Technology.

Conversations with Robert Barro, Gene Grossman, Elhanan Helpman, and Danyang Xie about their work on related issues have been very helpful, as were comments by Ray Riezman and Robert Staiger on earlier versions of this paper. The work of the second author was supported by NSF grant #SES88-22052, by a Sloan Foundation Fellowship, and by the Center for Advanced Studies in the Behavioral Sciences, which received support from NSF grant #BNS87-00864.

We know what some of the basic elements of such a growth model would be. Historical analysis (e.g., Rosenberg [1980]) shows that the creation and transmission of ideas has been extremely important in the development of modern standards of living. Theoretical arguments dating from Adam Smith's analysis of the pin factory have emphasized the potential importance of fixed costs and the extent of the market. There is a long tradition in trade theory of using models with Marshallian external effects to approach questions about increasing returns. More recently, static models with fixed costs and international specialization have been proposed that come closer to Smith's description of the sources of the gains from trade [Dixit and Norman, 1980; Ethier, 1982; Krugman, 1979, 1981; Lancaster, 1980]. There are also dynamic models with fixed costs and differentiated products in which output grows toward a fixed steady state level [Grossman and Helpman, 1989a].

Recent models of endogenous growth have used these ideas to study the effects that trade can have on the long-run rate of growth. (See, for example, the theoretical papers by Dinopoulos, Oehmke, and Segerstrom [1990]; Feenstra [1990]; Grossman and Helpman [1989b, 1989c, 1989d, 1989e, 1990]; Krugman [1990, Ch. 11]; Lucas [1988]; Romer [1990]; Segerstrom, Anant, and Dinopoulos [1990]; and Young [1990]. Backus, Kehoe, and Kehoe [1991] present both theoretical models and cross-country empirical evidence that bears on their models.) These models permit a distinction between a one-shot gain (i.e., a level effect) and a permanent change in the growth rate (i.e., a growth effect) that is extremely important in making an order of magnitude estimate of the benefits of economic integration. Conventional attempts to quantify the effects of integration using the neoclassical growth model often suggest that the gains from integration are small. If these estimates were calculated in the context of an endogenous growth model, integration might be found to be much more important.

The papers written so far have already demonstrated, however, that the growth effects of trade restrictions are very complicated in the most general case. Grossman and Helpman [1989b, 1989c, 1989e, 1990] have been particularly explicit about the fact that no universally applicable conclusions can be drawn. There are some models in which trade restrictions can slow down the worldwide rate of growth. There are others in which they can speed up the worldwide rate of growth.

To provide some intuition for the conjecture described in the first paragraph, that trade between the advanced countries does foster growth, we narrow the focus in this paper. We do not consider the general case of trade between countries with different endowments and technologies. Instead, we focus on the pure scale effects of integration. To set aside the other "comparative advantage" effects that trade induces in multisector trade models, we consider integration only between countries or regions that are similar. Therefore, we do not address the kinds of questions that are relevant for modeling the effects that trade between a poor LDC and a developed country can have on the worldwide rate of growth.

In the early stages of our analysis of integration and growth, it became clear that the theoretical treatment of ideas has a decisive effect on the conclusions one draws. In many of the existing models, flows of ideas cannot be separated from flows of goods. In others, flows of ideas are exogenously limited by national boundaries regardless of the trade regime. In either of these cases, economic integration can refer only to flows of goods along cargo networks. We consider a broader notion of integration, one that assigns an effect to flows of ideas along communication networks.

Flows of ideas deserve attention comparable to that devoted to flows of goods, for public policy can influence international communications and information flows to the same extent that it influences goods flows. Governments often subsidize language training and study abroad. Tax policies directly affect the incentive to station company employees in foreign nations. Immigration and visa policies directly limit the movement of people. Telecommunications networks are either run by government agencies or controlled by regulators. Some governments restrict direct foreign investment, which presumably is important in the international transmission of ideas. Others have made the acquisition of commercial and technical information a high priority task for their intelligence agencies.

Although these are the only ones we consider, it should be clear that flows of goods and flows of ideas are not the only elements in economic integration. Under some assumptions about nominal variables and the operation of financial markets, economic integration will also depend on monetary and institutional arrangements. The growth models we consider are too simple to consider these effects. It should also be clear that economic integration is not synonymous with political integration. Firms in Windsor, Ontario, may be more closely integrated into markets in the United States than they are to markets in the neighboring province of Quebec. Moreover, the notion of full economic integration does not entail the abolition of citizenship distinctions that have taken place in Germany's reunification.

The structure of the paper is as follows. Section 1.2 lays out the basic features of the production structure on which all arguments rely. It describes preferences, endowments, and the nature of equilibrium under the two specifications of R&D. Section 1.3 describes the equilibrium for both models in the closed economy and complete integration cases, and illustrates the scale effects that are present. Section 1.4 presents the three main thought experiments concerning partial integration. Sections 1.5 and 1.6 describe the general lessons that can be learned about the relation between the scale of the market and growth and discuss limitations of the models, extensions, and the relation to other models of endogenous growth.

1.2   Specification of the Models

1.2.1   *Functional Forms and Decentralization in the Manufacturing Sector*

The specification of the production technology for the manufacturing sector is taken from Romer [1990]. Manufacturing output is a function of human capital H, labor L, and a set $x(i)$ of capital goods indexed by the variable i. To avoid complications arising from integer constraints, the index i is modeled as a continuous variable. Technological progress is represented by the invention of new types of capital goods.

There are two types of manufacturing activities: production of consumption goods and production of the physical units of the types of capital goods that have already been invented. A third activity, research and development (R&D), creates designs for new types of capital goods. This activity is discussed in the next section. Both manufacturing activities use the same production function. Let $x(i)$ denote the stock of capital of type i that is used in production, and let A be the index of the most recently invented good. By the definition of A, $x(i) = 0$ for all $i > A$. Output Y is assumed to take the form,

$$Y(H, L, x(\cdot)) = H^\alpha L^\beta \int_0^A x(i)^{1-\alpha-\beta} di. \qquad (1)$$

Since the production function for manufacturing consumption goods is the same as that for manufacturing units of any type of existing capital, the relative prices of consumption goods and all types of existing capital goods are fixed by the technology. For simplicity, we choose units so that all of these relative prices are one. Fixed prices imply that the aggregate capital stock $K = \int_0^A x(i) di$ is well defined, as is aggregate output Y.

In this specification one unit of any capital good can be produced if one unit of consumption goods is forgone. This does not mean that consumption goods are directly converted into capital goods. Rather, the inputs needed to produce one unit of consumption are shifted from the production of consumption goods into the production of a capital good. Since inputs are used in the same proportions, it is easy to infer the allocation of inputs between the different production activities from the level of output of those activities. Because all the outputs here have the same production function, the consumption sector and all of the sectors producing the different capital goods can be collapsed into a single sector. We can therefore represent total manufacturing output as a function of the total stock of inputs used in the combined manufacturing sectors and can describe the division of inputs between sectors by the constraint $Y = C + K$. For one of the models of R&D described in the next section, we can use this same observation to combine the research sector and the aggregate manufacturing sector into a single sector describing all output in the economy. In the other model the R&D and manufacturing sectors must be kept separate.

There are many equivalent institutional structures that can support a decentralized equilibrium in manufacturing. For instance, the holder of a patent on good j could become a manufacturer, producing and selling good j. Alternatively, the patent holder could license the design to other manufacturers for a fee. Formally, it is useful to separate the manufacturing decision from the monopoly pricing decision of the patent holder, so we assume that patent holders contract out manufacturing to separate firms. It is also easier to assume that the patent holder collects rent on its capital goods rather than selling them. For analytical convenience, we therefore describe the institutional arrangements in the following, slightly artificial way. First, there are many firms that rent capital goods $x(i)$ from the patent holders, hire unskilled labor L, and employ skilled human capital H to produce manufactured goods. Each of these firms can produce consumption goods for sale to consumers. It can also produce one of the capital goods on contract for the holder of the patent. All of the manufacturing firms have the production function given in equation (1), which is homogeneous of degree one. They are price takers and earn zero profit. Manufacturing output is taken as the numeraire.

The firm that holds the patent on good j bids out the production of the actual capital goods to a specific manufacturer. It purchases physical units of the good for the competitive price, by normalization equal to one. The patent holder then rents out the units to all manufacturing firms at the profit-maximizing monopoly rental rate. It can do this because patent law prohibits any firm from manufacturing a capital good without the consent of the patent holder. The patent is a tradable asset with a price of P_A that is equal to the present discounted value of the stream of monopoly rent minus the cost of the machines. It is easy to verify that this set of institutional arrangements is equivalent to other arrangements. For example, the equivalent licensing fee for each unit of capital sold by a licensee is the present value of the stream of monopoly rent on one machine minus the unit cost of manufacturing it.

1.2.2 *Functional Forms and Decentralization in R&D*

We consider two specifications of the technology of R&D that permit easy analytic solutions. Each specification captures different features of the world, and neither alone gives a complete description of R&D. We use both of them because they help us isolate the exact sense in which economic integration can influence long-run growth. As the example in the next section shows, it would be easy to come to misleading conclusions about integration and growth if one generalized from a single example.

The first specification of the technology for producing designs for new capital goods assumes that human capital and knowledge are the only inputs that influence the output of designs:

$$\dot{A} = \delta H A, \tag{2}$$

where H denotes the stock of human capital used in research. The stock of existing designs A is a measure of general scientific and engineering knowledge as well as practical know-how that accumulated as previous design problems were solved. (See Romer [1990] for additional discussion of this specification.) New designs build on this knowledge, so we refer to this type of R&D process as the knowledge-driven specification of R&D. This specification imposes a sharp factor intensity difference between R&D and manufacturing. Neither unskilled labor nor physical capital has any value in R&D. Because of this difference, the resulting model must be analyzed using a two-sector framework.

A useful polar case is a technology for R&D that uses the same inputs as the manufacturing technology, in the same proportions. If H, L, and $x(i)$; denote inputs used in R&D and B denotes a constant scale factor, output of designs can be written as

$$\dot{A} = B H^\alpha L^\beta \int_0^A x(i)^{1-\alpha-\beta} di. \tag{3}$$

This specification says that human capital, unskilled labor, and capital goods (such as personal computers or oscilloscopes) are productive in research. But in contrast to the previous specification, knowledge per se has no productive value. Access to the designs for all previous goods, and familiarity with the ideas and know-how that they represent, does not aid the creation of new designs. We refer to this as the lab equipment specification of R&D.

As noted above, the growth model with the knowledge-driven specification for R&D has an unavoidable two-sector structure. The production possibility frontier in the space of designs and manufactured goods takes on the usual curved shape. In the lab equipment model the production functions of the goods and R&D sectors are the same, so the production possibility frontier is a straight line. If the output of goods is reduced by one unit and the inputs released are transferred to the R&D sector, they yield B patents. Thus, the price P_A of a patent in terms of goods is determined on the technology side as $P_A = 1/B$. Since capital goods and consumption goods have the same production technology, we integrated them into a single manufacturing sector in the last section. In the lab equipment model we can go farther and aggregate manufacturing and research into a single sector. Let H, L, and $x(i)$ denote the entire stock of inputs available in the economy at date t. Then we can express the value of total output $C + \dot{K} + \dot{A}/B$ in terms of the total stock of inputs.

$$C + \dot{K} + \frac{\dot{A}}{B} = H^\alpha L^\beta \int_0^A x(i)^{1-\alpha-\beta} di. \qquad (4)$$

The model's symmetry implies that $x(i) = x(j)$ for all i and j less than A. We can therefore substitute $K/A = x(i)$ in equation (4) to obtain a reduced-form expression for total output in terms of H, K, L, and A:

$$C + \dot{K} + \frac{\dot{A}}{B} = H^\alpha L^\beta A (K/A)^{1-\alpha-\beta}$$

$$= H^\alpha L^\beta K^{1-\alpha-\beta} A^{\alpha+\beta}. \qquad (5)$$

The knowledge-driven and lab equipment specifications of the R&D sector lead to different assumptions about how equilibrium in the R&D sector is decentralized. In the knowledge-driven model, output of designs is homogeneous of degree two. By Euler's theorem it is not possible for both of the inputs A and H to be paid their marginal product. We make the assumption that A receives no compensation. Holders of patents on previous designs have no technological or legal means of preventing designers of new goods from using the ideas implicit in the existing designs. The stock of A that can be put to use, with no compensation, by any individual researcher is therefore the entire stock of knowledge about previous designs, provided that there exists a communication network that makes this information available. The equilibrium is one with knowledge spillovers or external effects in the R&D sector (but not in the manufacturing sector). In this case, we can describe research as if it were done by independent researchers who use their human capital to produce designs, which they subsequently sell.

In the lab equipment model, output of designs is the same, homogeneous-of-degree-one production function as in the manufacturing sector. As is the case for the manufacturing sector, the equilibrium is one in which patents convey market power but in which there are no other entry restrictions. There are no external effects and no knowledge spillovers. There is free entry into both R&D and manufacturing. The only restriction is that no one can manufacture capital of type i without the consent of the holder of the patent on good i. In this case we conceive of R&D as being undertaken by separate firms that hire inputs, produce patentable designs, and sell them for a price P_A.

1.3   Balanced Growth and Integration

The description of the technology given so far represents output as a function of the inputs H, L, K, and A, and specifies the evolution equations for K and A. To facilitate the simple balanced growth analysis that we undertake, the stocks of L and H are each taken as given. Increases in either L or H could be accommodated if we undertook the more complicated task of solving a nonlinear system of differential equations with growth rates that vary over time.

The calculation of a balanced growth equilibrium for each of the two specifications of the R&D technology can be summarized in terms of two linear relations between the rate of growth and the interest rate that hold along a balanced growth path. One relation

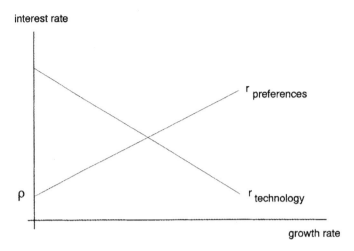

Figure 1.1. The Balanced Growth Equilibrium in the Knowledge-Driven Model.

comes from the conditions of equilibrium in production and the other from preferences.

As shown in the Appendix and as illustrated in Figure 1.1, the interest rate implied by equilibrium in the production sector is decreasing in the rate of growth of output for the knowledge-driven model:

$$r_{technology} = (\delta H - g)/\Lambda. \tag{6}$$

The term in the denominator depends only on the production function parameters, $\Lambda = \alpha(\alpha + \beta)^{-1}(1 - \alpha - \beta)^{-1}$.

The corresponding expression for the interest rate from the lab equipment model is shown in the Appendix to be a function of the production parameters and the stock of H and L. It does not, however, depend on the rate of growth:

$$r_{technology} = \Gamma H^\alpha L^\beta, \tag{7}$$

where Γ is defined by $\Gamma = B^{\alpha+\beta}(\alpha + \beta)^{\alpha+\beta}(1 - \alpha - \beta)^{2-\alpha-\beta}$.

In the knowledge-driven specification the negative relation between the interest rate and the growth rate arises because an increase in the interest rate reduces the demand for capital goods. The calculations in the Appendix show that an increase in the interest rate reduces the number of units of each capital good that are rented, and thereby reduces the value of a patent. According to the curved production possibility frontier between designs and manufactured goods, the reduction in the price of the patented design causes a shift in human capital out of the production of new designs and into the production of manufactured goods. This shift slows down the creation of technology and thereby slows growth. In the lab equipment model only a single value of the interest rate is consistent with production of both goods and designs. The relative price of patents and final goods is fixed, so the interest rate is technologically determined.

It remains to specify the preferences that provide the other balanced growth relation between the interest rate and the rate of growth. The simplest formulation to work with is Ramsey preferences with constant elasticity utility,

$$U = \int_0^\infty \frac{C^{1-\sigma}}{1-\sigma} e^{-\rho t} dt, \quad \sigma \in [0, \infty).$$

Under balanced growth the rate of growth of consumption must be equal to the rate of growth of output. Thus, for any fixed rate of growth $g = \dot{C}/C$, we can calculate the implied interest rate from the consumer's first-order conditions for intertemporal optimization:

$$r_{preferences} = \rho + \sigma g. \tag{8}$$

These preferences yield a positive relation between the interest rate and the growth rate because when consumption is growing more rapidly, current consumption is more valuable compared with future consumption, so the marginal rate of substitution between present and future consumption is higher. Consumers would therefore be willing to borrow at higher interest rates.

There is a parameter restriction that is necessary to ensure that the growth rate is not larger than the interest rate. If it is, present values will not be finite, and the integral that defines utility will diverge. In terms of Figures 1.1 and 1.2, the restriction is that the intersection of the two curves must lie above the 45 degree line. This will always be true if σ is greater than or equal to one, since in this

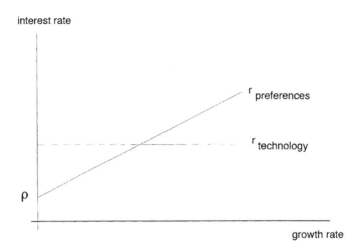

Figure 1.2. The Balanced Growth Equilibrium in the Lab Equipment Model.

case, the $r_{\text{preferences}}$ curve always lies above the 45 degree line. If σ is less than one, the $r_{\text{technology}}$ curve must not lie too far up and to the right.

Because the rate of growth under each specification is determined by the intersection of two straight lines, it can be calculated directly from the relation between r and g determined on the preference side, equation (8), and the relation between r and g determined by the technology, either equation (6) or (7). The balanced rate of growth for a closed economy under the knowledge-driven model of the research sector is

$$g = (\delta H - \Lambda\rho)/(\Lambda\sigma + 1). \tag{9}$$

The balanced rate of growth for the lab equipment model is

$$g = (\Gamma H^{\alpha} L^{\beta} - \rho)/\sigma. \tag{10}$$

Both of these models have a dependence on scale that is crucial to the analysis of the effects of trade. To see this, consider two economies that have identical endowments of H and L. In the long run these economies will have the same stocks of accumulated inputs as well, so that scale effects offer the only lasting source of gains from trade and economic integration.

Suppose that the two economies are physically contiguous, yet are totally isolated from each other by an impenetrable barrier that impedes the flow of goods, people, and ideas. If these economies evolve under isolation, the balanced rate of growth in each is characterized by Figures 1.1 and 1.2 and calculated in equations (9) and (10). Now suppose that the barrier is removed, so that the economies are completely integrated into a single economy. The change from two economies with endowments H and L to one economy with stocks $2H$ and $2L$ causes an upward shift in the $r_{\text{technology}}$ curve in both figures. Both the rate of growth and the interest rate increase after complete economic integration takes place, regardless of the specification of the technology for R&D. In both models (even the knowledge-driven model with no knowledge spillovers) the rate of growth is too low compared with the rate that would be selected by a social planner.[1] As a result, one would expect integration to be welfare improving. A full welfare analysis, however, would require explicit consideration of the dynamics along the transition path.

With this discussion as background the examples in the next section are designed to address three questions. First, can free trade in goods between countries induce the same increase in the balanced growth rate as complete integration into a single economy? If not, can the free movement of goods, combined with the free movement of ideas, reproduce the rate of growth under full integration? And finally, what is the underlying explanation for the dependence of the growth rate on the extent of the market?

1.4 Trade in Goods and Flows of Ideas

In this section we conduct a series of thought experiments about partial integration. In the first two experiments we focus on the knowledge-driven specification for R&D because it permits a sharp distinction between flows of goods and flows of ideas. In the third we consider the lab equipment specification in which ideas have no direct effect on production.

In the analysis of the knowledge-driven specification, we start with two identical, completely isolated economies that are growing at the balanced growth rate. We first allow for trade in goods, but continue to restrict the flow of ideas. To emphasize the distinction between goods and ideas, we assume that trade in goods does not induce any transmission of ideas. For example, we assume that it is impossible to reverse engineer an imported good to learn the secrets of its design. Under these assumptions we show that trade in goods has no effect on the long-run rate of growth. Then in the second experiment we calculate the additional effect of opening communications networks and permitting flows of ideas. We show that allowing flows of ideas results in a permanently higher growth rate.

In the third experiment we consider the effects of opening trade in goods under the lab equipment specification. In this case trade in goods alone causes the same permanent increase in the rate of growth as complete integration. Since ideas per se have no effect on production, the creation of communications networks has no additional effect.

1.4.1   *Flows of Goods with No Flows of Ideas in the Knowledge-Driven Model*

In all of the experiments considered here, the form of trade between the two countries is very simple. By symmetry there are no opportunities for intertemporal trade along a balanced growth path, hence no international lending. Because there is only a single final consumption good, the only trades that take place are exchanges of capital goods produced in one country for capital goods produced in the other.

With the knowledge-driven model of research, it is straightforward to show that opening trade in goods has no permanent effect on the rate of growth. In balanced growth the rate of growth of output is equal to the rate of growth of A, $\dot{A}/A = \delta H_A$, which is determined by the split of human capital $H = H_y + H_A$ between the manufacturing sector and the research sector. Opening trade in goods has two offsetting effects on wages for human capital in these two sectors. Before trade is opened, the number of different types of machines that are used in the manufacturing sector must equal the number that has been designed and produced domestically. Along

the new balanced growth path after trade is opened, the number of
types of machines used in each country approaches twice the number
that has been produced and designed domestically. In their pursuit
of monopoly rents, researchers in the two countries will specialize in
the production of different types of designs and avoid redundancy,
so the worldwide stock of designs will ultimately be twice as large as
the stock that has been produced in either country.

With trade in the specialized capital goods, domestic manufacturers can take advantage of foreign designs and vice versa. Ultimately,
the level $\bar{x}$ at which each durable is used in each country will return
to the level that obtained under isolation. From equation (1) it
follows that the increase in A doubles the marginal product of human
capital in the manufacturing sector, increasing it from $\partial Y/\partial H = \alpha H_A^{\alpha-1} L^\beta \bar{x}^{1-\alpha-\beta} A$ to $\partial Y/\partial H = \alpha H_A^{\alpha-1} L^\beta \bar{x}^{1-\alpha-\beta}(A + A^*)$, where
A^* is the set of durables available from abroad.

For the research sector, opening of trade implies that the market
for any newly designed good is twice as large as it was in the absence
of trade. This doubles the price of the patents and raises the return
to investing human capital in research from $P_A \delta A$ to $2P_A \delta A$. The
knowledge represented by A^* is not available for use in research
because flows of ideas are not permitted. Since the return to human
capital doubles in both of the competing sectors, free trade in goods
does not affect the split of human capital between manufacturing and
research. Hence, it does not change the balanced rate of economic
growth or the interest rate. In terms of Figure 1.1, opening trade in
goods does not change the position of either the $r_{\text{preferences}}$ locus or
the $r_{\text{technology}}$ locus.

This result does not imply that free trade in goods has no effect
on output or welfare. Consider, for example, the extreme case in
which two isolated economies start from completely nonintersecting
sets of capital goods A and A^* that have the same measure. Before
trade in goods, the home country will use capital at the level $\bar{x}$ for A
types of capital goods and the foreign country will use capital at the
same level $\bar{x}$ for A^* different types of capital goods. If existing capital
is freely mobile, each country will immediately exchange half of its
capital stock for half of the capital stock of the other country when

trade in capital goods is allowed. Each will then be using capital at the level $\bar{x}/2$ on a set of capital goods of measure $A + A^*$. (Over time, the level of usage will climb back to $\bar{x}$ as capital accumulation takes place because the level of x is determined by r and g, and on the new balanced growth path these are the same as before.) From the form of production in manufacturing given in equation (1), it follows that immediately after trade is opened output in each country jumps by a factor of $2^{\alpha+\beta}$. This is analogous to the kind of level effect one encounters in the neoclassical model and in static models of trade with differentiated inputs in production (e.g., Ethier [1982]). In the specific model outlined here, free trade in goods can affect the level of output and can therefore affect welfare, but it does not affect long-run growth rates.

If the two different economies start from a position with exactly overlapping sets of goods prior to the opening of trade, the timing of the effect on output is different, but the ultimate effect is the same. The level of output at future dates will differ from what it would have been without trade in goods and will generally be higher. But once the transitory effects have died out, the underlying growth rate will be the same as it was prior to the opening of trade in the capital goods.

1.4.2 *Flows of Information in the Knowledge-Driven Model of Research*

This second example shows that greater flows of ideas can permanently increase the rate of growth in the knowledge-driven model of research. Once we allow for flows of information, we must make some assumption about international protection of intellectual property rights. In each country we have assumed that patents protect any designs produced domestically. Once ideas and designs created abroad become available, the government could try to expropriate the monopoly rents that would accrue to the foreigners by refusing to uphold their patents. To simplify the discussion here, we assume that neither government engages in this practice. A patent in one country is fully respected in the other. (For a discussion of incomplete protection of intellectual property rights, see Rivera-Batiz and Romer [1991].)

Consider the two identical economies with the knowledge-driven specification of the research sector described in the first experiment. Trade in goods has already been allowed, and this creates the incentive for researchers to specialize in different designs. Over time the sets of designs that are in use in the two countries will be almost entirely distinct, so the worldwide stock of knowledge approaches twice the stock of designs in either country. In the absence of communications links, this means that researchers in each country will ultimately be using only one half of the worldwide stock of knowledge. In the domestic country the rate of growth of A is given by $\dot{A} = \delta H_A A$. In the foreign country it is given by $\dot{A}^* = \delta H_A^* A^*$.

Now suppose that flows of ideas between the two countries are permitted. Research in each country now depends on the total worldwide stock of ideas as contained in the union of A and A^*. If the ideas in each country are completely nonintersecting, the effective stock of knowledge that could be used in research after communication opens would be twice as large as it was before: $\dot{A} = \dot{A}^* = \delta H_A(A + A^*) = 2\delta H_A A$. Even if the allocation of $H = H_Y + H_A$ between manufacturing and research did not change, the rate of growth of A would double. But the increase in the set of ideas available for use in research increases the productivity of human capital in research and has no effect on its productivity in manufacturing. This change in relative productivity induces a shift of human capital out of manufacturing and into research. For two reasons communication of ideas speeds up growth.

Increasing the flow of ideas has the effect of doubling the productivity of research in each country. Compared with the closed economy model, the formal effect is the same as a doubling of the research productivity parameter δ. This would shift the $r_{\text{technology}}$ curve in Figure 1.1 upward and lead to a higher equilibrium growth rate and interest rate. The algebraic solution for the balanced growth rate of A (and therefore also of Y, C, and K) can be determined by replacing δ with 2δ in equation (9) to obtain $g = (2\delta H - \Lambda\rho)/(\sigma\Lambda + 1)$.

Doubling the value of the productivity parameter δ has exactly the same effect on the rate of growth of output and designs as a doubling of H. And according to the discussion in Section 1.2, doubling H has the same effect on growth as complete integration of the two economies into a single economy. Flows of ideas and goods together have the same effect on the growth rate as does complete integration. Complete integration would permit permanent migration as well, but since ideas and goods are already mobile and because the ratio of H to L was assumed to be the same in the two countries, migration is not necessary to achieve productive efficiency. For symmetric economies, allowing both trade in goods and free flows of ideas is enough to reproduce the resource allocation under complete integration.

So far, we have considered the additional effect that free flows of information would have if free trade in goods were already permitted. It is useful to consider the alternative case in which flows of information are permitted but flows of goods are not. In this case the results hinge on the degree of overlap between the set of ideas that are produced in each country.

In the absence of trade in goods, there would be no incentive for researchers in different countries to specialize in different designs either before or after flows of information are permitted. Moreover, after flows of information are opened, there would be a positive incentive for researchers in one country to copy designs from the other, and little offsetting incentives to enforce property rights. If the firm that owns the patent on good j is not permitted to sell the good in a foreign country, it has no economic stake in the decision by a foreign firm to copy good j and sell it in the foreign market. (The domestic firm would of course have both the incentive and the legal power to stop exports of the copies from the foreign country.) In the extreme case in which identical knowledge is created in each country, opening flows of information has no effect at all on production.

Alternatively, one could imagine that discovery is a random process with a high variance so that truly independent discoveries would take place in the different isolated countries. In this case, permitting the international transmission of ideas would speed up worldwide growth rates to some extent, even in the absence of trade in goods. With free communication each researcher would be working with a larger stock of ideas than would otherwise have been the case. For example, when the first overland routes to China were opened in the Middle Ages, transportation of goods was so expensive that the economic effects of trade in goods was small. But the economic consequences of the ideas that travelers brought back (e.g., the principle behind the magnetic compass and the formula for gunpowder) were large.

1.4.3   *Flows of Goods in the Lab Equipment Model of Research*

The two previous examples show that there is sometimes a separation between growth effects and level effects. In the first experiment, opening trade in goods had level effects but no growth effects. In the second experiment, opening flows of ideas had both a growth effect and a level effect. (Manufacturing output goes down when H shifts into research, and research output goes up.)

From the first two examples it is tempting to conclude that flows of goods will generally have level effects of the type that are familiar from neoclassical analysis and that it is only flows of ideas that have growth effects. The third example considered shows that this conclusion is wrong. The lab equipment model is constructed so that ideas per se have no effect on production. Hence, permitting international flows of ideas can have no economic effect. Yet we know from the discussion in Section 1.3 that complete integration causes a permanent increase in the rate of growth. The experiment considered in this example shows that trade in goods is all that is needed to achieve this result.

Recall that, when trade in goods is permitted in the knowledge-driven model, this increases the profits that the holder of each patent can extract because it increases the market for the good. By itself this increase in the return to producing designs would tend to increase the production of designs, but in the knowledge-driven specification, this effect is exactly offset by the increase in the marginal productivity of human capital in manufacturing.

In the lab equipment specification, opening trade in goods would cause the same kind of increase in the profit earned at each date by the holder of a patent if the interest rate remained constant. But as was noted in subsection 1.2.2, the price of the patent $P_A = 1/B$ is determined by the technology. The only way that the larger market can be reconciled with a fixed price for the patent is if the interest rate increases. A higher interest rate reduces the demand for capital goods, thereby lowering the profit earned by the monopolist at each date. The calculation in the Appendix shows that the required increase in the interest rate is by a factor of $2^{\alpha+\beta}$. When two identical economies are integrated and $2H$ is substituted for H and $2L$ is substituted for L in equation (7), the same increase in r obtains. In each case the higher interest rate leads to higher savings. From Figure 1.2 or from equation (10), it follows that this increase in the interest rate leads to the same faster rate of growth as complete integration.

1.5   Scale Effects and Growth

In the last example we noted one incorrect conjecture about why tighter economic integration leads to faster growth. From the knowledge-driven model one might conclude that flows of ideas are crucial to the finding that economic integration can speed up growth. But the lab equipment model shows that closer integration can speed up growth even in a model in which flows of ideas have no effect on production. A related conjecture is that knowledge spillovers are fundamental and that increasing the extent of the spillovers is how integrations speeds up growth. The lab equipment model shows that this too is incorrect, for it has no knowledge spillovers.

Finally, one might conclude that it is the increasing returns to scale in the production function for designs, $\dot{A} = \delta H_A A$, that causes integration to have a growth effect in the knowledge-driven model. This conjecture seems to us to come closest to the mark, but it needs to be interpreted carefully. To see why, recall that the production function for designs in the lab equipment model, $\dot{A} = BH_A^\alpha L_A^\beta \int_0^A x_A(i)^{1-\alpha-\beta} di$, exhibits constant returns to scale as a function of H, L, and the capital goods $x(i)$. There is, nonetheless, a form of increasing returns that is present in this model. It comes from the fixed cost that must be incurred to design a new good.

With integration this fixed cost need be incurred only once. Under isolation it must be incurred twice, once in each country.

To bring out the underlying form of increasing returns, recall from equation (5) that we can substitute $x = K_A/A$ into the expression for $\dot{A}$ and write it as a function of H, L, K, and A that is homogeneous of degree $1 + \alpha + \beta$: $\dot{A} = BH_A^\alpha L_A^\beta K_A^{1-\alpha-\beta} A^{\alpha+\beta}$. Interpreted as a statement about this kind of reduced-form expression, it is correct to say that both models exhibit increasing returns to scale in the production of new designs as a function of the stocks of basic inputs. Consequently, operating two research sectors in isolation is not as efficient as operating a single integrated research sector. To operate an integrated research sector in the knowledge-driven model, two things are required. First, one must avoid redundant effort, that is, devoting resources in one economy to rediscovering a design that already exists in the other. Trade in goods provides the incentive to avoid redundancy. Second, one must make sure that ideas discovered in one country are available for use in research in both countries. Flows of ideas along communications networks serve this function.

In the lab equipment model trade in goods once again provides the incentive to avoid redundant effort. Beyond this, all that is needed to create a single worldwide research sector is to ensure that all types of capital equipment available worldwide are used in all research activities undertaken anywhere in the world. Since ideas do not matter in research, trade in the capital goods is all that is needed.

There is one final point worth emphasizing. Rebelo [1991] offers a general observation about multisector models that is relevant for the experiments considered here. Consider a single sector model of the form, $C + \dot{K} + \dot{A} = B_0 F_0(K, A)$, where $F_0(\cdot)$ is a homogeneous of degree one function. In this example, K and A can denote any two arbitrary capital goods. If the productivity parameter B_0 increases, the balanced growth rate increases. Consider next a two-sector model in which there is an essential fixed factor L that enters as an input in the homogeneous of degree one production function for consumption and capital of type K: $C + \dot{K} = B_1 F_1(K, A, L)$ The capital good A, however, is produced by a homogeneous of degree one function $F_2(\cdot)$ of K and A alone: $\dot{A} = B_2 F_2(K_2, A2)$. In this case a change in the productivity parameter B_1 has no effect on the balanced rate of growth. It has only level effects. In contrast, an increase in B_2 increases the balanced rate of growth.

The connection between Rebelo's observation and our results is as follows. We do not consider changes in technology parameters like B_1 and B_2, but we do induce changes in scale for functions that are homogeneous of some degree greater than one. Increases in scale are analogous to increases in the productivity parameters. In the knowledge-driven model trade in goods exploits increasing returns in the sector that produces C and K, but not in the sector that produces A. It is like an increase in B_1 in Rebelo's two-sector model, and induces only level effects. In contrast, flows of ideas increase the productivity in the research sector that produces A, and are analogous to an increase in Rebelo's coefficient B_2. Finally, trade in goods in the lab equipment model induces a scale effect that is like an increase in B_0 in Rebelo's one-sector model.

1.6   Limitations of the Models and Extensions

As noted in the Introduction, the analysis carried out in this paper takes the form of thought experiments for idealized cases. These experiments reveal the following general insight about the connection between economic integration and the rate of economic growth. In a model of endogenous growth, if economic integration lets two economies exploit increasing returns to scale in the equation that represents the engine of growth, integration will raise the long-run rate of growth purely because it increases the extent of the market. Depending on the form of the model, this integration could take the form of trade in goods, flows of ideas, or both.

This conclusion must be tempered by a large number of qualifications. First, there is no consensus yet about whether the equation that is the engine of growth is homogeneous of some degree that is greater than one in the basic inputs (as it is in both of the models considered here) or instead is homogeneous of degree one (as it is, for example, in the papers by Rebelo [1991] and Lucas [1988]).

Second, as noted in the Introduction, we have focused on trade between economies with identical endowments and technologies to highlight the scale effects induced by economic integration. In a general two-sector framework, trade between economies that have different endowments or technologies will induce allocation effects that shift resources between the two sectors in each country. For example, Grossman and Helpman [1990] show that trade between countries that have different endowments or technologies will induce shifts between the manufacturing sector and the R&D sector that can either speed up or slow down worldwide growth. If one wants to take the optimistic conclusions reached in this paper literally, they are most likely to apply to integration between similar developed regions of the world, for example, between North America, Europe, and Japan.

There are many details of R&D at the micro level that have been ignored in all of the analysis. We have assumed that giving participants in the economy an incentive to avoid redundancy in research is sufficient to ensure that no redundancy takes place. We have also assumed that patents are infinitely lived and, implicitly, that the institutional structure avoids patent races. We have not considered the role of secrecy in preserving economic value for ideas. All of these restrictions are very strong. Grossman and Helpman [1989d] show how one element of the microeconomic literature on patents, the destruction of monopoly profits by new discoveries, can be included in an aggregate growth model. Other extensions will no doubt follow.

The functional forms used here cannot be literally correct. For example, in both of our models the output of patents at any date increases in proportion to the resources devoted to R&D. This permits the solution for balanced growth paths using linear equations, but it cannot be a good description of actual research opportunities. We would expect that a doubling of research effort would lead to a less than two-fold increase in R&D output, in large part because of the coordination and redundancy problems at the micro level that we have ignored. Addressing these issues would help reconcile a model in which growth rates increase linearly in H in one case, or as a power of H and L in the second, with a historical record showing that growth rates have indeed increased over time, but not nearly as much as the functional forms used here would suggest. More precision in the definition of the input H that is most important for research would also be helpful in this regard. In terms of their effects on research output, one presumably does not literally want to equate two people holding high school degrees with one person holding a Ph.D. degree.

Perhaps the most interesting limitation of the models considered here is one that it shares with many other models: there is no description of how ideas or information affect the production of goods. Once one admits that ideas per se can influence research output, it is apparent that they can influence the output of goods as well. Presumably this is what learning-by-doing models try to capture with the assumption that some production parameter increases with cumulative experience: producing goods yield both goods and ideas, and the ideas raise the productivity of the other inputs. Formal models in the tradition of Arrow [1962] have not yet addressed the importance of communication networks and information flows. When the learning-by-doing models are used in international trade, it is implicitly assumed that there is a communication network that extends throughout one national economy, yet does not cross national boundaries. Little theoretical attention has been given to the analysis of policy choices that can affect the efficiency of international communication networks and to explaining historical episodes (e.g., the emergence of the textile industry in the United States and of the automobile industry in Japan) that reflect large flows of information from developed industries in one country to developing industries in another.

Given these limitations and qualifications, our only claim is to have formalized, and we hope illuminated, an effect that is potentially important. If the discovery of new ideas is central to economic growth, one should expect that increasing returns associated with the opportunity to reuse existing ideas will be present. If the increasing returns extend to the sector of the economy that generates growth, economic integration will induce scale effects that will raise the long-run rate of growth. And because of the remarkable growth of the exponential function, policies that affect long-run rates of growth can have very large cumulative effects on economic welfare. Many other effects may be present as well, but in future theoretical and empirical work, we argue that scale effects on growth that are induced by economic integration are worth watching out for.

1.7   Appendix

1.7.1   *Derivation of Equation (7)*

In the lab equipment model the value of total production in manufacturing and research depends only on the aggregate stocks of inputs, not on their allocation between the two sectors:

$$Y + \frac{\dot{A}}{B} = H^\alpha L^\beta \int_0^A x(i)^{1-\alpha-\beta} di.$$

Taking its supply of H and L as given, each representative firm in the manufacturing sector chooses levels of $x(i)$ to maximize profits. Consequently, the first-order condition for the problem of maximizing $Y + \dot{A}/B$ minus total input cost $\int p(i)x(i)di$ with respect to the use of input i yields the economy-wide inverse demand curve for good i. The rental rate p that results when x units of the capital good are supplied is

$$p = (1 - \alpha - \beta) H^\alpha L^\beta x^{-(\alpha+\beta)} \qquad (A.1)$$

Input producers choose x to maximize the present value of monopoly rent minus x times the unit cost of each piece of capital, $P_A = \max(px/r) - x$. Using equation (A.1), the first-order condition that determines the number of machines $\bar{x}$ that the holder of the patent on good i rents to manufacturing firms is

$$(1 - \alpha - \beta)^2 H^\alpha L^\beta \bar{x}^{-(\alpha+\beta)} r^{-1} - 1 = 0, \qquad (A.2)$$

which implies that $p/r = (1 - \alpha - \beta)^{-1}$. The present discounted value of profit collected by the holder of the patent can then be simplified to

$$P_A = \left(\frac{p\bar{x}}{r}\right) - \bar{x} = \frac{\alpha + \beta}{1 - \alpha - \beta}\bar{x}. \tag{A.3}$$

Since $P_A = 1/B$, this implies that $\bar{x} = (1 - \alpha - \beta)/B(\alpha + \beta)$. Substituting this expression into equation (A.2) yields equation (7) in the text:

$$r_{technology} = B^{\alpha+\beta}(\alpha + \beta)^{\alpha+\beta}(1 - \alpha - \beta)^{2-\alpha-\beta}H^{\alpha}L^{\beta}.$$

1.7.2 *Derivation of Equation (6)*

The demand for the capital goods in this model has exactly the same form as in the lab equipment model, with the qualification that since all of the demand comes from the manufacturing sector, H must be replaced by H_Y. If we use equation (A.1) with this replacement to substitute for p in the expression for P_A, we have

$$P_A = (\alpha + \beta)\frac{p\bar{x}}{r} = \frac{\alpha + \beta}{r}(1 - \alpha - \beta)H_Y^{\alpha}L^{\beta}\bar{x}^{1-\alpha+\beta}.$$

Equating the wages of human capital in manufacturing and research yields $P_A\delta A = \alpha H_Y^{\alpha-1}L^{\beta}A\bar{x}^{1-\alpha-\beta}$. Combining these expressions and solving for H_Y yields $H_Y = (1/\delta)\alpha(\alpha + \beta)^{-1}(1-\alpha-\beta)^{-1}r = (\Lambda/\delta)r$. Hence, $g = \delta H_A = \delta H - \delta H_Y = \delta H - \Lambda r$.

1.7.3 *Trade in Goods in Lab Equipment Model Is Equivalent to Complete Integration*

If the interest rate remained constant, the value of a patent $P_A = \pi/r$ would double when trade in goods between two identical markets is introduced in this model. The monopolist that sells in two identical markets and faces constant marginal costs of production will maximize profits in each market independently and earn twice the flow of profits that would accrue from one market alone. Since the value of the patent must remain fixed at $1/B$ by the specification of the technology for producing patents, the interest rate must increase to restore equilibrium.

As shown above, maximization of profit by the monopolist implies that p/r is constant, so profit is proportional to $\bar{x}$. To offset the doubling of profit that the opening of trade would otherwise induce, r must increase by enough to make the number of units of capital supplied by the monopolist in each country fall by one half. From equation (A.2) this will happen if r increases by a factor of $2^{\alpha+\beta}$. This is the same as the increase in r that results from doubling H and L when the two countries are combined.

Notes:

[1]For the knowledge-driven model, this is shown in Romer [1990]. For an early version of the lab equipment model, this is shown in Romer [1987]. See Barro and Sala i Martin [1990] for a discussion of the optimality of the no-intervention equilibrium and of tax and subsidy policies that can achieve the socially optimal balanced rate of growth in a variety of endogenous growth models.

References

Arrow, Kenneth J., "The Economic Implications of Learning By Doing," *Review of Economic Studies*, XXIX (June 1962), 155–73.

Backus, David, Patrick Kehoe, and Timothy Kehoe, "In Search of Scale Effects in Trade and Growth," Working Paper No. 451, Federal Reserve Bank of Minneapolis, 1991.

Barro, Robert, and Xavier Sala i Martin, "Public Finance in Models of Economic Growth," National Bureau of Economic Research, Working Paper No. 3362, 1990.

Dinopoulos, Elias, James Oehmke, and Paul Segerstrom, "High Technology Industry Trade and Investment: The Role of Factor Endowments," University of Florida Working Paper, 1990.

Dixit, Avinash, and V. Norman, *The Theory of International Trade* (Cambridge, England: Cambridge University Press, 1980).

Ethier, Wilfred J., "National and International Returns to Scale in the Modern Theory of International Trade," *American Economic Review*, LXXII (June 1982), 389–405.

Feenstra, Robert, "Trade and Uneven Growth," National Bureau of Economic Research, Working Paper No. 3276, 1990.

Grossman, Gene, and Elhanan Helpman, "Product Development and International Trade," *Journal of Political Economy*, XCVII (December 1989a), 1261–83.

———, and ———, "Endogenous Product Cycles," National Bureau of Economic Research, Working Paper No. 2113, 1989b.

———, and ———, "Growth and Welfare in a Small Open Economy," National Bureau of Economic Research, Working Paper No. 2809, 1989c.

———, and ———, "Quality Ladders in the Theory of Growth," National Bureau of Economic Research, Working Paper No. 3099, 1989d.

———, and ———, "Comparative Advantage and Long Run Growth," *American Economic Review*, LXXX (September 1990), 796–815.

———, and ———, "Quality Ladders and Product Cycles," *Quarterly Journal of Economics*, CVI (1991), 557–86.

Krugman, Paul, "Increasing Returns, Monopolistic Competition, and International Trade," *Journal of International Economics*, IX (November 1979), 469–79.

———, "Intraindustry Specialization and the Gains from Trade," *Journal of Political Economy*, LXXXIX (October 1981), 959–73.

———, *Rethinking International Trade* (Cambridge MA: MIT Press, 1990).

Lancaster, Kevin, "Intraindustry Trade under Perfect Monopolistic Competition," *Journal of International Economics*, X (1980), 151–75.

Lucas, Robert E., Jr., "On the Mechanics of Economic Development," *Journal of Monetary Economics*, XXII (1988), 3–42.

Rebelo, Sergio, "Long-Run Policy Analysis and Long-Run Growth," *Journal of Political Economy*, 99, 3 (June 1991), 500–521.

Rivera-Batiz, Luis A., and Paul M. Romer, "International Trade with Endogenous Technological Change," *European Economic Review*, 35, 4 (May 1991), 971–1001.

Romer, Paul M., "Growth Based on Increasing Returns Due to Specialization," *American Economic Review*, LXXVII (May 1987), 56–62.

———, "Endogenous Technological Change," Journal of Political Economy, XCVIII (October 1990), S71–8102.

Rosenberg, Nathan, *Inside the Black Box* (Cambridge, England: Cambridge University Press, 1980).

Segerstrom, Paul, T. C. A. Anant, and Elias Dinopoulos, "A Schumpeterian Model of the Product Life Cycle," *American Economic Review*, (1990), 1077–91.

Young, Alwyn, "Learning by Doing and the Dynamic Effects of International Trade," *Quarterly Journal of Economics*, CVI (1991), 369–405.

1.8   Economic Integration and Endogenous Growth: An Addendum

The note by Devereux and Lapham [1994] shows why it is important to check the robustness and stability of results that rely on symmetry assumptions. It shows that one of the equilibria for one of the two models that we consider in our paper [Rivera-Batiz and Romer 1991] is not stable. If the economy starts from initial conditions other than the symmetric ones that we examine, it will not converge to the symmetric equilibrium we describe.

Their analysis also sheds additional light on the general result that emerges from our analysis of this "knowledge-driven" model of growth. When there are flows of knowledge between countries, we showed that researchers in one country work with a larger portion of the entire worldwide stock of knowledge and that growth is faster. (As Devereux and Lapham show elsewhere, the equilibrium with knowledge flows is locally stable.) When there are no flows of knowledge, we showed in our (unstable) symmetric equilibrium that opening trade in goods does not let workers in different countries work with a larger stock of knowledge, and therefore does not lead to an increase in the rate of growth. Workers in each country continue to do research, and they can take advantage of only local knowledge.

Devereux and Lapham show that if countries start from initial stocks of knowledge, trade in goods creates incentives for the workers in the country with the smaller stock of knowledge to stop doing research and to specialize in the production of goods. (For additional discussion of the forces leading to specialization, see chapter 8 of Grossman and Helpman [1990] and Rivera-Batiz and Xie [1993].) As a result, a larger fraction of the worldwide stock of knowledge is available to the workers who continue to do research because now they all work in the country with the larger initial stock of knowledge and now all increments to the stock of knowledge come in the country where they work.

The results of Devereux and Lapham therefore add additional force to the point that we made. The finding that trade in goods per se does not affect the rate of growth is not robust. The general point is that trade policies that increase the stock of knowledge available to workers doing research will increase the rate of growth.

References

Devereux, M. B. and B. J. Lapham, "The Stability of Economic Integration and Endogenous Growth," *Quarterly Journal of Economics*, CIX (1994), 299–305.

Grossman, G. and E. Helpman, *Innovation and Growth in the Global Economy*, (Cambridge: MIT Press, 1991).

Rivera-Batiz, L. and Paul M. Romer, "Economic Integration and Endogenous Growth," *Quarterly Journal of Economics,* CVI (May 1991), 531–555.

Rivera-Batiz, L. and Danyang Xie, "Integration Among Unequals," *Regional Science and Urban Economics*, XXIII (July 1993), 337–354.

Chapter 2

International Trade with Endogenous Technological Change*

2.1 Introduction

In a model of endogenous growth with increasing returns, one of us [Romer (1990b)] showed that a reduction in the extent of the market brought about by trade restrictions leads to a decrease in the worldwide rate of growth. Using essentially the same model of growth, Grossman and Helpman (1990) showed that in some circumstances, trade restrictions could nevertheless increase the worldwide rate of growth.

In this paper, we relate these apparently contradictory results by using a decomposition of the change in the growth rate that is similar to the decomposition of a change in demand into a substitution effect that can be signed based on a priori reasoning and an income effect that cannot. We identify two effects of trade restrictions,

---

*This chapter was co-authored by Luis A. Rivera-Batiz and Paul M. Romer and was originally published in *European Economic Review*, Vol. 35, No. 4 (May 1991), pp. 971–1004. ©1991 Elsevier Science Publishers.

We have benefited from several conversations with Gene Grossman and Elhanan Helpman about their work on related issues. Comments from Ray Riezman, Robert Staiger and Danyang Xie were also very helpful. The work of the second author was supported by NSF grant No. SES88-22052, by a Sloan Foundation Fellowship, and by the Center for Advanced Studies in the Behavioral Sciences, which received support from NSF grant No. BNS87-00864.

which we label the integration effect and the redundancy effect, that unambiguously decrease worldwide growth rates. We identify a third effect of trade, the allocation effect, that can either increase or decrease the rate of growth.

We use a model with two fundamental sectors: a research and development sector that produces the new ideas that make continued growth possible, and a manufacturing sector that makes use of these ideas and produces physical capital and consumption goods. Output from each of these sectors can be described in terms of a reduced form equation that depends on basic inputs such as physical capital, human capital, and labor used in the sector. The allocation effect refers to changes in sectorial output induced by changes in the allocation of basic inputs between the sectors. After trade opens, each country reallocates resources toward the sector in which it has a comparative advantage. As is clear from the classical theory of trade, allocation effects will be larger when the differences in the endowments or technologies of two trading partners are large.

In contrast to allocation effects, which link different sectors in the same country, integration effects link the same sector in different countries. Trade induces integration effects in a sector if its reduced form equation exhibits increasing returns. Increasing returns at the level of the sector could be associated with external effects arising from knowledge spillovers or with monopolistic competition between firms that supply a diverse set of specialized inputs used in production in the sector. If they are present, worldwide output from this sector will be larger when the two national sectors are integrated.

Trade restrictions will have a redundancy effect if they induce redundant research effort. When we measure the integration effect, we take as given the set of specialized inputs and pieces of knowledge available in each country. We ask merely whether output increases as the existing inputs and ideas flow more easily between the two countries. Redundancy is an inherently dynamic effect. Since the set of goods and ideas are growing over time, closer economic ties between nations can influence the new inputs and ideas that are produced. Redundancy occurs when the same specialized input or idea is invented or discovered twice, once in each country.

The integration or redundancy effects are defined holding constant the allocation of basic inputs between the manufacturing and research sectors, so it is possible to talk of an effect that takes place in one sector only. By definition, redundancy occurs only in the research sector. Since trade restrictions impede the exploitation of international increasing returns and since both integration and redundancy effects arise from increasing returns, both effects have unambiguously negative effects on output. Through its action in the manufacturing sector, the integration effect of trade restrictions decreases the level of income. Through their action in the research sector, both integration and redundancy effects decrease the rate of growth.

Since allocation effects link the manufacturing and research sectors, allocation effects always induce offsetting changes in the output of the sectors. If resources are shifted into manufacturing, they are shifted out of research. Hence, if the allocation effects of trade restrictions have a positive level effect, they have a negative growth effect. Moreover, there are no simple conditions that characterize which sector gains resources when trade policy is changed. In general, allocation effects can increase or decrease the rate of growth.

With these informal definitions, the apparent conflict between the results described in the beginning can be resolved. In the thought experiment undertaken in the first paper [Romer (1990b)], the trading partners are identical, so the allocation effect of trade is small, and in fact tends to reinforce the integration and redundancy effects. Trade restrictions between identical nations unambiguously decrease the worldwide rate of growth. In the experiment carried out by Grossman and Helpman (1990), trading partners have different technologies, so the allocation effect can be large. As they show, it can overwhelm the other effects. Growth can therefore speedup when trade restrictions are imposed.

To illustrate the use of our decomposition, we study two specific examples of trade restrictions. These examples extend the analysis of trade between identical nations. Our decision to focus on identical countries was guided partly by the belief that the decomposition is easier to grasp in this context. It applies, nonetheless, in all settings. Our decision also reflects the division of labor in research. To get a comprehensive picture of trade and growth, readers should also consult the growing literature on the growth effects of trade between asymmetrical countries, e.g., Dinopoulos, Oehmke and Segerstrom (1990), Feenstra (1990), Grossman and Helpman (1989a, b, c, d), Lucas (1988), Segerstrom, Anat and Dinopoulos (1990) and Young (1990).

In our first example, trade restrictions take the form of an across the board tariff, and we focus on allocation effects. One of the surprising results is that allocation effects can be present at all in the context of trade between countries with identical technologies and endowments. Besides showing why this is so, this example illustrates the ambiguity of the connection between allocation effects and growth. Starting from the point where the tariff equals zero, the growth rate decreases as the tariff rate increases. As the tariff continues to increase, the growth rate reaches a minimum, and then begins to increase. In our example, the growth rate does not, however, return all the way back to the free trade growth rate. (See Figure 2.3 below for a plot of the growth rate as a function of the tariff rate.)

In our second example, we consider selective protection of specific goods in a world in which intellectual property rights are less than perfect. This lets us consider the simultaneous effects of reallocation and redundancy. To keep the length of paper manageable, we focus only on these two effects. In a companion paper [Rivera-Batiz and Romer (1991)] we concentrate on the integration effect, with special emphasis on its action in the research sector that is the engine of growth.

Our examples in both papers were chosen primarily with a view toward illustrating the decomposition that we propose into allocation, integration, and redundancy effects. The strong conclusions that emerge from these examples are nevertheless of some interest in their own right. Taken together, our two papers show that there is a strong presumption that trade restrictions between similar regions like North America and Europe will reduce worldwide rates of growth.

The structure of the paper is as follows. In Section 2.2, we describe a generic two sector model of endogenous growth that can be used to define scale, redundancy and allocation effects more formally. Section 2.3 then presents the specific model of endogenous growth that is used in this paper. Sections 2.4 and 2.5 present the two main examples. A conclusion summarizes the results and describes limitations and extensions. Detailed algebraic calculations are presented in an Appendix.

2.2   Scale, Allocation, and Redundancy

Before delving into the specifics of the model considered here, it is useful to describe integration, allocation and redundancy effects in a more general context. Consider the following representation of a growth model. Suppose that there are two broad sectors in the economy. The growth sector produces the input that makes sustained growth possible. In the model presented below, we refer to this input as the state of the technology and denote it by the letter A. We call the sector that produces A the R&D sector. Other models give a different interpretation to the input that sustains growth (e.g., a special form of capital or education) and to the sector that produces it, but the two sector structure of these models is similar to the structure we consider here.

The second sector in our generic model behaves like the neoclassical growth model. It makes use of A and produces all tangible goods such as consumption goods and physical capital. We need a name for this sector, and it is convenient to refer to this sector as the manufacturing sector, in a very broad sense of the term. It includes all activities in the economy other than R&D.

The usual formulation of the neoclassical model describes output Y as a function of capital K, labor L, and the state of the technology A. We distinguish human capital H from labor L and add it to the list of inputs because we assume that research is relatively human capital intensive and that manufacturing is relatively labor and physical capital intensive. Using a subscript Y to denote inputs that are used in the sector that produces physical goods, we can write output Y as

$$Y = C + \dot{K} = F(H_y, L_y, K_y, A). \tag{1}$$

As in the usual one sector formulation, manufacturing output Y can be split between consumption C and increases in the capital stock $\dot{K}$.

Output in the R&D sector can be written as

$$\dot{A} = R(H_A, L_A, K_A, A). \tag{2}$$

The mnemonic here is R for research. The subscript A denotes the inputs devoted to the research sector, which produces increases in the stock of A. In both equations (1) and (2), the input A is treated differently from the other basic inputs. Inputs like H, L, and K are rivalrous. They can be used in only one sector at a time. In contrast, the knowledge represented by A is nonrival. No subscript on A is necessary because the entire stock of knowledge represented by A can be used in both sectors at the same time.

As noted in the introduction, we allow for the possibility of increasing returns in both of the reduced form eqs. (1) and (2). How integration between the same sector in different countries is achieved depends on the way in which sector-wide increasing returns are supported in a decentralized equilibrium with many firms. We consider two alternatives. The increasing returns could be purely external, arising from knowledge spillovers. In this case, closer integration between firms in the same sector and in different nations is achieved by international flows of ideas. Alternatively, the basic inputs could be connected to the final sectorial output through a large set of specialized activities and intermediate inputs that are provided by monopolistically competitive firms. In this case, integration is achieved by permitting flows of the intermediate inputs between the countries. In either case, if the reduced form equation for the sector exhibits increasing returns, the combined output of all firms in the sector will fall when the flow of ideas or intermediate inputs between the two countries is limited by trade restrictions, and will reach a minimum when the sector in one country operates in isolation from the other.

We assume that there are increasing returns with knowledge spillovers in the R&D sector, and increasing returns with specialized inputs in the manufacturing sector. This means that the degree of integration in the manufacturing sector is determined solely by trade in specialized inputs in production. In the research sector, it is the process of communication of ideas, as fostered by telecommunications networks, printed media, international travel, study, and investment by multinational corporations that determines the degree of integration.

This strict separation is convenient and captures what we think are the most important effects in these different sectors, but it paints a stylized picture that is too simple. Knowledge spillovers are doubtless important in manufacturing, and anyone who has ever seen a laboratory knows that a vast number of specialized inputs are used in research. The formal model can be extended to take account of the world where both mechanisms are present in both sectors. For example, in the companion paper, we use a model with specialized inputs in both R&D and manufacturing [Rivera-Batiz and Romer (1991)]. Devoting too much attention to how increasing returns are decentralized would, however, detract from one of the basic points of our analysis: it is the presence of sector-wide increasing returns that generates integration effects. How the increasing returns are decentralized is of secondary importance.

The three channels through which trade policy can affect the rate of growth are most clearly distinguished if one contrasts the extremes of total isolation and complete integration into a single economy. Let Z_Y and Z_A represent the vectors of inputs used in manufacturing and R&D respectively. With total isolation between two identical economies, worldwide manufacturing output is twice the output in each country, $2Y = 2F(Z_Y)$. If the reduced form function $F(\cdot)$ exhibits increasing returns because of the underlying specialized intermediate goods that make use of the nonrival input A, integration will increase worldwide output. [For a discussion of why nonrival inputs induce increasing returns, see Romer (1990a)]. In the definition of a pure integration effect, we assume that the split between Z_Y and Z_A in each country is held constant. Integration would cause worldwide manufacturing output to increase from $2F(Z_Y)$ to $F(2Z_Y)$. This is the integration effect in manufacturing. It increases the level of output associated with any given value of A, but it does not affect the rate of growth of A. Thus we say that the integration effect in manufacturing has a level effect but no growth effect.

When two research sectors operate in isolation using inputs Z_A, worldwide research output can lie anywhere in the interval between $R(Z_A)$ and $2R(Z_A)$. The advantage of a nonrival good like an idea is that once it has been produced, it can be used by everyone in the world. This means that there is no economic value to devoting resources to produce the idea again if it already exists somewhere else. When resources are used to produce a design idea that already exists, the worldwide stock of A does not increase. If the two R&D sectors operating in isolation produce solutions to exactly the same problems, then total worldwide production of A will be exactly equal to the production in either country, $R(Z_A)$. If, on the other hand, there is no redundant research effort, worldwide research output will be twice that in either country, $2R(Z_A)$.

As a result, when two isolated research sectors become more closely linked, worldwide research output can increase for two reasons. First, redundancy can be reduced or eliminated. The communication links and competitive pressures induced by closer ties will create incentives to avoid rediscovering the wheel. This is what we call the redundancy effect. Second, if there are increasing returns in the R&D sector, then even if there is no redundancy, integration will increase research output from $2R(Z_A)$ to $R(2Z_A)$. This is the integration effect in the R&D sector.

The analysis of any change in policy toward other nations can therefore be separated into three conceptual steps. The first step is to hold constant the degree of integration of the two economies (that is, hold constant any constraints on flows of existing goods, services, and ideas) and to hold constant the allocation of resources between the different sectors in each economy. Then one can observe the degree to which firms and individuals reduce the degree of redundancy in their innovative activities in anticipation of increased future flows of goods, services, and ideas. Thus, for example, an announced plan to open trade in goods (say in the near future) could induce a firm to stop trying to produce copies of goods available abroad and to start producing some unique specialized input. This isolates the redundancy effect of the policy change. By definition, it arises only in the research sector.

Next, the degree of integration between the different sectors is permitted to change as additional flows of existing goods and ideas take place. As ideas flow more readily between the two national research sectors and as firms take advantage of greater diversity in specialized inputs in manufacturing, the integration effects increase output in each sector. For example, integration could take place as an existing idea previously known only to researchers in one country becomes available for use in the second country. Alternatively, integration could increase because an existing piece of specialized equipment that previously had been used in manufacturing in only one country becomes available for use in the second. At this stage we are still holding constant the stock of basic inputs in the two different sectors in the two economies.

Finally, in the last step, it is possible to compare the rate of return to the different basic inputs in the two sectors. These will generally not be equal after the change in trade policy, and it is then possible to analyze the allocation effect — the reallocation of inputs needed to bring rates of return back into equality.

The functions $F(\cdot)$ and $R(\cdot)$ described in this section are reduced form expressions for manufacturing and research output as functions of the amounts of the basic inputs devoted to each sector. The next section describes structural production functions and the market arrangements that lead to reduced forms of this kind. For a heuristic comparison of isolation and complete integration, reduced form expressions are sufficient; but to characterize the intermediate degree of integration induced by policies like across the board tariffs or selective protection, a structural specification is required.

2.3   Specification of the Model

2.3.1   *Functional Forms in the Manufacturing Sector*

The detailed structure of the production technology for the manufacturing sector is taken from Romer (1990b). The fundamental assumptions are that many types of capital goods are used in production, that these are not perfect substitutes, and that technological progress arises from the invention of new types of capital goods. To formalize this, let i index the different types of capital goods and let $x(i)$ denote the usage of each type of good. Producers of consumption or capital goods face a production function of the form

$$Y = H^\alpha L^\beta \int_0^\infty x(i)^{1-\alpha-\beta} \mathrm{d}i. \tag{3}$$

This production function is homogeneous of degree 1 in H, L, and the list of durables $x(i)$. Firms in this sector can therefore be assumed to be price takers. This production function has the feature that it is possible to produce output even if $x(i)$ is equal to 0 for many goods i. At every date, there are many durables that are potentially usable but that cannot be used because they have not been invented yet. Good i has been invented if $i \leqq A$. Hence, the upper limit of integration can be changed from ∞ to $A(t)$ at each date t; however, it must be recognized that what changes over time is not the production function itself, but rather the set of inputs that are available. This specification exploits the kind of additively separable functional form used by Dixit and Stiglitz (1977) to model differentiated consumption goods. It also follows Ethier (1982) in that the relevant differentiated commodities are inputs in production rather than consumption goods. Here, there is a single final consumption good.

To derive a reduced form expression for Y as a function of H, L, A, and K, one must also specify how $x(\cdot)$ is related to K and A. The different capital goods are produced in an intermediate goods sector that the reduced form specification of output $Y = F(H, L, K, A)$ hides. It uses designs for new types of capital goods from the research sector. If firm i owns a design for capital good i, we assume that it can produce physical units of the capital good according to the same manufacturing technology as that used in the production of consumption goods. As a normalization of the unit of measurement of the durables, assume that one unit of forgone consumption generates one unit of any capital good. (Strictly speaking, one unit of consumption goods corresponds to one unit of capital for all different types of capital on a set of types of measure 1.)

Let K denote the total amount of capital goods in existence in the economy, $K = \int_0^A x(i)\mathrm{d}i$. Because all of the different $x(i)$ goods are produced according to the same production technology, this sum across different types of goods makes sense. It represents the cost of the total quantity of durable capital goods in units of forgone consumption goods, and is close to the usual national income account measure of total physical capital.

It is now a simple matter to solve for the list $x(\cdot)$ and write down the reduced form expression for Y as a function of H_y, L_y, K and A. Because the production technology for consumption goods and for each of the different capital goods is the same, total output in the manufacturing sector is the sum $Y = C + \dot{K}$. Given A, it follows by symmetry that $x(i)$ will take on a common value $\bar{x} = K/A$ for all i between 0 and A. Substituting the expression for $\bar{x}$ into eq. (3) then yields

$$Y = F(H_y, L_y, K, A) = (HA)^\alpha (LA)^\beta K^{1-\alpha-\beta}.$$

Even though the underlying production function for manufacturing goods described in eq. (3) is homogeneous of degree 1, this reduced form expression is homogeneous of degree $1 + \alpha + \beta$ in H, L, A, and K. By Euler's theorem, it is impossible for this sector to be decentralized using perfect competition; paying each of the inputs H, L, K, A its marginal product would more than exhaust total output. There are no spillovers and no external effects in the manufacturing sector. The increasing returns to scale are decentralized in this model through imperfect competition. The producer of good i is the only supplier of this good. It therefore charges the monopoly price for it. Because of competition between different firms to produce good i, the present discounted value of the stream of monopoly profits will be equal to the price that is paid for the design for good i. This is how compensation is generated for the research sector.

2.3.2   *Functional Forms and Decentralization in the Research Sector*

We assume that neither labor nor durables are used in research. Output of new designs is a function only of the stock of human capital employed and the stock of ideas that someone who does research has access to. This simple assumption is intended to reflect the fact that research is relatively intensive in human capital and ideas. Let A and A^* denote the stock of designs that have been produced in the home and foreign countries respectively. Let A^{world} denote total stock of designs in the world as a whole. Because of redundancy, $A^{world} \leqq A + A^*$. To isolate the effects of restrictions on trade in goods, we will assume throughout this paper that integration in the sense of full communication of ideas is possible. Thus the entire stock of ideas contained in A^{world} is available for researchers in each country. The effects of limitations of communication are described in a separate paper [Rivera-Batiz and Romer (1990)]. Then the output of designs for new goods in the home country can then be written as

$$\dot{A} = \delta H_A A^{world}. \tag{4a}$$

In the foreign country it is,

$$\dot{A}^* = \delta H_A^* A^{world}. \tag{4b}$$

This kind of specification is discussed in Romer (1990b). This model of research is easy to work with, but it has the disadvantage that it lets none of the specialized durable goods enter as inputs in research. Machine tools probably are not important inputs in research, but other durables like computers are. Our companion paper [Rivera-Batiz and Romer (1990)] describes a parallel model that does let physical capital enter as inputs in research.

Decentralization of production decisions in the research sector involves spillovers of knowledge. The direct dependence of $\dot{A}$ on A^{world} reflects the role of external effects of spillovers of ideas from previous patents both at home and abroad. Holders of patents on the previous designs do not have any technological or legal means for preventing designers of new goods from using the ideas implicit in existing designs for purposes of discovering new designs. For this reason A is not compensated in the research sector.

On the other hand, the holder of a patent on a design does have a legally enforceable property right on the use of the design for the purpose of manufacturing the associated good. Patents on designs confer monopoly power, and the associated monopoly rents provide the compensation for the researcher. Decentralization in manufacturing relies entirely on monopolistic competition while decentralization in research relies entirely on external effects.

2.3.3 *Preferences*

The technology so far describes the accumulation equations for K and A. The stocks of L and H are taken as given. It would be useful to consider an extension that allowed H to increase over time as the average level of human capital in the population increases, but doing so here would add an additional state variable and require analysis off of a balanced growth path. This modification would contribute little to the analysis of trade policy and would greatly increase the complexity of the arguments.

It remains to specify the preferences that determine the split of resources between consumption C, investment in K, and investment in A. For comparability with other work, it is useful to evaluate this model in the context of the standard Ramsey preferences,

$$U = \int_0^\infty \frac{C^{1-\sigma}}{1-\sigma} e^{-\rho t} \mathrm{d}t.$$

The only way in which these preferences enter the computation of the balanced growth equilibrium is through the relationship that they imply between the rate of growth of consumption and the market interest rate:

$$r = \rho + \sigma(\dot{C}/C). \tag{5}$$

(For a derivation of this result, see the Appendix.) Any other rule that pins down the interest rate and the savings rate would suffice to close the model.

2.4 Across the Board Protection

This section describes the equilibrium in a world with two perfectly symmetric countries that impose the same tariff on all imported goods used in production. As noted above, throughout the paper, we assume that ideas can flow freely between different countries and focus only on flows of goods. In this section, we will also assume that international patent protection for designs is perfect so no copying of existing designs takes place.

With these assumptions, we have ruled out any change in the degree of integration of the research sectors in the different countries and any change in redundancy in research. (The tariff will induce integration effects in the manufacturing sector that will reduce the level of income, but the focus here is not growth effects, not level effects.) For the example considered in this section, trade restrictions can therefore affect the rate of growth only by reallocating inputs between the growth and manufacturing sectors. In the next section we weaken the assumption that international patent protection is perfect and analyze a situation entailing redundant R&D. As noted above, consideration of the integration effects in the research sector is sufficiently intricate to merit a separate treatment in the companion paper.

To describe a model with trade in goods explicitly, more notation is needed. Without trade, the quantity of an intermediate input i that is used in a country is identical to the amount that is produced, and both usage and domestically produced stock can be denoted by the variable $x(i)$. With trade, production and usage in a country will differ. In what follows, $x(i)$ still denotes the stock of durable good i that has been produced by firms in the home country; $x^*(i^*)$ denotes the production of a different good in the foreign country. The goods indexed by i and i^* are completely different goods by assumption. Input 10 on the i list could be a hard disk made in the United States; input 10 on the i^* list could be a computer display screen made in Japan. By our strong assumption on international patent protection, no firm creates a design for a good that already exists.

The notation used here reflects the fact that the index labels i and i^* are merely names. The properties of a good are independent of which index is used to represent the good or the magnitude of the index. One can think of a master list of intermediate inputs from which all of the goods indexed by i or i^* are drawn. Particular intermediate inputs are placed on the i and i^* lists as they are introduced, according to the country in which they are discovered.

To describe the use of durable inputs by a final output firm in the home country, it is useful to have a separate notation for domestically produced and imported inputs. Let $d(i)$ denote domestic usage of durables produced in the home country, and let $m(i^*)$ denote home usage of durables produced in the foreign country. Then manufacturing output can then be written as

$$Y(H, L, d, m) = H_Y^\alpha L^\beta \left[\int_0^A d(i)^{1-\alpha-\beta} di + \int_0^{A^*} m(i^*)^{1-\alpha-\beta} di^* \right].$$

(6a)

Symmetrically, foreign output is

$$Y^*(H^*, L^*, d^*, m^*) = H_{Y^*}^\alpha L_{Y^*}^\beta \left[\int_0^A d^*(i^*)^{1-\alpha-\beta} di \right.$$

$$\left. + \int_0^{A^*} m^*(i)^{1-\alpha-\beta} di^* \right].$$

(6b)

The home country imports i^* goods while the foreign country imports i goods. Some portion of these goods are used at home, the rest are exported. Figure 2.1 shows the usage of both domestically produced i durables and imported i^* durables in the home country. Figure 2.2 illustrates the production of i goods in the home country. Because of the symmetry between the different types of durables, domestic and foreign goods would be used at the same level if there were no tariffs. Both of the figures are drawn under the assumption that a positive tariff is charged by each government on imports of durables.

A domestic producer of an i-type good buys a design from someone who has developed it in the research sector. The firm that rents out durable good i maximizes profit, choosing a level of output $d(i)$ to supply in the domestic market and a separate level $m^*(i)$ to supply in the foreign market. Because of the tariff charged on goods sold in the foreign market, the firm is free to segment these two markets and price discriminate, subject to the arbitrage constraint

Quantity of each input used in production

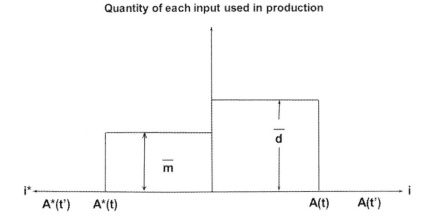

Figure 2.1.   Use in Manufacturing of Foreign and Domestic Inputs at Dates t and $t' > t$.

Quantity of each input produced

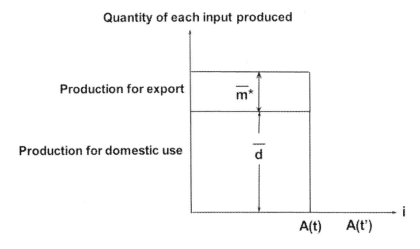

Figure 2.2.   Production of Domestic Inputs at Dates t and $t' > t$.

that the domestic price for the good must lie between the foreign price less the tariff and the foreign price inclusive of the tariff.

The domestic government imposes a tariff τ on the imports of m, so the price paid by domestic purchasers is $(1 + \tau)$ times the price received by the foreign seller. The foreign government imposes a tariff τ^*. In both countries, the tariff revenue is rebated to the consumers via a lump sum distribution. By the symmetry assumption, τ and τ^*

are assumed to be the same, as are L and L^* and H and H^*. The symmetric case has the advantage that the trade balance equation is always satisfied automatically.

Figures 2.1 and 2.2 also illustrate the evolution of the set of durables over time. Because of the symmetry among the goods, the durable good i is supplied in the same quantity $\bar{d}$ in the home market for all i. Because of the tariff, a smaller quantity $\bar{m}^*$ is supplied in the foreign market. In the figure, A denotes the range of inputs produced at home, A^* the comparable range of inputs produced abroad. Over time, A, A^*, and $A^{world} = A + A^*$ all grow, but $\bar{d}$ and $\bar{m}^*$ remain constant. (For derivations of these results, see the Appendix.)

As noted above, tariffs change the degree of integration in the manufacturing sector, but they do not affect integration in the research sector. We have also assumed that international protection for patents is perfect, so no redundancy occurs. As a result, the only growth effects that changes in the tariff rate can have stem from allocation effects which shift human capital between manufacturing and research. As noted in the introduction, the surprising result in this model (explicitly derived in the Appendix) is that the level of human capital used in research $H_A(= H_A^*)$ is not a monotonic function of the tariff rate, and hence neither is the rate of growth. The expression for the common rate of growth in the two countries is

$$g(\tau) = \frac{2\delta H - \Lambda\rho f(\tau)}{\Lambda\sigma f(\tau) + 1},$$

where the function $f(\tau)$ is defined by,

$$f(\tau) = \frac{1 + (1 + \tau)^{-(1-\alpha-\beta)/(\alpha+\beta)}}{1 + (1 + \tau)^{-1/(\alpha+\beta)}}.$$

Figure 2.3 plots an illustrative graph of the growth rate $g(\tau)$. (The specific parameter values used to generate this graph are described in the Appendix.) For any $\tau > 0$, the growth rate is strictly less than the rate of growth $g(0)$ with no tariffs. The growth rate $g(\tau)$ first falls with τ, reaches a minimum, and then begins to increase. In the limit as τ goes to ∞, $g(\tau)$ approaches the free trade growth rate $g(0)$. As

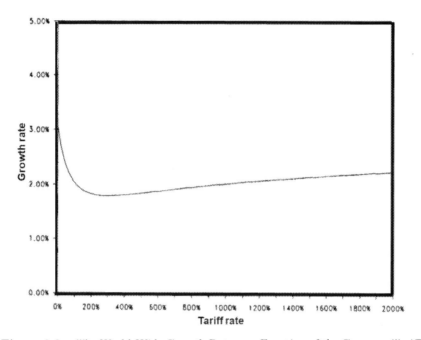

Figure 2.3. The World-Wide Growth Rate as a Function of the Common Tariff Rate.

the figure shows, however, the return back to the zero tariff growth rate is very slow.

This nonmonotonicity of the growth rate in the tariff rate arises because two offsetting forces influence the allocation of human capital. Symmetric increases in the tariff rate $\tau(= \tau^*)$ have effects on the return to human capital in both research and in manufacturing. An increase in τ^* represents a tax by the foreign government on the monopoly rents that the purchaser of a new design can extract from exports of the good. A higher tariff reduces imports by the foreign country m^* and therefore depresses the price of new designs. Everything else equal, this would cause human capital to shift out of research.

Everything else, however, is not equal. An increase in τ (which under our symmetry assumption also implies an increase in τ^*) also reduces the quantity of imported intermediate inputs m used by domestic manufacturers of final output. This reduces the marginal productivity of human capital in manufacturing. The net effect on the allocation of human capital depends on which of these effects is larger. Equation (A.12) in the Appendix shows that the marginal product of human capital in manufacturing depends on a term proportional to $m(\tau)^{1-\alpha-\beta}$, whereas the revenue extracted by the holder of a patent on a new design depends on a term proportional to $(1+\tau)^{-1}m^*(\tau)^{1-\alpha-\beta}$. By symmetry, $m(\tau) = m^*(\tau)$. Initially, the effect on patent revenue,

$$-(1+\tau)^{-2}m(\tau)^{1-\alpha-\beta} + (1+\tau)^{-1}(1-\alpha-\beta)m^{-\alpha-\beta}\frac{\partial m}{\partial \tau}$$

has a larger absolute value than the effect in manufacturing,

$$(1-\alpha-\beta)m^{-\alpha-\beta}\frac{\partial m}{\partial \tau}.$$

As τ goes to ∞ and $(1+\tau)^{-1}$ goes to 0, the relative magnitudes reverse.

When there are two effects that conflict, there will typically exist modifications of the model that will cause the effect that dominates to change. The correct general conclusion that can be drawn is that to the extent that trade restrictions have only allocation effects, the restrictions can have an ambiguous effect on the rate of growth. This is especially true in cases where there is an important asymmetry between two trading partners because the allocation effects of trade are likely to be larger in this case.

The example presented here shows that starting from realistic levels of tariffs, if two similar countries increase their tariffs on imports produced in a monopolistically competitive sector, the net effect will be to drive resources out of that sector. This will reduce the rate at which goods in these sectors are introduced because the dominant effect of an increase in the tariffs is to reduce the rents that provide compensation for research. If the assumption made here is correct — that goods with high fixed research and development costs play an important role in generating growth — then starting from realistic levels of tariffs, symmetric worldwide increases in tariffs on the goods that result from research and development will reduce the worldwide rate of growth.

2.5 Selective Protection with Imperfect Intellectual Property Rights

In the last section, the assumption that ideas flowed freely between nations meant that trade policy had no effect on integration in the research sector. The assumption that patent protection for ideas was perfect meant that regardless of the trade regime, no redundancy occurred. As a result, trade policy could affect the rate of growth only because of the induced allocation effects. In this section, we weaken the assumption that patent protection is perfect and show that trade in goods can reduce redundancy as well.

2.5.1 *Patent Protection, Copying and Trade Barriers*

If there is no trade in goods, there is no competitive reason to design a good that is different from one that exists in a foreign market. If we assume that it is cheaper to copy a foreign good than it is to design a new one, there is an incentive to copy if the costs of circumventing the legal protection are not too high. If, on the other hand, there is trade in goods, a firm faces an offsetting incentive to produce an entirely new design; a new good generates monopoly rents, whereas an existing good will lead to a duopoly game with another producer. Holding constant the degree of legal protection, trade in goods alone can therefore reduce redundant research effort by reducing the payoffs to someone who copies.

We formalize the idea that it is possible to circumvent patent protection and copy an existing design in the following way. Given a stock of general knowledge A^{world} and a quantity H of human capital, it is possible to produce δHA new designs per unit time or θHA copies of existing designs, with $\theta > \delta$. Part of the design cost required for copying a good might be needed to uncover aspects of the good that are not immediately apparent. An additional part of the design work is needed to make design changes that have no effect on how the good functions, but are intended merely to avoid patent infringement charges under the legal system. The assumption that θ is bigger than δ then implies that the amount of research needed to understand an existing good and to circumvent the patent is smaller than the research needed to design a new good.

To make our point as simply as possible, we want to make assumptions which guarantee that a firm that can copy a good and compete with an existing producer will not choose to do so, but that a firm that can copy a foreign good and sell in a market that is protected from the foreign producer's competition will choose to do so. For simplicity, protection from the foreign producer is assumed to take the form of selective quantity limits imposed by the government on imports. Imports for a fixed fraction q of the durable goods produced abroad will be set to zero. Equivalently, a prohibitive tariff is applied to these goods.

A researcher in the domestic country then has three options:

(1) designing a new good and earning monopoly rents in the world market;

(2) copying a good from abroad that is not allowed to enter the domestic market and earning monopoly rents from the domestic market alone; and

(3) copying a good that is already being sold in the domestic market and playing a duopoly game.

In the second case, the copying firm is assumed to be unable to sell in the foreign market because the foreign firm whose good has been denied entry into the home market can induce its government to restrict imports of the copies.

In the symmetric case considered here, the world market is twice the size of either domestic market. For the constant elasticity demand curves used here, prices are independent of market size so that profits are proportional to the size of the market. It is therefore more profitable to copy an excluded foreign good and sell it in the protected domestic market than it is to develop an entirely new good whenever copying is more than twice as easy as innovating, i.e., whenever θ is greater than 2θ. We assume that this is true. We also need an upper bound on how easy it is to copy. If copying were arbitrarily inexpensive (i.e., if θ were arbitrarily large) it would be worthwhile to copy a good that has not been excluded and play a duopoly game even if that game yields a very small profit. We impose a second restriction on θ that avoids this possibility. Specifically, we assume that θ is not too large and that the expected payoff from the duopoly game that would ensue after copying is not large. For example, if firms expect Bertrand competition in the duopoly game copying will never take place in the absence of protection, no matter how big θ is relative to δ. If firms expect Cournot competition, copying will not take place unless θ exceeds 2δ by a large enough margin to make duopoly a feasible equilibrium. For instance, in the case in which $\alpha + \beta$ equals 0.7, copying is not profitable if θ is less than 3δ.

Given these assumptions on θ and δ and implicitly on the duopoly game, the most profitable strategy is to copy an excluded foreign good and sell it in a protected market if this is possible. The next most profitable strategy is to design a new good and sell it worldwide. The third strategy, to copy a good that is not excluded and play a duopoly game, is dominated by the second strategy.

The notation must now reflect the existence of three types of goods. Goods indexed by i continue to represent durable inputs designed and produced at home that are sold in both the domestic and foreign markets. Symmetrically, goods indexed by i^* represent inputs designed and produced abroad that are sold in both markets. A new index j ranging from 0 to J represents nontraded goods. The range of nontraded goods indicates the total number of goods that have been designed in one country and copied in the other. The total measure of copied goods J is proportional to the total amount of effort by human capital that has been devoted to the socially worthless activity of producing redundant designs.

From the point of view of the home country, a good can become a j good in one of two ways. Either it is a newly designed good that is refused entry into the foreign market by the foreign government, or it is a copy of a foreign good that is refused entry into the home market by the domestic government. Since copying goods for sale in a protected market generates pure profits, all goods that are denied entry into a country are copied. As a result, the set of j goods is the same in the two countries. The arbitrary timing assumed here is as follows. Over a small interval of time, some new goods are introduced in the foreign market and are prohibited from entry into the domestic market. The right to earn a pure profit by copying one of these goods and selling it in the protected home market is allocated to a domestic firm. To allocate this opportunity to copy, domestic firms could be required to bid for a license from the government to produce such a good. To highlight the effects of trade alone, we assume that no resources are wasted in deciding which domestic firm gets the right to produce copies in the domestic market. That is, we assume away rent seeking activities in the usual sense. All of the unproductive effort expended here arises purely from effort exerted to reverse engineer a good that has already been designed.

Some researchers at home are engaged in reverse engineering of the foreign, excluded durable goods. Others produce new designs and sell them to firms that will manufacture the new inputs. A firm begins manufacturing, attempts to export the good, and then is told by the foreign government whether its good will be refused entry (which happens with probability q) or allowed to enter (with probability $1 - q$). In keeping with the symmetry assumption, the foreign and home governments exclude the same fraction q of goods from the other country. Because this represents a diversifiable risk, the price the manufacturer pays for a design is the expected monopoly profit that it will generate. This is equal to q times the monopoly profit that can be extracted from sales in the domestic market alone plus $1 - q$ times the monopoly profit that can be extracted from sales in the home market and the foreign market taken together.

The incentive for a government to prohibit imports of foreign goods comes from the fact that this offers a way to capture ex post monopoly rents that would otherwise flow to foreign nationals. A more direct way to expropriate these rents from foreigners is to intentionally weaken patent protection, especially if this can be done in a selective way that preserves intellectual property rights for domestic citizens but undermines them for foreigners. Here we focus only on trade in goods and defer consideration of policy decisions about patent rights and the legal system for future work. In the example we consider here, we focus only on the ways in which restrictions on flows of goods can be used to aid in this process of expropriation. We assume that patent protection applies equally to all designs regardless of the ownership, and that the extent of patent protection is not varied when the barriers to goods flows are varied (i.e., when the fraction of excluded goods q is varied.)

2.5.2   *Redundancy and Growth*

Output of final goods in the home country can be written as

$$Y(H, L, d(\cdot), m(\cdot), n(\cdot))$$

$$= H_Y^\alpha L^\beta \left[\int_0^I d(i)^{1-\alpha-\beta} di + \int_0^{I^*} m(i^*)^{1-\alpha-\beta} di^* + \int_0^I n(j)^{1-\alpha-\beta} dj \right].$$
$$(7)$$

A producer of final goods in the home country can make use of the three types of goods. For $0 \le i \le I, d(i)$ represents use of domestically designed and produced goods that are sold in both markets. For $0 \le j \le J, n(j)$ represents the use of nontraded goods that are produced at home. The total stock of designs produced in the home country A is equal to the sum $A = I + J$. As before, $m(i^*)$ represents imports of goods designed and produced abroad, i^* indexes these goods. Now, however, i^* ranges from 0 to I^* instead of from 0 to A^*. The total stock of goods designed and produced in the foreign country is $A^* = I^* + J$, but only the I^* goods trade.

The expression for the output of final goods in the foreign country is symmetric with that of the domestic country. A firm in the foreign country will use $d^*(i^*)$ of locally produced traded goods for $0 \le i^* \le I^*$. It will also use $m^*(i)$ of goods designed and produced in the home country for $0 \le i \le I$, and $n^*(j)$ units of nontraded goods for $0 \le j \le J$. Note the difference in the notation that is induced by the redundancy. Both lists $n(\cdot)$ and $n^*(\cdot)$ depend on the same index j. Good 34 on the j list is the same good in each country, regardless of the country in which it was first designed and produced. Since I and I^* measure the disjoint sets of traded inputs produced in each country, and J measures the set of nontraded inputs available in each, the measure of the worldwide stock of distinct inputs and distinct design knowledge is $A^{world} = I + I^* + J < A + A^*$.

To complete the specification of this model, it remains to describe how A^{world}, I, I^*, and J evolve. Now there are three different activities in which human capital can be used: manufacturing, denoted by H_Y; research on new goods, denoted now by H_N ('N' for new); and copying of existing designs, denoted by H_C ('C' for copy). When human capital H_N is used in research at home, the implied rate of growth of designs I that trade internationally is

$$\dot{I} = (1 - q)\delta H_N A^{world}. \tag{8}$$

A quantity of human capital equal to H_N produces $\delta H_N A^{world}$ new designs per unit time, but only a fraction $1 - q$ of these are allowed to trade internationally. Symmetrically, the growth of I^* is given by

$$\dot{I}^* = (1 - q^*)\delta H_N^* A^{world}. \tag{9}$$

The quantity of nontraded intermediate inputs grows as new inputs produced at home are excluded from the foreign market and as copying of foreign goods takes place at home:

$$\dot{J} = q^*\delta H_N A^{world} + \theta H_C A^{world}. \tag{10a}$$

The range J grows by the same amount, for the same reasons, in the foreign country:

$$\dot{J} = q\delta H_N^* A^{world} + \theta H_C^* A^{world}. \tag{10b}$$

Because copying generates pure profits, it is constrained only by the supply of goods produced abroad that are excluded from the home market. Consequently, H_C is determined by $\theta H_C A^{world} = q\delta H_N^* A^{world}$. It follows by substitution and symmetry that

$$\dot{J} = q\delta H_N^* A^{world} + q^*\delta H_N A^{world}. \tag{11}$$

By adding eqs. (8), (9), and (11), it follows that $\dot{A}^{world} = \dot{I} + \dot{I}^* + \dot{J}$ is given by

$$\dot{A}^{world} = \delta(H_N + H_N^*)A^{world}. \tag{12}$$

All human capital devoted to research on new goods contributes to the growth of A^{world}. The difference now is that a portion $H_C + H_C^*$ of the total worldwide stock of human capital is devoted to the socially unproductive activity of copying existing designs.

Given the discussion so far, it should come as no surprise that increases in the restrictions on trade in this model unambiguously reduce growth. First, the human capital $H_C + H_C^*$ that is induced into copying acts like a reduction in total worldwide human capital. Since the growth rate is increasing in the total stock of human capital, this reduces the rate of growth. This is the redundancy effect of trade protection. In the absence of the trade restrictions that create the incentive for copying, this amount of human capital would be put to a socially productive use.

In addition, growth is lower still because copying acts like a tax on the revenue generated by a new design. With probability q, all of the profit that would otherwise be collected from the foreign market is taken away. This reduction in the marginal productivity of human capital in research is not offset by any reduction in the marginal productivity of human capital in manufacturing. The manufacturing industries in both countries always use all of the inputs that exist in the world. Thus in this case, the allocation effect of the copying acts unambiguously to reduce growth.

The formal expression for the growth rate as a function of $q = q^*$ derived in the appendix is

$$ g = \left(2\delta H - \frac{2\Lambda\rho}{2-q} \right) \Big/ \left(\frac{2\Lambda\sigma}{2-q} + q\frac{\delta}{\theta} + 1 \right). \tag{13} $$

This expression for g is monotonically decreasing in q.

2.6   Conclusions

The first of our two examples shows that if North Americans were to use a tariff to apply broad restrictions on all newly invented goods imported from Europe, and Europeans put the same tariff on all newly invented goods from the United States, then invention would be a less rewarding activity in both places and technological progress would slow down. Formally, the result allows for the possibility that at very high levels of protection, the effect of higher trade restrictions might be to reduce other opportunities so much that more people become inventors despite the fact that returns to invention fall. The theoretical results, like common sense, suggest that while logically possible, this possibility is not important in practice.

The second example suggests that if Europeans and North Americans use targeted protection for specific goods to extract ex post monopoly rents that would otherwise flow to foreigners, research effort on new goods will be less rewarding, and valuable resources will be diverted from manufacturing and research into socially useless redundant activities. For both reasons, growth rates will fall.

Unambiguous results emerge in these two examples because of the specific details of the experiments that we consider. Of particular importance, we impose symmetry throughout our analysis, in both the endowments and technologies faced by each country, and in the policies that are implemented. This lets us highlight the sense in which trade exploits international increasing returns, and lets us minimize the obscuring effects that arise when trade induces large flows of resources between different sectors.

Our focus should not be taken to imply that differences in endowments, technologies, or policies are always unimportant. For example, in their analysis of product cycle model of trade between a developed North and a less developed South, Grossman and Helpman (1989b, d) have shown that policy changes making it easier for a less developed Southern country to imitate goods invented in the North may speed up the worldwide rate of growth. In this case, the redundancy effects of copying (which are bad for growth) are overwhelmed by the allocation effect of shifting manufacturing from the North to the South, and thereby freeing resources in the North for additional research. Additional copying in this setting can increase the worldwide rate of growth.

In some settings, the policies chosen by different countries will also be different. As first noted by Frank Graham (1923) in his analysis of trade policy with Marshallian increasing returns, the kind of policy favored by a developing country may be very different from that favored by an advanced country. Followers may prefer some kind of infant industry protection while leaders prefer free trade. For a recent analysis of this kind of issue in an endogenous growth model [see Lucas (1988) and Young (1990)].

Our results are therefore specific to a particular context — trade between similar developed countries. Other questions posed in other contexts may well lead to different answers. There results show, nonetheless, that the emerging theory of trade and growth can generate unambiguous conclusions in cases of practical interest.

With the formalization of the new theory of trade [as carried out by Krugman (1979, 1981), Lancaster (1980), Helpman (1981), and Ethier (1982)], it is now clear that the gains from trade can arise from at least fundamental sources: differences in comparative advantage and economy wide increasing returns. One of the difficulties that these two effects present for theorists is that they sometimes offset each other. Consequently, it is no longer possible to make completely general, unqualified statements about what the effects of trade restrictions will be. When the model under consideration is augmented from a static model or a dynamic model with steady states into a model with endogenous growth, the multiplicity of possible outcomes can at first be all the more daunting.

But even though we know that demand curves sometimes slope down and sometimes slope up, economists still have something useful to say about demand theory. We know that in some problems (e.g., the response of savings to changes in the interest rate) income effects can be very important and upward sloping demand curves are a real possibility. We also know that in many other cases, income effects will reinforce substitution effects, or will be small and can be ignored. In either of these cases, demand curves will slope down. By combining a theoretical decomposition of price changes into income and substitution effects with accumulated evidence about income elasticities, we have learned that there are many cases where the effects of price changes can be predicted with confidence. We hope that the decomposition proposed here can serve a similar purpose. Once economists have developed similar evidence about the magnitude and direction of the allocation effects of trade restrictions, we should be able to predict the effects that trade restrictions have on growth with the same confidence as when we predict the effect of a price change on demand.

2.7 Appendix

2.7.1 *Results from Section 2.4 in the Text*

The production function for the final output sector in the home country is given in eq. (6a). This constant returns to scale production function leads to the usual indeterminacy in the number of price-taking firms and the scale of production for each firm. Since aggregate output is determined, we can focus on the sector's total output and derive the aggregate demand for each good $x(i)$ by solving a maximization problem that is conditional on given levels of H_Y and L for the industry as a whole. Leaving aside the exogenous wage bill, the maximization problem can be represented as:

$$\max_{d,m} Y(H_Y, L, d(\cdot), m(\cdot)) - \int_{R^+} P_d(i)d(i)di - \int_{R^+} (1+\tau)^*_m (i^*)m(i^*)di^*,$$
(A.1)

where P_d refers to the home price of domestic inputs and P^*_m is the price received by foreign producers for their exports. (Both of these prices, and all other prices quoted for durables are rental prices.) We will henceforth treat the range of integration as being $\mathbb{R}_+$ and implicitly treat any good with $i > A$ or $i^* > A^*$ (that is any good that has not been invented yet) as having an infinite price. The price $P^*_m(1+\tau)$ is paid by domestic users of foreign inputs; it is greater than the price received by foreign producers due to the tariff τ applied in the home country. The price of the single final output good, which is freely traded, must be the same in the two countries. It is taken as the numeraire.

The first order necessary conditions for the choice of $d(i)$ and $m(i^*)$ in the domestic manufacturing sector are:

$$(1 - \alpha - \beta)H_Y^\alpha L^\beta d(i)^{-\alpha-\beta} - P_d(i) = 0, \qquad \text{(A.2)}$$

$$(1 - \alpha - \beta)H_Y^\alpha L^\beta m(i^*)^{-\alpha-\beta} - (1+\tau)P^*_m(i^*) = 0. \qquad \text{(A.3)}$$

The implied derived demands for domestic and imported inputs are:

$$d(i) = (1 - \alpha - \beta)^{1/(\alpha+\beta)} H_Y^{\alpha/(\alpha+\beta)} L^{\beta/(\alpha+\beta)} P_d(i)^{-1/(\alpha+\beta)}, \quad (A.4)$$

$$m(i^*) = (1 - \alpha - \beta)^{1/(\alpha+\beta)} H_Y^{\alpha/(\alpha+\beta)} L^{\beta/(\alpha+\beta)}$$
$$\times (1 + \tau)^{-1/(\alpha+\beta)} P_m^*(i^*)^{-1/(\alpha+\beta)}. \quad (A.5)$$

An analogous procedure yields the first order necessary conditions for the foreign country's choice of $d^*(i^*)$ and $m(i^*)$ in the symmetric tariff case $(\tau = \tau^*)$:

$$(1 - \alpha - \beta) H_Y^{*\alpha} L^{*\beta} d^*(i)^{-\alpha-\beta} - P_{d^*}^*(i^*) = 0, \quad (A.6)$$

$$(1 - \alpha - \beta) H_Y^{*\alpha} L^{*\beta} m^*(i)^{-\alpha-\beta} - (1 + \tau) P_{m^*}(i^*) = 0. \quad (A.7)$$

The implied derived demands for locally produced and imported inputs abroad are:

$$d^*(i^*) = (1 - \alpha - \beta)^{1/(\alpha+\beta)} H_Y^{*\alpha/(\alpha+\beta)}$$
$$\times L^{*\beta/(\alpha+\beta)} P_{d^*}^*(i^*)^{-1/(\alpha+\beta)}, \quad (A.8)$$

$$m^*(i^*) = (1 - \alpha - \beta)^{1/(\alpha+\beta)} H_Y^{*\alpha/(\alpha+\beta)} L^{*\beta/(\alpha+\beta)}$$
$$\times (1 + \tau)^{-1/(\alpha+\beta)} P_{m^*}(i)^{-1/(\alpha+\beta)}. \quad (A.9)$$

$P_{d^*}^*$ is the price (set by foreign firms on foreign goods) of foreign inputs. P_{m^*} (set by home firms on goods imported by foreigners) is the price received by home producers. $(1 + \tau^*)P_{m^*}$ is the price paid by the foreign users of these goods.

In equilibrium, the production $x(i)$ of a representative domestic input is equal to the sum of domestic usage $d(i)$ and exports $m^*(i)$. Since all domestic producers face the same demand and have identical cost functions, we can ignore the index i and write the demand as a function of the appropriate price, $d(P_d)$ and $m^*(P_{m^*})$. Total production x of an intermediate input in the home country can then be expressed as $x(P_d, P_{m^*}) = d(P_d) + m^*(P_{m^*})$.

The presence of a tariff barrier generates a range $P_{m^*} < P_d < (1 + \tau)P_{m^*}$ within which domestic producers can engage in price discrimination between foreign and domestic markets. Outside of this range, purchasers in one country could earn arbitrage profits by reselling in the other country. Domestic firms will set output levels in each market and charge prices to maximize total profits. Recalling that the prices are rental prices, revenue as a function of the quantities d and m^* is $P_d(d)d + P_{m^*}(m^*)m^*$. Because it costs one unit of forgone output to produce one unit of capital, the flow opportunity cost of these units is $r(d + m^*)$. The instantaneous rate of profit earned by the holder of the patent is therefore

$$\pi = \max_{d,m^*} P_d(d)d + P_{m^*}(m^*)m^* - r(d + m^*).$$

Equating each market's marginal revenue to marginal costs and substituting for $P_d(d)$ and $P_{m^*}(m^*)$ from (A.2) and (A.7), yields a pair of pricing equations for domestic and foreign sales: $P_d = r/1 - \alpha - \beta$ and $P_{m^*} = r/1 - \alpha - \beta$. These pricing functions represent identical markups over marginal cost, r. Thus we can drop the distinction between domestic prices P_d and prices received in foreign markets P_{m^*} and represent both of them by the symbol p. Similar considerations applied to foreign firms show that their optimal pricing functions are $P_{d^*}^* = P_m^* = r^*/1 - \alpha - \beta$. Furthermore, free flows of the final consumption good and free borrowing and lending imply that and interest rates must be equalized across countries ($r = r^*$). As a result, durables bear the same price $p = p^*$ in both countries. We can therefore conclude that

$$p = p^* = r/(1 - \alpha - \beta). \tag{A.10}$$

This fixed price is associated with constant values for $d = d^*$ and $m^* = m$ that are denoted with over bars: $\bar{d}, \bar{m}$.

Free entry into the durables sector ensures that the discounted value of revenue minus variable costs equals design costs P_A.

$$P_A(t) = \int_{\mathbb{R}+} e^{-\int_t^{s'} r(s)ds} \pi(s')ds'.$$

Differentiating with respect to time yields an arbitrage equation relating the interest rate to current profits per dollar invested plus the percentage change in the value of designs over time,

$$r = \pi(t)/P_A + \dot{P}_A/P_A.$$

We seek a solution characterized by a constant value for P_A, in which case the arbitrage equation reduces to:

$$P_A = \pi(t)/r = (1/r)[p(\bar{d} + \bar{m}^*)] - r(\bar{d} + \bar{m}^*) = (p/r - 1)(\bar{d} + \bar{m}^*). \tag{A.11}$$

Substituting $p/r = 1 - \alpha - \beta$ from (A.10), and using $p = (1 - \alpha - \beta)H_Y^\alpha L^\beta(\bar{d})^{-\alpha-\beta} = (1+\tau)^{-1}(1 - \alpha - \beta)H_Y^\alpha L^\beta \bar{m}^{*-\alpha-\beta}$ from (A.2) and (A.7), we obtain a relation between $P_A, r, \bar{d}$, and m^*,

$$P_A = (\alpha + \beta)\frac{P}{r}(\bar{d} + \bar{m}^*)$$

$$P_A = \frac{\alpha + \beta}{r}(1 - \alpha - \beta)H_Y^\alpha L^\beta [\bar{d}^{1-\alpha-\beta} + (1+\tau)^{-1}\bar{m}^{*1-\alpha-\beta}].$$

Equating the marginal product of labor in research, $\delta P_A A^{world}$, to that in manufacturing, $\partial Y/\partial H_Y$, yields

$$\delta((\alpha + \beta)/r)(1 - \alpha - \beta)H_Y^\alpha L^\beta A^{world}[\bar{d}^{1-\alpha-\beta} + (1+\tau)^{-1}\bar{m}^{*1-\alpha-\beta}]$$

$$= \alpha H_Y^{\alpha-1} L^\beta [A\bar{d}^{1-\alpha-\beta} + A^*\bar{m}^{1-\alpha-\beta}]. \tag{A.12}$$

To solve for H_Y, we impose the symmetry condition $A/A^{world} = A^*/A^{world} = 1/2$, and make use of the relation $\bar{m} = \bar{m}^* = \bar{d}(1+\tau)^{-1/(\alpha+\beta)}$, which follows from (A.4), (A.5), and (A.9) since $P_d = P_m^* = P_{m^*}$. This yields a formula for H_Y in terms of r:

$$H_Y = (\Lambda/2\delta)f(\tau)r, \tag{A.13}$$

where

$$\Lambda = \frac{\alpha}{(\alpha + \beta)(1 - \alpha - \beta)}$$

and

$$f(\tau) = \frac{1 + (1 + \tau)^{-(1-\alpha-\beta)/(\alpha+\beta)}}{1 + (1 + \tau)^{-1/(\alpha+\beta)}}.$$

Equation (A.13) provides the basic technological relation between g and r for the model. In order to solve for r and $H_A = H - H_Y$, we must consider the preference side of the model, which will determine the other relation involving r.

Let $T(t)$ denote the redistribution of tariff revenues through rebates, let w denote the wage for labor, and let w_H denote the wage for human capital. Also, let $D(t)$ denote the consumer's holdings of debt instruments, and assume that all firms are 100% debt-financed. (With no uncertainty, debt is equivalent to equity.) The utility maximization problem can be written as

$$\max_{C(\cdot)} U(C(\cdot)) = \int_0^\infty e^{-\rho t} \frac{C(t)^{1-\sigma}}{1-\sigma} dt$$

subject to $\dot{D} = rD + w(t)L + w_H(t)H + T(t) - C(t)$.

For now we treat r as a constant in the consumers problem. We show below that this is consistent with the equilibrium conditions on the production side as well. The Hamiltonian for this problem is

$$\mathcal{H} = \max \frac{C(t)^{1-\sigma}}{1-\sigma} e^{-\rho t} + \lambda[rD + w(t)L + w_H(t)H + T(t) - C(t)],$$

with associated Hamiltonian equations

$$0 = \partial\mathcal{H}/\partial C = C^{-\sigma} e^{-\rho t} - \lambda$$

which implies that $-\lambda = \partial H/\partial K = \lambda r$. Differentiating the expression $C^{-\sigma} e^{-\rho t} = \lambda$ with respect to time and then using the fact that $\dot{\lambda}/\lambda = -r$, we obtain eq. (5) in the text,

$$r = \rho + \sigma(\dot{C}/C). \tag{A.14}$$

The level of $C(\cdot)$ is determined by the requirement that the consumer's intertemporal budget constraint be satisfied. It can be verified that after substitution of the equilibrium values of $w(t), w_H(t)$ and $T(t)$, this forces $C(t)$ to be equal to the aggregate output of consumption goods at each time t.

Under balanced growth, the growth rate g is determined by the rate of growth of the total number of inputs, $\dot{A}^{world}/A^{world}$, where

$A^{world} = A + A^*$. From eqs. (4a, b) in the text, this is equal to

$$g = \delta H_A + \delta H_A^*. \tag{A.15}$$

Inserting this into the expression for r gives

$$r = \rho + 2\sigma\delta H_A. \tag{A.16}$$

In order to solve out for H_A and hence for r, and g, one must combine this preference condition with the technological condition in (A.13). Substituting into (A.13) we obtain

$$H_A = H - H_Y = H - \frac{\Lambda}{2\delta}f(\tau)(\rho + 2\sigma\delta H_A) = \frac{2\delta H - \Lambda f(\tau)\rho}{2\delta\left[1 + \Lambda\sigma f(\tau)\right]}. \tag{A.17}$$

with Λ and $f(\tau)$ defined as in (A.13).

Along a balanced growth path the growth rate in the world and in each country is given by $g = g^* = \delta H^{world} = 2\delta H_A$, so

$$g = \frac{2\delta H - \Lambda\rho f(\tau)}{1 + \Lambda\sigma f(\tau)}. \tag{A.18}$$

Because $f(0) = 1$, this reproduces the formula from Romer (1990b) for the growth rate in a two-country symmetric world economy with $\tau = \tau^* = 0$.

In the presence of tariffs, both the amount of R&D and the growth rate depend negatively on the function $f(\tau)$. This function is equal to 1 when $\tau = 0$, increases with τ up to a unique maximum, and asymptotically approaches 1 as τ goes to infinity. This generates the qualitative behavior reproduced in Fig. 2.3. This figure plots g as a function of τ for the following parameter values: $\alpha + \beta = 2/3, \delta H = 0.07, \rho = 0.05, \sigma = 1$. The value for $\alpha + \beta$ should be equal to the share of manufacturing income that is paid as salaries. Only the product δH is determined in this model, and the value of 0.07 was chosen to make the feasible rates of growth reasonable. Setting $\sigma = 1$ corresponds to the choice of logarithmic utility.

2.7.2   *Results from Section 2.5 in the Text*

Output of final goods in the home country is given in eq. (7) in the text. The profit maximization's problem for given levels of H_Y and L is

$$\max_{d,m,n} Y(L, H_Y, d(\cdot), m(\cdot), n(\cdot)) - \int_{\mathbb{R}+} P_d(i)d(i)di$$

$$- \int_{\mathbb{R}+} P_m^*(i^*)m(i^*)di^* - \int_{\mathbb{R}+} P_m(j)n(j)dj. \qquad \text{(A.19)}$$

As above, the first order necessary conditions for profit maximization yield the derived demands for d, m, and n and symmetrical expressions for d^*, m^*, and n^*.

Producers of traded durables choose output levels that equate marginal revenue in each location to marginal costs. Since there are no tariffs, producers face the same demand functions locally and abroad when they can sell in both markets. As a result, they will charge identical prices in both locations,

$P_d = P_{m^*} = r/1-\alpha-\beta$. With free trade in final goods and interest rate equalization, symmetric arguments give $P_d^* = P_m^* = r/1-\alpha-\beta$.

The maximization problem for producers of the j goods, which are not traded, is

$$\max_{n} \pi_n = p_n(n)n - rn.$$

It can be easily verified that constant marginal costs and a constant elasticity demand imply that $P_n = r/1 - \alpha - \beta$ for these goods as well. Consequently, $\bar{d} = m^* = \bar{n}$, and profit π_t, for traded goods is twice the profit π_n for the nontraded goods.

Ex ante, a producer of new product does not know whether it will be able to sell its output abroad. When bidding for a new design, the firm calculates the expected profit, which is equal to the probability $1 - q$ the good is not subject to foreign protection times π_t, plus the probability q that it is denied access to the foreign market times π_n. (By symmetry, the probabilities of exclusion in the two countries, q and q^*, are the same.) The price of new designs is equal to the discounted value of expected profits. The price bid for a new patent can then be written as

$$P_A = \frac{1}{r}[(1-q)\pi_t + q\pi_n],$$

$$= \frac{1}{r}(1-q)[p(\bar{d}+\bar{m}^*) - r(\bar{d}+\bar{m}^*)] + \frac{1}{r}q[p\bar{n} - r\bar{n}],$$

$$= \left(\frac{p}{r}-1\right)(1-q)(\bar{d}+\bar{m}^*) + \left(\frac{p}{r}-1\right)q\bar{n}.$$

Then using the result $(p/r)(1 - \alpha - \beta) = 1$, the expressions for p in terms of d, m^*, and n that are derived from the demand curves, and the fact that the quantities chosen by the monopolist are the same, $\bar{d} = \bar{m}^* = \bar{n}$, this can be expressed as

$$P_A = \frac{(1-q)(1-\alpha-\beta)}{r}(\alpha+\beta)H_Y^\alpha L^\beta(\bar{d}^{1-\alpha-\beta} + \bar{m}^{*1-\alpha-\beta})$$

$$+ \frac{q(1-\alpha-\beta)}{r}(\alpha+\beta)H_Y^\alpha L^\beta \bar{n}^{1-\alpha-\beta},$$

$$= (2-q)\frac{(1-\alpha-\beta)}{r}(\alpha+\beta)H_Y^\alpha L^\beta \bar{d}^{1-\alpha-\beta}. \qquad (A.20)$$

As in the previous section, the result linking the growth rate and the interest rate on the production side follows by equating the return to human capital in the research and manufacturing sectors:

$$\delta P_A A^{world} = \frac{\partial Y}{\partial H_Y} = \alpha H_Y^{\alpha-1} L^\beta [I + I^* + J]d^{1-\alpha-\beta}. \qquad (A.21)$$

Inserting the expression from eq. (A.20) in for P_A in eq. (A.21) and solving for H_Y, we obtain,

$$H_Y = (1/\delta)\Lambda(1/(2-q))r,$$

where $\Lambda = \alpha/(\alpha+\beta)(1-\alpha-\beta)$ as before.

We solve for the rate of growth as in the tariff example, by using eq. (A.14) to express the interest rate in terms of the balanced rate of growth for the economy, $r = p + \sigma g$, where $g = \dot{C}/C = \dot{A}^{world}/A^{world}$. Using eq. (12) from the text to substitute for $\dot{A}^{world}/A^{world}$ yields

$g = 2\delta H_N$. Together these two substitutions give

$$H_Y = \frac{\Lambda}{\delta} \frac{[p + 2\sigma\delta H_N]}{2 - q}. \tag{A.22}$$

H_Y can be removed from this expression by using the adding up constraint $H = H_Y + H_N + H_C$ and the fact that all of the goods that are available for copying are copied, to that $q\delta H_N^* A^{world} = \theta H_C A^{world}$. By symmetry $H_N^* = H_N$, so $H_Y = H - (1 - q(\delta/\theta))H_N$. Substituting this into eq. (A.22) and clearing for H_N yields

$$H_N = \left[H - \frac{\Lambda\rho}{\delta(2 - q)} \right] \Big/ \left[\frac{2\Lambda\sigma}{2 - q} + q\frac{\delta}{\theta} + 1 \right].$$

Equation (13) in the text then follows from $g = \delta H^{world} = 2\delta H_N$.

References

Dixit, Avinash and Joseph Stiglitz, 1977, "Monopolistic competition and optimum product diversity," *American Economic Review* 67, 297–308.

Dinopoulos, Elias, James Oehmke and Paul Segerstrom, 1990, "High technology industry trade and investment: The role or factor endowments," Working paper (University of Florida, Gainesville, FL).

Ethier, Wilfred J., 1982, "National and international returns to scale in the modern theory or international trade," *American Economic Review* 72, 389–405.

Feenstra, Robert, 1990, "Trade and uneven growth," Working paper No. 3276 (National Bureau of Economic Research).

Graham, Frank D., 1923, "Some aspects or protection further considered," *Quarterly Journal of Economics* 37, 199–227.

Grossman, Gene and Elhanan Helpman, 1989a, "Growth and welfare in a small open economy," National Bureau of Economic Research, Working paper No. 2809.

Grossman, Gene and Elhanan Helpman, 1989b, "Endogenous product cycles," National Bureau of Economic Research, Working paper No. 2913.

Grossman, Gene and Elhanan Helpman, 1989c, "Quality ladders in the theory or growth," National Bureau of Economic Research, Working paper No. 3099.

Grossman, Gene and Elhanan Helpman, 1989d, "Quality ladders and product cycles," National Bureau of Economic Research, Working paper No. 3201.

Grossman, Gene and Elhanan Helpman, 1990, "Comparative advantage and long run growth," *American Economic Review* 80, 796–815.

Helpman, Elhanan, 1981, "International trade in the presence of product differentiation, economies of scale, and monopolistic competition: A Chamberlin-Heckscher-Ohlin approach," *Journal of International Economics* 11, 305–340.

Krugman, Paul, 1979, "Increasing returns, monopolistic competition, and international trade," *Journal of International Economics* 9, 469–479.

Krugman, Paul, 1981, "Intraindustry specialization and the gains from trade," *Journal of Political Economy* 89, 959–973.

Lancaster, Kelvin, 1980, "Intraindustry trade under perfect monopolistic competition," *Journal of International Economics* 10, 151–175.

Lucas, Robert Jr., E., 1988, "On the mechanics or economic development," *Journal of Monetary Economics* 22, 3–42.

Rivera-Batiz, Luis A. and Paul M. Romer, 1991, "Economic integration and endogenous growth," *Quarterly Journal of Economics*, 106(2), 531–555.

Romer, Paul, 1990a, "Are nonconvexities important for understanding growth?," *American Economic Review* 80, 97–103.

Romer, Paul, 1990b, "Endogenous technological change," *Journal of Political Economy* 98, S71–Sl02.

Segerstrom, Paul, T.C.A. Anat and Elias Dinopoulos, 1990, "A Schumpeterian model or the product life cycle," *American Economic Review*, 80 (5), 1077–1091.

Young, Alwyn, 1991, "Learning by doing and the dynamic effects of international trade," *Quarterly Journal of Economics*, 106 (2), 369–405.

Chapter 3

GATT, Trade, and Growth*

3.1 Introduction

Time-series data on product and income show that the worldwide economic growth rate accelerated in the post-World War II period in comparison with previous decades. The GATT-sponsored dismantling of the heavily protectionist structures that took hold in the 1930's moved the world toward freer trade as it gradually opened up previously restricted markets. It supported renewed growth worldwide for three decades. During 1950–1980 world trade and output grew at average annual rates of 6 percent and 4 percent, respectively.

In the 1980's, the world economy dragged under the weight of reduced trade and surging nontariff barriers to trade. The GATT lost effectiveness, and bilateral agreements began to take its place. The GATT's accent on merchandise trade lost comprehensiveness as economic structures and world trade shifted toward services and information. World trade grew at about 4 percent per year and output at less than 3 percent, which represents the poorest performance since 1950. For many, the 1990's represent an era of diminished expectations.

*This chapter was co-authored by Luis A. Rivera-Batiz and Danyang Xie and was originally published in *American Economic Review*, Vol. 82 No. 2 (May 1992), pp. 422–427. ©1992 The American Economic Association.

We thank Paul Romer for helpful discussions.

In order to understand these events, we offer an endogenous-growth perspective that traces underlying sources of worldwide growth back to policy variables relating to trade among nations. We develop an open economy endogenous-growth model, pioneered by Gene Grossman and Elhanan Helpman (1991), and undertake various experiments that illustrate the growth mechanisms of the GATT and international trade, broadly conceived to include trade in goods and in ideas.

3.2   Growth Effects of Integration and Tariff Cuts

Consider the growth effect of a move from complete isolation to free trade in goods without knowledge diffusion. We find that whether growth rates are affected depends on whether or not countries are symmetric.

It is shown in Rivera-Batiz and Paul M. Romer (1991a) that if countries are symmetric, free trade in goods alone does not increase the attractiveness of the R&D sector vis-à-vis the final goods sector. The reason is that goods-market integration raises the value of the marginal product of human capital in both sectors, but in this model, these effects exactly cancel out so that there is no reallocation of human capital toward one sector or the other. The upshot is that there is a scale effect in manufacturing but no reallocation of resources toward the R&D sector. The scale effect in manufacturing produces a level effect on per capita income but does not affect the growth rate permanently.

With asymmetric countries, this note shows that integration through trade in goods generates an allocation effect. The allocation effect shifts resources toward manufacturing in the high-human-capital country and reduces the growth rate compared with isolation. The opposite happens in the initially low-growth country. We obtain that the resulting worldwide growth rate lies between the highest and the lowest growth rates under isolation. In other words, integration in goods without knowledge diffusion restricts growth in the high-growth regions and speeds it up in the low-growth regions. For a case in which no diffusion of technology can lead to uneven growth, see Feenstra (1990). For the case in which the world moves from complete isolation to free trade with full diffusion of technology, it is shown in Rivera-Batiz and Xie (1992) that all countries will unambiguously grow faster.

The case of no diffusion of technology can be interpreted as a situation in which patents are unenforceable. Inventors will protect their ideas through secrecy. In an extreme case, there is no knowledge diffusion at all due to secrecy. The case of full diffusion of technology is the case of an internationally enforced patent system through GATT-type arrangements. A patent allows the inventors to receive a profit while it also permits transmission of knowledge internationally. The system of patents promotes innovation and leads to faster world-wide growth.

Suppose now that full diffusion of technology has been achieved. What would be the growth effects of trade liberalization in the form of reciprocal reductions in tariffs à la GATT? For the case of two asymmetric countries, it is shown in Rivera-Batiz and Romer (1991b) that the relation between tariff rate and the growth rate is not monotonic. There is a critical rate τ^* below which lower tariffs lead to faster growth and above which further increases in tariffs speed up growth.

We show in this note that the critical rate τ^* increases with the number of countries engaging in the reciprocal reduction of trade restrictions. In one example, an increase from two to ten countries increases the critical tariff rate from 300 percent to 800 percent. As a consequence, a group of ten countries will fall below the critical value even if two countries by themselves would not. This also suggests that multilateral negotiations for reductions in trade barriers are more likely to speed up growth than are bilateral agreements.

3.3 A General Model of Endogenous Growth

There are N countries. We focus on describing one of them, namely country 1. The economic behavior of other countries will be clear once that of country 1 is well understood. Therefore, in this section, domestic country is always meant to be country 1. Superscripts $2, \ldots, N$ are used to identify foreign countries; the superscript for country 1 is omitted.

The economy in country 1 consists of two distinct sectors: an R&D sector and a manufacturing sector.

3.3.1 *The R&D Sector*

The R&D sector provides the designs for producer durables. Let A denote both the set of producer durables designed domestically and the measure of this set. We sometimes refer to A as knowledge capital, or technology. The production of new knowledge capital takes the following form:

$$\dot{A} = \delta H_R A_R \tag{1}$$

where H_R is the amount of human capital devoted to research and development, and A_R is the knowledge capital available for conducting research. When there is no international knowledge diffusion, A_R will simply be equal to domestically generated knowledge A. Otherwise, A_R can be greater than A.

The model of research embodied in equation (1) is labeled the "knowledge-driven" model of research because it stresses the intellectual inputs in the creation of new technology. A distinction is introduced between human capital and technology. Human capital is a private good that obtains a market return. Technology does not receive a return when it is applied in the R&D sector. A researcher can freely use for his research all the ideas, A_R, obtainable, for example, from a scientific paper or a patent document. To be able actually to manufacture a specific good from its design, however, one must hold or purchase the patent rights.

3.3.2 *The Manufacturing Sector*

The manufacturing sector produces two types of goods: a homogeneous consumption good and producer durables, the designs of which have been invented in the R&D sector. For mathematical tractability, we assume that the production function for making producer durables is the same as that for making consumption goods. As a result, the model behaves as one in which the consumption good and any specific type of producer durable can be converted into each other on a one-for-one basis. At any given time, the output of the manufacturing sector, Y, depends on the amount of human capital employed there (H_Y), unskilled labor (L), and the set of producer durables used. This latter set consists of domestically produced inputs, $\{x(a), a \in A\}$, and the set of imported inputs $\{m(a), a \in A_Y - A\}$.

$$Y = H_Y^\alpha L^\beta \left[\int_A x(a)^\gamma da + \int_{A_Y - A} m(a)^\gamma da \right] \qquad (2)$$

where parameters and are positive and sum to 1, so that the production function exhibits constant returns to scale in human capital, unskilled labor, and durable inputs.

3.3.3 The Market Structure

The consumption good is chosen as the numeraire (i.e., $P_Y = 1$). Since we will be focusing on the balanced-growth paths, the real interest rate, r, is taken to be constant over time. The markets for consumption goods, labor, and human capital are assumed to be perfectly competitive. The market for producer durables is assumed to be monopolistically competitive.

Suppose a firm owns the patent for producing a specific domestically designed durable input. Let p be the rental price charged by the firm. The demand curve for such a durable input by the domestic country's manufacturing sector will be given by $p = \gamma H_Y^\alpha L^\beta x^{\gamma-1}$. If all manufacturing sectors around the world have the same parameters α, β, and γ, then the demand curve for foreign country i is given by $p(1 + \tau^i) = \gamma (H_Y^i)^\alpha (L^i)^\beta (m_1^i)^{\gamma-1}$, where τ^i is the tariff rate imposed by country $i, i = 2, \ldots, N$. Since these demand curves have the same constant price elasticity, they can be aggregated to yield the following worldwide demand curve:

$$p = EX^{\gamma-1} \qquad (3)$$

where $X = x + m_1^2 + \cdots + m_1^N$ is the worldwide demand for the durable input and the letter E stands for the economic "environment" facing this country. This environmental factor incorporates the sizes of the manufacturing sectors around the world and the tariff rates imposed on the durable input by other countries.

The firm that produces the durable input chooses a profit-maximizing price, p, taking as given the environment, E. Since one unit of the durable input can be converted from one unit of the consumption good, the opportunity cost for the firm to provide one unit of service from the durable input is just the real interest rate, r. The profit-maximizing rental price for the durable input is therefore the standard Chamberlin markup over marginal cost, given by $p = r/\gamma$. Let $\bar{X}$ be the quantity demanded worldwide at the profit-maximizing price. The resulting profit, π, is then equal to $p\bar{X} - r\bar{X} = r\bar{X}(1 - \gamma)/\gamma$.

In equilibrium, the present value of the whole stream of profits that the firm can extract must equal the cost of obtaining the patent to produce the specific durable input. Suppose that all the domestically designed durable inputs are subject to the same tariff rates, perhaps a zero level. The symmetry of these durable inputs in the manufacturing sectors ensures that the values of the patents for those designs are the same and thus can be given a common notation P_A:

$$P_A = \int_0^\infty \pi e^{-rt} dt = \frac{\pi}{r} = \frac{\bar{X}(1 - \gamma)}{\gamma}. \tag{4}$$

The simplicity of formula (4) is due to our assumption that any patent is indefinitely lived.

3.3.4   *Preferences*

The examples to be discussed utilize a Ramsey-type utility function with constant intertemporal elasticity of substitution. Specifically, the instantaneous utility function is given by $u(c) = c^{1-\sigma}/(1 - \sigma)$. It is well known that this utility function yields a relation between the interest rate and the rate of growth of consumption of the form: $r = \rho + \sigma g_c$, where ρ represents the rate of time preference. Along a balanced-growth path, the growth rate of consumption is equal to the growth rate of technology, $\dot{A}/A = \delta H_R A_R/A$. Therefore, we have

$$r = \rho + \sigma\delta H_R \left(\frac{A_R}{A}\right). \tag{5}$$

3.3.5 *Market Equilibrium*

Market equilibrium requires that the returns to human capital in the manufacturing sector and in the R&D sector be equal:

$$\alpha H_Y^{\alpha-1} L^\beta \left[A\bar{x}^\gamma + \int_{A_Y - A} \bar{m}(a)^\gamma da \right] = P_A \delta A_R \tag{6}$$

where domestic demand $\bar{x}$ for domestically designed inputs is given by

$$\frac{r}{\gamma} = \gamma H_Y^\alpha L^\beta \bar{x}^{\gamma-1}. \tag{7}$$

Domestic demand $\bar{m}(a)$ for the durable inputs designed abroad (i.e., $a \in A_Y - A$), is given by the following equation:

$$\frac{r}{\gamma}[1 + \tau(a)] = \gamma H_Y^\alpha L^\beta \bar{m}(a)^{\gamma-1} \tag{8}$$

where $\tau(a)$ is the tariff rate imposed by domestic government on the imports of the durable input of type a.

Notice that $\bar{m}(a) = \bar{x}[1 + \tau(a)]^{-1/(1-\gamma)}$. Using this relation and equation (4) to substitute for $\bar{m}(a)$ and P_A in equation (6), and then recalling that $r = p\gamma = \gamma^2 H_Y^\alpha L^\beta \bar{x}^{\gamma-1}$ and using the market equilibrium condition $H_Y = H - H_R$, we obtain a general expression for the real interest rate:

$$r = \Omega \left[\frac{A_R \bar{X}}{(A + \int_{A_Y - A} [1 + \tau(a)]^{-\gamma/(1-\gamma)} da)\bar{x}} \right] \times (H - H_R) \tag{9}$$

where $\Omega = \gamma(1 - \gamma)\delta/\alpha$, and H is the total amount of human capital in this country.

3.4 Integration and Reciprocal Tariff Reductions

In the last section, we summarized equilibrium conditions in any single country by a pair of equations (5) and (9) under a general specification of country sizes and tariff policies. In this section, we use some specific examples to illustrate the growth effect of integration and of reciprocal tariff reductions.

Example 1. *Free Trade in Durable Inputs with No Knowledge Diffusion*

This is the case in which $A_Y^j = A^{world}$ and $A_R^j = A^j$, for $j = 1, \ldots, N$. Note that superscripts are added to identify countries. By assumption of free trade in goods, we have $\tau(a) = 0$ for any $a \in A^{world}$. Because of this, country i's demand for its domestically designed durable input, $\bar{x}^i$ is the same as country i's import, $\bar{m}_j^i$ of any specific durable input designed by its trading partner j. As a result, the worldwide demand for any durable input invented and produced by country j, $\bar{X}^j$ equals $\bar{x}^j + \sum_{i \neq j} m_j^i = \bar{x}^1 + \bar{x}^2 + \cdots + \bar{x}^N$, which is the same for all countries $j = 1, 2, \ldots, N$. Let us denote the common value as $\bar{X}$. Hence, for any country j, we have

$$r^j = \rho + \sigma \delta H_R^j \tag{5'}$$

$$r^j = \Omega \left[\frac{A^j \bar{X}}{A^{world} \bar{x}^j} \right] (H^j - H_R^j). \tag{9'}$$

Free trade in durable inputs equalizes the real interest rate across countries. Thus $r^j = r^{world}$, for any j. Then equation $(5')$ implies that all countries devote the same amount of human capital HR to research. Manipulating equation $(9')$ for all the countries yields

$$r^{world} = \Omega \left[\frac{1}{\bar{X}} \sum_{j=1}^{j=N} \frac{\bar{x}^j}{H^j - H_R} \right]^{-1}. \tag{10}$$

Note that the bracketed term is a weighted average of the reciprocals of $H^j - H_R$. This weighted average is always greater than or equal to $1/(H^{max} - H_R)$ and less than or equal to $1/(H^{min} - H_R)$, where H^{max} and H^{min} represent the greatest and smallest human-capital endowments in the countries considered. Hence the right-hand side of equation (10) is greater than or equal to $\Omega(H^{min} - H_R)$ and less than or equal to $\Omega(H^{max} - H_R)$. These properties allow us to conclude the following when there is free trade in goods without technology diffusion:

(1) Assuming there are no corner solutions, all countries will devote the same amount of human capital H_R in research, and hence grow at the same rate $g = \delta H_R$.

(2) The worldwide real interest rate and the growth rate are less than or equal to the real interest rate and the growth rate that can be sustained in the fastest-growing country in isolation.

(3) The worldwide real interest rate and growth rate are greater than or equal to the real interest rate and the growth rate sustained under isolation in the slowing-growing country.

If the N countries have the same endowments of human capital and labor, then $H^{min} = H^{max}$, and we obtain the same growth rate as under isolation. Free trade in goods expands the range of the durable inputs available in the manufacturing sector to N times the original range. Therefore the productivity of human capital in that sector is N times the before-trade productivity. Without knowledge diffusion, the productivity of human capital in the research sector is unaffected by opening trade in durable inputs. However, free trade in a durable input increases its demand to N times the before-trade demand. The value of a piece of design is therefore N times its value when the country was isolated. As a result, the values of the marginal product of human capital in both sectors increase by the same amount after trade. No sectorial reallocations of human capital are required. The worldwide growth and interest rates remain unchanged.

If the N countries have different endowments of human capital, free trade in goods will be able to affect the marginal product values of human capital in the manufacturing sector and the R&D sector in an unbalanced way and, therefore, can affect the worldwide growth and interest rates.

Example 2. *Reciprocal Tariff Reductions*

Due to the complexity of the model with tariffs, we will only consider the simplest case in which all tariffs are assumed to be equal. We denote the common tariff by τ. In contrast to the first example, we assume that international knowledge diffusion is now perfect. That is, $A_R^j = A^{world}$. Manipulating equations (5) and (9) for all the countries, we obtain:

$$r^{world} = \rho + \sigma\delta H_R^{world} \qquad (5')$$

$$r^{world} = \Omega\Gamma(\tau)(H^{world} - H_R^{world}) \qquad (9')$$

where $H^{world} = H^1 + \cdots + H^N$, $H_R^{world} = H_R^1 + \cdots + H_R^N$, and $\Gamma(\tau)$ is defined as

$$\Gamma(\tau) = \left[\sum_{j=1}^{j=N} \frac{(A^j + (1+\tau)^{-\gamma/(1-\gamma)}(A^{world} - A^j))\bar{x}^j}{A^{world}(\bar{x}^j + (1+\tau)^{-1/(1-\gamma)})\sum_{i\neq j}\bar{x}^i} \right]^{-1}.$$

Note that $\tau = 0$ is the case of free trade in durable inputs with perfect knowledge diffusion, and $\tau = \infty$ is the case of no trade in durable inputs with perfect knowledge diffusion. The observation $\Gamma(0) = \Gamma(\infty) = 1$ shows that the worldwide growth and interest rates are the same in these two cases. It means that perfect knowledge diffusion alone can generate the same worldwide growth rate as does the complete integration.

Other properties of the complicated function $\Gamma(\tau)$ are discussed in Rivera-Batiz and Xie (1992). A typical shape of $\Gamma(\tau)$ is described here when countries are symmetric:

(1) $\Gamma(\tau)$ slides down from 1 at zero tariff rate to a minimum value at a tariff rate τ^* and then climbs up forever, approaching 1 as the tariff rate goes to infinity.
(2) The turning point τ^* is greater when the number of countries involved is larger.
(3) The minimum value, $\Gamma(\tau^*)$, is smaller when the number of countries involved is larger.

For a numerical example that considers two countries with parameter γ set to $\frac{1}{3}$, it is shown in Rivera-Batiz and Romer (1991b) that the turning point τ^* is at 300 percent. Our calculation in this paper shows that when there are ten countries, the turning point τ^* is as high as 800 percent. Therefore, in the realistic region of tariffs,

$\Gamma(\tau)$ is a decreasing function of $\Gamma(\tau)$. Since a greater $\Gamma(\tau)$ induces a higher worldwide real interest rate and growth rate, a simultaneous reduction in tariffs is therefore recommended. When countries are highly asymmetric, counterexamples can arise. Nonetheless, our analysis is suggestive of the growth consequences of tariff reductions under GATT.

3.5 Conclusions

We have presented a model in which a move from isolation to free trade in goods without an internationally enforced patent system may restrict growth in the originally fastest-growing regions, because secrecy will obstruct international knowledge diffusion. Knowledge diffusion and trade in ideas through a GATT-type internationally enforced patent system are needed for the whole world to grow faster. We also show that under perfect knowledge diffusion, a movement toward economic integration through reductions in trade restrictions leads to faster long-term worldwide growth. Comprehensive multilateral liberalization that comprises trade in goods and ideas is likely to lead to faster growth in this model.

References

Feenstra, Robert, "Trade and Uneven Growth," *National Bureau of Economic Research* (Cambridge, MA) Working Paper No. 3276, 1990.

Grossman, Gene and Helpman, Elhanan, *Innovation and Growth in the Global Economy*, Cambridge, MA: MIT Press, 1991.

Rivera-Batiz, Luis A. and Romer, Paul M., (1991a) "Economic Integration and Endogenous Growth," *Quarterly Journal of Economics*, May 1991, 106, 531–55.

——— and ———, (1991b) "International Trade with Endogenous Technological Change," *European Economic Review*, May 1991, 35, 971–1001.

——— and Xie, Danyang, "World Trading Systems and Endogenous Growth," mimeo, University of Montreal, January 1992.

Chapter 4

Integration among Unequals*

4.1 Introduction

When nations get together to form larger economic units, the presumption is that they do so to attain a higher level of income per capita and to achieve a faster rate of economic growth. Europe 1992 has been understood as a mechanism to improve long-term economic growth by exploiting the gains from economies of scale in production. The fast-track process for negotiating a North American Free Trade Agreement (NAFTA) among Canada, the United States, and Mexico, also proceeded on the faster growth presumption. Should we really expect all these integration experiments to yield miracle expansions in all participating countries? The key theoretical issues concern the conditions under which integration is expected to be growth-enhancing in particular countries.

The first order of business into an investigation of the economies of integration is to define the experiment precisely. For instance, Europe 1992 entails a single internal market, establishing free trade in goods and capital, and allowing free migration. On the other hand, NAFTA proposes to integrate goods and capital markets, but not the

*This chapter was co-authored by Luis A. Rivera-Batiz and Danyang Xie and was originally published in *Regional Science and Urban Economics*, Vol. 23, No. 3 (July 1993), pp. 337–354. ©1993 Elsevier Science Publishers.

We have benefited from the comments of two anonymous referees and Francisco Rivera-Batiz. This work was supported by Centre de Recherche et Developpement en Economique (CRDE), Universite de Montreal.

labor markets. Also, integration can be interpreted to cover diffusion of technology in addition to the usual trade in goods. The importance of technology diffusion stems from empirical investigations that have shown that technological change is a significant determinant of secular increases in per capita income. Language barriers and inadequate patent laws that make technological transfer difficult can impede economic growth.

In order to incorporate the technological concomitant of integration one needs to provide a formulation of the problem that allows for a form of endogenous technological change. Recent work on models of growth driven by the creation of new goods [Grossman (1990), Grossman and Helpman (1990, 1991), Romer (1990)] provides a treatment of technology as a choice variable. We will adopt a two-country version of Romer's model to address issues of economic integration among countries that have unequal endowments of factors of production Lucas (1988) and Stokey (1991) provide alternative models for the study of trade between asymmetric countries.

The experiments performed here should be conceived as thought experiments that serve to highlight central factors at work. Two economies are initially isolated. The consequences of various forms of integration are then analyzed. Two distinct situations are considered. In one case, two innovating countries of unequal size are integrated The other case involves highly asymmetric countries in the sense that one of the countries does not initially count with the human-capital endowments needed to support a research sector. The first case can be interpreted as involving integration between industrialized, innovating countries, the second refers to North–South integration experiments. When innovating countries integrate, we show that integration through trade in goods alone results in a reduced growth rate for the initially faster-growing country and an increased growth rate for the slower-growing nation. We also show that the in-between growth rate can be affected by the extent of migration of human capital, but not by unskilled labor migration.

Once we also open the door for diffusion of technology, however, integration is growth-enhancing for both innovating countries. In the model presented, the faster growth result when there is free trade and full technology diffusion is not affected by whether or not migration is allowed to take place.

When one of the countries is not innovating under pre-integration conditions, two subcases arise. In one subcase, the non-innovating country remains so after integration, we call this country 'chronically non-innovating'. In the second subcase, the South is transformed into an innovating region after integration, we call this country 'newly innovating'.

Our results show that whether a country participates or does not participate in the research sector after integration hinges on the human capital endowments. When these endowments are not too low, a larger market post-integration will induce the shift to participation in the research sector. If human-capital endowments are too low, however, the non-innovating country remains so after the integration.

In the highly asymmetric case, the distribution of international factor endowments affects the growth rates. In particular, we show that greater endowments of skilled and unskilled labor in the non-innovating nation result in faster growth in the innovating economy and hence in the world. Greater endowments of unskilled labor in the innovating economy are growth-reducing here since they induce a shift of resources toward manufacturing and away from research in the innovating region.

A corollary is that migration of unskilled labor from the non-innovating to the innovating country is growth-reducing. Nonetheless, our analysis and a numerical calculation suggest that the extent of growth reduction from unskilled labor migration to the North is small compared with the integration effect. In one example, integration through trade in goods yields a 20% increase in the growth rate of the North and an even higher increase in the chronically non-innovating country. If integration is accompanied by emigration of 25% of the unskilled population of the South, the gain in the North from the integration is reduced from 20% to 16%.

Section 4.2 sketches the economics of R&D production and the determination of the market price of designs in a general asymmetric model. Section 4.3 deals with the determination of the growth rate in the case of two unequal, innovating countries. Section 4.4 focuses on highly asymmetric countries, one of which innovates while the other is initially non-innovating. The paper concludes with an application to Europe and a discussion of policy issues, difficulties, and extensions of the model.

4.2   A Two-Country Model of Technological Change and Growth

Our setting consists of a domestic and a foreign economy each of which can potentially engage in two sectors: an R&D sector, and a manufacturing sector that produces both a final consumption good and differentiated producer durables. The R&D can be constituted by either independent firms or by divisions within a corporate umbrella that are treated as engaged in the separate activity of producing designs for new differentiated goods. Growth is assumed to proceed deterministically through the creation of new durables that increase the productivity of the production process. We search for a balanced growth path equilibrium and focus on its properties.

4.2.1   *The Manufacturing Sector*

The output of the manufacturing sector, Y is given by a constant returns to scale function in three factors human capital H_Y, unskilled labor L, and producer durables. The producer durables consist of domestically-produced inputs, $\{x(a), a \in A\}$, and imported inputs, $\{m(a), a \in A^*\}$. Following Ethier (1982), the production function is

$$Y = H_Y^\alpha L^\beta \left[\int_A x(a)^\gamma \mathrm{d}a + \int_{A^*} m(a)^\gamma \mathrm{d}a \right], \qquad (1)$$

where $\alpha + \beta + \gamma = 1$.

Similarly, for the manufacturing sector in the foreign country, we have

$$Y^* = H_Y^{*\alpha} L^{*\beta} \left[\int_{A^*} x^*(a)^\gamma \mathrm{d}a + \int_A m^*(a)^\gamma \mathrm{d}a \right], \qquad (2)$$

Note that we use variables without asterisks and with asterisks to represent the domestic and the foreign economies, respectively.

In both countries, the output can be consumed or converted into capital in the form of intermediate producer durables. In order to manufacture a producer durable, however, the design specifying how to do so must be used. We assume that one unit of output can be converted into one unit of a producer durable provided the manufacturer pays or acquires the manufacturing rights from the patent holder.

4.2.2 The R&D Sector

The products of R&D are blueprints and designs for new producer durables. We will identify a country's technology with the range of producer durables it invents and produces. The domestic and foreign production of new designs, A and A^*, is a function of the amount of human capital employed, H_R and H_R^*, and the stock of knowledge capital, A_R and A_R^*, accessible for research activities

$$A = \delta H_R A_R,$$

$$A^* = \delta H_R^* A_R^*. \tag{3}$$

When knowledge capital for research is purely local, $A_R = A$ and $A_R^* = A^*$. If technological diffusion makes locally available the full set of designs existing in the world, and if there is no redundancy in the designs produced by the domestic and foreign countries, then $A_R = A_R^* = A + A^*$. For a general discussion of redundancy, see Rivera-Batiz and Romer (1991b).

The model of research embodied in eqs. (3) is labeled the 'knowledge-driven' model of research because it stresses the intellectual inputs in the creation of new technology. In order to stress the public good nature of technological knowledge capital, we establish a sharp distinction between the human-capital and technology inputs. Human capital is the only factor that obtains a market return in the research sector. Accessible technology can be acquired, free of charge, from a scientific paper or a patent document.

4.2.3   *Patents and Their Pricing*

We are treating existing technology as a public good, but only when used in the research sector. In the manufacturing sector, the use of the designs developed through research is subject to patenting. A manufacturer of a patented durable must pay or acquire the manufacturing rights from the patent holder. We assume that these patents are infinitely lived. The patents carry a positive value because the attached durables can be sold or rented for a profit to be used in the manufacturing sector. Patenting provides the incentive for innovation and makes technology partly a private good. The dual character of technology as both a public and a private good underlies the role of property rights in the production of technology and economic growth in this model.

What is the relative price of a patent in terms of consumption goods? The answer depends on the market structure. We assume that the market for producer durables is monopolistically competitive. Hence, in equilibrium, the relative price P_A (the consumption good is chosen as the numeraire so that $P_Y = 1$) is the present value of the monopoly rents obtainable from selling the durable. Since we will be focusing on the balanced growth paths, we can take the interest rate, r to be constant over time.

Suppose a firm has purchased the patent for producing a domestically-designed producer durable. Let p be the rental price charged by the firm. The demand curve for such a durable by the domestic country's manufacturing sector will be given by $p = \gamma H_Y^\alpha L^\beta x^{\gamma-1}$. Under free trade, the demand by the foreign country is given by $p = \gamma H_Y^{*\alpha} L^{*\beta} m^{*\gamma-1}$, where m^* represents the imports by the foreign country. Let $X = x + m^*$ denote the worldwide demand for this durable. The worldwide demand curve can then be expressed as

$$p = \gamma [H_Y^{\alpha/(1-\gamma)} L^{\beta/(1-\gamma)} + H_Y^{*\alpha/(1-\gamma)} L^{*\beta/(1-\gamma)}]^{1-\gamma} X^{\gamma-1}. \quad (4)$$

Under conditions of isolation, however, we have $p = \gamma H_Y^\alpha L^\beta x^{\gamma-1}$.

The producer of the durable chooses a price p that maximizes profit, $\pi = pX - rX$. Notice that, since we assume that one unit of producer durable can be produced by one unit of the consumption good, the rental cost for the firm to provide one unit of service of the durable is just the interest rate, r. The profit-maximizing price is therefore the standard Chamberlinian markup over marginal cost, given by $p = r/\gamma$. Notice that this price applies both under free trade and under isolation. Let $\bar{X}$ be the quantity demanded worldwide at the profit-maximizing price. The resulting profit is

$$\pi = p\bar{X} - r\bar{X} - r\bar{X} = \frac{r}{\gamma}\bar{X} - r\bar{X} = r\bar{X}\frac{(1-\gamma)}{\gamma}. \tag{5}$$

In equilibrium the present value of the whole stream of profits that the firm can extract must be equal to the cost of purchasing the patent for producing the specific durable. The symmetry of producer durables in the manufacturing sectors ensures that the value of the patents for all domestic designs are the same and thus can be given a common notation, P_A

$$P_A = \int_0^\infty \pi e^{-rt}\mathrm{d}t = \frac{\pi}{r} = \bar{X}\frac{(1-\gamma)}{\gamma}. \tag{6}$$

The simplicity of formula (6) is due to our assumption that any patent is infinitely lived, and the fact that r is constant along the balanced growth path.

Similarly, the rental price, p^* of producer durables designed in the foreign country equals r^*/γ. And the values of the patents for foreign designs are P_A^*

$$P_A^* = \bar{X}^*\frac{(1-\gamma)}{\gamma}, \tag{7}$$

where $\bar{X}^* = \bar{x}^* + \bar{m}$ under free trade, $\bar{X}^* = \bar{x}^*$ under isolation.

4.2.4 *Equilibrium in the Labor Market*

Labor market equilibrium requires the full employment of unskilled labor and human capital, that is, $L = L_Y + L_R$ and $H = H_Y + H_R$. Similar conditions hold for the foreign country. Since L_R is assumed to be nil in our model, there is no decision to be made concerning the sectorial allocation of unskilled labor.

Achieving the full employment of human capital involves its allocation between the manufacturing and the research sectors. The wage of human capital received in the manufacturing sector, W_{H_Y} is equal to its marginal product, $\alpha H_Y^{\alpha-1} L^\beta [A\bar{x}^\gamma + A^*\bar{m}^\gamma]$. This can be rewritten as $W_{H_Y} = \alpha r H_Y^{-1} \bar{x}^{1-\gamma} \times [A\bar{x}^\gamma + A^*\bar{m}^\gamma]/\gamma^2$ by recalling that $r = \gamma p = \gamma^2 H_Y^\alpha L^\beta \bar{x}^{\gamma-1}$. The wage (or shadow wage when the research sector is not active) of human capital in the research sector is $W_{H_R} = P_A \delta A_R = (\bar{x} + \bar{m}^*)(1 - \gamma)\delta A_R/\gamma$, with P_A substituted from (6). Utilizing the market equilibrium condition $H_Y = H - H_R$ we obtain

$$\frac{W_{H_R}}{W_{H_Y}} = \frac{\frac{\delta}{\Lambda}\left[\frac{A_R(\bar{x}+\bar{m}^*)}{\bar{x}^{1-\gamma}(A\bar{x}^\gamma+A^*\bar{m}^\gamma)}\right](H - H_R)}{r}, \tag{8}$$

where $\Lambda = \alpha/[\gamma(1 - \gamma)]$.

When a country does not engage in research in equilibrium (i.e., $H_R = 0$), it must be true that $W_{H_R}/W_{H_Y} \leqq 1$, i.e.

$$r \geqq \frac{\delta}{\Lambda}\left[\frac{A_R(\bar{x} + \bar{m}^*)}{\bar{x}^{1-\gamma}(A\bar{x}^\gamma + A^*\bar{m}^\gamma)}\right](H - H_R). \tag{9}$$

When both sectors are active in equilibrium, $W_{H_R}/W_{H_Y} = 1$. This yields

$$r = \frac{\delta}{\Lambda}\left[\frac{A_R(\bar{x} + \bar{m}^*)}{\bar{x}^{1-\gamma}(A\bar{x}^\gamma + A^*\bar{m}^\gamma)}\right](H - H_R). \tag{10}$$

Equation (10) relates the interest rate to the amount of human capital devoted to research, as derived from the conditions determining the allocation of human capital between sectors. In order to solve the model, we need to consider the role of preferences and consumption behavior, which will provide a second relation between the interest rate and the amount of human capital devoted to research.

4.2.5   *Preferences and Consumption*

Preferences are represented by a Ramsey-type constant elasticity of substitution utility function, with instantaneous utility given by $u(c) = [c^{(1-\sigma)} - 1]/(1 - \sigma)$. With this utility function, it is easy to derive [for an explicit derivation, see Rivera-Batiz and Romer (1991b, appendix)] the following relation between the interest rate and the rate of growth of consumption

$$r = \rho + \sigma \left(\frac{\frac{dc}{dt}}{c} \right), \tag{11}$$

where ρ is the rate of time preference.

Along a balanced growth path, the growth rate of consumption is equal to the growth rate of technology, $(\frac{dA}{dt})/A = \delta H_R A_R / A$. Therefore we have

$$r = \rho + \sigma \delta H_R \left(\frac{A_R}{A} \right). \tag{12}$$

Similarly, we have for the foreign country

$$r^* = \rho + \sigma \delta H_R^* \left(\frac{A_R^*}{A^*} \right). \tag{13}$$

We are now ready to apply this model to address issues concerning economic integration.

4.3   Integration between Unequal, Innovating Economies

This section examines integration between two innovating countries that differ in terms of factor endowments. By 'innovating country' we mean a country in which some amount of human capital is devoted to the R&D sector.

Consider first the pre-integration situation in which two economies are totally isolated. By definition, in an 'innovating country' the wage equalization condition (10) must hold. There is no international trade, and international technology diffusion is not occurring. Hence, $\bar{m} = \bar{m}^* = 0$, and A^* is not available to the domestic research sector, which means that $A_R = A$. Consequently, eqs. (10) and (12) simplify to

$$r = \frac{\delta}{\Lambda}(H - H_R) \tag{14}$$

and

$$r = p + \sigma \delta H_R. \tag{15}$$

Combining these two equations yields $H_R = [H - (\Lambda\rho/\delta)]/[1 + \Lambda\sigma]$. This is the result obtained by Romer (1990) and, with the appropriate change of notation, applies here to both isolated economies. Since the growth rates equal $g = \delta H_R$ and $g^* = \delta H_R^*$ the faster-growing economy will be the one with greater endowment of human capital. The research sector of this economy will be larger than that of the slower-growing economy. The higher interest rate will sustain greater savings and growth.

4.3.1   *Free Trade between Unequally Endowed Countries*

Suppose now that these two economies establish free trade in goods among them, but technology does not diffuse. This means that the manufacturing sectors in both countries can use the full set of the producer durables ever designed by the two countries. The R&D sectors, however, do not benefit from each other. Due to the lack of technology diffusion, A_R is still equal to A, and A_R^* is still equal to A^*. As a result, eq. (12) still reduces to $r = \rho + \sigma\delta H_R$, and eq. (13) reduces to $r^* = \rho + \sigma\delta H_R^*$.

Under free trade and perfect capital movement, interest rate equalization implies that domestically-designed and foreign-designed inputs have the same price $p = p^*$. Hence $\bar{m} = \bar{x}$ and $\bar{m}^* = \bar{x}^*$. Equations (8) and (10) then simplify to

$$\frac{W_{HR}}{W_{HY}} = \frac{\frac{\delta}{\Lambda}\left[\frac{A(\bar{x}+\bar{x}^*)}{(A+A^*)\bar{x}}\right](H - H_R)}{r} \tag{16}$$

and

$$r = \frac{\delta}{\Lambda}\left[\frac{A(\bar{x} + \bar{x}^*)}{(A + A^*)\bar{x}}\right](H - H_R), \tag{17}$$

where $\Lambda = \alpha[\gamma(1-\gamma)]$. For the foreign country, there is also a similar equation to (17) that relates the interest rate to the human capital employed in the R&D sector.

One observation we want to make is that interest rate equalization, $\rho + \sigma\delta H_R = \rho + \sigma\rho H_R^* \equiv r^{world}$, implies that the two countries will devote the same amount of human capital to research.

Consequently they will grow at the same rate. As a result, with no knowledge diffusion, the low-human-capital country devotes a larger proportion of its human capital to research than the human-capital-abundant country.

The equilibrium world interest rate is determined as follows. Equation (17) can be transformed into $\bar{x}/[(\bar{x} + \bar{x}^*)(H - H_R)] = [\delta/(\Lambda r^{world})][A/(A + A^*)]$. A similar equation holds for the foreign country. Summing over these two equations and then solving out for r^{world} yields

$$r^{world} = \frac{\delta}{A} \left[\frac{\bar{x}}{(\bar{x} + \bar{x}^*)(H - H_R)} + \frac{\bar{x}^*}{(\bar{x} + \bar{x}^*)(H^* - H_R^*)} \right]^{-1}. \quad (18)$$

What is the relation between the growth rate in the integrated region and the pre-integration growth rates? To determine this relation, assume that the domestic economy has greater endowments of human capital than the foreign economy, that is H exceeds H^*. First, note that the bracketed term in eq. (18) is weighted averaged of the reciprocals of $H - H_R$ and $H^* - H_R^*$. This weighted average is always greater than $1/(H - H_R)$ and smaller than $1/(H^* - H_R^*)$ because H exceeds H^* and $H_R = H_R^*$. Hence, the right-hand side of eq. (18) is smaller than $(\delta/\Lambda)(H - H_R)$ and greater than $(\delta/\Lambda)(H^* - H_R^*)$. This property allows us to reach the following conclusions when there is free trade in goods without technology diffusion.

(1) The worldwide interest rate and the growth rate are lower than the interest rate and the growth rate that can be sustained in the originally faster-growing country.
(2) The worldwide interest rate and the growth rate are higher than the interest rate and growth rate sustained under isolation in the originally slower-growing country.

4.3.2 *Discussion of the Results*

We have obtained that integration slows down economic growth in the country that would grow faster before integration and speeds it up in the pre-integration slower-growing economy. What is the intuition behind this 'in-between' growth rate result?

Notice that there is no diffusion of technology here. Consequently there are no scale effects in research activities to be exploited through integration. The worldwide growth rate is then a function of the independent research activities in each country. Therefore, the allocation effect of integration bears the whole responsibility for the 'in-between' growth rate result.

In order to visualize the allocation effect of integration, one can evaluate the sectorial wage ratio of human capital, W_{H_R}/W_{H_Y}, at the pre-integration equilibrium interest rate $r(\text{pre})$ and equilibrium level of research activity $H_R(\text{pre})$. From eq. (16), we obtain

$$\frac{W_{H_R}}{W_{H_Y}} = \frac{\frac{\delta}{\Lambda}\left[\frac{A(\bar{x}+\bar{x}^*)}{(A+A^*)\bar{x}}\right](H - H_R(\text{pre}))}{r(\text{pre})}$$

$$= \left[\frac{A(\bar{x}+\bar{x}^*)}{(A+A^*)\bar{x}}\right] \equiv \Phi, \tag{19}$$

which is derived using eq. (15), $r(\text{pre}) = (\delta/\Lambda)(H - H_R(\text{pre}))$.

If the sectorial wage ratio, Φ, is equal to 1 when evaluated at the pre-integration $r(\text{pre})$ and $H_R(\text{pre})$, then there is no pressure for reallocating human capital. If $\Phi \neq 1$, reallocation is necessary after integration to restore the equilibrium, $\Phi > 1$ means that the research sector expands, $\Phi < 1$ means that it shrinks.

The above equation highlights the key factors underlying the reallocation of resources caused by integration. On the one hand, a larger market due to integration means an appreciation of the value of patents. This appreciation benefits the human capital in the domestic R&D sector and that is what the numerator in Φ captures. On the other hand, the access to the durable inputs produced by the foreign country raises the productivity of the human capital in the domestic manufacturing sector and this effect is what the denominator in Φ captures.

Also, note that the condition $\Phi > 1$ is equivalent to $A\bar{x}^* > A^*\bar{x}$, or that the exports of differentiable inputs exceed the imports of differentiable inputs. Analogously, the condition for a movement of human-capital resources toward research is that the country experiences a surplus in the account for durables after integration.

The intuition for this result is quite clear. Recall from our discussion of research that its value relates positively to the size of the market for the innovative products, and hence, to the size of the market for exports of the durables. The productivity of manufacturing relates positively to the availability of differentiable producer durables and thus to the imports of those goods. The functional forms used here reflect this comparison quite neatly. When a country's exports of durables exceed its purchases of durables abroad, the integration increases the productivity of human capital in research more than in the manufacturing sector, the research sector expands. When the durables account is in deficit after integration, the integration increases the productivity of human capital in the manufacturing sector more than in R&D, and the research sector contracts.

We still need to explain why, along a worldwide balanced growth path after integration, the initially fast-growing economy must go into a trade deficit in durables and the originally slow-growing country must achieve a surplus in these goods. Or, what is the same here, we must explain why there is a reduction in the research sector of the rapid-growth country and an expansion of the research sector of its trading partner.

Since both countries cannot have a surplus in the *same* group of commodities, only three possibilities can arise trade in producer durables is balanced after integration, the fast-growth country has a surplus in durables, or the slow-growth country experiences it. We proceed to show that only the third possibility can hold.

If trade remains in balance, then integration does not favor any sector over the other The research sectors remain the same as before the integration, and the difference between the interest rates in the two countries will not disappear, which contradicts the assumption of free trade in goods Thus, this case cannot happen.

If the research sector expands in the domestic economy (i.e., it runs a surplus), then research must contract in the foreign economy (which must hold a deficit). But this means that the difference in the size of the research sectors becomes even greater than before integration, which is again inconsistent with the equalization of the interest rates.

The only possible equilibrium yields a deficit in durables and reduced research for the faster-growing economy and a corresponding surplus and increased research in the initially slower-growing economy. This serves to equalize the research sectors and the interest rates after integration.

With the intuition given above, it is easy to understand the conclusion reached in the study of two symmetric countries by Rivera-Batiz and Romer (1991a). They show that free trade without technological diffusion has no allocation effect on human capital and does not affect growth rates. This result should come up naturally because, with two symmetric countries, the trade surplus in the durables account must necessarily be zero for both countries.

4.3.3   *Free Trade with Perfect Knowledge Diffusion*

This is the case in which $\bar{m} = \bar{x}$, $\bar{m}^* = \bar{x}^*$, and $A_R = A_R^* = A + A^*$. For the domestic country, eqs. (10) and (12) become

$$r = \frac{\delta}{\Lambda} \frac{(\bar{x} + \bar{x}^*)}{\bar{x}} (H - H_R) \tag{20}$$

and

$$r = \rho + \sigma \delta H_R \frac{(A + A^*)}{A}. \tag{21}$$

Similar conditions hold for the foreign country.

Free mobility of capital with international interest rate equalization after integration yields

$$\rho + \sigma \delta H_R \frac{(A + A^*)}{A} = \rho + \sigma \delta H_R^* \frac{(A + A^*)}{A^*} \equiv r^{world}. \tag{22}$$

This condition then implies that the relative number of researchers in the two countries is equal to the relative number of designs invented in each country

$$\frac{H_R}{H_R^*} = \frac{A}{A^*}.$$

This relation differs from the case of free trade with no diffusion, in which research efforts are equalized in absolute terms across countries.

In order to determine the interest rate and the size of the research sectors, we manipulate eqs. (20) and (21), and their counterparts in the foreign country. Perhaps surprisingly, the manipulation yields

$$r^{world} = \frac{\delta}{\Lambda}(H^{world} - H_R^{world}) \tag{23}$$

and

$$r^{world} = \rho + \sigma\delta H^{world}, \tag{24}$$

where $H_R^{world} = H_R + H_R^*$ and $H_R^{world} = H + H^*$. Therefore, the above two equations share exactly the same form as eqs. (14) and (15). The only difference is that in one case we refer to worldwide variables, and in the other case we refer to individual country variables.

Solving eqs. (23) and (24) as before for H_R^{world}, we obtain the worldwide growth rate as follows

$$g = \delta(H_R + H_R^*) = \frac{\delta(H + H^*) - \Lambda\rho}{1 + \Lambda\sigma}.$$

Since worldwide real interest rates and growth rates depend only on $H^{world} = H + H^*$, the distribution of human capital among countries is not an issue. Relative country size does not matter for the determination of the worldwide growth rate in this example. Only the aggregate size matters. This result depends crucially on two assumptions. One is that country borders do not place a restriction on the full diffusion of ideas across countries. The other is that the distribution of human capital is such that no country abstains from participating in the research sector. In the next section we discuss integration between two countries, one of which does not innovate.

4.4 Integration between Highly Asymmetric Countries

This section deals with the case in which one country does not generate new technology when it is in isolation. Two subcases are studied. In the first subcase the country does not find it worthwhile to devote part of its scarce human capital to research, even when free trade in goods is established and full knowledge diffusion is present.

We label this country as 'chronically noninnovating'. In the second subcase the country begins to participate in R&D activities after integration. We label this country as 'newly innovating'. In both subcases we want to study the growth consequences of integration and labor migration.

The absence of positive R&D in equilibrium is not due to an assumed relative inefficiency in research or to financial factors. All countries considered are assumed to face the same interest rate, to have the same R&D production function, and to be equals concerning production possibilities for all goods. They fully share existing knowledge. What underlies the no-innovation condition is that a small amount of human capital in the South does not make R&D a profitable activity there, even in the presence of instantaneous worldwide diffusion of knowledge.

4.4.1 *'Chronically Non-Innovating'*

If a country devotes no human capital in R&D when it is in isolation, the range of its intermediate inputs stays at its initial level, A_0^*. Its long-run interest rate, r^*, must equal the rate of time preference, ρ. Also, the wage to human capital in the manufacturing sector, $W_{H_Y} = \alpha H^{*\alpha-1} L^{*\beta} A_0^* \bar{x}^{*\gamma}$, must be greater than or equal to the potential wage to the human capital doing research, $W_{H_R} = P_A^* \delta A_0^*$. The last condition underlies inequality (9), which yields a necessary and sufficient condition for the country not to participate in R&D under isolation.

$$H^* \leqq \frac{\Lambda \rho}{\delta} \qquad (25)$$

Suppose that this country opens free trade with a Northern partner in the presence of knowledge diffusion. If, after integration, the South is still noninnovating, its output growth will be at the rate $A/(A+A_0^*)$ because $Y^* = H^{*\alpha} L^{*\beta}(A + A_0^*)\bar{x}^{*\gamma}$. Consequently, the output growth is not constant if the Northern partner is on a balanced growth path. Put differently, the South will not be on an exact balanced growth path in this situation. Asymptotically, however, it is true that $A/(A + A_0^*) = \dot{A}/A$. As a result, the following discussions should be interpreted in terms of an asymptotic balanced growth path.

The equilibrium conditions on the allocation of human capital for the 'chronically non-innovating' country and the North are derived from eqs. (9) and (10) as follows

$$r^{world} \geqq \frac{\delta}{\Lambda}(1+s)H^*$$ (26)

and

$$r^{world} \geqq \frac{\delta}{\Lambda}(1+s^*)(H - H_R),$$ (27)

where s^* and s are defined as

$$s^* \equiv \left(\frac{H^*}{H - H_R}\right)^{\alpha/(1-\gamma)} \left(\frac{L^*}{L}\right)^{\beta/(1-\gamma)} \equiv s^{-1}.$$ (28)

In deriving eq. (27), we have implicitly used $A_R = A + A_0^*$, $s^* = \bar{x}^*/\bar{x}$, and $\bar{m} = \bar{x}, \bar{m}^* = \bar{x}^*$.

Solving $r^{world} = \rho + \sigma\delta H_R$ and eq. (27) simultaneously, and substituting the definition of s^*, we immediately obtain an equation in H_R only

$$\rho + \sigma\delta H_R = \frac{\delta}{\Lambda}(H - H_R) + \frac{\delta}{\Lambda}H^{*\alpha(1-\gamma)}\left(\frac{L^*}{L}\right)^{\beta/(1-\gamma)} \times (H - H_R)^{\beta/(1-\gamma)}.$$ (29)

Figure 4.1 shows the determination of H_R by means of eq. (29). The left-hand side of (29) is a linear function of H_R that we label the $r_{preference}$ curve. The right-hand side is a concave decreasing function of H_R that we label the $r_{technology}$ curve. Fig 4.1 shows that the solution to (29) exists and is unique.

It is easy to see that the solution of (29) yields a greater H_R than the isolation case. Since the second term in the left-hand side of (29) is always positive, the r-technology curve always lies above the one for the isolation case, $r = (\delta/\Lambda)(H - H_R)$. Therefore, integration between a Northern country and a chronically non-innovating Southern country shifts human capital toward R&D in the North and promotes worldwide growth.

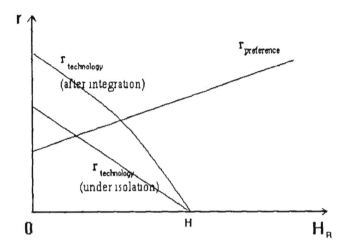

Figure 4.1. Equilibrium Human Capital Dedicated to R&D.

To make sure that it is not profitable for the South to do any research, the inequality condition in (26) must be satisfied. In view of eq. (27), the inequality condition (26) can be rewritten as

$$H^* \lesseqgtr s^*(H - H_R). \tag{30}$$

Since s^* is a variable that depends on the equilibrium value of H_R, and depends on the relative size of unskilled labor between the two countries, etc, this condition is rather complicated. A numerical example is helpful to show both the existence of 'chronically non-innovating' countries in which (30) is satisfied, and the existence of 'newly innovating' countries in which (25) is satisfied but (30) is violated.

In our numerical example, we set $\alpha = \beta = 0.3, \gamma = 0.4, \rho = 0.04$, $\sigma = 0.5$, $\delta = 0.001$, $H = 100$, $L = 1000$. Given these parameter values, eq. (25) implies that when a country has an H^* below 50, t will not engage in R&D under isolation. Assuming $L^* = L$, solving (30) implies that when a country has an H^* less than or equal to 42.86, then it fits our label for 'chronically non-innovating'. The country labeled 'newly innovating' has an H^* greater than 42.86 and less than or equal to 50.

Before we say anything about the 'newly innovating country', let us consider the issue of integration and of migration between the North and the 'chronically non-innovating South' with an $H^* = 20$. When the two countries are in isolation, the North grows at 3.08%, and the South stagnates. After integration, the North spends more on research because the increase in its patent value due to an extended market for its producer durables moves more human capital into R&D. As a result, it grows at 5.02%, a gain of 2% for the North, and a big jump for the South.

A migration of unskilled labor from the South to the North has three effects. First, this increases the marginal productivity of human capital in the North's manufacturing sector due to an increase in unskilled labor. Second, the increase in the unskilled labor in the North increases the demand for durables. This raises the value of patents and hence makes the research sector more attractive to human capital. Third, a reduction in the amount of unskilled labor in the South represents weak demand from the South for the durables produced in the North. This devalues the patents and therefore weakens the North's incentive to do research. We can show that the negative effect dominates [see eq. (29)], but we believe that the net effect of migration of unskilled labor on growth might not be significant compared with the positive effect of integration. In our example, a migration of 25% of the unskilled labor force from the 'chronically non-innovating' country reduces the growth rate from 5.02% to 4.64%, only a loss of less than 0.4%.

The migration of skilled labor from the South to the North has two offsetting effects. The growth-enhancing effect is that the stock of human capital in the North has increased, part of which will thus be spent in R&D. The growth-reducing effect is that the demand by the South for each producer durable designed by the North will decline because smaller human capital in the South's manufacturing sector means reduced marginal productivity of the durables. The value of patents thus will be lower, which depresses research. The net effect is ambiguous. In our example, if 25% of human capital in the 'chronically non-innovating' country moves to the North, the growth rate increases from 5.02% to 5.13%, a gam of only 0.11%.

4.4.2 *'Newly Innovating'*

It is possible that, after integration, the incentive for the human capital to engage in R&D in the South may be so enhanced that it starts to innovate in the case of full knowledge diffusion, its analysis is similar to the case of two innovating countries in section 4.3. Basically, integration increases the world-wide interest rate and growth. Migration of human capital and unskilled labor do not have any effects on growth provided that the extent of the migration is not so large as to change the 'newly innovating' to a 'chronically non-innovating'. The arguments for these results have been presented in section 4.3 and are not repeated here.

4.5   Conclusions

European integration presents situations quite similar to those studied here. Germany, France, Italy, and Britain are innovating countries to differing degrees. Spain has received a push from the integration process and is emerging as a 'newly innovating' country. Portugal, Greece, and Turkey (associate members) are non-innovating. In North America, Canada and the United States are innovating countries with similar income per capita, while Mexico remains non-innovating The model suggests that integration of the research sectors of European countries must be promoted in order to ensure a positive growth effect. Inappropriate patent laws, language barriers, and lack of cooperation in research that makes technological diffusion difficult can prevent a positive growth effect from integration.

There is other literature that suggests the centrality of technological diffusion for the outcome of integration. Results obtained by Feenstra (1990) show conditions under which the initially slow-growth economy will slow down after integration. In Feenstra's no diffusion of technology example, the growth rates will not be equal for both partners after integration. In that case, the smaller country will experience a decline in the growth rate after integration.

A host of unanswered questions remain to be examined that are of relevance if the emerging world of trading blocs comes into its own. What are the economics of multiple trading blocs in a growing context? Surprisingly little research has been conducted on these issues in the context of a growing world or regional economy. Exceptions include Rivera-Batiz and Xie (1992a, b).

A different source of inequality develops regionally within countries. Economic activity is not homogeneously distributed across space. Rather, it is characterized by agglomeration and interregional exchange. The economics of regions evolves in a context of free migration and absence of artificial barriers imposed by frontiers. For that reason, the economics of interregional trade and location within a country lies at the heart of the exchange process. Why some locations boom and attract economic activities while others stagnate is a key issue in development economics with a clear geographic connotation. The geographic question of location in space, however, has been addressed only in static models of trade with differentiated goods by Krugman (1991a, b), Rivera-Batiz (1988), and others. The growth economics of cities and regions, however, remains unexplored.

References

Ethier, Wilfred J, 1982, "National and international returns to scale in the modern theory of international trade," *American Economic Review* 72, 389–405.

Feenstra, Robert, 1990, "Trade and uneven growth," NBER Working Paper No. 3276.

Grossman, Gene M, 1990, "Explaining Japan's innovation and growth: A model of quality competition and dynamic comparative advantage," *Bank of Japan Monetary and Economic Studies* 8, 75–100.

Grossman, Gene M and Elhanan Helpman, 1990, "Comparative advantage and long run growth," *American Economic Review* 80, 796–815.

Grossman, Gene M and Elhanan Helpman, 1991, *Innovation and growth in the global economy*, (MIT Press, Cambridge, MA)

Krugman, Paul, 1991a, *Geography and trade* (MIT Press, Cambridge, MA)

Krugman, Paul, 1991b, "Increasing returns and economic geography," *Journal of Political Economy* 99(3), 483–499.

Lucas, Robert E Jr, 1988, "On the mechanics of economic development," *Journal of Monetary Economics* 22, 3–42.

Rivera-Batiz, Francisco L., 1988, "Increasing returns, monopolistic competition, and agglomeration economies in consumption and production," *Regional Science and Urban Economics* 18, 125–153.

Rivera-Batiz, Luis A and Paul M Romer, 1991a, "Economic integration and endogenous growth," *Quarterly Journal of Economics* 106(2), 531–555.

Rivera-Batiz, Luis A and Paul M Romer, 1991b, "International trade with endogenous technological change," *European Economic Review* 35(4), 971–1001.

Rivera-Batiz, Luis A and Danyang Xie, 1992a, "GATT, trade and growth," *American Economic Review* 82(2), 422–427.

Rivera-Batiz, Luis A and Danyang Xie, 1992b, "World trading systems and endogenous growth," University of Montreal.

Romer, Paul M, 1990, "Endogenous technological change," *Journal of Political Economy* 98, S71–S102.

Stokey, Nancy L, 1991, "The volume and composition of trade between rich and poor countries," *Review of Economic Studies* 57, 63–80.

Chapter 5

The Economics of Technological Progress and Endogenous Growth in Open Economies*

5.1 Introduction

Is international trade an "engine of growth"? Do trade liberalization and increased openness lead to higher rates of economic expansion? This has been one of the most controversial issues in international economics. From Adam Smith and John Maynard Keynes to Hans Singer and Raul Prebisch, the debate between pro-traders and protectionists has raged over the years.

In the 1950s and 1960s, the vision that trade restrictions and protectionism lead to higher growth rates took hold among many policymakers, particularly in Latin America. In the form of import-substitution strategies, trade restrictions proliferated. More recently, in the 1980s and 1990s, there has been a rising perception among the public, policymakers and many academics that the question of whether or not trade leads to greater economic growth should be answered affirmatively. The proliferation of free trade zones,

*This chapter was authored by Francisco L. Rivera-Batiz and was originally published in Georg Koopmann and Hans-Eckart Scharrer, eds., *The Economics of High Technology Competition and Cooperation in Global Markets*, Nomos Verlagsgesellschaft, Baden-Baden, Germany, 1996, pp. 31–62. ©1996 Nomos Verlagsgesellschaft.

The author is grateful to the comments of Richard Baldwin.

trade liberalization initiatives, and the successful completion of the Uruguay Round of the General Agreement on Tariffs and Trade (GATT) are testimony to the rising faith in trade as an engine of growth. Yet, there is a vocal and influential minority which continues to assert that trade liberalization is deleterious for growth. For instance, economist Lance Taylor, of the New School for Social Research, affirms that there are "no great benefits (plus some loss) in following open trade and capital market strategies...development strategies oriented internally may be a wise choice towards the century's end" (Taylor 1991, p. 141).

As the debate on the issue of how trade and growth are connected continues, economic research on the topic accumulates. New ideas about how trade and growth are interconnected emerge, refueling the controversy. This paper presents a summary of the key economic mechanisms postulated in recent years about how openness is linked — or not linked — to increased rates of growth of domestic output.

A simple correlation of openness with income growth rates in a cross-section of countries does not show a clear directional pattern. Figure 5.1, for example, plots nominal levels of protection (as measured by nominal tariff rates) versus output growth for a sample of European countries in the nineteenth century. These data do not result in a statistically significant relationship between protectionism and economic growth; if anything, the figure appears to indicate a positive connection between protectionism and growth.[1]

Unfortunately, such casual empiricism is misleading. In examining the simple correlation between protectionism and growth, other factors that influence economic expansion are ignored. Since these other factors may be related to both trade and growth, they may generate a spurious relationship between the two variables. In order to examine more adequately the connection between trade and growth, a multivariate analysis is required. Such an analysis can then be used to examine how protectionism affects economic growth, holding other variables constant.

The existing empirical literature studying in a more rigorous way the connection between openness and growth overwhelmingly

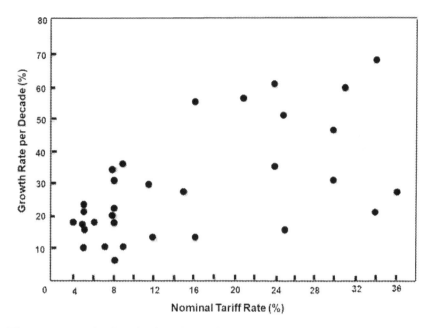

Figure 5.1. The Simple Correlation between Economic Growth and Protectionism in the Nineteenth Century.

Source: Forrest Capie, *Tariffs and Growth* (Manchester: Manchester University Press, 1994). Table 2, p. 41.

suggests that increased trade or reduced protectionism are linked to greater economic growth. For instance, in a recent paper, Sebastian Edwards finds that: "after taking into account the roles of capital accumulation, growth in the labor force, and technological gap, countries with higher degrees of trade intervention tend to grow, on average, slower than countries with lower trade restrictions" (Edwards 1989, p. 51).[2] Similarly, Barro and Xala-i-Martin included tariff rates in a regression analysis of variables explaining economic growth in a cross-section of countries, finding that "the estimated coefficient is significantly negative," and concluding that: "This result brings out another channel through which distortions of markets can reduce the growth rate (Barro and Xala-i-Martin 1995, p. 438)."[3]

Even when a negative relationship between protectionism and economic growth has been established, holding other things constant, there is still an ambiguity arising from the fact that correlation does not necessarily imply causality. As a growing literature on the political economy of protectionism indicates, reduced growth may generate a reaction against international trade, resulting in the imposition of tariffs and reduced openness. In this case, the causality goes from reduced growth to reduced trade, not the other way around.[4] One is, therefore, motivated to look explicitly at the various ways through which openness causes growth. Further empirical analysis would then be dictated on testing whether these particular connections are empirically valid.

What are the mechanisms through which trade affects economic growth? The modern theory of economic growth suggests that, although increased supplies of factors of production such as physical capital and labor, account for a substantial portion of growth, it is technological change that explains most of the increased productivity of the labor force and, therefore, income per-capita. As Paul Krugman has aptly summarized the issue: "Mere increases in inputs, without an increase in the efficiency with which those inputs are used, must run into diminishing returns, input-driven growth is inevitably limited. How, then, have today's advanced nations been able to achieve sustained growth in per capita income over the past 150 years? The answer is that technological advances have led to a continual increase in total productivity — a continued rise in national income for each unit of input" (Krugman 1994, p. 68).

In order to investigate how trade affects growth, one must focus on how openness influences technological change. This paper provides a survey of the effects of trade on growth by examining the various ways through which openness affects technical change.

Our approach follows the recent literature on endogenous growth theory in assuming that technological change is not exogenous but affected instead by a myriad of economic parameters. Openness, of course, is one of these parameters. Commercial policy, for example, which restricts trade, can influence technological change by influencing domestic rivalry and competition, thus inducing local firms to change their innovation investments, or by reallocating resources among sectors and industries in the economy, fostering or discouraging domestic research and development sectors. Note that the interest of this analysis is not to predict technological change, a matter which may be problematic, but instead to explain better some of the forces that influence it. As Zvi Griliches has noted: "Given the fundamental uncertainties entailed in the creative act, in invention, and in innovation, there is no reason to expect the fit of our models to be high or for the true residual to disappear. We should, however, be able to explain it better *ex post* even if we cannot predict it (Griliches 1994, p. 18).

The impact of trade on economic growth can be examined within two time frames: medium term and long-run.[5] Within a medium-term context, trade alters growth over a certain period of time but the impact is only temporary, disappearing after a while. In a long-run growth context, however, the focus is on how trade alters the economy's growth rate in the long run. In the latter case, the interest is not on how trade influences technical change and growth in the short run or during a transition period. Rather the focus is on how trade shifts the economy's steady state growth rate.

In this paper, we start by considering the impact of trade on medium-term growth. Later sections then focus attention on long-run growth. The next section begins the discussion by reviewing how endogenous growth theory fits into the historical analysis of growth accounting.

5.2 Endogenous Technological Change and Economic Growth

Based on Solow (1956, 1957), growth accounting seeks to explain the growth rate of aggregate output into various components, mainly the growth of factor supplies — usually capital and labor — and technological progress. The discussion begins with a standard neoclassical production function:

$$Y(t) = A(t)F[K(t), L(t)], \tag{1}$$

where $Y(t)$ refers to domestic output at time t, $A(t)$, defined as total factor productivity, denotes an index that relates to the technological level of the economy or its stock of knowledge, $K(t)$ is the amount of capital services, and $L(t)$ is the labor input. Taking proportional changes in both sides of the equation yields:

$$\dot{Y}/Y = \dot{A}/A + \frac{KAF_K}{Y}\dot{K}/K + \frac{LAF_L}{Y}\dot{L}/L, \qquad (2)$$

with dots representing the time derivatives ($\dot{A} = \mathrm{d}A/\mathrm{d}t$), and F_K and F_L denoting the partial derivatives of the production function, F, with respect to capital and labor, respectively. Equation (1) shows that output growth can be explained by the rate of technological progress or by the growth of capital and labor inputs employed in production.

On the assumptions of perfect competition in factor markets and constant returns to scale, then the marginal value product of capital, $P_Y AF_K$, equals the rental rate on capital, r (with P_Y denoting the price of output, Y), and the marginal value product of labor, $P_Y AF_L$, equals the wage rate, W. In addition, the sum of the share of capital in costs of production, $\Theta_k = rK/P_Y Y$, and the share of labor, $\Theta_L = WL/P_Y Y$, add up to one. Incorporating these relationships and definitions into equation (2) results in:

$$\dot{Y}/Y = \dot{A}/A + (1 - \Theta_L)\dot{K}/K + \Theta_L\dot{L}/L, \qquad (3)$$

In order to measure the relative roles played by input growth and technological change in explaining output growth, one would have to measure the various components of equation (3). Usually, the technological change growth, $\dot{A}/A$, is difficult to measure. As a result, Solow (1957) and others proceeded to compute available information on the growth of output and inputs, imputing the role of technological change, as a residual. This is easily seen from equation (3) by rearranging terms so that:

$$\dot{A}/A = \dot{Y}/Y - (1 - \Theta_L)\dot{K}/K + \Theta_L\dot{L}/L. \qquad (4)$$

This provides an imputation of how much technological change accounts for growth, based upon information available on output and input growth.

In his classic paper on this issue, Solow (1957) obtained that technological change, as measured by the residual, explains 87.5 percent of the increase in gross output per man-hour in the U.S.

during the period of 1909 through 1949. For the post-war period, recent estimates put technological change as 49 percent of the increase in the total factor productivity in the U.S. from 1948 to 1985. A similar calculation for France yields 76 percent, 78 percent for Germany, 55 percent for Japan and 73 percent for the United Kingdom (Boskin and Lau 1992, p. 47).

A myriad of other studies has confirmed the significance of the residual in accounting for a large share of long-run growth.[6] In the medium term, though, many countries have sustained high rates of growth in income per-capita through extended accumulation of capital per worker. In the case of the fast-growing Singapore, for example, Alwyn Young has suggested that its expansion since the 1960s has been totally due to increases in the supplies of capital and labor, as conventionally measured (Young 1992). In assessing these results, though, one should consider that technological changes are often linked to increases in the stock of capital or labor. Laboratories producing the latest new inventions, for example, may use highly sophisticated equipment and a variety of workers may be employed in such ventures. Similarly, new technology may be embodied in new machines. So, in part, physical capital accumulation is determined by technological developments, with changes in A and K in the earlier equations intimately linked to each other.[7]

Growth accounting has been a useful tool in identifying the significant role played by the residual in explaining long-run growth. However, one needs to go further in specifying the economic forces that determine the residual. Technological change, for example, constitutes a large chunk of what is symbolically referred to as $\dot{A}/A$ in equation (4), but how is the rate of technical change determined? Some authors, for instance, have focused on the role played by research and development expenditures in determining innovation [See Griliches (1994)]. Others have emphasized the local availability of human capital in fostering technological change [See Romer (1990) and Lucas (1993)]. Yet some others have focused on learning externalities [See Stokey (1988), Young (1991) and Lucas (1993)]. And some recent literature has looked at the impact of cities and urban agglomeration on medium-term productivity growth [See Rivera-Batiz (1988a, 1988b, 1994), Eaton and Eckstein (1993), Hanson (1994), and Rauch (1995)]. What these approaches have in common is that they endogenize technological change, looking at the forces that increase or decrease the rate of technical progress in the economy. In terms of equation (1), A is an endogenous variable, determined by economic forces.

The next section provides a model of endogenous technological change showing how trade influences total factor productivity and medium-term growth.

5.3   Rivalry, Trade and Technological Change

In examining the reasons why some firms have higher rates of innovation and are more competitive than others in different countries, one factor emerges as critical: the extent of rivalry and competition faced by firms is a key determinant of their innovative activities. Insofar as openness and international competition increase rivalry and competition among domestic firms, innovation will be stimulated and growth will rise. By contrast, protectionism and policies that restrict trade would result in reduced innovation and a slowdown of growth. As Michael E. Porter concludes in his far-ranging study of innovation and competition: "Competitive advantage emerges from pressure, challenge and adversity, rarely from an easy life. Pressure and adversity are powerful motivators for change and innovation... Complacency and an inward focus often explain why nations lose competitive advantage. Lack of pressure and challenge means that firms fail to look constantly for and interpret new buyer needs, new technologies, and new processes... Protection, in its various forms, insulates domestic firms from the pressure of international competition" (Porter 1990, pp. 170–171 and 665).

The economist F.M. Scherer has noted that "even the most casual observer cannot escape noticing the invigorating effect rivalry commonly has on industrial firms' research and development efforts" (Scherer 1986, p. 83). In this section, we develop a simple model showing how international trade, by increasing rivalry and competition, induces firms to engage in greater research and development (R&D) thus leading to technological progress.

Consider an economy of the type examined by Krugman (1990), specialized in the production of slightly differentiated goods in a market structure of monopolistic competition. We first assume that the economy is operating under autarky, determining its equilibrium in the absence of trade. The effects of opening the economy to international trade are then discussed. Consumers exhibit the following Dixit-Stiglitz utility function:

$$U = \left[\sum_{k=1}^{n} C_k^{\Theta} \right]^{1/\Theta} \tag{5}$$

where C_k is the quantity consumed of each differentiated good produced in the economy, k is an index for denoting each differentiated product, with $k = 1, \ldots$, n and Θ is a parameter with a numerical value between zero and one. Note that Θ is related to the strength of tastes toward product diversity: as Θ increases towards 1, the products in the industry become less differentiated and product variety loses its value.

Consumers maximize profits subject to a budget constraint, given by:

$$I_o = \sum_{k=1}^{n} P_k C_k \tag{6}$$

where P_k is the price of commodity k and I_o is the income of consumers. Maximization of equation (5) subject to (6) leads to the following first order condition:

$$C_k = \left[\frac{I_o}{P_k U^{\Theta}} \right]^{1/(1-\Theta)}, \tag{7}$$

whose price elasticity is given by:

$$\varepsilon_k = \frac{1}{1 - \Theta \left[1 - 1/n\right]}. \tag{8}$$

This elasticity is always greater than one and rises with the number of firms operating in the economy. This embodies the fact that a larger number of firms causes each single producer to lose some of its influence on aggregate demand, its monopoly power, making the market more competitive. Each firm faces this increased rivalry or competition through an increase in the price elasticity of demand for its own (differentiated) product.[8]

Each firm requires the use of unskilled labor in production, given by:

$$L_k = \mu_k + \beta X_k, \tag{9}$$

where L_k is the unskilled labor used by firm k, X_k denotes the output of each firm, the parameter β represents the amount of variable labor per unit of output and μ represents a fixed amount of labor, giving rise to fixed costs of production. Unskilled labor is hired at a wage rate denoted by W.

In addition to unskilled labor, each firm uses skilled labor, H_k, in activities relating to research and development (R&D). This labor is hired at a wage rate W_H, and is associated with a supply of R&D which is by denoted A_k. The amount of R&D produced by each unit of skilled labor (the productivity of human capital in research and development activities) is denoted by $1/\phi$. The amount of skilled labor used by a firm is then:

$$H_k = \phi A_k. \tag{10}$$

The use of human capital in research and development activities is assumed to produce a benefit for the firm in the form of reduced variable costs. More specifically, it is assumed that the fixed labor requirement, μ_k, is reduced according to the R&D undertaken by the firm, according to:

$$\mu_k = \mu_o A_k^{-\alpha}. \tag{11}$$

Where the parameter α is related to the productivity of research and development in reducing costs in the firm.[9]

Each firm maximizes profits, which — using equations (9), (10) and (11) — are given by:

$$\pi_k = P_k X_k - W\beta X_k - W\mu_o A_k^{-\alpha} - W_H \phi A_k. \tag{12}$$

The first order conditions for profit maximization, for the choice variables, X_k and A_k, respectively, are:

$$P_k = [\varepsilon_k/(\varepsilon_k - 1)]\,\beta W \tag{13}$$

and

$$A_k = \left[\frac{\alpha W\mu_o}{W_H \phi}\right]^{1/(1+\alpha)}. \tag{14}$$

Equation (13) shows that price is a markup above marginal cost (βW), where the markup is related to the elasticity of demand facing a producer. Using equation (8), one can transform equation (13) into:

$$P_k = (\Theta\sigma)^{-1}\beta W \tag{15}$$

where $\sigma = 1 - 1/n$. Note that the price markup declines when the number of producers rises in the market. This is the mechanism through which increased rivalry benefits consumers in the economy: by reducing the extent to which price is above marginal cost.

Equation (14) shows that R&D activities are positively related to the cost of unskilled labor (since the higher this cost, the greater the fixed costs of the firm and, therefore, the larger the benefits of spending on R&D). The R&D engaged by each firm is negatively related to the price of human capital, W_H, since R&D activities require expenditures on skilled labor. Finally, R&D is related to the productivity of R&D in reducing costs (α) and the productivity of human capital in generating knowledge in the economy (ϕ).

For simplicity, a symmetric equilibrium will be examined here. All firms are thus assumed to face the same cost and demand parameters. Free entry into the industry guarantees zero profits, from which the equilibrium output of each firm is determined by setting equation (12) equal to zero and substituting the values of P_k and A_k

in equations (14) and (15). The result is:

$$X_k = \frac{\Theta\sigma(1+\alpha)\mu_o}{(1-\Theta\sigma)\,\beta}A^{-\alpha}. \tag{16}$$

The employment of unskilled labor on the part of each firm is then specified by substituting the expression for X_k into equation (9), yielding:

$$L_k = \frac{1+\Theta\sigma\alpha}{1-\Theta\sigma}\mu_o A_k^{-\alpha}. \tag{17}$$

On the symmetry assumption, aggregating over all firms in the economy, the equality of unskilled labor demand, nL_k, with the economy-wide endowment of skilled labor, $\bar{L}$, yields:

$$\bar{L} = n\left[\frac{1+\Theta\sigma\alpha}{1-\Theta\sigma}\right]\mu_o A_k^{-\alpha} \tag{18}$$

where use has been made of equation (17).

Since $\bar{L}$ is exogenous, equation (18) has two endogenous variables, n and A_k. Observe also that the number of firms enters in equation (18) directly through n but also through σ, which is a rising function of n $(\mathrm{d}\sigma/\mathrm{d}n > 0)$. Taking into account these nuances, some algebraic manipulation of the total differential of equation (18) leads to the conclusion that the equation establishes a positive connection between the number of firms, n, and the amount of R&D of each firm, A_k. The economic intuition behind this result is that, as the number of domestic firms rises, with other things held constant, the demand for unskilled labor increases. This augments the wage rate received by unskilled workers and increases the marginal benefits of R&D, whose purpose is precisely to reduce the costs of unskilled labor for the firm. As the marginal benefits of additional units of R&D shift upwards, with the marginal cost of R&D held constant (the price of skilled labor, W_H, held fixed), an increase in the amount of R&D, A_k, would occur. This positive linkage between the number of domestic firms and the amount of R&D each firm engages in, A_k, is represented by the AA curve in Figure 5.2.

An additional constraint is imposed by the fixed supply of skilled labor in the economy, $\bar{H}$. The economy-wide equality of demand for

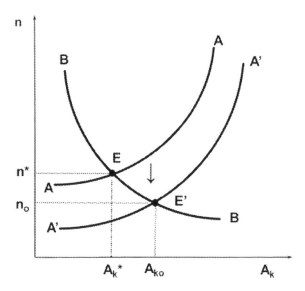

Figure 5.2.   Domestic Equilibrium under Autarky and Free Trade.

and supply of skilled labor is:

$$n\phi A_k = \bar{H}. \tag{19}$$

Equation (19) gives a tradeoff between the number of domestic firms
in the economy and the volume of R&D of each firm. An increase in
the number of firms, with other things held constant, increases the
demand for skilled labor. With a fixed endowment of human capital,
to sustain equilibrium in the skilled labor market, each firm would
have to reduce its demand for skilled labor. This implies that the
R&D activities of each firm would decline, reducing A_k. This tradeoff
is reflected by the downward-slopping BB curve in Figure 5.2.

Equations (18) and (19) implicitly define the equilibrium number
of firms in the economy under autarky, n^*, as well as the expenditures
on R&D and the accumulation of knowledge, A_k^*. In Figure 5.2, this
equilibrium occurs at point E, where the AA and BB curves intersect.

Up to this point we have considered an economy under autarky.
What is the impact of international trade in this context? The
simplest setting to consider is one where the two economies are
identical. Both countries would then have the same number and type

of consumers, equal factor endowments, identical technology, and so on. When the two economies trade, intraindustry trade will emerge. Since all products are differentiated from each other, consumers will wish to purchase not only the domestic varieties but also the foreign varieties. This increases the number of products consumed in each country. Each economy, however, would spend the same fraction of income on domestic and foreign products, and therefore, there would be balanced trade.

In terms of the equilibrium at point E in Figure 5.2, the first thing to notice is that the domestic skilled labor market equilibrium condition (equation (19)) remains unchanged and, therefore, the BB curve remains unaltered. On the other hand, the AA curve, which is determined by the unskilled labor market equilibrium, is changed by trade. Equation (18) shows the algebraic depiction of the domestic unskilled labor market equilibrium. The only item of equation (18) that is altered by trade is the variable σ, which determines the price markup charged by firms above marginal cost. Under autarky, σ depends on the number of domestic firms, n. Under free trade, however, σ is related to the total number of firms in the market, not just domestic firms. With a greater set of competitors in the now global market, there is more rivalry and this is reflected in a reduced price markup above marginal cost. Algebraically, the variable σ rises with trade, narrowing the gap between P_k and βW (marginal cost).

In terms of Figure 5.2, an increase in σ shifts the AA curve to A‘A’. The outcome is that domestic equilibrium is achieved at point E’. The opening of trade is thus associated, first of all, with a drop in the number of domestic firms from n^* to n_o. Although the total number of competitors in the domestic market rises with trade due to the access to foreign products, the increased competition lowers price markups and induces some domestic firms to exit the market. At the same time, Figure 5.2 indicates that trade is associated with increased R&D expenditures per firm, A_k. The increased R&D per firm is a reaction to the rivalry generated by foreign competition. As the number of competitors rises and price markups decline above marginal cost, the mirror image of this phenomenon is an increase in the real wage of unskilled labor, W/P_k. This higher real cost of unskilled labor increases the marginal benefit of R&D expenditures, thus leading each firm to demand more human capital. The increased use of skilled labor per firm then results in technical improvements that lower costs.

In this model, trade is associated with technological change and, therefore, economic growth. What is the impact of this growth on domestic economic welfare and how does it compare with traditional trade models under monopolistic competition (such as Krugman (1990))? The utility derived by domestic consumers is given by equation (5). On the symmetric equilibrium assumption, all C_k's in equation (5) are identical and, therefore:

$$U = n^{(1-\Theta)\Theta} n C_k. \tag{20}$$

But from the income constraint, $nC_k = I/P_k$, where $I = w\bar{L} + W_H \bar{H}$. Substitution into equation (20) results in:

$$U = n^{(1-\Theta)\Theta} \left[(W/P_k) \bar{L} + (W_H/P_k) \bar{H} \right]. \tag{21}$$

Equation (21) shows that domestic utility rises by means of three mechanisms: (1) the number of differentiated products consumed rises from n^* to $2n_o$ due to the availability of foreign varieties; (2) as the number of producers increases, the real wage rate of unskilled labor, W/P_k, also increases (this is the mirror image of the reduction in price markups suffered by producers; and (3) as R&D per firm rises, the demand for skilled labor increases, which, given a fixed stock of human capital, leads to a hike in the real wage rate of skilled labor, W/P_k.

Utilizing expressions derived earlier, equation (21) becomes:

$$U = n^{(1-\Theta)\Theta} \Theta \sigma/\beta \left[\bar{L} + \left(\phi A_k^{1+\alpha}/\alpha\mu_o \right) \bar{H} \right]. \tag{22}$$

Algebraically, this shows three mechanisms through which utility is increased: through n directly, by rising σ, and by augmenting A_k. Note that in the simplified models in the previous literature [such as Krugman (1990)], there is no investment in R&D and the last two mechanisms would not arise.

The present model incorporates gains from trade related to the increased domestic productivity that foreign competition induces through increased rivalry and competition. This increases domestic total factor productivity and, therefore, economic growth. The impact of trade on growth described in this section, however, is medium term. It would disappear over time, as the economy settles at the new equilibrium, algebraically described by point E' in Figure 5.2.[10] The next section focuses on the effects of trade on long-run growth.

5.4   Trade, Technological Change and Long-Run Growth

In examining the impact of trade on long-run growth, it is useful to review first some of the key forces associated with innovation and long-run growth, as they have been postulated in the literature.

Studies of innovation and technological change suggest that the invention and development of new goods and new inputs constitute one of the major sources of modern economic growth. Insofar as international trade stimulates the creation of new goods and inputs, long-run growth will rise. However, as the recent literature, on trade and endogenous growth makes clear, there are mechanisms through which increased trade may actually discourage innovation and thus, *reduce* growth.

Human capital is one of the key resources used in innovative activities. The amount of human capital dedicated to innovation in an economy is closely linked to technological change. Increased international trade can severely constrain innovation and growth if it tends to generate wide sectoral shifts that reduce the use of scarce human capital in research and development activities. Such is the case, for example, if trade raises the production of manufacturing industries intensive in the use of human capital. The increased demand and employment of skilled labor within the production activities of these industries would drive human capital away from research and development, reducing innovation and growth.

These sectoral effects constitute a potentially pernicious impact of trade on growth for some countries. Their importance is directly to the economy's endowment of human capital relative to that of other inputs, and whether comparative advantage dictates that human capital-intensive sectors expand or contract under trade. It is possible that trade liberalization and economic integration with the rest of the world can reduce growth. As Gene Grossman and Elhanan Helpman have noted: "A country that imports human-capital-intensive goods finds that international integration reduces derived demand for human capital and thereby lowers the cost of innovation. In such a country the indirect effect of trade also is to encourage growth. But trade may impede growth in a country that exports human capital-intensive goods because the exportables sector draws human capital away from research activities" (Grossman and Helpman 1991, p. 170).[11]

Sectoral effects imply that increased trade or economic integration can raise or lower economic growth.[12] There are, however, other mechanisms through which trade can influence technical change and growth. A pre-condition for most innovative activity is a body of knowledge and ideas upon which new concepts emerge. Very few innovations totally break with the past. Most are based on existing ideas.

Insofar as international trade fosters the transmission of knowledge and ideas across any two countries, the additional information now available in each economy will tend to spur technological change and growth. As Northwestern University's historian, Joel Mokyr has noted in relation to some historic periods of innovation and growth: "When two previously unconnected civilizations establish contact, technical information is exchanged that may yield potential economic gains to both... Technologically creative societies started off as borrowers and typically turned soon into the generators and then the exporters of technology. In the seventeenth century, England was regarded as a backward society that depended on foreigners for its engineering and textile industries; by the nineteenth century, the directions were reversed. Modern day East Asia finds itself in the same position" (Mokyr 1990, p. 188–189).

Within this context, restrictions on international trade which reduce flows of technological information across borders are associated not only with the distortionary losses examined exhaustively in the trade literature but also with negative effects on technical change and long-run growth. As David Mowery and Nathan Rosenberg have noted in reference to the United States: "efforts to restrict the international flow of basic scientific and technological information and research... will impoverish U.S. citizens..." (Mowery and Rosenberg 1989, p. 292).

Although international trade can greatly increase the local stock of information available in an economy, this is a necessary but not a sufficient condition for growth. The impact on economic growth may be limited if the domestic innovation system is not able to handle the new knowledge. Such is the case if key local resources are not available that can gainfully use the new information generated by openness. The next section presents a simple model of endogenous growth incorporating the role played by national innovation systems on growth.

5.5   National Innovation Systems and Long-Run Economic Growth

A national system of innovation is the network of institutions that support the initiation, modification and diffusion of new technologies (Cantwell 1992, p. 166). More specifically, a national innovation system includes "home-based suppliers and related industries in those products, components, machines, or services that are specialized and/or integral to the process of innovation in the industry" (Porter 1994, p. 453). This section will show how the state of development of national innovation systems influences technological change and growth. The economy considered is a closed economy. The implications regarding the impact of trade on domestic growth are examined in the next section.

To simplify the analysis, the model used is a straightforward extension of Romer-type endogenous growth models (Romer 1990). We consider an economy whose aggregate production function is given by:

$$Y = H_Y^\alpha L_\mu^\beta \sum_{i=1}^{A} X(i)^\sigma \qquad (23)$$

where Y is output of final, consumer goods, H_Y represents the use of human capital in the production of consumer goods, L_μ denotes the amount of unskilled labor used in production, and $X(i)$ is the amount of an intermediate or capital good i used in final goods production, where there are A of these intermediate goods, all slightly differentiated from each other. It is assumed that $\alpha + \beta + \sigma = 1$. Given the symmetric way in which capital goods enter the production function, and the similarity of their cost, and therefore supply, functions — to be established below — the amount of each capital good that industry will purchase is identical. As a result, the aggregate quantity demanded of each capital good will be $X(i) = X_o$. The total demand for capital goods is then given by: $X_m = nX_o$. Equation (23) can therefore be transformed into:

$$Y = A^{1-\sigma} H_Y^\alpha L_\mu^\beta X_m^\sigma. \tag{24}$$

Equation (24) states that final goods production is related to the quantities of labor, capital and human capital demanded *and* to the number of capital goods used, A. That the number of capital goods used by industry has an effect on output independent of that of their quantity demanded is an outcome of the form of the sub-production function for capital goods and reflects the presence of specialization economies in the use of intermediate goods. Note that the form of (24) is such that it can be interpreted as representing a standard Cobb-Douglas production function with inputs given by human capital, unskilled labor and physical capital, with a shift parameter equal to $A^{1-\sigma}$. As noted earlier, most growth theory previously assumed that this shift parameter was exogenously-determined [see Solow (1956)]. In endogenous growth theory, though, A represents the equilibrium number of capital goods produced in the economy and is thus endogenous.

Profits in the final goods sector, π, are given by:

$$\pi = P_Y H_Y^\alpha L_\mu^\beta \sum_{i=1}^{A} X(i)^\sigma - W L_\mu - W_H H_Y - \sum_{i=1}^{A} P(i) X(i) \tag{25}$$

where W is the wage rate for unskilled labor, and W_H is the wage or return received by human capital, $P(i)$ represents the rental cost of each "real" capital good i used in final goods production, and P_Y is the price of final goods. The latter is normalized to equal 1.

From the first order conditions for profit maximization, the following expressions can be derived:

$$H_Y = \alpha Y / W_H \qquad (26)$$

$$L_\mu = \beta Y / W \qquad (27)$$

and

$$P(i) = (1 - \alpha - \beta) H_Y^\alpha L_\mu^\beta X(i)^{-\alpha-\beta}. \qquad (28)$$

These implicitly define the final goods demands for unskilled labor, human capital and each capital good.

What determines the number and output capital goods? The production of a capital good by a firm or entrepreneur requires some investment funds (venture capital) plus owning a design for the capital good. The investment funds come from the savings decisions of consumers. As in the Solow model, out of total output, a certain amount, C, is consumed and an amount S is saved, where $S = dK/dt$ represents the investment funds available to firms at a rate of interest, r. It is assumed that the amount of financial capital required by each capital goods firm, $K(i)$, varies with output:

$$K(i) = \mu X(i) \qquad (29)$$

where u is a fixed parameter denoting the venture capital per output required by firm i. The cost of borrowing financial capital for each firm is then $rK(i) = r\mu X(i)$.

In addition to the investment funds, in order to produce a capital good, a firm has to purchase a design or blueprint for the capital good. These designs are produced, in turn, by a research and development sector composed of various types of specialized human capital, all of them operating within the environment of a national innovation system. It is assumed that there are N different types of specialized human capital in the research sector of the economy. The production function for the research and development sector is postulated to be:

$$\dot{A} = dA/dt = \delta \left(\sum_{j=1}^{N} H_j^{\varepsilon} \right)^{1/\varepsilon} A \tag{30}$$

where H_j represents the amount of each specialized type of human capital used in innovation activities (involving engineering, design, legal services, etc.), ε is a parameter between zero and one to be interpreted shortly, and δ is a parameter reflecting the productivity of the domestic research and development sector in creating new product designs out of the stock of knowledge, A, available to it.

On the simplifying assumption that the amounts of each specialized type of human capital used in the national innovation system are equal to each other, then, equation (30) becomes:

$$\dot{A} = dA/dt = \delta N^{(1-\varepsilon)/\varepsilon} H_A A \tag{31}$$

where $H_A = NH_j$. Equation (31) states that number of new capital goods designed over any given time period is related to: (1) the total amount of human capital used in the research and development sector, H_A, (2) the productivity of that human capital in designing new products out of the existing knowledge, δ, (3) the existing body of knowledge, as reflected in the number of existing product designs, A, (4) and the number of different types of specialized human capital in the research and development sector, N.

The status of the national innovation system of a country determines the values of δ and N in equation (31). High values of δ are related to highly productive innovation systems. Low-yielding national innovation environments would have small values of δ. If, for instance, the innovation system in a country is rooted in old, declining technological paradigms, then its productivity in using the available knowledge to develop new ideas will decline and the parameter will be smaller. Even though new knowledge may be flowing into the economy at a fast rate (increasing A very quickly), the development of new products will lag because of the inability of the local innovators to take the new ideas and design new capital goods based on them. This may occur if, for instance, new technologies are being developed abroad, which reflect either new industrial innovations or otherwise new areas of scientific discovery. In this case, as John Cantwell has observed: "with the emergence of a new paradigm, technological leadership tends to move away from a society whose institutions were particularly geared towards problem-solving activity within the confines of the previously-prevailing paradigm" (Cantwell 1992, p. 166).

The degree of specialization among a country's skilled labor force may also influence its rate of technological change. Urban historian Jane Jacobs, among many others, has noted that one of the key factors behind the economic growth associated with urbanization historically has been the great diversity of the specialized labor services in the cities. As she notes: "Graphics consultants, stationary engravers and designers, specialists in the ventilation of buildings, lighting consultants, and advertising agents are some examples. They simultaneously serve other local organizations producers' goods and services, exporters, and enterprises supplying consumer goods and services to local people" (Jacobs 1969, p. 195). The specialized labor allows inventions of all types to be more easily designed, engineered and marketed.

Equations (30) and (31) incorporate the productivity of specialized skilled labor in generating innovation by adopting a Dixit-Stiglitz-Ethier production function which relates the number of new products developed in any given time period to the array of specialized types of labor available domestically, N. The exponent ε measures the extent of specialization economies in the use of skilled labor for innovation purposes. The stronger the specialization economies, the closer the value of ε to zero, and the greater the impact of increased division of skilled labor on the rate of technical change. On the other hand, as ε approaches 1, specialization loses its value and the role played by N in equation (31) tends to disappear.

Within the present model, the extent of specialization among skilled workers is assumed to be exogenous. A recent literature on economic geography, however, endogenizes this variable.[13] By increasing the extent of the market, urban agglomeration allows a greater division of labor, leading to a more diversified labor force. It is precisely the availability of such a diversified labor force that boosts innovative activities and stimulates economic growth.[14]

Equation (31) retains the traditional role played by increased human capital on technical change, but its impact on technological change is mediated by the economy's innovation system. Note also that the production of new designs is augmented by the total level of knowledge in the economy, other things the same. Such knowledge is reflected in equation (31) by the total number of designs, A. This is so because of the non-excludable nature of technology. Everybody has access to the designs and blueprints involved in producing all capital goods. This information is freely-available.

In order to produce a capital good i, a firm must make an investment, $K(i)$, plus buy a design for the capital good as supplied by the research and development sector, which represents a fixed cost for each firm. This gives the firm the right to produce using the design. The profits of each firm producing capital goods — excluding the fixed cost of purchasing the design — is then:

$$\pi(i) = P(i)X(i) - r\mu X(i). \tag{32}$$

Making use of equation (28), the first order condition for profit maximization for producer i leads to:

$$P(i) = r\mu/(1 - \alpha - \beta). \tag{33}$$

Since the marginal cost of producing a capital good is $r\mu$, equation (33) suggests that the price of capital good i is at a markup above marginal cost.

Substituting the equilibrium price in equation (33) into the profit equation in (32) yields:

$$\pi(i) = (\alpha + \beta)P(i)X(i). \tag{34}$$

These would be the production profits of each capital goods firm during a given time period. From these profits, each firm must pay for the price of the design it must purchase in order to produce the capital good i. Denoting the price of a design by P_A, then potential entrants into the capital goods market drive the present value of the profits from selling the capital good to equal the price of a design, or:

$$P_A = \pi(i)/r = (\alpha + \beta)P(i)X(i)/r$$

$$= (\alpha + \beta)(1 - \alpha - \beta)H_Y^\alpha L_\mu^\beta X(i)^{1-\alpha-\beta}/r. \qquad (35)$$

This determines the price of a design.

Human capital is used in the production of final goods and in the research and development sector. If the supply of human capital in the economy is fixed at H, then:

$$H = H_A + H_Y. \qquad (36)$$

If the human capital market is competitive, the wage rate for human capital in the two sectors — final goods and research/development — must be equalized. The marginal product of human capital in the production of designs (in the research and development sector) is:

$$d\dot{A}/dH_A = \delta N^{(1-\varepsilon)/\varepsilon} A. \qquad (37)$$

And if the price of a design is denoted by P_A, then the wage rate received by human capital in the research sector is equal to the marginal value product of human capital in that sector:

$$W_H = P_A \delta A N^{(1-\varepsilon)/\varepsilon}. \qquad (38)$$

From equation (26), the marginal product of human capital in the final goods sector is:

$$W_H = \alpha A H_Y^{\alpha-1} L_\mu^\beta X(i)^{1-\alpha-\beta}. \qquad (39)$$

Equating (38) and (39) results in:

$$P_A \delta A N^{(1-\varepsilon)/\varepsilon} = \alpha A H_Y^{\alpha-1} L_\mu^\beta X(i)^{1-\alpha-\beta}. \qquad (40)$$

And substituting the expression for P_A in equation (35) into (40) results in:

$$H_Y = [\alpha/\delta N^{(1-\varepsilon)/\varepsilon}(1 - \alpha - \beta)(\alpha + \beta)]r. \qquad (41)$$

Equation (41) shows that the higher interest rate, the greater the amount of human capital allocated to final goods. The reason is that, as r rises, the present value of the profits generated by producing a capital good declines. This pushes down the price of a design and, therefore, the value of the marginal product of human capital in the research sector. As a consequence, human capital shifts out of research and into final goods production.

Using the full employment equation (36):

$$H_A = H - H_Y$$

$$H_A = H - [\alpha/\delta N^{(1-\varepsilon)/\varepsilon}(1-\alpha-\beta)(\alpha+\beta)]r \qquad (42)$$

If the economy is at a steady state, its rate of growth, g, will be:

$$g = \dot{Y}/Y = \dot{A}/A$$

$$g = \delta N^{(1-\varepsilon)/\varepsilon} H_A = \delta N^{(1-\varepsilon)/\varepsilon} H$$

$$- [\alpha/(1-\alpha-\beta)(\alpha+\beta)]\, r = \delta N^{(1-\varepsilon)/\varepsilon} H - \tau r \qquad (43)$$

where $\tau = [\alpha/(1-\alpha-\beta)(\alpha+\beta)]$ is a constant.

In order to complete the model, the interest rate must be determined. This requires modeling the consumption/savings decision of households. Following Romer (1990), it is assumed that consumers maximize the utility derived from an infinite stream of consumption beginning at time t = 0, discounted to the present:

$$U_o = \int_0^\infty e^{-\Theta t}\frac{C(\tau)^{1-\phi_1} - 1}{1-\phi} \qquad (44)$$

where the utility function is assumed to be of the constant elasticity type:

$$U(\tau) = \frac{C(\tau)^{1-\phi_1} - 1}{1-\phi}. \qquad (45)$$

Maximization of utility subject to the budget constraint then leads to:

$$\frac{\dot{C}}{C} = \frac{r - \Theta}{\phi}. \qquad (46)$$

If the economy is at a steady state, its rate of growth, g, will be:

$$\dot{g} = \dot{Y}/Y = \dot{C}/C = (r - \Theta)/\phi. \tag{47}$$

Combining equations (43) and (47) results in the economy's steady state growth rate:

$$g = \frac{\delta N^{(1-\varepsilon)/\varepsilon} H - \tau\Theta}{\phi\tau + 1}. \tag{48}$$

In addition, the equilibrium interest rate is given by:

$$r = \frac{\Theta + \phi\delta N^{(1-\varepsilon)/\varepsilon} H}{\phi\tau + 1}. \tag{49}$$

Equation (48) shows the long-run growth of the economy under autarky. Note that, the higher the stock of human capital, the greater the growth rate. By allowing greater human capital employment in research and development, economies with higher endowments of skilled labor will grow faster. This, of course, is the traditional explanation for high rates of growth in many countries. As Gary Saxonhouse notes of Japan: "Throughout the past century, relative to these other economies [other industrialized nations], Japan, with uniquely poorly endowed with natural resources, has also been well endowed with a high-quality labor force and with unusually thrifty households. These distinctive Japanese circumstances may go a long way toward explaining its superior economic growth performance. . ." (Saxonhouse 1993, p. 150).

Still, cross-country differences in human capital endowments fail to explain a substantial portion of growth differentials (Lucas 1993). In the model developed in this paper, the impact of human capital on the growth rate is mediated by the status of the national innovation system. The more developed the innovation system of an economy, the greater its long-run growth rate, given the aggregate endowment of human capital. This is reflected in higher values of δ and N, as discussed earlier.

What is the impact of trade on long-run economic growth in the present model? The next section examines this issue.

5.6   The Impact of International Trade on Endogenous Growth

Suppose that, within the framework developed in the previous section, two identical economies are originally under autarky and suddenly engage in free trade. What is the impact on economic growth?[15]

In this framework, there is production of only one, homogenous final good. We are therefore precluded from examining international trade in final goods, which requires at least two differentiated products. However, the impact of trade in intermediate goods (trade in the capital goods) and in ideas (the flow of designs or blueprints) can be examined in great detail. This simplifies the analysis by excluding the sectoral effects noted earlier. It would straightforward, though, to extend the model to a two-sector economy. Within that context, the issues raised by the present model would also apply, though the overall impact on growth would depend on how production is altered across sectors and the relative intensity of human capital utilization in each sector.

For purposes of the analysis, we assume that under autarky the two economies considered are producing capital goods which are totally different from each other. A rationale for this assumption is that technological change tends to be localized. Innovations follow particular paradigms which may take divergent paths in different countries, even if those countries have identical factor endowments and consumer tastes. Countries isolated from each other are likely to follow different paths of invention.

When trade occurs, each country has now available the ideas and knowledge of the other, as represented by the stock of blueprints, A. The greater body of knowledge (twice as much as before) increases the rate of invention and, therefore, growth would rise in both economies. In fact, the steady state growth rate under free trade would be given by:

$$g = \frac{2\delta N^{(1-\varepsilon)/\varepsilon} H - \tau \Theta}{\phi \tau + 1}. \qquad (50)$$

The effects of trade on growth can be severely limited by the extent to which the national innovation system can in fact utilize effectively the new information and knowledge in the production of new ideas. It may be that the specialized human capital required to use effectively the new ideas and knowledge is not locally available. Symbolically, the value of N in equation (50) mediates the extent to which the foreign ideas have an impact on domestic innovative activities. If N is small, openness will result in a very small growth improvement. At the same time, if N is large, the impact on growth could be substantial. The same applies to other aspects of the local innovative atmosphere: the more limited their ability to develop new products with the newly-available ideas, the smaller the impact of trade on growth.

Whatever the impact of the increased flows of ideas and technology across borders on long-run growth, the present model suggests a definite positive impact of trade on medium-term growth. The Dixit-Stiglitz-Ethier technology emphasized by endogenous growth models is one where the availability of additional types of capital goods increases productivity. As the two economies trade with each other, final goods producers find it profitable to expand the use of capital goods by adopting those produced abroad. If the two economies are identical, then there is a doubling of the number of capital goods and this has a positive impact on total factor productivity in each country. Indeed, the effect on aggregate production is:

$$Y_1/Y_o = 2^{\alpha+\beta} \tag{51}$$

where Y_1 represents output under free trade and Y_o is the output under autarky. Medium-term growth is thus augmented by trade by making available a wider variety of capital goods in production.

5.7   Summary and Conclusions

Is international trade an "engine of growth"? The existing empirical literature studying in a rigorous way the connection between openness and growth overwhelmingly suggests that increased trade or reduced protectionism are linked to greater economic growth. However, when one studies the mechanisms through which trade affects economic growth, good reasons emerge to suspect that, while openness and trade may stimulate economic expansion in some countries, it could *reduce* growth in others.

What are the mechanisms through which trade affects economic growth? The modern theory of economic growth suggests that increased supplies of factors of production such as physical capital and labor account for a substantial portion of growth, but that it is technological change that explains most of the increased productivity of the labor force and, therefore, income per-capita. In order to investigate how trade affects growth, one must focus on how openness influences technological change.

Openness can influence technological change in many ways. This paper has focused on several key mechanisms through which trade and innovation are related. Firstly, by increasing domestic rivalry and competition, trade can induce domestic producers to increase their R&D activities, augmenting innovation and raising medium-term growth. In examining the reasons why some firms have higher rates of innovation and are more competitive than others in different countries, one factor emerges as critical: the extent of rivalry and competition faced by firms is a key determinant of their innovative activities. Insofar as openness and international competition increase rivalry and competition among domestic firms, innovation will be stimulated and growth will rise. By contrast, protectionism and policies that restrict trade would result in reduced innovation and a slowdown of growth.

Secondly, trade can affect growth by reallocating resources among sectors and industries in the economy, thus fostering or discouraging domestic research and development. For instance, human capital is one of the key resources used in innovative activities. The amount of human capital dedicated to innovation in an economy is closely linked to technological change. Increased international trade can severely constrain innovation and growth if it tends to generate wide sectoral shifts that reduce the use of scarce human capital in research and development activities. Such is the case, for example, if trade raises the production of manufacturing industries intensive in the use of human capital. The increased demand and employment of skilled labor within the production activities of these industries would drive human capital away from research and development, reducing innovation and growth.

Thirdly, insofar as international trade fosters the transmission of knowledge and ideas across any two countries, the additional information now available in each economy will tend to spur technological change and growth. Within this context, restrictions on international trade which reduce flows of technological information across borders are associated not only with the distortionary losses examined exhaustively in the trade literature but also with negative effects on technical change and long-run growth.

Although international trade can greatly increase the local stock of information available in an economy, this is a necessary but not a sufficient condition for growth. The impact on economic growth may be limited if the domestic innovation system is not able to handle productively the new knowledge. Such is the case if key local resources are not available that can gainfully use the new information generated by openness. Substantial supplies of specialized labor services are required to engage in the research and development involved in the creation of new goods. Such supplies may be absent in slow-growing economies. By contrast, economies with a diversity of specialized, highly-skilled workers available for the research and development of new goods (possibly located within proximity of each other in cities) are likely to grow faster. Under these conditions, trade is more likely to stimulate higher rates of long-run growth.

Notes:

[1] On the basis of these data, Bairoch (1972) has made the argument that income growth is positively affected by protectionism; see, however, the different interpretation made by Capie (1994).

[2] In another paper (Edwards 1993), Edwards has surveyed the empirical literature on trade and growth.

[3] See also Lee (1993).

[4] A discussion of these, and other issues, relating to the connection between trade and growth are explored by Bhagwati (1988), chapter 1.

[5] This distinction has been made by Richard Baldwin in a number of papers; see Baldwin (1992) and (1994).

[6]For a recent survey, see Barro and Xala-i-Martin (1995), chapter 10.

[7]An argument made by Lucas (1993) in reply to Young.

[8]In the present framework, how much ε_k can increase is bounded by the form of the utility function, which determines the elasticity of substitution between any two given products in the economy. As n rises to ∞, ε_k approaches the value of: $1/(1\text{-}\Theta)$.

[9]This type of R&D function has been used by Dasgupta (1986) and Dasgupta and Stiglitz (1980).

[10]Medium-term growth effects may last a long time. If the economy does not move immediately from autarky to free trade, but it does so gradually, eliminating trade restrictions over time, the growth effects can be long-lasting.

[11]In another paper, Rivera-Batiz and Xie (1992) show that integration in goods restricts growth in the high-growth region and speeds it up in the low-growth region.

[12]For a summary of the various effects of economic integration on medium- and long-term growth, public finance, and regional development, see Rivera-Batiz and Gingsberg (1993).

[13]See Rivera-Batiz (1988a) and (1988b), and Krugman (1991). A model of economic growth based on the growth of cities is presented in Rivera-Batiz (1994). This model determines the division of skilled labor endogenously.

[14]See Glaeser and Mare (1994) and Rauch (1993).

[15]This is the type of experiment carried out by Rivera-Batiz and Romer (1992).

References

Ades, Alberto and Edward L. Glaeser, "Evidence on Growth. Increasing Returns and the Extent of the Market", National Bureau of Economic Research Working Paper No. 4714, April (1994).

Aghion, P. and P. Howitt, "A Model of Growth Through Creative Destruction," *Econometrica*, 60(2) (1992): 323–352.

Bairoch, Paul, "Free Trade and European Economic Development in the Nineteenth Century," *European Economic Review*, (1972).

Baldwin, Richard E., *Towards an Integrated Europe* (London: Center for Economic Policy Research, 1994).

Baldwin, Richard E., "Measurable Dynamic Gains from Trade," *Journal of Political Economy*, 100 (1), February (1992): 162–174.

Baldwin, Richard E., "On the Growth Effects of Import Competition," National Bureau of Economic Research Working Paper No. 4045, (1994).

Baldwin, Richard E., "Growth Effects of 1992," *Economic Policy*, 9 (1989).

Barro, Robert J. and Xavier Xala-i-Martin, *Economic Growth*, (New York: McGraw Hill, 1995).

Bhagwati, Jagdish N., *Protectionism*, (Cambridge: The MIT Press 1988).

Boskin, Michael J. and Lawrence J. Lau, "Capital, Technology, and Economic Growth," in N. Rosenberg, R. Landau and D.C. Mowery, eds., *Technology and the Wealth of Nations* (Stanford: Stanford University Press, 1992).

Cantwell, John, "Japan's Industrial Competitiveness and the Technological Capability of the Leading Japanese Firms," in T.S. Arrison, C. Fred Bergsten, E.M. Graham, M. Caldwell Harris, eds., *Japan's Growing Technological Capability: Implications for the U.S. Economy*, (Washington, D.C.: National Academy Press 1992).

Capie, Forrest, *Tariffs and Growth: Some Insights from the World Economy*, (Manchester: Manchester University Press, 1994).

Dasgupta, Partha, "The Theory of Technological Competition," in J.E. Stiglitz and G. Frank Mathewson, eds., *New Developments* in *the Analysis of Market Structure*, (Cambridge: the MIT Press, 1986).

Dasgupta, Partha and Joseph Stiglitz, "Industrial Structure and the Nature of Inventive Activity," The *Economic Journal*, 90 June (1980): 266–293.

Dinopoulos, Elias and Constantinos Syropoulos, "Trade Liberalization and Schumpeterian Growth," paper presented at the AEA Meetings, January 1995.

Eaton, Jonathan and Zvi Eckstein, "Cities and Growth: Theory and Evidence from France and Japan," Conference on *Regional Integration and Growth*, Centre for Economic Policy Research, Barcelona, Spain, November (1993).

Edwards, Sebastian, "Openness, Trade Liberalization and Growth in Developing Countries," *Journal of Economic Literature*, 31, September (1993).

Edwards, Sebastian, "Openness, Outward Orientation, Trade Liberalization and Economic Performance in Developing Nations," NBER Working Paper No. 2908, March (1989).

Findlay, Ronald, "Growth and Development in Trade Models," in R.W. Jones and P. Kenen, eds., *Handbook of International Economics*, (Amsterdam: North Holland Publishing Company, 1984).

Glaeser, Edward L. and David C. Mare, "Cities and Skills," National Bureau of Economic Research Working Paper No. 4728, May (1994).

Griliches, Zvi, "Productivity, R&D, and the Data Constraint," *American Economic Review*, 84 (1) March (1994): 1–23.

Grossman, Gene M. and Elhanan Helpman, "Technology and Trade," in G. Grossman and K. Rogoff, eds., *The Handbook of International Economics*, (Amsterdam: North Holland Publishing Company, 1995).

Grossman, Gene M. and Elhanan Helpman, *Innovation and Growth in the Global Economy*, (Cambridge: The MIT Press, 1991).

Grossman. Gene M. and Elhanan Helpman, "Trade, Knowledge Spillovers and Growth," National Bureau of Economic Research Working Paper No. 3485, October (1990).

Hammond, Peter J. and Andres Rodriguez-Clare, "On Endogenizing Long-Run Growth," in Torben M. Andersen and Karl O. Moene, *Endogenous Growth*, (Oxford: Blackwell Publishers, 1993): 1–36.

Hanson, Gordon H., "Regional Adjustment to Trade Liberalization," National Bureau of Economic Research Working Paper No. 4713, April (1994).

Head, Keith, John Ries and Deborah Swenson, "Agglomeration Benefits and Location Choice: Evidence from Japanese Manufacturing Investment in the United States," NBER Working Paper No. 4767, June (1994).

Hertel, Thomas W., "The Pro-Competitive Effects of Trade Policy Reform in a Small, Open Economy," *Journal of International Economics*, 36 (1994): 391–411.

Jacobs, Jane, *The Economy of Cities*, (New York: Random House, 1969).

Krugman, Paul, "The Myth of Asia's Miracle," *Foreign Affairs*, November/December (1994): 62–78.

Krugman, Paul, "Increasing Returns and Economic Geography," *Journal of Political Economy*, 99 (1991): 483–199.

Krugman, Paul, "Increasing Returns, Monopolistic Competition, and International Trade," in P. Krugman, *Rethinking International Trade*, (Cambridge: The MIT Press, 1990): 165–182.

Lee, Jong-Wha, "International Trade, Distortions, and Long-Run Growth," *IMF Staff Papers*, 40 June (1993): 299–328.

Lucas, Robert E., "Making a Miracle," *Econometrica*, 61(2) March (1993).

Lucas, Robert E., "On the Mechanics of Economic Development," *Journal of Monetary Economics*, 22 (1988): 3–42.

Mankiw, N. Gregory, David Romer and David N. Weil, "A Contribution to the Empirics of Economic Growth," *Quarterly Journal of Economics*, 107 (1992): 407–437.

Mokyr, Joel, *The Lever of Riches: Technological Creativity and Economic Progress*, (Oxford: Oxford University Press, 1990).

Mowery, David C. and David J. Teece, "The Changing Place of Japan in the Global Scientific and Technological Enterprise," in T.S. Arrison, C. Fred Bergsten, E.M. Graham, M. Caldwell Harris, eds., *Japan's Growing Technological Capability: Implications for the U.S. Economy*, (Washington, D.C.: National Academy Press, 1992).

Mowery, David C. and Nathan Rosenberg, *Technology and the Pursuit of Economic Growth*, (Cambridge: Cambridge University Press, 1989).

Murphy, Kevin, Andrei Shleifer and Robert Vishny, "The Allocation of Talent: Implications for Growth," National Bureau of Economic Research Working Paper No. 3530, December (1990).

Porter, Michael E., "Toward a Dynamic Theory of Strategy," in R.P. Rumelt, D.E. Schendel and D.J. Teece, eds., *Fundamental Issues in Strategy: A Research Agenda*, (Boston: Harvard Business School Press, 1994).

Porter, Michael E., *The Competitive Advantage of Nations*, (New York: The Free Press, 1990).

Rauch, James, "Productivity Gains from Geographic Concentration of Human Capital: Evidence from the Cities," *Journal of Urban Economics*, 34(3) (1993): 380–400.

Rivera-Batiz, Francisco L., "The Effects of Immigration on Economic Growth," paper presented at the American Economic Association Meetings, Washington, D.C., January 5, (1995).

Rivera-Batiz, Francisco L., "Urban Agglomeration, Innovation and Economic Growth," mimeo, Dept. of Economics, Columbia University, New York, (1994).

Rivera-Batiz, Francisco L. and Ralph B. Ginsberg, "European Regional Economic Integration: Introduction," *Regional Science and Urban Economics*, 23(3), July (1993).

Rivera-Batiz, Francisco L. and Luis A. Rivera-Batiz, "Europe 1992 and the Liberalization of Direct Investment Flows: Services Versus Manufacturing," *International Economic Journal*, 6(1), Spring (1992).

Rivera-Batiz, Francisco L. and Luis A. Rivera-Batiz, "The Effects of Direct Foreign Investment in the Presence of Increasing Returns due to Specialization," *Journal of Development Economics*, 34 (1991): 287–307.

Rivera-Batiz, Francisco L., "Modeling Urban Agglomeration: Producer Services, Linkage Externalities and Specialization Economies," in William G. Vogt and Marvin H. Mickle, eds., *Modeling and Simulation*, Vol. 19, Instrument Society of America, Research Triangle Park, North Carolina, (1988). (a).

Rivera-Batiz, Francisco L., "Monopolistic Competition, Economies of Scale, and Agglomeration Economies in Consumption and Production," *Regional Science and Urban Economics*, Vol. 18, 1, February (1988). (b)

Rivera-Batiz, Luis A. and Danyang Xie, "GATT, Trade and Growth," *American Economic Review*, May (1992).

Rivera-Batiz, Luis A. and Paul M. Romer, "Economic Integration and Endogenous Growth," in G. Grossman, ed., *Imperfect Competition and International Trade*, (Cambridge, Mass.: The MIT Press, 1992).

Romer, Paul M., "New Goods, Old Goods and the Welfare Costs of Trade Restrictions," *Journal of Development Economics*, February (1994).

Romer, Paul M., "Endogenous Technological Change," *Journal of Political Economy*, 98(5) (1990): S71–S102.

Romer, Paul M., "Capital, Labor and Productivity," *Brookings Papers on Economic Activity: Microeconomics 1990*, (1990): 337–367.

Saxonhouse, Gary, "Economic Growth and Trade Relations: Japanese Performance in Long-Term Perspective," in T. Ito and A. Krueger, eds., *Trade and Protectionism*, (Chicago: The University of Chicago Press, 1993).

Scherer, F.M., *Innovation and Growth: Schumpeterian Perspectives*, (Cambridge: The MIT Press, 1986).

Solow, Robert M., "A Contribution to the Theory of Economic Growth," *Quarterly Journal of Economics*, (1956): 65–94.

Solow, Robert M., "Technical Change and the Aggregate Production Function," *Review of Economics and Statistics*, (1957): 312–320.

Stokey, Nancy, "Learning by Doing and the Introduction of New Goods," *Journal of Political Economy*, 96 (1988): 701–717.

Taylor, Lance, "Economic Openness: Problems to the Century's End," in T. Banuri, ed., *Economic Liberalization: No Panacea*, (Oxford: Oxford University Press, 1991): 99–147.

Young, Alwyn, "A Tale of Two Cities: Factor Accumulation and Technical Change in Hong Kong and Singapore," in O.J. Blanchard and S. Fischer, eds., *NBER Macroeconomics Annual 1992*, (Cambridge: The MIT Press, 1992).

Young, Alwyn, "Learning By Doing and the Dynamic Effects of International Trade," *Quarterly Journal of Economics*, (1991): 369–405.

Part 2

Trade, Increasing Returns
and Economic Geography

Chapter 6

Increasing Returns, Monopolistic Competition, and Agglomeration Economies in Consumption and Production*

6.1 Introduction

Over the years, a wide array of hypotheses have been postulated to explain the existence of spatial concentrations of producers and consumers as well as the agglomeration of economic activity into urban areas. One line of thought looks at agglomeration economies from the production side, examining the role played by economies of scale at the level of the firm, industry or urban market area [see the review by Mulligan (1984), and Goldstein and Moses (1975), Dixit (1973), Henderson (1977), Fujita and Ogawa (1982), and Kim (1987), among others]. A second set of theories explores the consumption aspects of agglomeration, showing the utility gains that consumers can obtain by concentrating in space. These include

*This chapter was authored by Francisco L. Rivera-Batiz and was originally published in *Regional Science and Urban Economics*, Vol. 18, No. 1 (February 1988), pp. 125–153. ©1988 Elsevier Science Publishing.

This paper was written while the author was a visiting professor at the University of Pennsylvania. He is grateful to an anonymous referee and to the participants of seminars at the University of Pennsylvania and the Thirty-Third Annual North American Meetings of the Regional Science Association held in Columbus, Ohio, November 1986, for helpful comments and suggestions.

the presence of economies of scale in the provision of local public goods and amenities or the access to a greater variety of local goods and services in larger market areas [see Arnott (1979), Stahl (1983), and Diamond and Tolley (1982)]. Very few studies, however, have integrated both the consumption and production aspects of agglomeration. It is the purpose of this paper to provide an integrated view of agglomeration by considering the role of the service sector in generating agglomeration economies in both production and consumption.

The service sector is here exclusively identified with local services that are not traded (exported, imported) in national or international markets. This means that the supply of and demand for services in any particular location (city) are constrained to be equal. Since both producers and consumers use services, service sector firms can be differentiated on the basis of whether they supply producer or consumer services. Producer services are related to the array of input requirements that the industrial base of a city demands, in the form of repair and maintenance services of all kinds, transportation and communication services, engineering and legal support, advertising, banking, security, etcetera. Consumer services, on the other hand, supply the final demands of consumers, among which can be considered restaurants, theatres, taxicabs, barbershops, and a whole variety of other personal services.

The service sector can generate agglomeration economies in two ways. Firstly, the agglomeration of producers in a particular industry will result in gains if the increased extent of the market allows producer services to proliferate and to become more specialized, raising the productivity of the industry that uses them. This is an example of localization economies, that is, economies that are external to the particular firms in an industry but internal to the overall industry in a particular city. There is recent evidence from the United States and Brazil suggesting that such economies constitute the main source of economies of scale associated with increased city size[1] and that they substantially explain the observed agglomeration of firms in an industry — or in similar industries — within the same SMSA.[2]

Secondly, the concentration of consumers in a city will provide gains since individuals generally value positively the increased variety of consumer services that such larger population generates. Indeed, there is widespread evidence that increased urban population (and increased population density) raises the variety of local goods and services available to consumers and that this explains why city density is sometimes correlated with lower real wages:[3] individuals tolerate a reduction in their real standard of living in denser cities if they are compensated by the existence of a wider array of local consumer services (restaurants, barbershops, theatres, etc.) relative to less densely populated areas.

That the service sector is closely associated with production and consumption agglomeration economies is well known. As Mills and Hamilton (1984, p. 13) remarks, 'large urban areas provide specialized cultural, legal, medical, financial, and other services that are not available in small urban areas'. Unfortunately, though casual observation and serious empirical evidence suggest the importance of such economies, the theoretical analysis in this field has not developed adequate frameworks specifying endogenously the degree to which services specialize in more agglomerated areas. This paper provides an integrated framework where agglomeration economies due to the service sector are endogenously determined and their impact on equilibrium city size specified.

Our modeling visualizes the service sector as supplying consumers and industrial goods producers with arrays of differentiated services sold under a market structure of monopolistic competition. Within this framework, the number of firms supplying services is an endogenous variable, making variety and specialization enter as equilibrium variables in the analysis, instead of as ad hoc restrictions, as usually considered in the literature. That the service sector can be characterized by monopolistic competition is a direct result of the fact that the markets for services are generally highly competitive, facing relatively minor entry and exit barriers, while, at the same time, both producers and consumers have highly specialized demands and/or tastes toward them, making each service sector firm differentiated from others in the minds of those that demand them.

Sections 6.2 and 6.3 describe the production side of the model, stressing how increased diversity and specialization of producer services are generated and how they determine external economies of scale in the industrial base of a city. Section 6.4 develops the consumption side, emphasizing the role played by diversity in the service sector, and then looks at the equilibrium of a single, closed city. Section 6.5 extends the discussion to a system of closed cities and section 6.6 specifies the equilibrium allocations of households among a system of open cities. Section 6.7 summarizes our conclusions and points out possible extensions.

6.2   Specialization in Producer Services and Industrial Economies

The first task in sight is to determine the production pattern among urban areas, that is, the goods and services (including both producer and consumer services) produced by each city in the economy. We assume that there is a range of industrial goods, indexed by m, that can be produced through the use of labor, L_m, space, K_m and a set n of producer services. Producer services are differentiated and assumed to be sold within a market structure characterized by Chamberlinian monopolistic competition.

Product differentiation among service sector firms arises from the fact that the industrial sector demands a wide array of different types of services requiring highly specialized tasks. Thus any modern industrial complex needs maintenance and support services requiring expertise in such diverse areas as electricity, water and heating, office equipment, industrial machinery service and maintenance, transport services, banking and insurance, legal services, and so on. Each of the tasks required of these professions is highly specialized, depending on the firm and type of industry considered.

It is assumed that the degree of specialization of the tasks demanded by the industrial sector can be so great that if each task was to be supplied by a single service sector firm, the number of firms would have to approach infinity. In that case, each service firm would respond to such a minimal number of service calls that it would not find it profitable to operate. The equilibrium number of service sector firms is therefore much smaller than the number of tasks that can potentially be demanded by industry, with each firm unable to supply ideal, perfectly specialized services. Still, the larger the number of service sector firms in the market, the more specialized the producer services that they can supply, the smoother industrial production can be sustained and the higher the productivity of the industrial sector. On the other hand, if there is a reduction in the equilibrium number of service sector firms, the services provided will be less specialized, resulting in reduced industrial production, even when the amount of resources that the industry spends on inputs is unchanged.[4]

In conclusion, an increased variety of specialized producer services shifts out the industrial sector's production function. Since the number of services is partially determined by the scale of the industry that demands them, the productivity gains involved here represent external economies of scale.[5] On this basis, the technology of producing each industrial good m is assumed to be given by the following production function:

$$X_m = L_m^a K_m^b V_{sm}^c, \quad a + b + c = 1, \tag{1}$$

where X_m is the output of good m, K_m is the amount of industrial space use by sector m, the parameters a, b and c are a function of technology and are associated with the factor shares and marginal products of labor, space and services, respectively, and V_{sm} is a sub-production function of the array of producer services used by industry m. For simplicity, the sub-production function V_{sm} is assumed to be of the CES type, given by

$$V_{sm} = \left(\sum_{i=1}^{n} S_{im}^{\sigma} \right)^{1/\sigma}, \quad 0 < \sigma < 1, \tag{2}$$

with S_{im} denoting the amount of each service demanded by industry m, σ is a parameter to be interpreted shortly, and n represents the number of services used by industry m.

Given the symmetric way in which services enter the production function V_{sm} and the similarity of their cost, and therefore supply, functions — to be established below — the amount of each service that industry m will purchase is identical for all $i = 1, \ldots, n$. As a result, the aggregate quantity demanded of producer services by industry m is equal to

$$S_m = \sum_{i=1}^{m} S_{im} = m S_{im}.$$

Equation (2) can then be transformed into

$$V_{sm} = S_m n^{(1-\sigma)/\sigma}. \tag{3}$$

Inserting this expression into Eq. (1), and some manipulation, yields

$$X_m = n^{c(1-\sigma)/\sigma} L_m^a K_m^b S_m^c. \tag{4}$$

Equation (4) states that the output of good m is related to the quantities of labor, space and producer services demanded by the sector *and* to the number of producer services used by the industry. Observe that the form of (4) is such that it can be interpreted as representing a standard Cobb-Douglas production function with inputs given by labor, space and services and a shift parameter equal to $n^{c(1-\sigma)/\sigma}$. Since, as will be shown shortly, the number of producer services is directly related to the aggregate output of industrial goods in the city, the shift parameter in Eq. (4) reflects endogenous agglomeration economies.[6]

That the number of services used by industry has an effect independent of that of their quantity demanded is an outcome of the form of the sub-production function for services, V_{sm}, and reflects the presence of specialization economies in the use of producer services. As noted earlier, a rise in the number of producer services available increases the output of industrial goods, even if the industry keeps their total quantity demanded the same (S_m constant), because the services used become more specialized and, hence, more effective, resulting in smoother production and increased output.

The parameter σ is positive, indicating that the sub-production function V_{sm} is concave and that increased variety of services results in specialization economies ($\partial X_m / \partial n > 0$). As the value of σ goes to 1, however, the exponent of the number of services, n, in Eq. (4)

approaches zero and the influence of n on X_m disappears. The reason
is that, as σ goes to 1, the sub-production function, V_{sm}, becomes
the simple sum of the quantities of services used by the industrial
sector. That is, in this case, services become perfect substitutes
for each other. With services homogeneous there is no influence of
the number of services on industrial production; only total quantity
demanded, S_m, has an impact. On the other hand, as the value of
σ declines towards zero, the exponent of n in Eq. (4) increases, and
the importance of diversity in services becomes more significant (the
exponent of n rises).

It is assumed that the services utilized by any industry m are
different from those used by other industries and that there is thus
no possible sharing by an industry on the external economies of
another industry. Since we assume that services cannot be traded
(exported, imported) among cities, in order to profit from the
external economies of scale associated with an increase in the number
of producer services, firms producing a given industrial commodity
m will desire to agglomerate in the same location.

For simplicity we consider an economy that consists of a large
number of areas that can potentially be developed for urban industrial and residential use. If developed, a city is assumed to consist
of a predetermined center (export) point around which there is a
circular business district where the city's industry is located. The
central business district (CBD) encloses a fixed amount of space
developed for industrial purposes equal to $\pi \underline{u}^2$, where $\underline{u}$ is the radius
of the CBD in miles. Surrounding the CBD are circular grids of
housing or space where households are located. The total amount
of space available for residential use is then $\pi(\bar{u}^2 - \underline{u}^2)$, where $\underline{u}$
denotes the city's boundary. All cities are assumed to be identical
in terms of the amount of land or space that can be developed
and is available for industrial and residential use. In addition,
commuting costs and other congestion effects are for now ignored.
These assumptions, of course, are limiting since they sweep aside the
whole range of factors that determine the amount and distribution
of land use endogenously in each city. However, in this paper, our
main interest is to specify the factors determining the equilibrium

allocation of firms and households among cities, and this justifies some degree of simplification regarding intracity land use. In any case, the last section does go into the details of modeling explicitly the determinants of city boundaries and specifies intracity bid-rent functions, showing that the analysis does not have to be significantly altered when the amount of space available for urban residential use is variable.

Of the large number of potential cities in which industries can locate only a fraction of them are actually developed since the number of industrial goods that can be produced competitively in international markets by the economy is assumed to be smaller than the number of potential cities. Note that, given the agglomeration economies described earlier, firms producing the same industrial good will prefer to locate in the same area. In addition, the assumption that there is an excess supply of potential locations or cities but a fixed amount of space available within each city means that each industry will desire to locate in a different urban area, as otherwise it would have to share a given amount of industrial space with other industries, resulting in higher land rental costs compared to possible alternative, undeveloped sites. From now on we will thus associate cities with industries, using the index m to identify a particular city.

Industrial sector profits, Pr, are given by

$$Pr = P_m L_m^a K_m^b V_{sm}^c - W_m L_m - r_m K_m - \sum_{i=1}^{n} P_{sim} S_{im},$$

where W_m is the wage rate in city m, r_m is the rental rate on industrial space, P_{sim} is the price charged for the services supplied by a service firm i in city m, and P_m is the price of commodity m in world markets. It is assumed that the latter is exogenously given.

First order conditions for profit maximization imply

$$P_m a \frac{X_m}{L_m} = W_m, \tag{5}$$

$$S_{im} = \left[\frac{c P_m X_m}{V_{sm}^\sigma P_{sim}} \right]^{1/(1-\sigma)}, \tag{6}$$

$$c P_m X_m = \sum_{i=1}^{n} P_{sim} S_{im}. \tag{7}$$

Equation (5) shows the equality of the wage rate to the marginal value product of labor (where the marginal product is aX_m/L_m), and will be used below to show how changes in the wage rate alter the quantity demanded of labor in the industrial base of the city. Equation (6), on the other hand, depicts the quantity demanded of each producer service, and Eq. (7) shows how the total expenditure of the industrial sector on producer services is equal to a constant function of the total revenues made by the industry, a standard implication of the Cobb-Douglas production function. Note finally that we are omitting the first-order condition specifying the demand for space since the rental rate, r_m, will adjust to equate the aggregate demand for industrial space, K_m, to the given, fixed supply of industrial space available in the city, $\pi \underline{u}^2$. In the background, however, there is a relationship establishing the equilibrium rental rate on industrial space in city m.

Substitution of the expression for X_m in Eq. (4) into the left-hand side of Eq. (5) results in the following expression for the wage rate in city m:

$$W_m = a P_m L_m^{a-1} (\pi \underline{u}^2)^b S_m^c n^{c(1-\sigma)/\sigma}. \tag{8}$$

This shows that the wage rate in city m is influenced by the price of the industrial good produced in the city, by the parameters a, b, c and σ (associated with the marginal products of labor, space and services), the amount of space available to the sector, and the number and quantity of producer services demanded. We now proceed to specify the determinants of the latter two variables, which are endogenous.

6.3 The Supply of Producer Services: Diversity, Pricing and Output Decisions

Ample evidence tends to indicate that, broadly speaking, services are relatively labor intensive. We thus assume, for simplicity, that each firm supplying producer services uses only labor as an input whose requirements are given by

$$L_{im} = c_0 + c_1 S_{im}, \tag{9}$$

where c_0 represents a fixed labor input requirement and c_1 is a variable labor input requirement. Following the standard Chamberlinian framework, the technology used by all service firms is considered to be identical, implying that c_0 and c_1 are the same for all firms i.

With the labor requirements depicted by (9), each firm's total costs are equal to $W_m L_{im}$. Average costs are then given by $AC_{im} = W_m c_1 + W_m c_0 / S_{im}$, reflecting the presence of internal economies of scale in the production of services. Marginal costs, finally, are equal to $W_m c_1$, a constant for each single firm in the market. The equality of marginal cost to marginal revenue suggested by profit maximization indicates that

$$W_m c_1 = P_{sim}(\varepsilon_i - 1)/\varepsilon_i. \tag{10}$$

Since marginal revenue is related to the price elasticity of demand facing each firm, $\varepsilon_i = -(P_{sim}/S_{im})(\partial S_{im}/\partial P_{sim})$. We must specify this variable in order to determine the profit-maximizing price and output of each service.

Equation (6) can be used to describe the demand curve facing a single service sector firm. By differentiating it with respect to P_{sim}, and some manipulation, the price elasticity of the demand for each service, ε_i, can be determined:

$$\varepsilon_i = \frac{-P_{sim}}{S_{im}} \frac{\partial S_{im}}{\partial P_{sim}} = \frac{1}{1-\sigma} + \frac{\sigma}{1-\sigma} \frac{P_{sim}}{V_{sm}} \frac{\partial V_{sm}}{\partial P_{sim}}, \tag{11}$$

where

$$\frac{P_{sim}}{V_{sm}} \frac{\partial V_{sm}}{\partial P_{sim}} = \frac{1}{\sum_{i=1}^{n} S_{im}^{\sigma}} \left[\sum_{j \neq i} P_{sjm} S_{jm}^{\sigma-1} \frac{\partial S_{jm}}{\partial P_{sim}} \right] - \varepsilon_i \frac{S_{im}^{\sigma}}{\sum_{i=1}^{n} S_{im}^{\sigma}}. \tag{12}$$

Equations (11) and (12) exhibit very well the complications involved in calculating the elasticity of demand facing one firm in a market composed of firms supplying: differentiated services. The discussion can be greatly simplified, however, if the market structure within which services are sold is assumed to be one of Chamberlinian monopolistic competition. Within this framework, each producer acts in a Cournot-Nash fashion in conjecturing that other firms in the sector will not change their output in response to changes in the firm's own price. In terms of Eq. (12), this assumption regarding the strategic behavior of firms under monopolistic competition implies that $\partial S_{jm}/\partial P_{sim} = 0$, for $i \neq j$. The first term in the right-hand side of Eq. (12) thus vanishes.

In addition, Chamberlinian monopolistic competition assumes that there is a large enough number of firms in the market such that the influence of each firm on the total output of the sector is insignificant. The implication of this assumption is that the term $S_{im}^{\sigma}/\sum_{i=1}^{n} S_{im}^{\sigma}$ in Eq. (9) becomes infinitesimal (if the number of firms, n, is sufficiently large). As a result, the second term in Eq. (12) also vanishes and the elasticity of demand facing a single firm becomes

$$\varepsilon_i = \frac{1}{1 - \sigma}. \tag{13}$$

Observe that since σ is a fixed parameter, the demand curve facing each service sector firm exhibits constant elasticity. However, as σ is exogenously increased toward 1, this elasticity tends to approach infinity. The explanation is that, when σ rises, the services demanded by the industrial sector require less specialization and, therefore, any service firm in the market can effectively supply them, increasing the competition among services and raising the responsiveness of quantity demanded to any particular firm's change in price. On the other hand, when the parameter σ declines, the services demanded by industry m become more differentiated, allowing each particular firm to have more leeway in affecting its demand, reducing the value of the elasticity.

Substitution of the expression for the elasticity of demand shown by Eq. (13) into Eq. (10), and some simplification, yields

$$P_{sim} = \sigma^{-1} c_i W_m. \tag{14}$$

Equation (14) can be interpreted a stating that each service sector firm sets its price at a mark-up above its marginal cost, $c_1 W_m$. The mark-up is inversely related to the parameter σ, reflecting the role played by product differentiation in allowing firms to increase price above marginal cost. As σ decreases toward 0, the services required by the industrial sector become more strongly differentiated from each other, allowing any given number of firms operating in the market to increase their price mark-ups.

Since all firms face identical cost and demand parameters — c_0, c_1, and σ are the same for all i — the profit-maximizing prices they charge will be the same. The subscript i can thus be eliminated with regard to the price variable: $P_{sm} = P_{sim}$ for all i. Note also that each service firm supplies only one service: in the Chamberlinian framework of monopolistic competition firms can differentiate their products costlessly, and since the demand available for each service is symmetric, it would not be profitable for a firm to share the demand for any given service with other firms.

Entry into the service sector guarantees that the industry's equilibrium is one with no unexploited profit opportunities. Zero profits exist when total revenue, $P_{sm}S_{im}$ equals cost, $W_m L_{im}$. Using Eqs. (9) and (14), the zero profits equilibrium occurs at a level of output equal to

$$S_{im} = \frac{\sigma c_0}{(1-\sigma)c_1}. \tag{15}$$

Since, as noted earlier, each firm faces the same σ, c_0 and c_1 parameters, Eq. (15) indicates that each service sector firm will produce the same equilibrium level of output. This output is positively related to the fixed labor requirement, given that an increase in c_0 raises the degree of economies of scale facing each firm (it shifts average costs upwards). Higher variable labor requirements, on the other hand, reduce equilibrium output since an increment in c_1 raises the marginal cost of producing any given level of output. Finally, a stronger degree of differentiation among services — a reduction in σ — reduces the equilibrium level of output by lowering the elasticity of demand facing each service firm.

The equilibrium number of firms in the producer services sector is also derived from the zero profits condition by noting that $P_{sm}S_m = P_{sm}nS_{im} = W_m L_{sm}$, where L_{sm} is the aggregate demand for labor in the sector. Using Eqs. (14) and (15), the equilibrium number of producer services is

$$n = \frac{c_1}{c_0}\frac{1-\sigma}{\sigma}S_m. \tag{16}$$

This reflects the fact that, given the aggregate demand for services, $S_m = nS_{im}$, the equilibrium number of firms in the sector is inversely related to the output supplied by each firm and, therefore, to the factors that influence such output. An increase in the aggregate demand for services, on the other hands raises the equilibrium number of firms.

Given that services and labor are the main variable inputs of the industrial sector, one can specify how the demand for one is related to the demand for the other. Using the relationships defining the demand for labor and services in Eqs. (5) and (7), and recalling that, due to the symmetry embedded in the model, each firm produces the same level of output and changes the same price level, it can be easily derived that

$$S_m = \frac{c\sigma}{ac_1}L_m \tag{17}$$

and

$$n = \frac{1-\sigma}{c_0}\frac{c}{a}L_m. \tag{18}$$

Equations (17) and (18) show that producer services and industrial labor are complements in production. An increase in the use of industrial labor shifts up the demand for producer services, increasing the equilibrium number of service firms and the aggregate quantity supplied by the sector.

Substitution of the expressions in Eqs. (17) and (18) into Eq. (8), and some manipulation, yields

$$W_m = aP_m L_m^{(c/\sigma+a-1)}\pi^b \underline{u}^{2b}\left(\frac{1-\sigma}{c_0}\frac{c}{a}\right)^{c/\sigma}\left(\frac{\sigma}{1-\sigma}\frac{c_0}{c_1}\right)^c. \tag{19}$$

This shows how the wage rate in city m is related to the employment of industrial labor and to an array of exogenous parameters that include the price of the industrial good produced in the city, P_m, the space available to the urban industrial base in the CBD; $\pi\underline{u}^2$, technology parameters regarding the production of industrial goods $(a, b, c$ and $\sigma)$, and parameters involving the producer services sector $(c_0$ and $c_1)$.

It can be concluded that, holding commodity prices and land use constant, the urban industrial labor demand function will vary from city to city depending on the differences in the production functions of industrial goods and services among cities. Urban wages, however, are related to both labor demand and labor supply. The next section specifies the labor supply function facing the industrial base of a city given the number of households located in the city. This is then used to specify the city's equilibrium wages as a function of exogenous parameters and the city's labor force.

6.4   Services, Variety and Agglomeration Economies in Consumption

Given a fixed number of households in a city, $\bar{L}$, each supplying a fixed amount of labor, $H = 1$, the assumption of perfect competition in the labor market implies the following full-employment condition:

$$L_m + L_{sm} + L_{cm} = \bar{L}, \tag{20}$$

where L_{cm} represents the amount of labor employed in the consumer services sector. Since the last section specified the determinants of the industrial labor demand of the city and the demand for labor in the producer services sector, we now proceed to examine employment in the consumer services sector.

Consumer services are assumed to supply output to households located within city bounds. Therefore, in contrast to the industrial sector — whose output can always be sold in the national and international market — the consumer services sector relies exclusively on urban demand. We proceed to consider the consumption decisions of the urban population.

Each household j consumes local services, space or housing, and an array of internationally traded, industrial sector goods that we aggregate into a composite, C_{jT}. The household utility function is, for simplicity, assumed to be log-linear:

$$U_j = \alpha_1 \ln C_{jT} + \alpha_2 \ln K_{jh} + \alpha_3 \ln Z_j, \tag{21}$$

where $\alpha_1 + \alpha_2 + \alpha_3 = 1$, K_{jh} is the household's demand for housing or space, and Z_j is a sub-utility function of the household's consumption of local consumer services, to be specified next.

Consumer services are assumed to be differentiated and to be sold in a market characterized by Chamberlinian monopolistic competition. Following Dixit and Stiglitz (1977); the sub-utility function describing the impact of this array of different consumer services on utility is assumed to be concave and, for exponential convenience, of the CES type, or

$$Z_j = \left(\sum_{k=1}^{N} C_{jk}^{\theta} \right)^{1/\theta}, \tag{22}$$

where C_{jk} denotes the household demand for a single service, N is the number of services available in city m, and $0 < \theta < 1$. The latter is a parameter representing preferences toward variety in consumer services, as is shown next by means of a simple transformation of Eq. (22).

Given the symmetry through which each service enters into Z_j and the identical pricing that each is assumed to follow — to be discussed later — the quantities demanded of each service, $k = 1, \ldots, N$, are identical. As a consequence, the aggregate quantity demanded of consumer services by a household in city m is equal to

$$C_{jm} = \sum_{k=1}^{N} C_{jk} = NC_{jk}.$$

And Z_j then becomes, through some manipulation,

$$Z_j = N^{(1-\theta)/\theta} C_{jm}. \tag{23}$$

This states that the utility households derive from services is related to the aggregate quantity consumed of services *and* the number of services available in the market. That the variety of services has an effect on utility independent of their quantity consumed is embodied in the parameter θ. As θ increases towards a value of 1, services become closer substitutes and product variety loses its impact on utility; in the limit, when θ equals 1, all services become perfect substitutes and variety loses all effect on utility. On the other hand, as θ declines toward zero, the significance of the variety of consumer services available in the city on household utility rises.

The utility function in (21) is maximized subject to the following budget constraint:

$$P_T C_{jT} + r_{hm} K_{jh} + \sum_{k=1}^{N} P_{km} C_{jk} = W_m, \qquad (24)$$

where P_T is an index of the prices of goods traded in international markets, r_{hm} is the rental rate on housing paid by households in city m, and P_{km} is the price charged by a given consumer service k in city m. It is assumed that each household supplies an amount H of man-hours over the given period of time under consideration, with H normalized to equal 1, implying that household labor income is equal to the market wage rate, W_m. In addition, it is assumed that spending is made out of labor income, meaning that rental income is either saved or accrues to non-city dwellers.[7] Finally, note that, for now, we assume locations within the city are homogeneous in that there are no commuting costs or other effects of this type that could generate intra-city rent gradients. A later section will relax this assumption, without major consequences.

Substitution of Eq. (22) into (21), and using (24), we can set the Lagrangean function L for the constrained optimization problem facing the individual worker j in city m:

$$L = \alpha_1 \ln C_{jT} + \alpha_2 \ln K_{jh} + \alpha_3 \ln \left(\sum_{k=1}^{N} C_{jk}^{\theta} \right)^{1/\theta}$$

$$- \lambda \left[P_T C_{jT} + \sum_{k=1}^{N} P_{km} C_{jk} + r_{hm} K_{jh} - W_m \right], \qquad (25)$$

where λ is a Lagrangean multiplier. On the assumption that all households have identical tastes, the first-order conditions for the individual household j derived from (25) can then be aggregated over all individuals to yield:

$$C_{Tm} = \alpha_1 W_m \bar{L}/P_T, \tag{26}$$

$$K_{hm} = \alpha_2 W_m \bar{L}/r_{hm}, \tag{27}$$

$$\sum_{k=1}^{N} P_{km} C_{km} = \alpha_3 W_m \bar{L} \tag{28}$$

and

$$C_{km} = \left[\frac{\alpha_3 W_m \bar{L}}{P_{km} Z_m^\theta} \right]^{1/(1-\theta)}, \tag{29}$$

where $Z_m = (\sum_{k=1}^{N} C_{km}^\theta)^{1/\theta}$ represents the sub-utility accruing to all consumers from their consumption of services, and C_{Tm}, K_{hm} and C_{km} denote the quantities demanded of internationally traded goods, housing and each kth service by all households residing in city m.

Note that with a fixed amount of space available in city m, denoted by $\pi(\bar{u}^2 - \underline{u}^2)$, the equality of the supply of and demand for space — with the latter given by (27) — can be manipulated to result in

$$W_m/r_{hm} = \pi(\bar{u}^2 - \underline{u}^2)/\bar{L}\alpha_2. \tag{30}$$

Equation (30) shows the inverse relationship between the city's labor force and the ratio of its nominal wage to the rental cost of housing: an increase in the number of households in the city raises the demand for space, resulting in an equilibrium increase in rental rates and a drop in the wage-rental ratio.

The set of eqs. (26)–(29) shows the symmetry of our analysis with respect to the firms supplying producer and consumer services. This can be easily discerned by comparing Eqs. (6) and (29). We now use this similarity to specify the price elasticity of demand facing each consumer service firm without going through the detailed derivations. In the same way that Eq. (13) is derived, under the standard assumptions of Chamberlinian monopolistic competition, the elasticity of demand facing a consumer service supplier, $\varepsilon_k = \frac{1}{1-\theta}$.

Note that since θ is fixed, each service's demand curve embodies a constant price elasticity.

Each firm supplying consumer services is assumed to be produced under a technology of increasing returns to scale, given the presence of some fixed set-up labor requirements which we denote by γ. Each producer also uses labor as a variable input, with the labor input-output coefficient given $\beta = L_{ck}/X_{ck}$, where β is assumed, for simplicity, to be a fixed, positive parameter given by technology. Each consumer service's total cost is the sum of fixed and variable cost, or

$$TC_{ck} = W_m\gamma + \beta X_{ck}W_m. \tag{31}$$

We assume that each service sector firm has the same technology (the same λ and β). And following the Chamberlinian assumption that firms can differentiate their product costlessly, it will pay each producer to specialize in supplying a single service.

Service sector firms set price and output so as to maximize profits, that are equal to total revenue, $P_{km}X_{ck}$, minus total cost TC_{ck}. The following price equation is obtained from the first-order condition for such optimization problem:

$$P_{km} = \theta^{-1}\beta W_m. \tag{32}$$

Equation (32) states that the profit maximizing price set by a consumer service firm is a fixed mark-up above the average variable cost of the firm, βW_m. Since all firms face the same θ, β and W_m, the price charged by each service is the same. This is a result of the Chamberlinian assumptions of symmetry in production and consumption.

Entry of firms into the sector guarantees zero profits and determines the following equilibrium output level for each firm:

$$X_{ck} = \frac{\theta}{1-\theta}\frac{\gamma}{\beta}. \tag{33}$$

The aggregate supply of consumer services is then given by

$$X_{cm} = NX_{ck} = N\frac{\theta}{1-\theta}\frac{\gamma}{\beta}. \tag{34}$$

And, from Eq. (28), the aggregate demand for services is given by

$$C_{sm} = NC_{km} = \alpha_3 W_m \bar{L}/P_{km}. \tag{35}$$

Equating the supply of and demand for services yields

$$N = \frac{1 - \theta}{\gamma} \alpha_3 \bar{L}. \tag{36}$$

Equation (36) states that the variety of services available in city m is a function of (1) tastes toward product variety: as θ goes to 0, consumers value variety in services more highly, and the equilibrium value of N increases [the term $(1 - \theta)$ rises]; (2) the fraction of income spent on services, α_3, in the obvious way; (3) the fixed labor requirements facing each consumer service firm: the stronger the requirement, the larger the equilibrium output of each firm and the smaller the equilibrium number of firms, everything else constant; (4) the labor force in the city: as $\bar{L}$ increases, urban spending rises, shifting upwards the demand for services.

This last result, associating population growth with an increase in the variety available to consumers is indeed at the kernel of the urban agglomeration economies arising from the consumption side.[8] By the same token, the inverse relationship between wages deflated by the cost of housing and urban population established earlier in Eq. (30) implicitly depicts the costs of urban agglomeration to consumers. Indeed, there is an analogy here to a result in the theory of urban public finance [see Arnott (1979)] stating that the value of differences in the provision of local public goods is embodied into the value of land, in the form of higher property values or housing rental rates. In the present case, the increased value to consumers of having a wider variety of services available in larger cities is embodied into higher housing rental costs.

Having examined the determination of output, prices and variety in the service sector, it becomes easy to specify the amount of labor used by the sector. Note that since $W_m L_{cm} = \alpha_3 W_m \bar{L}$, then $L_{cm} = \alpha_3 \bar{L}$. Both an increase in the labor force and a higher share of income spent on services (a larger value of α_3) raise the demand for consumer services, shifting upwards the demand for labor in the sector.

Since the demand for producer services is derived from the demand for industrial goods, and $L_{cm} = [c/a]L_m$, substitution into Eq. (20) yields the following supply of labor to the industrial sector of the economy:

$$L_m = a(1 - \alpha_3)\bar{L}/(a + c). \tag{37}$$

This shows that: (1) in increase in the factor share of labor in the industrial sector, a, will raise the demand for industrial labor and thus employment in the sector; (2) a lower share of income spent on consumer services, α_3, will also raise industrial employment since it will release labor from the service sector; (3) a larger factor share of producer services, c, raises the demand for labor in that sector and lowers the labor available to industry; and (4) an increase in the economy's labor force, $\bar{L}$, will raise industrial sector employment since only a fraction of the additional labor force can be employed in the service sector.

Substitution of the expression for industrial employment in (31) into (19) results in the following equation relating the city's nominal wage rate to a set of exogenous variables:

$$W_m = a^a P_m \left(\frac{1-\sigma}{c_0}c\right)^{c/\sigma} \left(\frac{\sigma}{1-\sigma}\frac{c_0}{c_1}\right)^c \pi^b \underline{u}^{2b}[(1-\alpha_3)\bar{L}/c+a]^{(c/\sigma)+a-1}. \tag{38}$$

It is fairly evident from Eq. (38) that an increase in the price of good m — assuming the prices of other industrial goods fixed — will elevate the wage rate in city m since it raises the marginal value product of labor. In addition, an increase in the supply of space results in a higher wage rate given that it shifts upwards the demand for labor. There are also parameters relating to the producer services sector, c_0, c_1 and σ, that influence the wage rate. For instance, if the fixed costs of supplying producer services rises, then, as a result, W_m declines, everything else constant. The explanation is that the hike in fixed costs reduces the equilibrium number of firms, decreasing their specialization and, therefore, their productivity to the industrial sector. This contractionary impact on agglomeration economies results in lower marginal products and, thus, lower wages.

In a similar way, one can specify the impact of other exogenous variables on the city's equilibrium wage rate.

The impact of changes in the labor force of the city, $\bar{L}$, on the wage rate, W_m, is of ambiguous sign. On the one hand, the traditional effect of an increase in the labor force is to induce an excess supply of labor that reduces the city's wage rate. However, in the present context, an increase in the size of the urban population increases the size of the industrial sector and, therefore, it shifts upwards the demand for producer services. The latter leads to an expansion of the service sector that raises the variety of such services. With a wider diversity of services available, the industrial sector can obtain more specialized services and its productivity is therefore enhanced. This productivity increase is then embodied into higher wages rates. The net impact of increased population on the equilibrium wage rate in city m is related to the relative importance of the 'excess supply' and the 'increased productivity' effects. A substantial amount of evidence exists suggesting that, due to the productivity effect of agglomeration economies, nominal wages are positively correlated with the size of the population in a city [see Goldfarb and Yezer (1976), and Segal (1976)]. In the following discussion we shall assume such connection, though the analysis is perfectly consistent with the opposite relationship.

The closed city's equilibrium and the reduced-form expressions for all variables in the model can be easily obtained by substituting the expression for the wage rate in (38) into earlier equations, either directly or sequentially.

6.5 Household Utility Differentials in a System of Closed Cities

Previous sections have determined the equilibrium of a given city m facing an exogenous population, $\bar{L}$. How does the utility of consumers in such a city compare with those of other cities? If differences in such utility can be determined, it would suggest the presence of incentives to migrate were the cities to be open, that is, subject to labor flows.

On the assumption that households have identical preferences one can use the household utility function in (21), in combination with

Eqs. (24), (26), (27), (28), (30) and (32), to derive — through some tedious manipulations — the following expression for the utility that a household receives from city m:

$$U_m = \alpha_1 \ln \frac{\alpha_1 W_m}{P_T} + \alpha_2 \ln \frac{\alpha_2 W_m}{r_{hm}} + \alpha_3 \frac{1-\theta}{\theta} \ln N_m + \alpha_3 \ln \alpha_3 \frac{W_m}{P_{km}}.$$
$$(39)$$

Equation (39) depicts the key variables affecting household utility in city m. These are the nominal wage rate, W_m, the cost of living — as represented by the prices of traded goods, P_T, the cost of consumer services, P_{km}, the rental price on housing, r_{hm} — and product variety in consumer services, N_m.

The utility level, U_m, is more fully specified by substituting the expressions we have determined for wage rates, real wages, and consumer product variety as given by Eqs. (30), (36) and (38) into Eq. (39). The result is

$$
\begin{aligned}
U_m = \alpha_1 & \left[\frac{c+a\sigma}{\sigma} \ln \alpha_1 - \ln P_T + a \ln a + \ln P_m + c \left(\frac{\sigma-1}{\sigma} \right) \ln c_0 \right. \\
& - c \ln c_1 + \left(\frac{c}{\sigma} \right) \ln c + c \ln \sigma + c \left(\frac{1-\sigma}{\sigma} \right) \ln(1-\sigma) + b \ln \pi \underline{u}^2 \\
& \left. + \left(\frac{c}{\sigma} + a - 1 \right) \ln \alpha_2/(a+c) \right] + \alpha_2 \ln \pi (\bar{u}^2 - \underline{u}^2) \\
& + (\alpha_3/\theta) \ln \alpha_3 + \alpha_3 \frac{1-\theta}{\theta} \ln \frac{1-\theta}{\gamma} + \alpha_3 \ln \frac{\theta}{\beta} \\
& + \left[\frac{\alpha_3}{\theta} + \alpha_1 \left(\frac{c+a\sigma}{\sigma} \right) - 1 \right] \ln L^m.
\end{aligned}
$$
$$(40)$$

This equation shows a connection between the total population in a city m, L^m (not to be confused with L_m, the labor force of the industrial sector in city m), and the utility that a representative household derives from that city, U_m, given a number of exogenous parameters. Figure 6.1 depicts one such relationship by means of the curve Eq, with the city's labor force measured in the horizontal axis and utility in the vertical axis. Setting $L^m = 0$ determines the vertical intercept at point E in the diagram. This represents the limit value of household utility as the population of the city declines towards zero; in order to ensure an interior solution for city m, we assume that this value is positive.

The slope of the curve depicting the relationship between city population and utility is determined by differentiating (40) with respect to L^m, the result of which is

$$\mathrm{d}U_m/\mathrm{d}L^m = (\Delta/L^m) \quad \text{where} \quad \Delta = \frac{\alpha_3}{\Theta} + \alpha_1 \left(\frac{c}{\sigma} + a\right) - 1. \quad (41)$$

This expression can be positive or negative, depending on the values of the parameters involved. The stronger (weaker) the production and consumption agglomeration economies associated with increased city population, the more (less) likely that Δ is positive.

The first two terms in the expression for Δ reflect the influence of agglomeration economies. The first one involves consumer agglomeration economies, associated with the increased utility provided by a more populated area as a result of its greater variety of services. Note that, the more valuable product variety is to consumers — the smaller the parameter θ is — the stronger the consumer agglomeration economies and the larger the value of the first term in Δ given by Eq. (41).

The second term in Eq. (41) is connected to the increased nominal wage effects as city size rises. First is the impact of higher productivity, a consequence of the more specialized producer services available to the industrial sector in a larger city. This is related to the magnitude of σ: as σ declines in value, the effect of increased variety in producer services — and their increased specialization — on productivity rises and any increase in population would have a steeper effect on urban wages. It is then more likely that a larger city would raise the utility level of households. In addition, an increase in the marginal productivity of labor and producer services in industrial production (larger parameters c and a) would shift upwards the demand for labor, strengthening the positive impact of additional population on wage rates and utility. Finally, the last term in Eq. (41) reflects the increased congestion on housing associated with an increment in population. It embodies the fact that increased population — everything else held constant — is associated with higher costs of living, lower real income and reduced household utility.

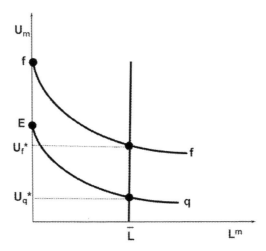

Figure 6.1.   Equilibrium Utility Differentials in a System of Closed Cities.

For expositional purposes, the population-utility locus Eq in Fig. 6.1 illustrates a particular case where an increase in the population of city m is associated with lower utility. In other words, the congestion effect on housing is assumed to dominate the agglomeration economies in consumption and production. Given an exogenous labor force in the city equal to $L^m = \bar{L}$, the equilibrium utility of each household is then given by U_q^*.

Different cities can exhibit different population-utility loci due to disparities in the world market price of the industrial goods that they produce and/or because of differences in the types of production functions used by industry and services in each city. For instance, consider two cities, f and q. If the price of industrial goods produced in f exceeds the price of the industrial goods produced in q (if $P_f > P_q$, in terms of a numeraire), then the population-utility locus of city f will lie above that of city q, everything else the same. This can be easily discerned by a quick glance at Eq. (40): for any given population level, city f will have a higher marginal value product of labor, higher wages and, therefore, greater utility relative to q.

Similarly, if cities f and q are identical except that producer services in city f have a lower fixed cost requirement than their equivalent in city q (if the value of c_0 is lower in city f), again the population-utility locus for city f will lie above that for q. In this case, the reason is that, at any given population level, a lower fixed cost requirement allows the number of producer service firms to rise, resulting in specialization economies that raise productivity and, thus, wage rates in city f relative to those in city q. Consequently, utility levels would be higher in f relative to q.

Diagrammatically, the two previous examples would be reflected in city f having population-utility loci with higher vertical *intercepts* than city q. Suppose, however, that production of industrial goods is city f is such that the parameter 'a' — affecting the marginal product of industrial labor — is higher than that prevailing in the production of goods in city q. For any given level of the population in the two cities, the population-utility locus of city f will now lie above that of city q because both its vertical intercept is higher and because its slope is less negative.

Other experiments can be carried out to specify the impact of differences in other exogenous variables on population-utility loci among cities. Depending on such differences, closed cities, might reflect varying household utility. Such is the case illustrated in Fig. 6.1, where the ff and Eq loci depict the relationship between population and utility in cities f and q, respectively. If the labor force in each city is equal to $\bar{L}$, city f would provide higher utility than city q. There would be incentives for workers to move from city q to city f. The next section examines the allocation of households among cities if such mobility is allowed.

6.6   Agglomeration Economies and the Equilibrium Allocation of Households among a System of Open Cities

Up to this point we have examined the equilibrium of cities on the assumption that their population is fixed. However, in a system of open cities, households are free to move within the economy and the population of any particular city must be considered an endogenous variable. This section examines how relative equilibrium city size (population size) is related to the array of exogenous variables in our model. On the basis of our earlier analysis, we assume that there is a given number of industrial goods that can be competitively produced by the economy in national and international markets, and that each urban area would specialize in producing one such good. There are, therefore $m = 1, \ldots, M$ potential locations or cities, and $\bar{L}$ households ($\bar{L}$ much larger than M) to be allocated among them. We have thus to perform two tasks: firstly, to specify which cities will be populated (that is, which cities will exist), and, secondly, to determine the equilibrium population of each city in existence.

The equilibrium distribution of households among cities is that allocation at which there is no incentive to migrate among locations. This occurs when the utility that a typical household derives from one city f, U_f, is equal to that in any other city q, U_q, for any f and q. Using Eq. (39), intercity equilibrium occurs when

$$0 = U_f/U_q = \alpha_1 \ln W_f/W_q + \alpha_2 \ln \frac{W_f/r_{hf}}{W_q/r_{hq}} + \alpha_3 \frac{1-\theta}{\theta} \ln \frac{N_f}{N_q}.$$

(42)

Equation (42) shows the essential variables that adjust to achieve intercity household equilibrium: nominal wages, rental rates on housing — insofar as they affect real wages — and consumer product variety. Presumably, if a city offers higher nominal wages and/or higher variety of consumer services, immigration to that city will flow from other urban areas. As a consequence, rental rates on housing in the city are pushed upwards until they compensate for the higher utility that the city would otherwise provide.

The distribution of households among cities f and q implied by Eq. (42) can be completely specified by substituting the expressions for wage rates, real wages, and consumer product variety in Eqs. (38), (30) and (36), respectively. Since the resulting equation is quite complicated it is not reproduced here. Instead, we describe the system's equilibrium diagrammatically.

Figure 6.2 depicts a system of two cities f and q with population-utility loci ff and qq, respectively. Equilibrium occurs when the labor force, $\bar{L}$ is fully allocated among the two cities *and* the utility that

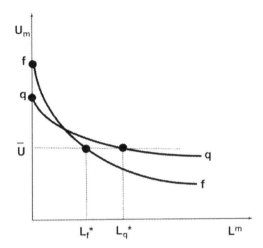

Figure 6.2. Equilibrium Distribution of Households in a System of Two Cities.

households derive from each city are equal. As can be observed, this equilibrium is reached at a level of utility equal to $\bar{U}$, with the equilibrium populations in each city given by L_f^* and L_q^*, where $L_f^* + L_q^* = \bar{L}$.

Though in the case illustrated by Fig. 6.2 the economy can potentially produce only two goods, f and q, both of which are produced in equilibrium, the discussion can be easily extended to consider any number of goods (cities). Figure 6.3 shows the population-utility loci associated with the potential production of four industrial commodities, that is, with four possible urban sites. Given the economy's labor force, $\bar{L}$, the equilibrium number of cities will be three, with the potential city z providing such a low level of utility that it cannot attract a positive amount of population. Cities f, q and g all exist in equilibrium, with their populations given by L_f, L_q and L_g, where $L_f + L_q + L_g = \bar{L}$.

One of the shortcomings of the existing literature on systems of cities is that heterogeneity in space (or variance in city size) is often obtained on the basis of ad hoc assumptions regarding differences in tastes, factor endowments or internal urban structure (such as differences in transportation systems or the availability of local public goods). In the present paper, the only ad hoc assumption that is need

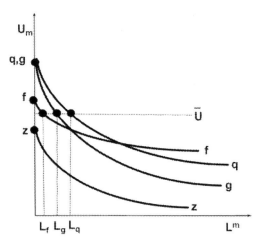

Figure 6.3.   Equilibrium Distribution of Households in a System of Open Cities.

to generate intercity spatial heterogeneity is that there be a range of industrial commodities requiring the use of different bundles of producer services. The following example shows this in a system of two cities.

We consider two cities, f and q, that have the same stock of housing or residential space available, identical supplies of industrial space (equal CBD radius), and equal parameters in their consumer services production functions. The key difference lies in the industrial sector of each city, that we assume requires the use of different types of producer services. This diversity is in the form of differences in the cost functions of these services, which generates a disparity in the number of firms supplying them in each city and, therefore, in the agglomeration economies facing each urban area.

Under the assumptions, and using Eq. (40), Eq. (42) can be manipulated to yield

$$\ln \frac{L_f}{L_q} = \frac{\alpha_1}{\Delta} \left[\ln \frac{P_f}{P_q} + c \left(1 - \frac{1}{\sigma} \right) \ln \frac{c_{0f}}{c_{0q}} + c \ln \frac{c_{1q}}{c_{1f}} \right], \qquad (43)$$

with Δ as defined before. The Δ coefficient must be negative in order for there to be an interior solution, that is, for households to allocate themselves to the two cities in equilibrium instead of agglomerating into a single one. In a system of open cities, it is possible that the agglomeration economies in the production of a particular good (a particular city) so dominate those in other goods (other cities) that equilibrium requires the agglomeration of all the population into that city. For instance, if the price of the industrial good in a particular city m rises relative to those in other cities, this tends to raise the wage rate of city m relative to other locations and to induce an increase in its population. But if production agglomeration economies in city m dominate those in other cities, this increase in population raises wages in city m relative to other cities even further. In addition, the increased population creates a boom in the consumer service sector, inducing agglomeration economies in consumption. The key variable reducing the incentives to immigrate to city m is the cost of housing, which rises with the population. However, if Δ is positive, as when the fraction of income that consumers allocate to housing is small, this real cost of living effect will not be sufficient to offset the agglomeration economies in consumption and production. The economy's population then ends up completely in city m, with industrial production specialized in commodity m.

Suppose that the prices of industrial goods are the same in cities f and q. Is there any difference in the populations of the two cities? Figure 6.4 depicts equilibrium on the assumption that city f has lower values of c_{0m} and c_{1m} relative to city q. The population-utility locus of city f has the same slope as that of city q — as given by Δ — but a higher intercept. With the economy's population equal to $\bar{L}$, the maximum that households can achieve is U_o, which occurs through an intercity distribution of labor equal to L_q and L_f. There is, therefore, spatial heterogeneity, in spite of the lack of differences in tastes, factor endowments and internal urban structure. Note finally that city f will have a larger equilibrium city size since it can offer higher nominal wages than city q, at any equal population allocation. In addition, consumer product variety in city f will exceed that in q, suggesting that, in equilibrium the cost of housing in city f must exceed by far that in q. The higher rental cost of housing must compensate for the utility advantages of a broader variety of consumer services and higher nominal wage rates.

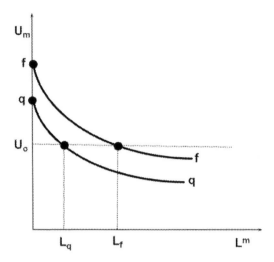

Figure 6.4. Interindustry Differences in the Use of Producer Services and City Size.

6.7   Conclusions

This paper has developed a model emphasizing the role played by the service sector in generating agglomeration economies in both production and consumption. Instead of relying on ad hoc specifications, our framework models agglomeration economies endogenously, showing precisely the origins of the external effects involved. From the production side our theoretical analysis describes how the agglomeration of industrial producers results in an upward shift of the demand for producer services, allowing increased specialization and exploitation of internal economies of scale in that sector. On the other hand, from the consumption side, the paper models explicitly tastes toward product diversity and describes how the agglomeration of households in the same location raises the variety of consumer services and, therefore, their utility. This gives rise to external effects on consumption.

Our analysis underscores the significance of developing explicitly the underpinnings of the market structure within which services are assumed to be sold. From both the production and consumption sides, we have concentrated on modeling the presence of product heterogeneity in the service sector, as we believe it is highly relevant empirically and provides critical clue to the origins of agglomeration. We have also assumed that service sector firms sell in markets characterized by imperfect competition, another aspect of the model that provides a closer approximation to the actual operation of this sector. In particular, the framework used assumes that service sector markets are monopolistically competitive. The symmetric structure and reliance on free entry and exit in this market structure simplify the analytics without an extreme sacrifice of realism.

In a significant part of the existing literature in urban economics, when the discussion turns to systems of open cities, heterogeneity in city size is usually explained by introducing ad hoc assumptions involving differences in tastes, factor endowments or internal city allocation mechanisms — such as differences in transportation systems or the availability of local public goods. In the present model, the only assumption that is exogenously specified on this regard is the fact that there exist a range of industrial commodities that use different technologies in production and, therefore, might require different bundles of producer services. This generates a divergence in the degree of agglomeration economies in production among cities, given that the analysis implies urban industrial specialization. The equilibrium allocation of households among a system of open cities then involves variation in city sizes. This heterogeneity can arise even if all households have identical tastes, all cities have the same amount of space available, and even if the industrial sector production function parameters are the same for different products. The factor that gives rise to the divergence among city sizes in this case is differences in the cost functions of the producer services supplying each city.

The integrated nature of our analysis of agglomeration economies has required some simplifications. We have, firstly, assumed that all consumers have identical tastes. This makes the computation of the equilibrium intercity allocation of households an easy task. The discussion, however, should be extended to consider taste heterogeneity since, within a city systems context, there is widespread evidence suggesting that individuals exhibit strong locational preferences, differentiating among alternative sites on the basis of climate, temperature, environmental scenery, etcetera.

A second key assumption is the lack of modeling of the internal land use pattern of cities. It is straightforward, though, to modify the analysis to incorporate distance from a Central Business District (CBD) and commuting costs as variables determining patterns of internal land use. Consider the following simple model where it is assumed that households demand a fixed lot size occupying $\bar{K}_{jh}$ of space. If the city's outer boundary is at a radius denoted by $\bar{u}$, an endogenous variable now, and the CBD encompasses a radius of $\underline{u}$, then the equality of demand for and supply of space implies

$$\bar{L}\bar{K}_{jh} = \pi(\bar{u}^2 - \underline{u}^2),$$

which can be solved for the equilibrium boundary radius of the city as a function of the city's population size and CBD radius:

$$\bar{u} = \left(\frac{\bar{L}\bar{K}_{jh}}{\pi} + \underline{u}^2\right)^{1/2}.$$

Assume that transportation cost to the CBD, $T(u)$, is directly related to distance from the CBD according to $T(u) = tu/2$, so that a household located at a radius u from the *CBD* has roundtrip transport costs given by tu. Denote the rental rate on housing or space at a radius $u > \underline{u}$ by $r(u)$ and assume that the opportunity cost of land at the city boundary is $\bar{r}$, the agricultural land rent. In this framework, the equality of utility among locations in the city implies that $tu + r(u)\bar{K}_{jh}$, be equal for all u within the city limits. Therefore, the following must hold:

$$t\bar{u} + r(\bar{u})\bar{K}_{jh} = tu + r(u)\bar{K}_{jh},$$

which can be transformed to yield

$$r(u) = \frac{t(\bar{u} - u)}{K_{jh}} + \bar{r},$$

which states that urban land rents will exceed the agricultural land rent by an amount proportional to the closeness of the location to the

CBD's outer limits. Substituting the expression for u derived earlier then results in

$$r(u) = -(tu/\bar{K}_{jh}) + \bar{r} + (t/\bar{K}_{jh}) \left(\frac{\bar{L}\bar{K}_{jh}}{\pi} + \underline{u}^2 \right).$$

This equation describes the bid-rent function for a given city with a population of $\bar{L}$. This expression can be substituted in place of Eq. (30), which specified rental rates on housing in our earlier model. Substitution of Eqs. (26)–(30) into the utility function in (21) would then provide the indirect utility function for a household located at a radius u from the center of city m. This utility, however, would be equal no matter what the location within the city is. As a consequence, since the rest of the analysis earlier is not significantly altered, the equilibrium in a system of open cities is determined by the equality of such a representative utility — for a household at distance u — among cities. The main difference with our discussion above would be that more populated cities would have higher housing rental-cum-commuting costs, but not necessarily higher rental rates on housing. Furthermore, residential rental rates will vary within the city. However, our main conclusions regarding the nature of production and consumption agglomeration economies would remain unaltered.

A third critical assumption made in the paper is that the service sector is perfectly labor intensive. It would be significant to extend the discussion to at least incorporate the use of space by the sector. Our results can be substantially altered in this case insofar as the prices of services can increase more than wages do as agglomeration occurs. Increased population can then lower utility by raising both housing costs and the prices of services; these two effects would then work together to compensate for the utility-enhancing impact of agglomeration economies.

Finally, even though the assumption of a monopolistically competitive market structure in the service sector is highly convenient for expositional purposes, within this market structure (in its Chamberlinian form) market power considerations do not play a major role. It is quite easy, however, to extend the discussion to an oligopolistic competition context in which the degree of market power of each firm is altered through the process of agglomeration. In this case, the increased extent of the market made possible by a larger population raises the degree of competition among service sector firms, lowering their price mark-ups above marginal cost. Larger cities, therefore, provide additional gains to consumers and producers. Relaxing this and other assumptions should be the task of future work.[9]

Notes:

[1] As opposed to 'agglomerative scale economies', defined as economies internal to the firm, and urbanization economies, which are external to the industry and internal to the city.

[2] See Henderson (1983, 1986), Segal (1976) and Moomaw (1985).

[3] Rosen (1979), using the 1970 Current Population Survey, finds that city density among a set of SMSAs is negatively related to real wages. Using Census Bureau data, Getz and Huang (1975) obtain similar results and then show a correlation between lower real wages and the number of leisure activities available in an SMSA (leisure activities include the number of restaurants, symphony orchestras, zoos, sports activities, etc., which are closely related to our definition of consumer services). See also Izraeli (1979).

[4] This particular approach has been utilized by Ethier (1982) to examine the role played by trade in intermediate goods on national and international economies of scale; see also Helpman and Krugman (1985, ch. 11). For an application to the analysis of urban agglomeration economies in production, see Rivera-Batiz (1988).

[5] Krugman (1987) has referred to this type of economies of scale as representing 'linkage externalities', see also Rivera-Batiz (1988).

[6] Some empirical evidence [see Segal (1976)] has found data for U.S. manufacturing consistent with a constant returns to scale equation such as (4), with a shift parameter that is significantly larger in more populated cities, reflecting localization economies.

[7] This simplifying assumption is widely utilized in urban models of systems of cities; see, for instance, Henderson (1977, p. 63).

[8] The possible role of increased product variety as a factor explaining urban growth is, of course, the basis of the old 'city lights' explanation for rural-urban labor migration. The first use of a formal model of product diversity to explain such labor migration was made by Krugman (1979) and Stahl (1983); Rivera-Batiz (1983) extended the analysis to incorporate the role played by diversity in consumer services. More recent work incorporating models of consumer product diversity and monopolistic competition into an urban economies context includes Fujita (1988), Hobson (1987) and Abdel-Rahman (1988).

[9]See, for instance, Rivera-Batiz (1984) on how to model oligopolistic competition. One further issue to consider within this context is that of optimal city size. In the present paper, the use of a Chamberlinian framework implies that city size is a second-best optimum (a first-best option optimum cannot be achieved except through the use of tax-subsidy schemes of questionable feasibility). If, oligopolistic competition is considered, and each service sector firm exerts its monopoly power, the market will produce an equilibrium with excess product variety, as compared with a constrained (second-best) Pareto optimum [see also Hobson (1987)].

References

Abdel-Rahman, H., 1988, "Product differentiation, monopolistic competition and city size," *Regional Science and Urban Economics*, 18 (1), 69–86.

Arnott, R., 1979, "Optimal city size in a spatial economy," *Journal of Urban Economics*, 6, 65–89.

Diamond, D. and G.S. Tolley, 1982, "The economic roles of urban amenities," in: D. Diamond and G.S. Tolley, eds., *The economics of urban amenities* (Academic Press, New York) 3–54.

Dixit, A.K., 1973, "The optimal factory town," *Bell Journal of Economics and Management Science*, 4, 637–654.

Dixit, A.K. and J. Stiglitz, 1977, "Monopolistic competition and optimum product diversity," *American Economic Review*, 67, 297–308.

Ethier, W., 1982, "National and international returns to scale in the modern theory of international trade," *American Economic Review*, 72, 389–405.

Fujita, M., 1988, "A monopolistic competition model of spatial agglomeration: A differentiated product approach," *Regional Science and Urban Economics*, 18 (1), 87–124.

Fujita, M. and H. Ogawa, 1982, "Multiple equilibria and structural transition of non-monocentric urban configurations," *Regional Science and Urban Economics*, 12, 161–196.

Getz, M. and Y. Huang, 1975, "Consumer revealed preference for city size," Mimeo. (Vanderbilt University, Nashville, TN).

Goldfarb, R.S. and A. Yezer, 1976, "Evaluating alternative theories of intercity and interregional wage differences," *Journal of Regional Science*, 16, 345–362.

Goldstein, G.S. and L.N. Moses, 1975, "Interdependence and the location of economic activity," *Journal of Urban Economics*, 2, 63–84.

Helpman, E. and P. Krugman, 1985, *Market structure and foreign trade: Increasing returns, imperfect competition and the international economy* (MIT Press. Cambridge, MA).

Henderson. J.V., 1977, *Economic theory and the cities* (Academic Press, New York).

Henderson. J.V., 1983, "Industrial bases and city sizes," *American Economic Review*, Papers and Proceedings 73, 164–168.

Henderson. J.V., 1986, "Efficiency of resource usage and city size," *Journal of Urban Economics*, 19, 47–70.

Hobson, P., 1987, "Optimum product variety in urban areas," *Journal of Urban Economics*, 22, 190–197.

Izraeli, O., 1979, "Externalities and intercity wage and price differentials," in: G.S. Tolley, P. Graves and J.L Gardner, eds., *Urban growth policy in an urban economy* (Academic Press, New York) 159–194.

Kelley, K.C., 1977, "Urban disamenities and the measure of economic welfare," *Journal of Urban Economics*, 4, 379–388.

Kim, S., 1987, "Diversity in urban labor markets and agglomeration economies," Papers of the Regional Science Association, 62 (1), 57–70.

Krugman, P., 1987, "Strategic sectors and international competition," in: R.M. Stern, ed., *U.S. trade policies in a changing world economy* (MIT Press, Cambridge, MA) 207–232.

Mera, K., 1973, "Urban agglomeration and economic efficiency," *Economic Development and Cultural Change*, 21, 309–321.

Mills, E.S. and B.W. Hamilton, 1984, *Urban Economics*, Third edition (Scott, Foresman, Glenview, IL).

Moomaw, R.L., 1981, "Productivity and city size: A critique of the evidence," *Quarterly Journal of Economics*, 95, 675–688.

Moomaw, R.L., 1985, "Firm location and city size: Reduced productivity advantages as a factor in the decline of manufacturing in urban areas," *Journal of Urban Economics*, 17, 73–89.

Mulligan. G.F., 1984, "Agglomeration and central place theory: A review of the literature," *International Regional Science Review*, 9, 1–12.

Rivera-Batiz. F., 1983, "The service sector, monopolistic competition and the impact of emigration," *Economics Letters*, 12, 183–187.

Rivera-Batiz, F., 1984, "Economies of scale, increased competition and the gains from intra-industry trade," Paper presented at the American Economic Association Meetings, Dallas, TX, December 30.

Rivera-Batiz, F., 1988, "Modeling urban agglomeration: Producer services, linkage externalities and specialization economies," in: V.G. Vogt and M.H. Mickle, eds., *Modeling and simulation* (Instrument Society of America, NC).

Rosen, S., 1979, "Wage-based indexes of urban quality of life," in: P. Mieszkowski and M. Straszhein, *Current issues in urban economics* (Johns Hopkins University Press, London) 74–104.

Segal, D., 1976, "Are there returns to scale in city size?," *Review of Economics and Statistics*, 58, 339–350.

Shefer, D., 1973, "Localization economies in SMSA's: A production function analysis," *Journal of Regional Science*, 13, 55–64.

Stahl, K., 1983, "A note on the microeconomics of migration," *Journal of Urban Economics*, 14, 318–326.

Chapter 7

Geography, Trade Patterns, and Economic Policy*

7.1 Introduction

Recent developments in the world economy have raised a number of issues in which the dimension of space plays a central role. Of paramount importance is the economic analysis of interregional trade, the environment, and their relation to economic development. Yet, there is no body of theory or general equilibrium models that can help us understand the delicate interaction between endogenous technological development, location patterns and environmental factors.

International trade theory originates in the notion of separate economies that differ in terms of factor endowments and national policies. Current theory focuses on the conditions under which these

*This chapter was co-authored by Carlos M. Asilis and Luis A. Rivera-Batiz and was originally published in *International Monetary Fund Working Paper No. WP/94/16*, Washington, D.C., February 1994. ©1994 International Monetary Fund.

This paper was written while the second author was a visiting scholar in the Developing Country Studies Division of the Research Department of the International Monetary Fund. We are grateful to seminar participants at the IMF and the 1993 CEPR Conference on the Location of Economic Activity held in Vigo, Spain for useful comments and discussion. Catherine Fleck provided helpful editorial assistance. The views expressed are those of the authors alone and do not necessarily represent those of the International Monetary Fund or any of the affiliated institutions.

economies interact and the benefits achieved through trade. This paradigm requires modifications to deal with recent developments in the world trading system, especially the trend toward integration. The European Single Internal Market, and to a large extent the North American Free Trade Agreement, are converting international trade into interregional trade. Within these markets factor mobility prevails. Integration is proceeding in Asia and further European integration may involve Eastern Europe. The economics of location and the impact of each region's environmental policies have naturally come to the foreground in public discussions.

This paper focuses on the geographic and regional basis for development, trade, and the environment. A geographical theory of interregional trade is developed, which can be used to examine policy issues in economic development and in environmental protection. Location is treated as an endogenous variable by firms, consumers and perfectly mobile workers. The model determines the potential range of locations of industrial centers and of associated land and labor use patterns. Space plays a central role owing to transportation costs, access to markets, and distance from polluting industrial centers.

The analysis presented here has interesting implications for central issues in regional development, trade, environment, and optimal government policy. This paper stresses:

(1) aspects of an equilibrium compensating differential theory of regional unevenness,
(2) the theoretical formulation of a "gravity" theory of trade patterns,
(3) the geographic basis for industrial and environmental policy,
(4) the interaction between technological change in transportation, location patterns, and other types of technological improvements.

One of the main traits of development is the regional unevenness in incomes. Even when convergence is observed, residual unevenness remains (Barro and Sala-i-Martin (1991, 1992a, 1992b)). Unevenness in intra-country per capita income is sustained in the face of labor mobility and national policies that are uniformly applied across regions. Region-based factors, such as regional and local policies, must be introduced to account for these divergencies (see Garcia-Mila and McGuire (1992), and Garcia-Mila, McGuire, and Porter (1993)).

The model presented below focuses on compensating differentials-based unevenness. These compensating differentials are location-specific and exhibit a regional component. Hence, the equilibrium factor rewards and utilization are location-dependent. Since labor is fully mobile, regional wage differentials reflect compensating differentials related to transportation costs and pollution levels. These compensating differentials offset the adverse effects of conditions such as high pollution levels or a high cost of living. As such, they remain as measured residual unevenness even when regional convergence is otherwise fully achieved. These regional disparities are associated with the determination of regional trade patterns.

Explanations of bilateral trade flows frequently rely on the so-called "gravity" model. The gravity model stresses that economic size relates positively to trade while transportation cost barriers cause distance to relate negatively with the extent of bilateral trade flows. While the gravity theory has been widely applied, its theoretical foundations are still not fully developed. As Frankel (1993a, p. 7) argues: "Although the importance of distance and transportation costs is clear, there is not a lot of theoretical guidance on precisely how they should enter."

Our model extends and formalizes the basic notions of the gravity model. The roles of distance and transportation costs are introduced in a geographic model in which space and distance enter explicitly. In particular, we examine how the interaction between size, distance and the divergence in regional productive structures lead to trade. The positive role of economic size and associated specialization in trade is validated in our analysis but the impact of distance is shown to be more complicated.

The role of distance is shown to depend crucially on regional specialization patterns. For instance, consider a region that is far away from the center and specializes in commodity x, for which it attains an above-average production concentration (i.e., it is a big exporter). This peripheral region engages in greater trade with the y-specialized center than with other regions that stand nearer to the center and specialize in x, but are not major centers of its production (i.e., they are small exporters or even importers of x). In this context, it is easy to see how the regional specialization effect explains the exchanges of machinery and beef between England and Argentina in the nineteenth century. At that time Argentine trade was far greater with Great Britain than with other Latin American countries. In our model this "unnatural" trading between distant partners emerges endogenously from factor endowments and regional location decisions.

An interesting industrial policy arises because agglomeration forces lead to multiple equilibria in industrial city locations. We show that there is a natural role for government to push the economy toward the utility-maximizing industrial center location. The location of government services and infrastructure investments entail an implicit industrial policy that can be used to achieve optimality. The sort of industrial policy that results is quite different from the usual discussions of industrial targeting. As with other expenditures, such as education, the government can steer the economy toward an optimal equilibrium. But there is no industrial targeting in the sense of choosing one industry over another. Actually, in this model manufacturing products are entirely symmetric and there is no basis for targeting one product over another.

The model is used to examine the interaction between transportation costs, location patterns and technological change. Technological change in this model can arise from the agricultural, manufacturing and transportation sectors. The analysis illustrates how change in the transportation technologies feeds back into new industrial technological developments. We show that the effects these developments have on location depend crucially on how strong the centralization forces are in particular industries. Reductions in transportation costs promote industrial expansion and hence growth and concentration in industrial centers. At the same time lower transportation costs push some activities away from the city. These are activities in which centralization forces are not strong. Increased industrial pollution thus causes a reallocation of resources away from the center. Paradoxically, this process enhances the mass of industrial concentration while simultaneously giving rise to a flight-to-the-periphery phenomenon if industrial transportation costs are sufficiently small.

Finally, the model also illuminates the sectoral basis for technological change. The model's comparative static results show that the source of technological change cannot be determined by simply looking at the expansion in size and productivity of individual sectors. These findings pose a number of caveats on recent studies of sectoral technological change that correlate the sources of technological change with high productivity growth or rapidly expanding sectors.

The analysis formalizes how the historical reductions in transportation costs encourage both industrial improvements and reallocation of regional resources. A reduction in transportation costs is equivalent to an increase in market size, which encourages innovation that is driven by market-size. Whether concentration or regional decentralization occurs depends on the nature of individual industries. Reductions in transportation costs lead to further concentration of industries that grow in response to such concentration. On the other hand, lower transportation costs encourage decentralization of those industries that are by nature not dependent on major industrial centers. Thus, in this case lower transportation costs operate to effectively bring the periphery and the center closer together and can lead to further decentralization. This two-way impact can help to explain how greater industrial concentration can subsist with increased dispersion of decentralized activities.

We proceed to briefly review models of trade that incorporate cities, regions, and the spatial variables. Sections 7.2 and 7.3 develop a theoretical model of economic geography and trade that analyzes location, environmental, and regional development issues. Regional inequalities and interactions are endogenously specified within the model. Section 7.4 examines a number of policy issues relating to employment, agriculture and the environment. The conclusion considers extensions and limitations of the analysis.

7.2   Models of Location, Agglomeration and Trade

7.2.1   *The Advent of Regional Analysis*

Work on regional analysis became an active field during the 1950s and has proceeded in the areas of regional planning, urban economics, and a host of related fields. A number of studies have addressed such issues as central market theory, land-rent gradients, and regional development and convergence (or divergence patterns). In a real sense much of the most recent work on regional economics reexamines work that has been conducted independently since that time.

Regional development must establish a balance between the opposite forces of agglomeration and those that work for the dispersion of economic activities. The outcome of this equilibrating process yields regional trade patterns as a by-product. A basic test of any regional theory is to model and illuminate the stylized facts that incorporate the consistency between the forces of agglomeration and dispersion.

Analysts have begun to construct new varieties of models of intra-country or regional development. An emerging theory of trade and development introduces explicitly the variable of space and models the location and interaction between economic agents in a geographic context. Most of these theories incorporate some form of regional specialization and interregional competition. The discussion that follows contains a highly-selected review of work on economic geography. This review is only intended to place this paper in the context of recent related work and does not purport to be a full or even a comprehensive survey of the subject.

7.2.2   *Models of Regional Development*

Henderson (1974, 1988) assumes localized external economies in production and contrasts the associated centripetal forces with the centrifugal ones, which stem from increasing land rents. The first factor generates pressures for agglomeration while the latter puts a cap on city expansion. A competitive market framework is utilized to examine the factors determining the number and the size of cities. The relative location in space is, however, not considered.

The models by Fujita (1988) and F. L. Rivera-Batiz (1988a) specify sources of the localized increasing returns to scale and consider the effects of imperfect competition among producers. F. L. Rivera-Batiz (1988a) develops a model with nontraded intermediate goods, a form of increasing returns to scale provided by diversity in services, and endogenous city size among a number of potential city locations (open cities model). Migration incentives and city population profiles in alternative locations are based on the exploitation of the localized benefits from nontraded services. Agglomeration permits the exploitation of economies of scale (and scope) but agglomeration is limited by the escalation of land values that accompanies economic aggrandizement. An equilibrium emerges in which city population, output, and a variety of productive services are endogenously determined and made consistent with the dispersion of economic activities.

Fujita (1988) considers a model with nontraded intermediate goods and city size as determined by urban concentration. Increasing returns to scale are based on Marshall-type economies of scale. Both Rivera-Batiz and Fujita derive increasing returns from the existence of a monopolistically competitive nontraded goods sector that exhibits increasing returns. The role of space is not made explicit and transportation costs are ignored.

Krugman (1991a, 1991b) uses a two-region model in which regions are regarded as dimensionless points. The equilibrium that obtains is interpreted as the endogenous differentiation between an industrialized "core" and an agricultural "periphery". Manufacturing firms chose a single location in order to maximize the gains from increasing returns to scale in production at the plant level; they locate in the higher-demand region in order to minimize transportation costs and to have greater access to markets.

7.2.3 *Explicit Spatial Models*

In all the models reviewed above, location along a space dimension is not explicitly modeled. Cities are treated as dimensionless points that interact with one another. There is no explicit treatment of the distance between locations, or of distance-related factors such as transportation costs, the set of communication facilities, or market access. A number of papers have introduced a more detailed specification of the space variable.

F. L. Rivera-Batiz (1988b) develops a model of intra-city activities and land use. He presents a three-level stratified spatial urban model. The city consists of a circle subdivided into three distinct layers. These comprise an industrial center (export node) around which lies a central business services district, and a peripheral residential zone. The population and activity level of each region are endogenous. The model is utilized to examine city population size, its effects on productivity, and the determinants of emigration or immigration. However, the total amounts of space devoted to industrial, service and residential purposes are considered fixed, as is the position of each on the circle. Since transportation costs are ignored, neither the size nor the distance between the different layers within a city affect the results.

Rauch (1991) constructs an explicit spatial model in which location is endogenous and international trade is explicitly considered. The model exhibits local external economies and offers a limited number of potential location sites. Transportation costs increase with the distance from an external trading partner. Trade takes the form of importation of a raw input and distance from trading center is measured as distance from the coast. City or regional size is a function of transportation costs in relation to a fixed point. The largest cites are located near the coast and city size declines as the distance from the coast increases, that is, as one moves inland. Rauch's model is based on the exploitation of the natural comparative advantage enjoyed by the coast location, and its interaction with the assumed local external economies.

Krugman (1992a) develops a model of endogenous location in continuous space, along a line and along a circle. The two-sector model consists of an agricultural sector and a manufacturing sector with increasing returns that produces a given number of differentiated goods sold in a monopolistically competitive market. Increasing returns at the manufacturing plant level are introduced through the presence of a fixed setup cost. All goods are considered tradable and manufacturing transportation costs vary directly with the distance between the production origin and the final market. No external economies are assumed and there are no transport costs in agriculture.

Manufacturing plant location decisions are based on the interaction of economies of scale at the manufacturing plant level (i.e., at individual production facilities), and transportation costs of final goods. At some equilibria no center emerges, but for some parameter values only one location becomes dominant, that is, a metropolis develops. A single metropolis develops if transportation costs are low enough. The metropolis has the character of a manufacturing center with increasing returns to scale that services the agricultural hinterland sector.

The center has a natural comparative advantage in manufacturing because of its location. In Krugman's model, however, the equilibrium is influenced also by created comparative advantages. Natural comparative advantages are viewed as first nature to the center's location. Created advantages, such as market access due to agglomeration in particular locations, are second nature to the locations but can nevertheless be dominant in determining the location of the metropolis. Multiple locational equilibria — the set of equilibria is represented as a band around the center — occur due to the fact that agglomeration points are to some extent arbitrary. Manufacturing cannot be located far away from the center but it does not have to be at the heart of the center.

Krugman (1992c) develops a dynamic spatial model that examines how locational patterns evolve over time, how multiple agglomerations evolve, and how the location patterns change when exogenous variables change. Analytical solutions are difficult to obtain in the dynamic, multiregional case so the author relies (as do we, below) on numerical examples. Locations grow by adding new products to the center's. Metropolises are characterized by product availability and diversity.

Krugman and Elizondo (1992) and Fujita (1993) extend Krugman's (1992c) model to generate diverse patterns of spatial agglomeration and multiple metropolises. They accomplish this by introducing multiple types of symmetric groups of manufacturing goods, which are subject to transport costs. The firms within each group agglomerate but different kinds of manufacturing goods can center at different places.

The spatial models discussed above and the related work by Thisse (1993) and others represent some first steps into a general equilibrium analysis of interregional trade. They provide us with a portfolio of economic geography models with which to work. For instance, the papers by F. L. Rivera-Batiz and Rauch focus on the analysis of intra-city and coastal location. The papers by Krugman examine a wide range of issues concerning location and number of cities as well as of economic geography, as broadly understood.

The influential papers by Krugman (1992a, 1992b, 1992c) rely on a number of strict assumptions that will be relaxed below. Agricultural and industrial labor are treated asymmetrically. The manufacturing sector is characterized by full locational mobility of workers but agriculture is assumed to utilize an immobile factor, agricultural labor (used as a proxy for land immobility). The one-to-one association between agricultural labor and land is accomplished by assuming that labor is permanently attached to the land. This means that agricultural labor cannot move from one parcel of land to another and cannot migrate. The fact that agricultural labor is attached to land generates population dispersion across space and provides a force against full concentration of economic activities in the city. This dispersion condition, however, is not a result of the model but, rather, is achieved by construction. On the other hand, migration of manufacturing workers is allowed and is needed to generate agglomeration of the urban population.

Since neither agricultural capital nor land are explicitly considered, agricultural production — both total and at each location — is given in this model. There is no possible intersectoral substitution and production conditions in agriculture play no role in the analysis (the only role of agriculture is to generate population dispersion). Furthermore, labor mobility from agriculture to industry is not allowed, which means that farmers are immobile both across locations and across industries. This model's property stems from the assumption of sector-specific labor in manufacturing and in agriculture.

7.3   A General Model of Interregional Trade

This section develops a two-sector general equilibrium model of location and interregional trade in a static framework. The two sectors, manufacturing and agriculture, use labor and land as inputs. The allocation of labor to agriculture and manufacturing, and along space, is endogenized by allowing workers to decide on their workplace, the choice being between manufacturing and agriculture as possible lines of work. Agricultural production decisions allocate labor to each plot of land along a line of range (0,1). Labor allocation decisions for manufacturing are discussed more fully below.

Location is treated as an endogenous variable by firms, consumers and perfectly mobile workers. Space plays a central role owing to transportation costs, access to markets, and distance from polluting industrial centers. The quality of land depends on its location in a nontrivial way. Total land availability and the fixed location of each plot plays the role of multiple differentiated, fixed factors. The model determines the potential range of locations of industrial centers and of associated land use patterns. In this paper we determine the range of parameters from which there is a single industrial center equilibrium and focus on this case.

Industrial interdependence arises from the benefits of a concentration of demand at one point and the associated reduction in transportation costs. Industrial firms prefer to locate where there are other industrial firms, and hence markets for their products. This interdependence in firms' location decisions means that the site of an industrial center is indeterminate within a band along the linear space [0,1]. As a result there are multiple equilibria in terms of city location and the associated resource allocation.

Initially, the industrial center will be fixed and the focus is on one particular equilibrium among those possible, that is, the focus is on a generic central point and the equilibrium attached to it. The analysis is general because the equations used are applicable to each central location, which are denoted by x_c, within the set of equilibria. There is no presumption that x_c must lie at the center in real space — the midpoint of the interval [0,1]. Note, however, that $x_c = 0.5$ is an element of the equilibrium set in all cases (see Asilis and Rivera-Batiz (1993a)).

Section 7.9 characterizes the multiple equilibria that arise in the single-city equilibrium case.

7.3.1 *Consumers' Choice of a Consumption-Residence Location*

In a geographic setting, consumers and firms face a two-stage decision problem. Consumers choose (1) a location in which to live and work, and (2) the allocation of consumer spending within a given budget constraint. The two decisions are related because the location determines both the consumer's budget and the prices of the goods he buys. In turn, the location decision must take into account wage and cost of living differentials. Let us examine the household budget allocation problem.

7.3.1.1 The budget allocation problem

Consumption decisions depend on income and the relative costs and availability of consumer goods. Both decisions are closely linked since the workplace location determines both the wages earned by the agent and the location where the agent makes purchases (and hence the cost of the goods purchased and the location-dependent utility obtained from them).

For any given location the consumer's budget allocation problem can be expressed in terms of a set of market commodities $\{c_i; \ i = 1, \ldots, N\}$, the agricultural good C_A, and monetary income Y:

$$\max_{[c_A, c_i; i=1,\ldots,N]} \left[\sum_{i=1}^{N} c_i^{\frac{\sigma-1}{\sigma}} \right]^{\mu_M \frac{\sigma}{\sigma-1}} c_A^{\mu_A},$$

$$\text{s.t.} \ \sum_{i=1}^{N} p_i c_i + P^A c_A \leq 1. \tag{1}$$

The demand function for a manufacturing good c_i is given by:

$$c_i = \left(\frac{\mu_M}{\mu_M + \mu_A}\right)^{\sigma} \frac{I^{\sigma}}{\left(\sum_{i=1}^{N} c_i^{\frac{\sigma-1}{\sigma}}\right)^{\sigma} P_i^{\sigma}}$$

$$= \left(\frac{\mu_M}{\mu_M + \mu_A}\right) \frac{I}{\left(\sum_{i=1}^{N} P_i^{1-\sigma}\right) P_i^{\sigma}}. \tag{2}$$

Multiplying both sides of equation (2) by P_i and summing up all manufacturing goods yields $\sum p_i c_i - (\frac{\mu_M}{\mu_M + \mu_A})I$, showing that the expenditure share of the aggregate of manufactures is the constant $(\frac{\mu_M}{\mu_M + \mu_A})$.

7.3.1.2 The consumer-worker location decision

The consumer's budget problem is not fully solved because the income I is not given but is determined endogenously by the consumer's location decision. The location decision will take into account both the location-specific wages and the difference in the cost and quality of living across locations. The cost of living differs across locations owing to a number of factors. First, prices of manufacturing goods paid by consumers are inclusive of transportation costs and are higher the farther away a location is from the center. Second, the cost of agricultural products could be higher or lower in the periphery than in the center depending on whether they are sold directly at the source or have to be taken to the center prior to distribution. Both cases can be incorporated into the model but, for simplicity, we will assume that agricultural goods transportation costs are zero and focus on the environment factor.

The quality of living is introduced through a consumption diseconomy called pollution — that is generated by the agglomeration of industrial centers. Pollution spreads in space and is higher near the city and declines at a decreasing rate with distance from the city. It affects location decisions of workers and generates a demand for rural residence (commuting is ignored here). It provides a balance to the strong centralization forces in the model given that the cost of manufacturing goods makes the cost of living higher in the countryside.

As we move farther away from the city, residential location puts a value on the declining impact of pollution. This utility value is represented by a residential location utility factor of the form:

$$R_x = R_{x_C}(1 + |x - x_C|)^\gamma = R_{x_C}e^{\gamma \ln(1+|x-x_C|)}, \quad 0 < \gamma < 1, \qquad (3)$$

where γ represents a positive health parameter associated with less incidence of pollution toward the countryside. A greater γ represents a superior quality of environment stemming from the lower incidence of pollution in the rural areas. The health factor $\gamma \ln(1+|x-x_C|)$ also embodies the condition that housing services are superior the farther away one is from the polluting focus (the industrial center x_C).

Since environment is a public good, the quality of the environment does not have an explicit market price, but it enters as a factor in utility maximization. The individual's consumption balance yields that the relative shadow price between residence at x and residence at the city or industrial center x_C is:

$$P_x^R = P_{x_C}^R e^{-\gamma(\mu_M+\mu_A)\ln(1+|x-x_C|)}. \qquad (4)$$

Since residential location, not housing space, is being considered, the supply is constant at every location. Residential utility services R are normalized at x_C to unity so that $R_x = \exp[\gamma \ln(1 + |x - x_C|)]$.

In the presence of perfect labor mobility, real wages received by agricultural workers living at location x must be equal to those paid at the center (i.e., the city). The "full" agricultural real wage rate is computed by taking into account a cost of quality living that in turn incorporates the effects of pollution (i.e., the shadow price of residential utility).

The full real $\frac{W_x^A}{P_X}$ at point x relative to that at point x_C corresponds to:

$$\frac{\frac{W_x^A}{P_x}}{\frac{W_{x_C}}{P_{x_C}}} = \frac{W_x^A}{W_{x_C}}\frac{P_{x_C}}{P_x} = \frac{W_x^A}{W_{x_C}}\frac{(P^A)^{\mu_A}(P_{x_C})^{\mu_M}(P_{x_C}^R)^{1-\mu_M-\mu_A}}{(P^A)^{\mu_A}(P_x)^{\mu_M}(P_x^R)^{1-\mu_M-\mu_A}}$$

$$= \frac{W_x^A}{W_{x_C}}e^{[-\tau\mu_M+\gamma(\mu_M+\mu_A)(1-\mu_M-\mu_A)]\|x-x_C\|} \qquad (5)$$

$$= \frac{W_x^A}{W_{x_C}} e^{-D\|x - x_C\|},$$

$$D \equiv \tau \mu_M - \gamma(\mu_M + \mu_A)(1 - \mu_M - \mu_A),$$

$$\|x - x_C\| \equiv \ln(1 + |x - x_c|),$$

where P represents the cost of living and p^A and p the prices of agricultural and manufacturing goods, respectively. The last equality obtains because manufacturing prices at x can be computed from those at x_C by simply multiplying by the transportation cost factor $(1 + |x - x_C|)^\tau = \exp[\tau \ln(1 + |x - x_C|)]$, while agricultural prices in locations x_C and x are equalized because of the assumed absence of transportation costs for agricultural goods. Also recall that the shadow price of the residential utility factor at x relative to that at x_C equals $e^{-\gamma(\mu_M + \mu_A) \ln(1 + |X - X_C|)}$.

Real wage equalization means that in equilibrium W_x^A equals the center wage multiplied by $e^{D\|x - x_C\|}$. The parameter $D \equiv \tau \mu_M - \gamma(\mu_M + \mu_A)(1 - \mu_M - \mu_A)$ represents a location compensating differential. When $D > 0$, nominal wages will be higher in the periphery that in the center. If $D < 0$, rural workers will receive lower nominal compensation in equilibrium.

The compensating differential $D = \tau \mu_M - \gamma(\mu_M + \mu_A)(1 - \mu_M - \mu_A)$ formalizes two geographic factors — transportation costs and environmental pollution — that enter into workers' residence-work decisions. The factor D increases with a higher transportation cost factor τ and a lower pollution-free health factor γ. Whether a rural workplace-residence commands premium wages or is offered at a discount depends on the relative size of these effects. The costs of transporting manufacturing goods to the periphery require a positive compensating differential to attract workers; the offsetting force comes from the benefits of being away from city-sourced pollution and other agglomeration-related disutilities.

In this model consumers face location-specific wages and prices but are identical and have full geographical mobility. Labor market equilibrium must be such as to eliminate the incentives for worker migration. For this reason, location is undetermined from the point of view of the individual. For the economy as a whole, residential patterns are uniquely determined as a function of the industrial center's location x_C. For each equilibrium x_C, the allocation of resources between agriculture and manufacturing is uniquely determined. The spatial distribution of productive activities implies the spatial shape of the population and associated trade patterns.

We have formulated a model of location-specific compensating differentials. To solve the model, wages and prices need to be determined at each location. In order to do this the productive sectors must be considered. First, production decisions and wage determination are examined in a model of dispersed agriculture. We will obtain a relationship between wages at different locations and the wage at the center. Subsequently, the requirements of full employment and labor market mobility across locations and between industry and agriculture are utilized to determine wages in the center, and the associated productive and spatial structure of the economy.

7.4   The Geography of Employment, Agriculture and Pollution Externalities

The agricultural sector produces a homogeneous product with labor and land inputs. Transportation costs in agriculture are ignored so that the agricultural price $p_x^A = p^A$ will be the same at all locations x, and will not affect the relative allocation of agricultural labor across space.

We consider a production function of the form $\int F(L_x^A, x)dx$ with labor and land inputs L and $x \in [0, 1]$. This production function exhibits what we denote as *space additive separability*. This property means that the productivities of labor at different plots of land are independent of each other. For any given point x in space at which a good is produced, labor use does not affect labor productivity in other plots no matter how close the plots of land are.

Space additive separability simplifies our spatial allocation problem because it allows point by point maximization over space in allocating labor over available land. In order to work out a computable equilibrium we specialize the form for the function F to the

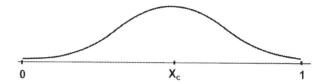

Figure 7.1. Agriculture Population Distribution; $D > 0$.

following:

$$F(L^A_x, x) = f(L^A_x) = \frac{1}{(1-\rho)}(L^A_x)^{1-\rho}, \quad 0 < 1 - \rho < 1. \quad (6)$$

Profit maximization leads to the equalization of the agricultural wage rate W^A_x and the value of the marginal product of agricultural labor. We obtain: $W^A_x = p^A(L^A_x)^{-\rho}$, where $F_L(L^A_x, x) = (L^A_x)^{-\rho}$ is the marginal product of labor. Given the fixed prices and wages faced agricultural firms face, the latter equation determines the amount of labor allocated to any given point in space.

The nominal wage W^A_x has a location-specific component. This is due to the need to compensate workers for cost of living and residential utility differentials. We have already shown that "full" real wage equalization across locations implies that $p^A(L^A_x)^{-\rho} = W^A_x$ equals the center wage multiplied by $\exp(D\|x - x_C\|)$. This condition allows us to rewrite the agricultural labor allocation relationship as:

$$L^A_x = \left[w_{x_C} \frac{e^{D\|x - x_c\|}}{P^A} \right]^{-\frac{1}{\rho}}. \quad (7)$$

Figures 7.1 and 7.2 show two illustrative plots of the spatial allocation of agricultural labor. When a positive $(D > 0)$ compensating differential is required to attract workers to the countryside, agricultural employment concentrates near the cities and gradually declines as we move away from the center on both sides (Figure 7.1). This pattern emerges because the real cost of labor is greater the farther the location is from the center. Consequently, the marginal productivity is greater the farther locations are from the center, implying that labor will be used less intensively the farther away from the center the production occurs.

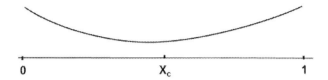

Figure 7.2.   Agriculture Population Distribution; $D < 0$.

On the other hand, when the rural sector carries a negative compensating differential, a U-shaped agricultural employment pattern arises, and real wages are lower in the pollution-free countryside. If the manufacturing goods transportation cost parameter τ goes up, D increases, the compensating rural-urban differential increases, and the population becomes more concentrated in the urban sector. An opposite centrifugal force arises if the health factor γ increases.

7.5   Industrial Centers Servicing Widespread Heterogeneous Markets

The decision process of manufacturing firms can be decomposed into two related stages. One stage entails allocating sales across spatially separated markets, given the production location. The other decision involves choosing the production place. In both stages firms take as given the spatial distribution of the population and the schedule of transportation costs from the production point to every possible market. As mentioned earlier, there is a band along which the manufacturing location might be centered in equilibrium (see Section 7.9 and Asilis and Rivera-Batiz (1993b)). The focus here is on a generic point x_c in the equilibrium set. The equations used are equally valid at any central equilibrium location so the analysis below is general.

7.5.1   *Location-Specific Monopolistic Competitive Pricing*

The pricing and sales allocation problem is modeled in terms of the Dixit-Stiglitz monopolistic competition framework, which is extended to allow sales in different locations. The producer enjoys a monopoly in each location because the firm is the only source of the differentiated good it specializes in and makes pricing decisions on the basis of two location-specific elements. First, the producer must take into account the transport costs of sending goods from the production base to each specific location. Second, the producer takes as given the spatial distribution of the population that in general is not uniform along the space dimension. Each market-location will thus bring about a different demand and fetch a different price.

Pricing-sales decisions are realized to maximize profits from total sales, given the production location at the industrial center x_C. Since demand at any given location does not depend on the price at other locations and because cost functions are linear, the firm's problem can be decomposed into individual maximization problems at each location.

The firm's decision at any given location is to choose its price and associated sales — which in the monopolistic competition case equals total consumption there — so as to maximize gross profits (of fixed costs). Since the firm is producing at the central location x_C, gross profits from sales at x are given by the solution to the following problem:

$$\max_{[c_x]} P_x e^{-\tau \|x - x_C\|} L_x^A c_x - \beta w_{x_C} L_x^A c_x. \tag{8}$$

The parameter β represents the labor input-output coefficient, and is assumed to be constant. Notice that the price received by the seller equals $p_x . \exp[-\tau \ln(1 + |x - x_C|)]$, that is, the price received by the firm is net of the transaction cost. The relevant wage rate is the one prevailing at the central location x_c, which is the point of production.

Using equation (2) again, for the price derived from the demand for manufactures, we obtain an explicit expression for the price (gross of transportation costs) in terms of wages:

$$P_x = \left(\frac{\sigma}{\sigma - 1}\right) \beta W_{xc} e^{\tau \|X - X_C\|} = p_{x_c} e^{\tau \|X - X_C\|}. \tag{9}$$

The previous equation is a spatial version of the traditional markup equation in monopolistic competition models. It tells us the price charged by the firm; in this framework firms will charge different prices at different locations in order to cover transportation costs. The price received by the firm is simply the markup $\sigma\beta/(\sigma-1)$ over the wage at the central location.

7.5.2 *Geographical Sales Allocation*

In order to solve for resource allocation in the manufacturing sector, quantities sold at different locations must be specified. That is, total quantities sold by a manufacturing firm located at x_C are given by the sum of two components: of manufacturing goods sold to L^M manufacturing workers at x_C and of sales to agricultural workers dispersed across the $[0,1]$ interval.

Aggregate quantity demanded from a manufacturing firm located at x_C, q^d is the sum of manufacturing workers' demand at x_C, plus the integral agricultural workers' demand located over the interval $[0,1]$:

$$q^d = \left(\frac{\mu_M}{\mu_M + \mu_A}\right) \frac{P_{x_c}^{1-\sigma}}{\sum_{i=1}^{N} P_{x_c}^{1-\sigma}} \frac{\sigma-1}{\beta\sigma}$$

$$\times \left[L^M + \left(\frac{w_{x_c}}{P^A}\right)^{-1/\rho} \int_0^1 e^{\left[D\left(1-\frac{1}{\rho}\right)-\tau\right]\|x-x_c\|} dx\right]. \quad (10)$$

Expression (10) is obtained by adding up the previous demand expressions (2), and using (9). Since all goods $i = 1,\ldots,N$ enter symmetrically in demand, have the same cost function, and are produced at the same location, the previous equation applies equally to all manufactured goods.

Expression (10) neatly illustrates a number of points that we want to formalize. The first term shows the unambiguously positive demand effect of the center's economic size as measured by its wage bill and negative substitution effect (including the term $p^{-\sigma}$). The second term incorporates the positive income demand effect of agricultural wages as well as the negative one resulting from the substitution effect and the inverse relationship between the agricultural population and the real wages at each location. Notice that a higher agricultural price p^A will increase the number of workers at location x and thus result in increased demand. The demand effect of the agricultural sector also depends on the value of the term $D(1 - \frac{1}{\rho}) - \tau$, with $D = \tau \mu_M - \gamma(\mu_M + \mu_A)(1 - \mu_M - \mu_A)$. It is instructive to take a close look at this term.

The integral term in (10) shows the complex role of distance in product demand. Transportation costs entail a price demand effect (related to the factor $\exp(-\tau)$). The distance of the agricultural workers' residence from the center induces an income effect (related to the factor $\exp(D)$) through the level of wages needed to induce workers to settle in a particular location. The sign of the income effect of greater distance from the center is ambiguous because the sign of the compensating differential D cannot be ascertained a priori. Finally, there is the population density effect of the level of wages which is required to compensate workers for transportation and pollution costs (related to the factor $\exp(-D/\rho)$). The population density effect strengthens demand when the compensating differential D has a negative sign and weakens it when D is positive.

In order to ascertain the net demand effect of a greater distance from the center the different channels of influence on demand must be taken into account. In this model the net demand effect of increasing the distance from the center is ambiguous because the compensating differential is ambiguous.

7.6 The Gravity Theory of Trade Patterns

A widely-used model in the empirical literature of trade patterns is the so-called "gravity theory." This theory was first applied by Armington (1969a and 1969b) and has recently been used by Frankel (1993) and others.

The "gravity theory" stresses that trade operates in a manner that is similar to the force of gravity on space. In the same way that larger and closer-positioned bodies attract each other, trade increases with size and proximity between trading patterns. Operationally, the gravity theory is taken to mean that the importance of trade declines with the distance between trading partners and increases with the economic size of the trading partners.

The model presented in this paper determines interregional trade patterns by the interaction between a manufacturing region

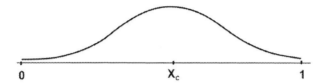

Figure 7.3.   Exports to Production Ratio; D > 0.

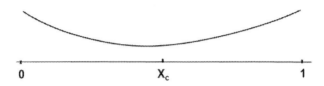

Figure 7.4.   Exports to Production Ratio; D < 0.

that imports agricultural goods and an agricultural region that imports manufactured goods from the center. It can also assess the role of distance and size. In this model, interregional trade patterns entail the interaction between a manufacturing region that imports agricultural goods and an agricultural region that imports manufactured goods from the center.

The geographical nature of trade patterns in our model can be determined by computing the ratio of exports to output at each point in space. The result of the calculation (see Asilis and Rivera-Batiz (1993a)) embodies the geographic position explicitly:

$$\left(\frac{exports}{output}\right)_x = 1 - \frac{e^{\frac{D}{\rho}\|x-x_c\|}}{constant}. \tag{11}$$

The relation between distance from the center and trade with it relates to the sign of the parameter $D = \tau\mu_M - \gamma(\mu_M + \mu_A)(1 - \mu_M - \mu_A)$. Figures 7.3 and 7.4 depict two possible patterns.

The hump-shaped pattern shown in Figure 7.3 illustrates the negative relation between distance and trade suggested by the gravity theory. The export-output ratio is higher near the center and declines as we move away from it. The humped-shaped pattern arises when the compensating differential D exceeds unity in value. It is not a general feature of the economies we model.

The U-shape curve pattern in Figure 7.4 illustrates how our framework generalizes the insights of gravity theory. First, notice that the relation between distance from the center and trade with it is positive, not negative as in the usual version of the theory. However, the notion that high-population centers trade with each other still holds. This case shows a situation in which there are various centers of gravity: the industrial center and two peripheral agricultural centers. The agricultural centers do not trade with each other (since they specialize in the same product) but each trades with the industrial center.

The pattern of trade is a consequence of specialization patterns and the population associated with the regions. In cases in which population concentrates far from the center, trade will increase with distance. The point is not taken to imply that by itself higher transportation costs tend to be beneficial to trade. But any detrimental role of transportation costs in trade can be offset by other factors, such as environmental pollution, which disperse production in favor of decentralized production centers. In the case of peripheral agricultural centers, represented by $D < 0$ in our model, distance relates positively with trade with the industrial center.

The analysis incorporates the detrimental effects of transportation costs but also alerts us to not focus exclusively on transportation costs or to associate distance with less trade. In fact, historically, distant regions trade substantially among themselves. The opposite forces for the centralization and decentralization of production must be taken into account to explain production and dispersion of production centers, and the associated trade patterns.

The theory of trade presented here differs in important respects from traditional theories that stress factor endowments and increasing returns. Factor endowment theories stress that countries differ in their endowments of labor and land. We have allowed regional labor endowments to be fully endogenous. Increasing returns models focus on trade between regions each of which is specialized in a particular product. These models, however, fail to explain why it is that all production activities fail to concentrate in the same location. In our model each country or region specializes endogenously instead of concentrating production in a single region.

What distinguishes the theory formulated here from alternative theories is that this paper has developed a theory of trade that is geographic in nature. Essentially, trade occurs as a result of the endogenous geographical dispersion of factors of production and population. A general theory of trade must explain the forces determining the geographical patterns of dispersion.

The theory of trade put forth in this paper is based on two factors that motivate dispersion in the presence of a factor — land — that is necessary to the production process. First, diminishing marginal product of labor at *a* given plot of land leads to production dispersion across the whole space, and hence, of trade. Second, city congestion, modeled here in terms of pollution, leads to population dispersion in space. Thus, regional labor endowments are endogenous here.

What makes one region different from another is its location in space. The spatial relation between a point in space and other regions is determined by the location, which cannot be changed since it is a fixed factor. For instance, how far a location is from the industrial center turns out to be crucial in the model. Increasing returns is crucial in generating industrial concentration but is not the determinant of trade patterns here. What determines trade patterns is the interaction between activities that show increasing returns, which creates forces for concentration in space and for others that are decentralized or naturally dispersed.

Some activities benefit from decentralization because of the decreasing returns to concentration. Agriculture is one such activity and is exploited in our model. However, other activities can also be mentioned. For instance, recent improvements in communications have promoted the dispersion of a myriad of service activities that used to be located near a center. Sports training and health-related activities benefit from distance or by being separated from industrial pollution. As a consequence of these factors, a number of gravity centers emerge endogenously in the economy and their interactions are what determine the trade patterns.

7.7 Patterns of Spatial Resource Allocation in Manufacturing and Agriculture

We are now ready to determine manufacturing employment, denoted by L^M. It is important to note, however, that the demand for manufacturing goods depends on the demand generated by agricultural workers, which in turn, depends on the size of the agricultural labor force, denoted as L^A. To determine L^M, we solve for L^A and then compute L^M from the full employment condition $L^M = \bar{L} - L^A$.

Total sales of a firm located at x_c are jth sum of total sales to manufacturing workers at x_c, plus the integral sum of sales to agricultural workers over the interval [0,1]. In order to obtain manufacturing employment for the good in question, the labor input requirement condition for N firms, which in equilibrium yields $L^M = N(\alpha + \beta q)$, ($\alpha$ and β positive) is used, where q represents total quantity sold by a single firm. Then, L^M is eliminated from the full employment condition $L^M = \bar{L} - L^A$ to obtain $q = (\bar{L} - L^A)/\beta N - \alpha/\beta$, which must equal the demand as determined above:

$$q = \frac{1}{\beta}\frac{(\bar{L} - L^A)}{N} - \frac{\alpha}{\beta} = \left(\frac{\mu_M}{\mu_M + \mu_A}\right)\frac{P_{x_c}^{1-\sigma}}{\sum_{i=1}^{N} P_{x_c}^{1-\sigma}}\frac{\sigma - 1}{\sigma\beta}$$

$$\times \left[\bar{L} - L^A + \left(\frac{w_{x_c}}{P^A}\right)^{-1/\rho}\int_0^1 e^{\left[D\left(1-\frac{1}{\rho}\right)\right]\|x - x_c\|}dx\right]. \quad (12)$$

This is the sum of our previous total sales expressions after collecting common terms. In symmetric equilibrium, the above corresponds to:

$$q = \frac{1}{\beta}\frac{(\bar{L} - L^A)}{N} - \frac{\alpha}{\beta} = \left(\frac{\mu_M}{\mu_M + \mu_A}\right)\frac{(\sigma - 1)}{\sigma\beta}\frac{(\bar{L} - L^A)}{N}$$

$$+ \left(\frac{w_{x_c}}{P^A}\right)^{-1/\rho}\left(\frac{\mu_M}{\mu_M + \mu_A}\right)\frac{(\sigma - 1)}{N\sigma\beta}\int_0^1 e^{\left[D\left(1-\frac{1}{\rho}\right)\right]\|x - x_c\|}dx.$$

$$(13)$$

Since all manufacturing goods enter symmetrically in demand, have the same cost function, and are produced at the same location, the previous equation applies equally to all of them.

Substituting the previous equation into the full employment condition, we can obtain a closed form solution for L^M:

$$L^M = \frac{\bar{L}\frac{\psi}{\Lambda} + \frac{N\alpha\sigma(\mu_M+\mu_A)}{\mu_M(\sigma-1)}}{\frac{\sigma(\mu_M+\mu_A)}{(\sigma-1)\mu_M} - 1 + \frac{\psi}{\Lambda}}, \tag{14}$$

where,

$$\psi(D,\rho,\tau) = \int_0^1 e^{[D(1-\frac{1}{\rho})-\tau]\|x-x_c\|}dx, \tag{15}$$

and,

$$\Lambda(D,\rho) = \int_0^1 e^{-\frac{D}{\rho}\|x-x_c\|}dx, \tag{16}$$

and where ψ/Λ corresponds to the average per capita sales ratio between the countryside and the industrial center.

Imposing full employment $L^M+L^A = \bar{L}$ and a zero profit industry equilibrium, we obtain the solution for the number of manufacturing goods N:

$$N = \frac{\frac{\bar{L}}{\alpha\sigma}\frac{\psi}{\Lambda}}{\frac{(\mu_M+\mu_A)}{\mu_M} - 1 + \frac{\psi}{\Lambda}}, \tag{17}$$

with $\psi(D, r, \rho)$ and $\Lambda(D, \rho)$ as defined in the expression for L^A above.

7.8 Technological Change, Transportation Efficiency and Externalities

Recent work on growth has stressed the wisdom of looking beyond the numbers at the national level toward the need to examine specific industries (Harberger (1993), Young (1993a, 1993b)). Aggregate data frequently hides industrial developments that constitute the sources of technological change. As Harberger (1993) observes concerning total factor productivity (TFP) growth:

> TFP growth tends to be highly concentrated, to pop up in the most unlikely places, and then to move to other arenas. If we think of successive great technical advances — in automobile making, in rubber tires, in refrigerators, in television sets, in plastics, in petrochemicals

generally, in telecommunications and most recently, of course, in the computing 'industry' — we see advances concentrated in relatively short time spans (like decades) for each industry group, and advances concentrated in specific industry groups in any particular decade.

There are three basic sources of technological change in our highly aggregated model. These are; innovation in manufacturing, improvement in agricultural technology, and reductions in transportation costs. The feedback from transportation efficiency to industrial variety shows how innovation can move from one industry to another. An examination of these three sources also suggests a series of caveats concerning the interpretation of data on technological change and industrial growth.

7.8.1 Searching for the Source of Technological Change

Manufacturing innovation is represented as a process of technological change in the form of a reduction in the marginal labor requirement β and as an increase in the number of manufacturing products N. The reduction in the marginal labor requirement β does not affect the resource allocation, L^M, L^A, or agricultural labor at any location. Since manufacturing efficiency increases, manufacturing output goes up and utility levels increase for all workers. In equilibrium, manufacturing output per man hour increases and agricultural output per man hour remains constant.

One way to expand the range of industrial products is through a reduction in the fixed cost coefficient α. Equation (17) shows that the consequence of a reduction in the fixed cost in manufacturing is to increase the range of available industrial goods. In this case, manufacturing employment expands and agricultural employment falls. Output per manhour increases in both sectors, as do real wages. Also, the utilities of both the urban and rural population are enhanced.

In the previous exercises, the output per manhour effects vary according to the source of the technological improvement. In the first example, there is no reallocation of resources. In the second example, there is an enhanced productivity in both sectors. It would be difficult to identify the source of the technological change either by looking at the sectoral productivity change or by examining which sector expands the most.

These considerations have a bearing on recent controversies concerning the relation between structural and technological change in Korea and other so-called Asian Tigers (Alwyn Young (1993a, 1993b)). The previous results are, of course, a consequence of the model's specifications. They should, however, alert us of the difficulty in identifying sources of technological change on the basis of market data that reflects an economy's equilibrium response. Similar caveats follow from a consideration of the effects of technological change originating in agriculture (for further discussion see Asilis and Rivera-Batiz (1993b, c)).

7.8.2   *The Feedback from Transportation to Industrial Technologies*

Improvements in transportation efficiency emerge as a force in innovation that is not always realized. Figure 7.6 shows the relation between transport costs, and the number N of manufacturing goods. A reduction in transportation costs exerts a secondary technological improvement in manufacturing through increased demand for manufacturing products. Because the gains from creating new goods are related to their market size, lower transportation costs will lead to innovation in the form of more manufacturing goods in equilibrium.

This effect helps to explain how innovation feeds upon itself and how historical declines in transport costs have led to a second round of related innovation. But it would be difficult to infer sources of technological effects from the data on wages or on equilibrium resource allocations.

Interestingly, the resource allocation effects of the reduction in transportation costs entail two opposite effects. Ceteris paribus, the increase in the number of manufacturing goods means that manufacturing grows at the expense of agriculture. But, recall that the transportation cost reduction itself leads to an increase in the size of the agricultural sector. Hence, the transportation cost driven innovation does not unambiguously alter the sectoral allocation of resources.

There is a feedback between reductions in transportation costs and industrial variety. Specifically, when transportation costs decrease the number of industrial products goes up and so do manufacturing employment and concentration around the industrial center. However, for the case in which pollution is increasing in the number of industrial polluters, there is a negative externality on consumers. In general, the benefits from greater industrial variety must be balanced against the negative consumption externalities created thereby. Notice that the pollution externality is partly internalized by firms through the higher wages they must pay to workers residing in the industrial center. Interestingly, increases in industrial variety lower the degree of internalization of the externality. To see this, consider the case of a symmetric two-firm industry. The marginal production of pollution affects each firm through the higher wages it must pay to its manufacturing workers. As industry size increases the impact of an increase in pollution on a firm's wages becomes smaller (see Asilis and Rivera-Batiz (1993a)).

7.9   Industrial Policy and Theory of Central Location

The model above analyzed the interregional equilibrium in an economy that produces manufacturing and agricultural goods. The model has two special traits which will be considered in this section. The first concerns the central location x_c, which was given at the outset and held constant throughout the analysis. The second is the pollution diseconomy that was not a function either of the number of plants in the city or of the levels of production realized by those plants. Therefore, this section will analyze the determinants of the central location and the case in which the number of plants in the city positively affects the health factor associated with being located away from the industrial center.

Residential location assigns an increasing utility value to the declining impact of pollution as work-living locations move farther and farther away from the industrial center. This utility value is an increasing function of the number of firms N producing manufacturing goods in the industrial center. The residential health factor can be formalized in terms of a location utility factor of the form:

$$R_x = R_{x_c} e^{\gamma N \ln(1+|x-x_c|)}, \tag{18}$$

where γ represents the positive health parameter associated with less incidence of pollution toward the countryside.

A greater value of the factor γN represents a superior quality of the environment stemming from a lower incidence of pollution in the countryside. The health factor $\gamma N \ln(1 + |x - x_c|)$ also embodies the condition that housing services are superior the farther away one is from the polluting source (the industrial center x_c). The solution of the model in the case where health is a function of the number of firms in the industrial center is detailed in Asilis and Rivera-Batiz (1993a).

We find that there are multiple single-city equilibria in the determination of location. The reason for this is that increasing returns tend to pull firms to wherever other firms are located and generates a band of potential equilibria. We also find that a single-city equilibrium cannot be sustained under certain parameter values. In this instance, even in the presence of increasing returns two-city equilibria emerge endogenously.

The possibility of multiple single-city equilibria raises the issue of whether there is a role for industrial policy. We examine the utility level associated with each single-city equilibrium. This utility level is unique among the population because all individuals have the same preferences and there is perfect labor mobility which, as explained before, equalizes full real wages.

The utility map associated with an alternative location for the city center, for the case of positive compensating differential $D > 0$ (this is the arguably more realistic case; for a discussion of optimal industrial policy for the case of negative compensating differential $D < 0$ see Asilis and Rivera-Batiz (1993c)), is given by Figure 7.5. In this model, there is a unique location that maximizes the utility

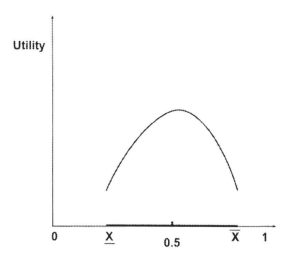

Figure 7.5. Pareto Optimality of Central Location in a $(\underline{x}, \bar{x})$, Single-City Equilibrium Space; D > 0.

level of the representative individual. The striking result is that the optimum location is the central location $x_c = 0.5$, that is, the central location maximizes welfare. This result confirms, in a very different model that explicitly considers environmental externalities, the results obtained by Quinzii and Thisse in their paper on "The Optimality of Central Places". In this paper the central location theory was based on minimization of transportation costs where transportation costs play a role but so does environmental pollution. The optimal polluting focus, if we are allowed to speak in those terms, is also at the center. The reason for this result is that the distortions caused by a non-central polluting center to economic allocation reduce the agents' utility.

The previous considerations suggest that a natural role for industrial policy emerges in terms of choosing the city center. However, the opportunity to exercise that choice is limited. After a city center has been established, the costs of moving the center might be too high. The analysis suggests that city and regional planners should be quite careful in the choice of the regional infrastructure spending. Once a city center is established the incentives are drastically changed and the first best optimum might be unattainable.

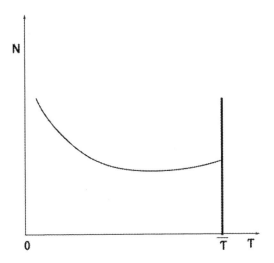

Figure 7.6.   Industrial Variety and Transportation Costs: Low ρ.

The inclusion of environmental costs that are positively associated to the number of plants in the city introduces a number of changes in the analysis of the relation between transportation costs and the creation of technology. Figure 7.6 shows that the relation between these values ceases to be monotone after environmental externalities are incorporated. At high levels of industrial transportation cost, a reduction in these costs will lead to a reduction in the number of industrial goods produced in the economy. This occurs mainly as a result of the interplay between two forces when the marginal productivity parameter in agriculture is high (low ρ). Specifically, increases in transportation costs lead to greater concentration of population around the industrial center, which increases demand for the manufacturing goods; however, increases in transportation costs also tend to reduce the quantity demanded of such goods. When the marginal productivity parameter in agriculture is high, the productivity effects of greater concentration are small enough so that the effect of increased demand for manufacturing goods dominates the negative transportation effect on demand.

7.10   Concluding Remarks

This paper has presented a fully-specified model of an interregional equilibrium allocation of resources. As a by-product of the analysis, a geographic theory of trade and trade patterns emerges. The theory turns out to be a generalization of the so-called "gravity theory" of trade patterns that has been widely applied by trade practitioners.

A number of extensions can be accomplished with the previous framework. First, the role of growth needs to be incorporated in the analysis. Second, a characterization of the multiple-city case would be of interest in understanding the factors in favor of or against integrationist policies between trading partners and trading blocs (Asilis and Rivera-Batiz (1993b) formulate the multiple city case and provide an algorithm to be used in its computation).

At least since the classic writings of Hecksher and Ohlin, economists have dealt with models of national trade and exchange. The straitjacket of national borders and of immobile factors have been the bread and butter of trade theories. As the linkages between countries and regions strengthen and the world globalizes, the traditional paradigms will have to be modified to accommodate the new realities. In this context, the usefulness of thinking in regional terms cannot be overemphasized. The economics of location and distance are not everything in today's global setting, but it might be useful to examine the perspectives offered by well-defined general equilibrium models of interregional market behavior.

References

Armington, Paul S., "A Theory of Demand for Products Distinguished by Place of Production," *Staff Papers*, 16(1) March (1969): 1–24.

―――, "The Geographic Pattern of Trade and the Effects of Price Changes," *Staff Papers*, Vol. 16(2) July (1969): 179–199.

Asilis, Carlos M. and Luis A. Rivera-Batiz, "A General Interregional Equilibrium Model," International Monetary Fund and University of Florida, Gainesville, (1993a).

―――, "A Spatial General Equilibrium Model with Environmental Externalities," mimeo, International Monetary Fund and University of Florida, Gainesville, (1993b).

————, "Growth and Geography," mimeo, International Monetary Fund and University of Florida, (1993c).

Barro, Robert J. and Xavier Sala-i-Martin, "Convergence Across States and Regions," *Brookings Papers on Economic Activity*, (1991): pp. 107–158.

————, "Convergence," *Journal of Political Economy*, 100 (1992a): 223–251.

————, "Regional Growth and Migration: A Japan-U.S. Comparison," National Bureau of Economic Research, Working Paper No. 4038, March, (1992b).

Frankel, Jeffrey, "Is Japan Creating a Trade Block in East Asia and the Pacific," in *Regionalism and Rivalry: Japan and the U.S. in Pacific Asia*, edited by Jeffrey Frankel and Miles Kahler (University of Chicago Press, Chicago, (1993a)).

Frankel, Jeffrey and Shang-Jin Wei, "Trade Blocks and Currency Blocks," CEPR conference on 'The Monetary Future of Europe, La Coruna, Spain.

————, "Is There a Currency Block in the Pacific," Conference on 'Exchange Rates, International Trade and Monetary Policy,' Federal Reserve Bank of Australia, (1993), July.

————, "Yen Block or Dollar Block: Exchange Rate Policies of the East Asian Economies" in Takatoshi Ito and Anne Krueger, editors, *Macroeconomic Linkage: Savings, Exchange Rates, and Capital Flows*, (Chicago: University of Chicago Press, 1992).

Frankel, Jeffrey, Ernesto Stein and Shang-jin Wei, "Trading Blocs: The Natural, the Unnatural, and the Super-Natural," *Journal of Development Economics*, 47 (1995): 61–95.

Fujita, Masahisa, "Monopolistic Competition and Urban Systems," *European Economic Review*, 37 (1988): 308–315.

————, "A Monopolistic Competition of Spatial Agglomeration: Differentiated Products Approach," *Regional Science and Urban Economics*, 18 (1993): 87–124.

Garcia-Milà, Teresa, and Therese J. McGuire, "The Contributions of Publicly Provided Inputs to States' Economies," *Regional Science and Urban Economics,* 22 June (1992): 229–241.

Garcia-Milà, Teresa, Therese J. McGuire and Robert H. Porter, "The Effect of Public Capital in State-level Production Functions Reconsidered," Universitat Pompeu Fabra, Economics Working Paper No. 36, (1993).

Gupta, Sanjeev, Kenneth Miranda, and Ian Parry, "Public Expenditures Policy and the Environment: A Review and Synthesis," IMF Working Paper 93/27, (Washington D.C.: International Monetary Fund, 1993).

Hanson, Gordon, Industry Agglomeration and Trade in Mexico, MIT Ph.D. thesis, (1992).

Harberger, Arnold, "Reflections of the Growth Process," mimeo, University of California, Los Angeles, (1993).

Henderson, J.V., "The Sizes and Types of Cities," *American Economic Review*, 64 (1974): 640–656.

————, *Urban Development: Theory, Fact and Illusion* (New York: Oxford University Press, 1988).

Krugman, Paul R., *Geography and Trade*, (Cambridge: MIT Press, 1991a).

———, "Increasing Returns and Economic Geography," *Journal of Political Economy*, June (1991b): pp. 483–499.

———, "First Nature, Second Nature, and Metropolitan Location," *Journal of Regional Science*, 33(2) (May 1993): 129–144.

———, "On the Number and Location of Cities," *European Economic Review*, 37 (1992b): 293–298.

———, "A Dynamic Spatial Model," National Bureau of Economic Research Working Paper No. 4219, (1992c).

———, "The hub effect, or, threeness in international trade," in *Trade and Policy* edited by Wilfred Ethier, Elhanan Helpman, and J. Peter Neary (Cambridge: Cambridge University Press, 1993).

Krugman, Paul and Raul Livas Elizondo, "Trade Policy and the Third World Metropolis," National Bureau of Economic Research Working Paper No. 4238, (1992).

Muzondo, Timothy R., "Mineral Taxation, Market Failure and the Environment," *Staff Papers*, 40(1) (March 1993): 152–177.

———, "Alternative Forms of Mineral Taxation, Market Failure and the Environment," IMF Working Paper No. 92/149 (Washington D.C.: International Monetary Fund, 1992).

Muzondo, Timothy R., Kenneth M. Miranda, and A. Lans Bovenberg, "Public Policy and the Environment: A Survey of the Literature," IMF Working Paper No. 90/56 (Washington D.C.: International Monetary Fund, 1990).

Quinzii, Martine, and Jacques-François Thisse, "On the Optimality of Central Places," *Econometrica*, 58 (5) (September 1990): 1101–1119.

Rauch, James, "Comparative Advantage, Geographic Advantage, and the Volume of Trade," National Bureau of Economic Research Working Paper No. 3512, (1991).

Rivera-Batiz, Francisco L., "Increasing Returns, Monopolistic Competition, and Agglomeration Economies in Consumption and Production," *Regional Science and Urban Economics*, (1988a).

———, "Modeling Urban Agglomeration: Producer Services, Linkage Externalities, and Specialization Economies," in William G. Vogt and Marvin H. Mickle, editors, *Modeling and Simulation*, (Instrument Society of America, North Carolina, 1988b).

Rivera-Batiz, Luis A., and Paul M. Romer, "Economic Integration and Endogenous Growth," *Quarterly Journal of Economics*, 106(2) May (1991b): 531–555.

Romer, Paul M., "Endogenous Technological Change," *Journal of Political Economy*, 98 October (1990): S71–S102.

———, "Two Strategies for Economic Development: Using Ideas, and Producing Ideas," in Proceedings of the World Bank Annual Conference on Development Economics 1992, (Washington D.C.: World Bank, 1993), pp. 63–91.

Taylor, Carol A., "Spatial Utility Equilibrium and City Size Distribution in a Central Place System," *Journal of Urban Economics*, 19 (1986): 1–22.

Thisse, Jacques-François, "Oligopoly and the Polarization of Space," *European Economic Review*, Vol. 37 (1993): pp. 299–307.

Young, Alwyn, "The Tyranny of Numbers: Confronting the Statistical Realities of the East Asian Growth Experience," mimeo, MIT (1993a).

――――, "Tales of Two Cities," *National Bureau of Economic Research Macroeconomics Manual*, (1993b).

Part 3
Public Sector Governance, Capital Flows and Economic Growth

Chapter 8

Democracy, Governance, and Economic Growth: Theory and Evidence[*]

8.1 Introduction

Is democracy associated with greater economic growth? Do increased political and civil rights lead to improved standards of living, compared with more authoritarian regimes? The debate on this issue has raged for centuries and it is often linked to the legitimacy of democracy as a political regime.

The existing evidence on the links between democracy and economic growth does not provide a clear-cut support of the idea that increased democracy causes growth. Some early studies, such as those by Kormendi and Meguire (1985) and Scully (1988), found statistically significant effects of measures of political freedom on growth. However, more recent studies have provided ambiguous results (see Helliwell, 1994; Przeworski and Limongi, 1993; and the survey by Brunetti, 1997). For instance, Barro (1996) concludes that the established links between democracy and growth are a result of the connections between democracy and other determinants of

[*]This chapter was authored by Francisco L. Rivera-Batiz and was originally published in *Review of Development Economics*, Vol. 6, No. 2 (June 2002), pp. 225–247. ©2002 Blackwell Publishers Ltd.

The author is grateful to two anonymous referees for useful comments.

growth, such as human capital. Similarly, Rodrik (1997) concludes that, after controlling for other variables, "there does not seem to be a strong, determinate relationship between democracy and growth."

This paper provides a theoretical and empirical analysis of how democracy affects long-run growth by influencing the quality of governance in a country. Section 8.2 examines the connections between quality of governance and democracy, providing empirical evidence of the strong linkage between these two variables. Section 8.3 then presents a general-equilibrium, endogenous growth model showing how a governance improving democracy can raise growth. In this model, the quality of a country's governance institutions makes domestic innovative activity more profitable, inducing greater technological change and growth. If democracy is associated with improved governance, then it will also lead to accelerated innovation and growth.

The impact of democracy on growth is examined under various assumptions regarding capital mobility. Section 8.4 presents an empirical model constructed to determine the connections between democracy, governance, and growth in a cross-section of countries between 1960 and 1990. This analysis shows that democracy is a statistically significant factor affecting total factor productivity and growth in GDP per capita between 1960 and 1990, but that the relationship is mediated by the quality of governance. Democracy influences growth mainly through its strong positive effects on the quality of governance. But once a measure of the quality of governance in a country is introduced into the growth regression equations, democracy ceases to be a statistically significant influence on growth. Section 8.5 summarizes the paper's results.

8.2   The Linkages between Democracy and Governance

The existing literature has developed various arguments that link democracy to both greater and lower quality of governance. First of all, by definition, democracies allow populations to peacefully and regularly oust inept, inefficient, and corrupt government administrations, while allowing people to keep more efficient, successful regimes, thus tending to make the quality of governance on average higher in the long run. Authoritarian regimes may randomly provide high-quality governance, but if they do not, they can be changed only by force, which may take years or decades longer than under democratic institutions. As Sen (2000, p. 152) succinctly summarizes: "[in considering the effects of democracy relative to authoritarian regimes] we have to consider the political incentives that operate on governments and on the persons and groups that are in office. The rulers have the incentive to listen to what people want if they have to face their criticism and seek their support in elections."

The potentially high cost of sustaining poor government policies under authoritarian regimes have been noted forcefully by Goetzmann (1999) in relation to recent financial crises:

> Suppose bankers lend to a dictatorship, as Indonesia was... suppose further that debt piles up, and the government of the borrowing country cannot service its obligations... This is in fact what has happened. Tens of millions of people in emerging markets have recently fallen back into poverty. Without a democratic voice, they had no control of the risks their governments assumed. Even more outrageous, without transparent political institutions and a free press they had no way to understand these risks... Some would call this taxation without representation. In fact, history is filled with examples of non-democratic governments causing great harm to their citizens.

On the other side of the coin, a number of authors have noted that the proliferation of interest groups lobbying for power or for rents under democratic institutions may lead to policy gridlock, preventing the major decisions that are required in the development process. The most popular of those voicing this view is the former prime minister of Singapore, Lee Kuan Yew, who has argued that Singaporean growth — one of the most remarkable over the last 30 years — would not have occurred without the stringent restrictions on political and civil rights under his regime. Some have also contrasted the successful experience of China in undertaking market reforms, contrasting it to the disorganized and distorted reforms in more democratic regimes, such as Russia.

A connected issue is the great variability that electoral democracies display in effectively promoting grassroots, participatory decision-making. The fact that electoral votes can be purchased may allow wealthy individuals or parties to control the electoral process in much the same way that an openly authoritarian regime would. As Piero Gleijeses observes of the situation in Latin America: "The box on the outside is labeled a democracy, but inside you have an authoritarian system."[1]

It can be concluded that the introduction of democratic institutions in the form of more ample political rights, civil rights, and freedom of the press, among others, may or may not be associated with improved governance. The real question, then, is the relative strength of the forces just discussed in the real world. Are the various cases of "enlightened dictatorship" the rule or the exception in the recent past? Do most democracies allow their population to choose more effective policymakers or are they generally window-dressing, used as a tool by specific classes and oligarchies to control political power and sustain ineffective, corrupt regimes? Let us look at the empirical evidence on this issue.

This section presents the results of a simple empirical exercise examining the connections between democracy and the quality of governance in a cross-section of countries. To measure the quality of governance, we utilize an index constructed by Hall and Jones (1999) that evaluates countries on the basis of the "institutions and government policies that determine the economic environment within which individuals accumulate skills, and firms accumulate capital and produce output."[2] Countries with a high value of this index get "the prices right so that ... individuals capture the social returns to their actions as private returns."[3]

The index of quality of governance is itself the average of two indexes. Included first is an index of the quality of government institutions based on data assembled by Political Risk Services, a firm that specializes in providing assessments of risk to international investors. The quality of government institutions is based on a comprehensive evaluation of each country's government institutions regarding: (1) law and order, (2) bureaucratic quality,

(3) corruption, (4) risk of expropriation, and (5) government repudiation of contracts. On the basis of this assessment, an index is constructed that ranges from 0 to 1, with larger values connected to higher quality of government institutions.

The second element composing the index of quality of governance is the extent to which the country is open to international trade. The idea here is that protectionist governments are more likely to engage in policies that distort prices and undermine the ability of the private sector to produce efficiently and innovate. This may be a direct result of the trade — and other — taxes and restrictions imposed by the policymakers but also the indirect cause of the rent-seeking activities that are almost inevitably associated with protectionist policies. The index of openness used is that constructed by Sachs and Warner (1995), which measures the fraction of years during the period 1950 to 1990 that the economy was open. The index thus ranges from 0 to 1, with a value of one being the most open and zero the least open.

An average of the indexes of the quality of government institutions and openness is used as the measure of quality of governance. This index, which I will refer to as *GOVERN*, ranges from 0 to 1, with larger values indicating higher quality of governance. Note that the index reflects the long-term competency of governance in the country during the period 1950 to 1990. Countries with high values include most industrialized countries — such as Switzerland (1.00), the United States (0.97), and Canada (0.966) — and a number of nations that were low-income countries in the 1950s and 1960s, including Singapore (0.930), Hong Kong (0.896), Barbados (0.869), and Mauritius (0.852). The countries with the lowest quality of governance are Congo/Zaire (0.113), Haiti (0.118), Bangladesh (0.156), Somalia (0.160), Sudan (0.167), and Myanmar (0.184).

To measure the strength of democratic institutions we utilize the Freedom House index of political rights. According to this measure, countries with broader political rights (more democratic institutions) "enable people to participate freely in the political process . . . this means the right of all adults to vote and compete for public office, and for elected representatives to have a decisive vote on public policies."[4] The Freedom House constructs an index of political rights based on a careful analysis of a country's political institutions. Based on this index, the strength of democratic institutions is measured through the variable *DEMOC*, which ranges from 1 to 7, with higher values indicating stronger democratic institutions and lower values reflecting more authoritarian regimes. As an example, the most democratic regimes in 1990 included industrialized countries — Canada, the US, Germany, France, etc. — all of which score at 7.0, as well as a number of developing nations, such as Costa Rica (7.0), Barbados (7.0), Dominican Republic (6.0), Botswana (5.9), Mauritius (5.8), and Gambia (5.6). Among the least democratic countries are Benin (1.0), Central African Republic (1.0), Mali (1.0), Somalia (1.0), and Afghanistan (1.0).

To estimate the links between democracy and governance, a simple linear regression model is first used, with the dependent variable represented by the index of quality of governance and the independent variable being *DEMOC*, which is the average of the values of the democracy index for 1960 and 1990, representing the long-term democratic environment of a country. The sample consists of 115 countries for which data are available. The first column of Table 8.1 presents the ordinary least squares (OLS) coefficients of this simple regression equation. As can be seen, there is a strong positive connection between the strength of democratic institutions and the quality of governance, with the variable *DEMOC* having a positive and statistically significant coefficient. The R-squared (adjusted for degrees of freedom) is 0.51 for this equation, suggesting that the democratic institutions variable alone explains close to half of the variance of the quality of governance among the countries in the sample.[5]

There are, of course, a variety of social and economic forces that explain the quality of governance in a country (La Porta *et al.*, 1999; Kaufmann *et al.*, 2000). It is possible that the correlation of democracy with some of these forces provides a spurious correlation between the indexes of governance and democracy. In order to take this into account, a multivariate analysis was carried out in which was added a set of variables that the literature considers to be related to the quality of governance in a country. According to the analysis of

Table 8.1.   Democracy and Quality of Governance.

Dependent variable: Hall-Jones Index of Quality of Governance
Sample mean = 0.48 (SD = 0.26)

Explanatory variable	Estimated coefficient (se) [t]	Estimated coefficient (se) [t]	Estimated coefficient (se)
Constant	0.1551*	0.2077*	—
	(0.0338)	(0.0650)	
	[4.6]	[3.2]	
DEMOC	0.0856*	0.0561*	3.8
	(0.0078)	(0.0087)	(2.2)
	[11.1]	[6.5]	
TERTIARY	—	0.4505	0.053
		(0.3134)	(0.063)
		[1.4]	
URBAN	—	0.0017	46.2
		(0.0010)	(25.0)
		[1.6]	
POOR90	—	−0.1034**	0.40
		(0.0473)	(0.49)
		[−2.2]	
Observations	115	115	
R−squared	0.51	0.62	

*Coefficient is statistically significant at the 99% confidence level.
**Coefficient is statistically significant at the 95% confidence level.

North (1990), as development occurs and economic activity expands, countries can afford to provide greater resources to the public sector and allow governments to function more efficiently. To include this in the empirical analysis, a dummy variable, *POOR*, was added which is equal to one if the country is poor and zero otherwise. We can expect this variable to be negatively associated with the quality of governance.

A wide dispersion of the population in a country can make transportation and communications difficult, and it can magnify ethnic divisions that can prevent an effective government (Easterly and Levine, 1997). To represent this influence, the variable URBAN is used, which is the percentage of the population residing in an urban area. We can expect that higher values of *URBAN* will be positively related to the quality of governance index.[6] Finally, the availability of an educated workforce can be expected to spill over into a more informed public sector. The variable *TERTIARY*, which is equal to the fraction of the population 25 years of age or older who have enrolled in a tertiary education institution is added. We can anticipate that this variable is positively connected to quality of governance.

The second column of Table 8.1 shows the results of a multivariate regression model where the quality of governance index is the dependent variable. As can be seen, the estimated coefficient on the *DEMOC* variable declines relative to the simple regression reported in the first column, but it retains a strong, statistically significant impact on governance. Of the other estimated coefficients reported in Table 8.1, only *POOR* is statistically significant, at a 95% confidence level. All coefficients have the expected signs and the value of R-squared rises to 0.62.

The results in Table 8.1 confirm that stronger democratic institutions are closely associated with greater quality of governance. Assuming that there is such a connection, what is the implication about the relationship of democracy to economic growth? The next section presents an endogenous growth model that examines the theoretical links between democracy, governance, and growth. A later section examines the issue empirically.

8.3   A Model of Democracy, Governance, and Endogenous Growth

The evidence presented in the last section shows how democracy is positively connected to the quality of governance, one key aspect of which is corruption. As the World Bank (1997) observes: "in democracies, citizens can vote officials out of office if they believe them to be corrupt. This gives politicians an incentive to stay honest and work for the interests of their constituents."[7] More democratic institutions can also facilitate the activities of the press, which can monitor corruption and disseminate information on corrupt government officials to the public so that they can be held accountable. This section constructs a theoretical model that captures how democracy affects economic growth through its impact on corruption.[8]

8.3.1   *The Equilibrium Level of Corruption*

Corrupt officials are assumed to impose a tax on the profits made by firms and entrepreneurs engaged in the innovation, design, and production of new goods in the economy. Each new good invented must be licensed by the government in order to be produced. Government officials ask license applicants for bribes in order to grant their approval. These officials are assumed to receive civil service income that is negligible compared to the bribes. The corrupt bureaucrats are thus residents of the country who do not produce at all but survive through the imposition of bribes on the producers of new goods.

The officials maximize their expected income by setting a bribery tax rate, t, on the profits made by producers of new goods in the country, π. They set this rate taking into account the impact of the bribery on profits and on the probability, θ, that the bribery scheme is revealed to the public and dismantled. Producer profits are assumed to decline with the tax rate ($\partial \pi / \partial t > 0$). The probability that the corrupt activities will be revealed and dismantled is assumed to depend on the bribery tax rate as well as on the strength of the democratic institutions in the country. The higher the bribery tax rate, the more likely that those being taxed will find it in their interest to obtain the political capital to eradicate corruption ($\partial \theta / \partial t > 0$). The more democratic the country, the higher the probability that corrupt activities will be revealed and dismantled: symbolically: $\partial \theta / \partial D > 0$, where D is an index of democracy, with higher values of D linked to stronger democratic institutions.

Under the assumptions, corrupt officials will seek to maximize their expected gain from bribes, G, which is equal to

$$G = [1 - \theta(t, D)]t\pi(t), \qquad (1)$$

with all symbols as defined before.[9] The first-order condition for the maximization of G is:

$$t^* = \frac{(1-\theta)(1-\varepsilon)}{\theta'}, \tag{2}$$

where $\varepsilon = -(t/\pi)(\partial\pi/\partial t) > 0$ is the elasticity of producers' profits with respect to the bribery tax rate, assumed to be less than one, and $\theta' = \partial\theta/\partial t > 0$ is the partial derivative of the probability that the bribery system will be dismantled with respect to the bribery rate.

Equation (2) suggests that, ceteris paribus, the bribery tax rate maximizing the officials' economic welfare decreases in response to stronger democratic institutions $(\partial t^*/\partial D < 0)$. As political rights and freedom of the press rise, the likelihood that corrupt officials will be discovered and their bribery schemes dismantled increases, which forces them to lower bribe rates so as to become less visible. Note that the level of corruption increases (t^* goes up) when the producers' profit function is relatively more inelastic with respect to the bribery rate (lower values of ε) and when increased tax rates cause a smaller impact on the probability that the corrupt regime will be dismantled (lower values of θ').

8.3.2   *Democracy, Corruption, and Growth*

The model of democracy and corruption presented in the last subsection is now embedded in an endogenous growth model, to show the linkages between democracy and growth.[10] We consider a small open economy trading in goods and services with the rest of the world. The country produces two final goods, X and Y, that are traded in world markets and whose prices are determined by global market conditions (P_x and P_y are exogenously given). No international capital mobility exists initially, but international trade in assets is introduced later.

Sector X is a human-capital intensive sector whose production function is of the Cobb–Douglas type, given by

$$X = I_x^\beta H_x^{1-\beta}, \tag{3}$$

where X is the output of good X, H_x is the amount of human capital used in production, β is a positive fraction, and I_x is a subproduction function given by

$$I_x = \left(\sum_{i=1}^{n} Z_{ix}^{\alpha} \right)^{1/\alpha}, \tag{4}$$

with $0 < \alpha < 1$, and Z_{ix} representing the use of physical capital good i in sector X, where there are n differentiated capital goods used in production at any given time, with the input of each represented by Z_{ix}.

Each capital good enters symmetrically into the sub-production function in (4). On the assumption that all the Z_{ix} are identical, then

$$I_x = n^{(1-\alpha)/\alpha} Z_x, \tag{5}$$

where $Z_x = n Z_{ix}$ is the total quantity demanded of capital goods by sector X.

Substitution of (5) into (3) yields

$$X = n^{\gamma} Z_x^{\beta} H_x^{1-\beta}, \tag{6}$$

where $\gamma = \beta(1 - \alpha)/\alpha$. This shows that the output of good X is a function of the total quantities of physical and human capital employed in the sector, Z_x and H_x, respectively, as well as of the number of differentiated capital goods used, n. The production function in equation (6) appears as a standard Cobb–Douglas production function with a shift parameter $A = n^{\gamma}$ that depends on the number of capital goods. Since the number of capital goods is a variable determined as part of the model, this makes total factor productivity growth endogenous, a staple of endogenous growth models (Romer, 1990).

Production of good Y is intensive in the use of unskilled labor and its production function is given by

$$Y = I_y^{\beta} L_y^{1-\beta}, \tag{7}$$

where Y is the output of good Y, L_y is the input of unskilled labor, β is a parameter defined above, and I_y is a subproduction function given by

$$I_y = \left(\sum_{i=1}^{n} Z_{iy}^{\alpha} \right)^{1/\alpha}, \tag{8}$$

where α is as defined earlier, and Z_{iy} represents the use of physical capital good i in sector Y. One can combine (7) and (8) into

$$Y = n^{\gamma} Z_y^{\beta} L_y^{1-\beta}, \tag{9}$$

where $Z_y = n Z_{iy}$ is the total demand for capital in sector Y. Equation (9) shows that output of good Y is dependent on the total quantities of unskilled labor and physical capital used plus the number of capital goods, n.

Both final goods, X and Y, are sold in perfectly competitive markets. As a consequence, cost-minimizing firms producing final goods will set price equal to unit costs:

$$P_x = n^{-\gamma} C_x(W_H, P_Z), \tag{10}$$

$$P_y = n^{-\gamma} C_y(W_L, P_Z), \tag{11}$$

with C_x and C_y equal to the unit cost functions in sectors X and Y, respectively, W_H is the wage rate of skilled labor or human capital, W_L is the wage rate of unskilled labor, and P_Z is the price of each capital good. (As is established next, all capital goods will have the same price, as determined from the symmetry of the demand for, and supply of, each capital good.)

The production function for each capital good is given by a constant-returns-to-scale production function:

$$Z_i = H_{zi}^{a} L_{zi}^{1-a} \tag{12}$$

where H_{Zi} is the demand for human capital in the firm producing capital good i, L_{Zi} is the demand for unskilled labor used by each firm, and the exponent "a" is an exogenous parameter between zero and one.

The profit of each producer of capital goods, π_i, is given by total revenue minus total cost (including the cost of both the skilled and unskilled labor):

$$\pi_i = P_z Z_i(1 - t^*) - W_H H_{zi} - W_L L_{zi}$$

$$= P_z(1 - t^*)H_{zi}^a L_{zi}^{1-a} - W_H H_{zi} - W_L L_{zi}, \quad (13)$$

where we have made use of equation (12). Note that the bribery rate, t^*, acts to reduce the firm's revenues, $P_z Z_i$. As examined earlier, corruption constitutes a tax on the producers of new capital goods, that need to have their product blueprints registered and licensed by government officials in order to start production.

Capital goods firms are assumed to maximize profits within a market structure characterized by monopolistic competition. First-order conditions for profit maximization establish the equality of the marginal revenue product of each input to the cost of hiring that input. For the use of human capital:

$$MR_i(\partial Z_i/\partial H_{zi}) = W_H. \quad (14)$$

where MR_i represents the marginal revenue facing each capital goods producer and $\partial Z_i/\partial H_{zi}$ is the marginal physical product of human capital. But marginal revenue is given by $MR_i = P_Z(\varepsilon_i - 1)/\varepsilon_i$, where ε_i is the price elasticity of demand facing each capital goods producer. The latter can be determined from the subproduction functions in equations (4) and (8) to be $\varepsilon_i = 1/(1 - \alpha)$. Furthermore, from the capital goods production function in equation (12): $\partial Z_i/\partial H_{zi} = aZ_i/H_{zi}$. Substitution of these relationships into equation (14) results in

$$a\alpha(1 - t^*)P_Z Z_i = W_H H_{zi}. \quad (15)$$

A similar set of derivations can be carried out for the first-order condition with respect to the use of unskilled labor, resulting in

$$(1 - a)\alpha(1 - t^*)P_Z Z_i = W_L L_{zi}. \quad (16)$$

Equations (15) and (16) can be combined by observing that

$$\alpha(1 - t^*)P_Z = (W_L L_{zi} + W_H H_{zi})/Z_i$$

$$= C_z(W_L, W_H), \quad (17)$$

where C_z is the unit cost of production for each firm in the capital goods sector. Note that corruption acts as a tax on capital goods producers, reducing the effective price, P_Z, that they receive per unit of the good sold. The greater the level of corruption, as represented symbolically by an increase in t^*, the greater the cut of the officials out of P_Z.

We can summarize the structure of the model so far as follows. Given the number of capital goods, n, and the exogenous prices of final goods, P_x and P_y, then equations (10), (11), and (17) constitute a system of three equations in three variables, W_L, W_H, and P_Z. What remains to discuss, then, is the dynamics of the economy, whose engine is the increase in the number of capital goods available for production. I will discuss shortly the equilibrium determinants of n, but the profile of the economy's steady-state equilibrium can be sketched now.

If we denote the steady-state growth rate in the number of capital goods by g, then equations (10), (11), and (17) imply that the wages of skilled and unskilled labor and the prices of capital goods will all rise at the rate γg. Taking time derivatives in equations (10), (11), and (17) yields

$$\gamma \hat{n} = \hat{C}_x = \Theta_{HX} \hat{W}_H + (1 - \Theta_{HX}) \hat{P}_Z, \tag{18}$$

$$\gamma \hat{n} = \hat{C}_y = \Theta_{LY} \hat{W}_L + (1 - \Theta_{LY}) \hat{P}_Z, \tag{19}$$

$$\hat{P}_Z = \hat{C}_Z = \Theta_{LZ} \hat{W}_L + (1 - \Theta_{HX}) \hat{W}_H, \tag{20}$$

where a circumflex denotes growth rate, so that $\hat{n} = \dot{n}/n$, with $\dot{n} = dn/dt$, etc. The Θ are factor shares, so that $\Theta_{HX} = W_H H_x/P_x X$, the share of skilled labor in the value of output in sector X, and so on for other values of Θ. Note that, if the number of capital goods rises at a rate equal to g, then in order for all three equations to be satisfied, the steady state of the economy will imply that W_H, W_L, P_Z will all rise at the rate γg.

In addition, at the steady state, the usage of inputs cannot be shifting across sectors, meaning that the steady-state values of Z_x, Z_y, L_y, L_Z, H_x, and ($H_z = nH_{zi}$) are fixed. But then, from equations (6) and (9), the levels of output X and Y will also grow at the steady-state rate γg. Consequently, the economy's aggregate output growth rate will also equal γg.

8.3.3 *Determinants of Technical Change*

Since the increase in the number of capital goods, n, determines the steadystate growth rate, the key question in the model is how new capital goods are created.

Following the literature,[11] I assume that new capital goods are created by a research or technology sector that uses human capital and has the following production function:

$$dn/dt = \dot{n} = nH_n/a_H, \tag{21}$$

where H_n is the amount of human capital used in the technology sector, and a_H is an exogenous parameter that reflects the productivity of human capital in generating new capital goods, with higher values of a_H representing lower productivity. Equation (21) states that the creation of new capital goods is positively related to the skilled labor used by the technology/research sector. It is also related to the number of capital goods, n. This reflects the fact that, as n rises, the existing ideas available for innovators to generate new products increase, stimulating innovation and, as a result, the number of new capital goods created; for more details, see Romer (1990a).

From equation (21):

$$g = \dot{n}/n = (H_n/a_H). \tag{22}$$

Equation (22) states that the rate of growth of new capital goods depends on the amount of human capital allocated to the research/technology sector and to an exogenous parameter reflecting the productivity of this human capital in producing new capital goods. The next step is to specify the equilibrium value of H_n.

The rate of return on producing a new capital good, r, is equal to the capital gain on the value of the capital good plus the dividend rate:

$$r = \dot{V}/V + \pi_i/V, \tag{23}$$

where V is the value of a new capital good and π_i denotes the profit obtained from the production of a capital good, so that π_i/V is the dividend rate.

The value of a new capital good is equal to the cost of production of the new capital good, which is given by

$$V = (W_H H_n/\dot{n}) = (W_H a_H/n), \tag{24}$$

where we have made use of equation (21). Taking changes in equation (24), one derives that the capital gain — the gain in the value of a new capital good — is given by

$$\dot{V}/V = \dot{W}_H/W_H - \dot{n}/n. \tag{25}$$

Substituting equation (25) into (23) results in

$$r = \dot{W}_H/W_H - \dot{n}/n + \pi/V. \tag{26}$$

But the profits in the production of each capital good are

$$\pi_i = P_Z Z_i - C_Z Z_i = [1 - \alpha(1 - t^*)]P_Z Z_I, \tag{27}$$

where use has been made of equation (17). Using equation (15) to modify equation (27) and then substituting into equation (26) yields

$$r = \dot{W}_H/W_H - \dot{n}/n + [1 - \alpha(1 - t^*)]H_Z/a\alpha(1 - t^*)a_H$$
$$= (\gamma - 1)g + [1 - \alpha(1 - t^*)]H_Z/[a\alpha(1 - t^*)]a_H, \tag{28}$$

where, at the steady state, the wage rate of skilled labor rises at the rate γg and the number of capital goods at the rate g.

Equation (28) determines the rate of return on new capital goods, but it includes the amount of human capital used in the capital goods sector as a variable. To finish solving the model we need to introduce the human capital endowment constraint:

$$H_n + H_x + H_Z = H, \tag{29}$$

where H is the total endowment of human capital available to the economy. Equation (29) can be further simplified by noting that, at the steady state, equation (22) implies that

$$H_n = ga_H. \tag{30}$$

In addition, from (9):

$$H_x = (1 - \beta) P_Z Z_X / \beta W_H; \tag{31}$$

and from (15):

$$a\alpha(1 - t^*) P_Z n(Z_{ix} + Z_{iy}) = W_H n H_{zi}. \tag{32}$$

If we define λ to be the ratio of the use of each capital good in the X and Y sectors at the steady state, then $Z_{iy} = \lambda Z_{ix}$, which can be substituted into equation (32) to obtain

$$P_Z Z_X / W_H = H_z / a\alpha(1 - t^*)(1 + \lambda). \tag{33}$$

Equation (33) can then be substituted into (31) to yield

$$H_x = (1 - \beta) H_Z / \beta a\alpha(1 - t^*)(1 + \lambda). \tag{34}$$

Equations (30) and (34) can be substituted into the human capital endowment constraint to obtain

$$ga_H + bH_Z = H, \tag{35}$$

where $b = [(1 - \beta) + \beta a\alpha(1 - t^*)(1 + \lambda)] / \beta a\alpha(1 - t^*)(1 + \lambda)$.

Equation (35) provides an expression for H_Z that can be substituted into equation (28) so that, with some manipulation, an expression for the steady-state rate of growth of the economy is obtained:

$$g = \{[1 - \alpha(1 - t^*)] / \delta a_H\} H - [ba\alpha(1 - t^*) / \delta] r, \tag{36}$$

where $\delta = 1 - \alpha(1 - t^*) + b(1 - t^*) a\alpha(1 - \gamma)$ is a parameter that is assumed to be positive to ensure a steady-state equilibrium.

Equation (36) establishes a negative connection between the growth rate and the rate of return to capital. It is depicted in Figure 8.1 by means of the downward-sloping curve PP. A higher rate of return to capital will be associated with a flow of human capital into the capital goods sector. This will reduce the human capital available for innovation, thus lowering the economy's growth rate. An increase in the country's endowment of human capital, H, allows both the research/innovation sector and the rest of the economy to expand, resulting in greater technological change and therefore accelerated growth, at any given level of the rate of return, r. The result is a shift of the PP curve to the right.

An increase in the strength of democratic institutions causes the level of corruption in the economy to decline, algebraically represented by a reduction in the bribery tax rate, t^*. Equation (36) clearly shows that a drop in t^* will result in an increase of the growth rate, g, everything else held constant. As a consequence, the PP curve in Figure 8.1 would shift to the right, to P'P'.

The analysis so far has established a connection between the rate of return to capital and growth. An additional relationship between growth and the rate of return to capital must be established to determine the steady-state growth rate. In an economy that does not trade in assets with the rest of the world, domestic consumers

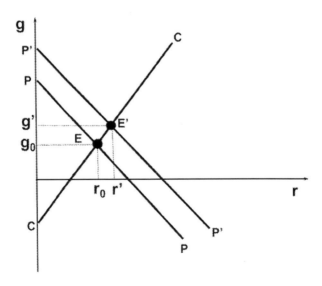

Figure 8.1. The Impact of Increased Democracy on Growth.

determine such a second relationship between the rate of return to capital and growth.

Consumers are assumed to maximize the utility derived from an infinite stream of consumption, discounted to the present time, t:

$$U = \int_t^\infty \exp[-\rho(\tau - t)] \log \ U[C_x(\tau), C_y(\tau)] d\tau, \qquad (37)$$

where ρ is a rate of discount. Equation (37) is maximized subject to a budget constraint:

$$\int_t^\infty \exp[-r(\tau - t)]\{W_H(\tau)H + W_L(\tau)(L_y + L_Z)\} d\tau$$

$$\geq \int_t^\infty \exp[-r(\tau - t)][P_x(\tau)C_x(\tau) + P_y(\tau)C_y(\tau)] d\tau, \qquad (38)$$

where the expression on the left-hand side represents the present discounted value of income and the right-hand side is the present discounted value of aggregate consumption spending. The outcome of this maximization problem is the following condition:

$$r = (\dot{E}/E) + \rho, \qquad (39)$$

where E is aggregate consumption expenditure.

Now, in the economy's steady state, as noted earlier, aggregate consumption expenditure will grow at the rate γg, and therefore:

$$r = \gamma g + \rho. \qquad (40)$$

Equation (40) displays a positive relationship between the rate of interest, r, and the growth rate, g. As the rate of interest increases, the rate of growth of consumption spending also rises, ceteris paribus, and with no external borrowing or lending so does the rate of growth of output. This is depicted by the curve CC in Figure 8.1. Note that an increase in the rate of time preference would reduce the rate of growth at a given interest rate and shift the CC curve to the left. In this case, consumers switch their spending towards the present, reducing the rate of growth of future spending and output.

8.3.4   *Democracy and the Steady-State Growth Rate*

Equations (36) and (40) constitute a system of two equations in two variables, g and r. Solving them produces the steady-state values of the growth rate, g, and the interest rate, r. The steady-state rate of growth of the economy is

$$g = \{[1 - \alpha(1 - t^*)]/\delta a_H\}H - \rho[a\alpha(1 - t^*)b/\delta]. \qquad (41)$$

This shows that the steady-state rate of growth is determined by the economy's endowment of human capital plus a wide array of parameters that include, among others, the rate of time preference, the degree of corruption, and the productivity of human capital in generating inventions.

Diagrammatically, as Figure 8.1 depicts, the steady state of the economy is determined by the intersection of the PP and CC curves at point E. This gives rise to a steady-state growth rate of g_0 and a rate of return to capital equal to r_0. How is democracy related to this steady state? Stronger democratic institutions would act to constrain the level of corruption in the economy. Such a change would reduce the bribery rate t^* and, as equation (41) suggests, it would cause an increase in the steady-state growth rate. Figure 8.1 illustrates the impact of an increase in the strength of democracy by means of the shift of the PP curve to P'P', which raises the steady-state growth from g_0 to g' and the rate of return to capital from r_0 to r'. By reducing the corrosive effects of corruption and thus raising the rewards from creating new capital goods, an increase in political rights stimulates innovation and raises both the rate of return to capital as well as the steady-state growth rate of the economy.

8.3.5   *Opening the Capital Account: Democratic versus Authoritarian Regimes*

So far this analysis has assumed that the economy is closed to international capital flows. What is the impact of an opening to global trade in assets? This is an issue that has created great controversy in recent years, with some authors claiming strong positive growth effects of liberalization (Levine, 2001) and others suggesting instead that there is no such impact (Rodrik, 1998) or even that the effects could be negative (Radelet and Sachs, 1998). The present analysis suggests that the impact of capital account liberalization on growth can be positive or negative, depending on whether the country has more democratic or more authoritarian regimes.

If we assume that the country is a small open economy, then free trade in assets with the rest of the world will cause the domestic rate of return to be determined by the world rate of return, r^*. Using equation (36), the equilibrium growth rate is then

$$g = \{[1 - \alpha(1 - t^*)]/\delta a_H\}H - [ba\alpha(1 - t^*)/\delta]r^*, \qquad (42)$$

where all the variables are as defined earlier. Note that if the equilibrium rate of return to capital before the liberalization lies below r^*, then equation (42) implies that the growth rate will decline after liberalization. The capital account opening causes capital flight, as domestic residents find higher rates of return in the rest of the world. This reduction in domestic investment causes the growth rate to drop. If the domestic rate of return before liberalization is above the world rate of return, on the other hand, there will be an increased growth rate, as the liberalization acts to attract foreign capital.

The stronger the democratic institutions in the country, the more likely that capital account liberalization will produce an expansion of the steady-state growth rate. The reason is that more democratic institutions act to limit corruption, lowering the bribery tax rate and raising the domestic rate of return to capital. As international trade in assets is permitted, democratic governments are more likely to have rates of return to capital that exceed the world rate of return, inducing capital inflows. More authoritarian governments are more likely to face capital flight instead.

Figure 8.2 shows the diametrically opposite effects of capital account liberalization in democratic and authoritarian regimes. The curves PP and CC and their intersection at point E represent the steady state before capital account liberalization in an authoritarian regime. The steady-state growth rate is g_0 and the rate of return to capital is r_0.

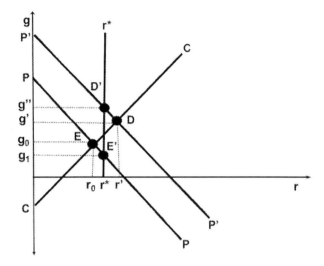

Figure 8.2.   Capital Mobility and the Impact of Democracy on Growth.

In this situation, if the world rate of return to capital is r^*, an opening of the capital account leads to a shift of the steady state from point E to point E'. This is associated with capital flight that causes the growth rate to decline, from g_0 to g_1.

Under more democratic institutions, the steady state is characterized by the curves P'P', CC, and their intersection at point D gives rise to a growth rate equal to g' and a domestic rate of return to capital of r'. Opening the capital account in this situation causes the steady state to move from point D to point D', raising the growth rate from g' to g''.

This section constructed an endogenous growth model showing how more democratic institutions are linked to reduced corruption, improved governance, and increased growth rates. This connection is stronger when countries are open to international capital flows, which magnify the growth impact of democracy.

What is the empirical evidence regarding the links between democracy and growth, particularly through the impact of democracy on the quality of governance, as established in the last section? The next section examines this issue.

8.4   The Empirical Evidence on Democracy and Growth

This section presents the results of cross-country growth regressions identifying the role of democracy on the growth of GDP per worker between 1960 and 1990. The analysis is based on the following aggregate production function for country i:

$$Y_i = A_i K_i^\alpha H_i^{1-\alpha}, \qquad (43)$$

where Y is gross domestic product (GDP), $0 < \alpha < 1$, H is a human capital-augmented measure of the labor force in the economy, K is the capital stock, and A is a parameter that reflects the influence of factors other than capital and labor on production. By definition, A represents total factor productivity (TFP). It is through A that our theoretical analysis in the previous section identified the impact of democracy. This analysis showed how stronger democratic institutions increase the quality of governance and spur technological change, shifting TFP upward.

We follow Hall and Jones (1999) and Krueger and Lindahl (2001) in postulating the following specification for human capital-augmented labor:

$$H_i = L_i exp\phi Ed_i, \qquad (44)$$

where Ed_i is the average number of years of schooling of the labor force, and ϕ represents the productivity of workers with Ed_i years of education relative to those with no schooling.[12]

Dividing equation (43) by the labor force and using (44) yields

$$Y_i/L_i = A_i (K_i/L_i)^\alpha [exp\phi Ed_i]^{1-\alpha}. \qquad (45)$$

Taking logarithms in both sides of the equation, one obtains

$$\log[(Y_i/L_i)^{90}/(Y_i/L_i)^{60}]$$
$$= [\log A_i^{90}/\log A_i^{60}] + \alpha \log[(K_i/L_i)^{90}/(K_i/L_i)^{60}]$$
$$+ (1-\alpha)\phi(Ed_i^{90} - Ed_i^{60}), \qquad (46)$$

where the superscripts 60 and 90 are used to denote values for 1960 and 1990, respectively.

The parameter A is equal to total factor productivity and it represents forces that affect GDP per worker other than physical and human capital. Traditionally, economists have assumed that changes in this coefficient are closely related to technological changes (Solow, 1956), but they may in fact reflect the influence of any other forces (wars, natural catastrophes, health and epidemics, ethnic conflict, geography, etc.). In terms of technological change, of course, there is a wide array of variables that influence innovations. We will include some of these variables in the empirical work, in order to identify their role as potential determinants of economic growth.

The endogenous growth model presented in the last section identified human capital as a key determinant of technological change (see also Romer, 1990a, b). One expects persons with higher education to be those most closely connected to the innovation sector. To proxy for changes in A_i, we add to the growth equation in (46) a variable *TERTIARY*, which is equal to the average of the 1960 and 1990 proportions of the population aged 15 or older who had attended some level of tertiary education. This represents a sample period average of the fraction of the labor force who have had some exposure to higher education.

The theoretical analysis also showed how democracy works in raising the rate of technical change, although this mechanism was shown to operate through the higher quality of governance (lower corruption) associated with democracy. To incorporate this into the analysis we first add to the growth regression the index of democracy discussed earlier, *DEMOC*, which ranges from 1 to 7, from weaker to stronger democratic institutions. We then also estimate another equation which adds the variable *GOVERN*, which represents the index of governance discussed earlier and which ranges from 0 to 1, with higher values denoting higher quality of governance.

There are other forces influencing technological change. Data limitations do not allow us to include most of these variables, but we shall include some popular influences on technical change. Urbanization, for example, has been postulated to be associated with agglomeration economies that allow new industries to emerge and new goods and services to be competitively produced, effectively raising the rate of innovation (Jacobs, 1969; Rivera-Batiz, 1988). To incorporate this force into the empirical work, the variable *URBAN* is added, which is equal to the percentage of the population in 1980 residing in an urban area. Also note that innovations intensive in research and development may be spurred by the presence of large, capital-intensive firms that allocate resources for these purposes, suggesting a positive relationship between the capital per worker in the economy and total factor productivity growth. We add $(K/L)^{60}$, which is the initial capital–labor ratio of the economy, to the growth equation.

We can summarize the determinants of total factor productivity changes through this equation:

$$\log A_i^{90} / \log A_i^{60}$$
$$= f(DEMOC_i, GOVERN_i, TERTIARY_i, URBAN_i, (K/L)^{60}). \tag{47}$$

Equation (47) can then be substituted into (46).

The growth equation (46) can be estimated using the following empirical model:

$$\log[(Y_i/L_i)^{90}/(Y_i/L_i)^{60}]$$
$$= \beta_0 + \beta_1 DEMOC_i + \beta_2 GOVERN_i + \beta_3 TERTIARY_i$$
$$+ \beta_4 URBAN_i + \beta_5 (K_i/L_i)^{60} + \beta_6 \log[(K_i/L_i)^{90}/(K_i/L_i)^{60}]$$
$$+ \beta_7 [Ed_i^{90} - Ed_i^{60}] + \varepsilon_i, \tag{48}$$

where the β_j are parameters to be estimated, and ε_i is a random error term assumed to be distributed normally with mean zero and constant variance.

The dataset includes 59 countries for which information on all variables is available. The dependent variable is measured by the log-change of real GDP per worker in constant, international dollars (base year 1985).[13] The K_i/L_i data are for capital stock per worker, as reported by the Penn World Tables 5.6 (measured in constant, 1985 international dollars).[14] The Ed_i is measured by the average years of schooling of the population 15 years of age or older,

Table 8.2.   Sample Means for Growth Accounting.

Variable	Sample mean (sd)
$\log[(Y_i/L_i)^{90}/(Y_i/L_i)^{60}]$	0.65
	(0.49)
$\log[(K_i/L_i)^{90}/(K_i/L_i)^{60}]$	1.02
	(0.78)
$Ed_i^{90} - Ed_i^{60}$	2.22
	(1.04)
$DEMOC$	4.7
	(1.9)
$GOVERN$	0.59
	(0.26)
$TERTIARY$	0.069
	(0.058)
$URBAN$	54.1
	(24.6)
$(K_i/L_i)^{60}$	7,482.0
	(8,031.0)
Observations = 59	

taken from the Barro–Lee (1994) database. The values of *DEMOC, GOVERN, TERTIARY*, and *URBAN* are as defined earlier.

Table 8.2 presents the sample means of the variables used in the analysis. The overall growth of GDP per worker between 1960 and 1990 was 0.65 in the sample of countries, which corresponds to an average of 2.2% per annum. The capital per worker grew an average of 102% between 1960 and 1990, or 3.4% per year. And the average educational attainment in the sample rose by 2.2 times between 1960 and 1990. The sample mean for the democracy index was 4.7, on a range of 1 to 7. The mean value of the governance index was 0.59, on a range of 0 to 1. Table 8.2 shows the sample means for the other variables in the analysis.[15]

Table 8.3 displays the ordinary least squares coefficients of the growth regressions corresponding to equation (48). Column 1 reports the results of a simple regression that includes only the capital per worker, educational attainment, and democracy index as explanatory variables. As can be seen, all three variables are statistically significant in explaining growth of GDP per worker.

Table 8.3.   Growth Accounting Regressions.

Dependent variable: Log of 1960–90 change in GDP per worker:
$$\log[(Y_i/L_i)^{90}/(Y_i/L_i)^{60}]$$
Sample mean = 0.588 (SD = 0.521)

Explanatory variable	Estimated coefficient (se) [t]	Estimated coefficient (se) [t]
Constant	−0.3269** (0.1656) [−1.9]	−0.3494** (0.1585) [−2.2]
$\log[(K_i/L_i)^{90}/(K_i/L_i)^{60}]$	0.4055* (0.0562) [7.2]	0.3288* (0.0606) [5.4]
$Ed_i^{90} - Ed_i^{60}$	0.1273* (0.0431) [3.0]	0.1182* (0.0407) [2.9]
DEMOC	0.0578** (0.0228) [2.5]	0.0052 (0.0312) [0.2]
GOVERN	—	0.9347* (0.2545) [3.7]
TERTIARY	—	−0.7264 (0.9739) [−0.7]
URBAN	—	−0.0016 (0.0025) [−0.7]
$(K_i/L_i)^{60}$	—	−0.00005 (0.000008) [−0.6]
Observations	59	59
$\bar{R}$−squared	0.55	0.62

*Coefficient is statistically significant at the 99% confidence level.
**Coefficient is statistically significant at the 95% confidence level.

In particular, the value of the democracy coefficient is positive and statistically significant. In fact, an increase of one standard deviation in the index of democracy (equal to 1.9 points) is associated with an increased growth rate of GDP per capita between 1960 and 1990 of 0.4 percentage points per year.

The second column of Table 8.3 reports the results of the full regression model, which includes all explanatory variables. Note that the adjusted R-squared rises substantially, from 0.55 to 0.62, indicating that the full model explains a significantly larger fraction of the variance of growth in GDP per capita. Most importantly, the democracy variable loses its statistical significance, the value of its estimated coefficient changes sign, and its magnitude becomes insignificant in terms of its impact of growth. Accompanying this result is the fact that the quality of governance variable, $GOVERN$, is statistically significant and a strong determinant of growth. In fact, an increase in the governance index of one standard deviation (an increase of 0.26 in the index) increases the growth rate of GDP per capita by 1.2 percentage points per year.

The results presented in Table 8.3 suggest that democracy is a key determinant of growth but only insofar as it is associated with improved governance. As the theoretical model implies, the key influence of democracy on growth is through its effects in raising the quality of governance in the economy, which is then closely linked to greater factor productivity growth.[16]

8.5   Conclusions

This paper has examined how democracy affects long-run growth through its impact on the quality of governance of a country. The issue is explored both at the theory level and through empirical evidence.

The paper focused first on presenting empirical evidence on the link between democracy and quality of governance. An index of quality of governance constructed by Hall and Jones (1999) was used as a dependent variable in a multivariate analysis of the determinants of quality of governance. The results show that the quality of governance is substantially higher in more democratic countries, even after holding other variables constant.

A general-equilibrium, endogenous growth model was then built to specify how a governance-improving democracy raises growth. In this model, stronger democratic institutions influence governance by constraining the actions of corrupt officials. The force of the vote means that, over the long run, inept, corrupt officials will be voted out of office. More democratic institutions also facilitate the activities of the press, which can monitor corruption and disseminate information on corrupt government officials to the public so that they can be held accountable.

The theoretical model visualizes corruption as a tax on the entrepreneurs and firms that sell new capital goods in the economy. This reduces the incentives to innovate and dampens technological change. By reducing the corrosive effects of corruption and raising the rewards from creating new capital goods, an increase in political rights stimulates innovation and raises both the rate of return to capital as well as the steady-state growth rate of the economy.

The theoretical analysis also shows that, the stronger the democratic institutions in the country, the more likely that capital account liberalization will produce an expansion of the steady-state growth rate in developing countries. The reason is that more democratic institutions are associated with higher domestic rates of return to capital. As international trade in assets is permitted, democracies are more likely to have rates of return to capital that exceed the world rate of return, inducing capital inflows. More authoritarian governments are more likely to face capital flight instead.

The paper concludes by providing empirical evidence showing that democracy is in fact a significant determinant of total factor productivity (TFP) growth between 1960 and 1990 in a cross-section of countries. But this contribution occurs only insofar as democratic institutions are associated with greater quality of governance. In a multivariate growth regression analysis where both quality of governance and democracy indexes are introduced, the democracy variable loses its statistical significance. The quality of governance variable, on the other hand, is statistically significant and a strong determinant of growth. In fact, an increase in the governance index of one standard deviation increases the growth rate of GDP per capita by 1.2 percentage points per year.

These results thus suggest that democracy is a key determinant of growth but only insofar as it is associated with improved governance. In cases where democracy is not associated with improved governance, it will have very little impact on growth. And in authoritarian countries where the quality of governance is high, growth is likely to also be at high levels.

Notes:

[1] As cited in Krauss (2000, p. D-4).

[2] See Hall and Jones (1999, p. 84).

[3] See Hall and Jones (1999, p. 84).

[4] See Freedom House (1997, p. 572).

[5] Of course, the issue of causality emerges in any exercise of this type. Although we have mentioned the strong reasons to hypothesize that more democratic institutions will cause improved governance, it is possible that the causal direction in examining the links between democracy and governance involves greater governance causing democracy, rather than vice versa. For instance, well-governed dictatorships, with successful economies, may have the political breathing space to allow greater democratic institutions to emerge. Countries with poor governance, on the other hand, may have the collapsing economies that cause repressive, authoritarian governments to flourish. To explore this hypothesis, a regression equation was estimated where the dependent variable was GOVERN and the explanatory variable was the value of the democracy index for 1960. The latter was found to be a strong, statistically significant determinant of the quality of governance in the period of 1960 to 1990. Although only indicative, this result is consistent with a causal influence of democracy on governance.

[6] Urbanization may also have a negative impact on the quality of governance. Historically, in a number of countries, political groups based in growing urban areas have managed to dominate national, state, or local governments, instituting populist, patronage systems that benefit their urban political base while taxing the rest of the country, state, or locality. These urban political machines — which can operate under both democratic and nondemocratic regimes — have often created deeply flawed governments (World Bank, 1997, p. 105).

[7] See World Bank (1997, p. 108).

[8] There is growing literature examining both the theory and evidence on the impact of corruption in developing countries; see, for instance, Shleifer and Vishny (1993), Mauro (1995), Gray and Kaufmann (1998), Ehrlich and Lui (1999), Paldam (1999), and Treisman (1999). The model in this paper was developed in Rivera-Batiz (2001a).

[9]It is assumed, for simplicity, that there are no penalties imposed when corrupt officials are discovered. They only lose their bribes. In this case, the expected gain, G, to the corrupt officials if their scheme is discovered and dismantled is just zero.

[10]The model is based on the endogenous growth models of the open economy developed by Grossman and Helpman (1991a, b); see also Rivera-Batiz and Romer (1991), Rivera-Batiz (1996, 1997).

[11]We again follow closely the models in Grossman and Helpman (1991a,b); see also Romer (1990a,b) for a detailed analysis.

[12]The exponential relationship between human capital and output per worker follows the widespread evidence available from microeconomic labor market studies establishing an exponential linkage between earnings and educational attainment of labor market participants. Unfortunately, this is not the functional specification that has been adopted in most cross-country studies linking education to growth; see, for example, Pritchett (1997), and Easterly and Levine (2001). A careful analysis of the two alternative functional specifications makes clear that the exponential form appears to fit the data more closely. For an analysis of this issue and estimates of the role of education on economic growth, see Rivera-Batiz (2001b).

[13]These data were obtained from the World Bank economic growth database, which relies on the Penn World Tables 5.6.

[14]The capital stock data were obtained from the World Bank economic growth database, which are derived, in turn, from the Penn World Tables 5.6, based on perpetual inventory estimates of capital stocks using disaggregated investment and depreciation statistics. These data are utilized by Easterly and Levine (2001) in their analysis.

[15]The comparatively small sample of countries (59) may give rise to a suspicion that the analysis is subject to sample selection bias. The technique developed by Ray and Rivera-Batiz (2002) was used to determine whether the growth regression coefficients would change significantly when adjusted for sample selection bias, but the changes were negligible.

[16]The possibility also exists that democracy can affect growth through its impact on the accumulation of physical and human capital, a possibility that is not examined in this paper; see Tavares and Wacziarg (2001).

References

Barro, Robert J., "Democracy and Growth," *Journal of Economic Growth*, 1 (1996): 1–27.

———, *Determinants of Economic Growth: A Cross-Country Empirical Study*, Cambridge, MA: MIT Press (1997).

Brunetti, Aymo, "Political Variables in Cross-Country Growth Analysis," *Journal of Economic Surveys*, 11 (1997): 163–90.

Easterly, William and Ross Levine, "Africa's Growth Tragedy: Policies and Ethnic Divisions," *Quarterly Journal of Economics*, 112 (1997): 1203–50.

———, "It's Not Factor Accumulation: Stylized Facts and Growth Models," *The World Bank Economic Review*, 15 (2001): 177–219.

Ehrlich, Isaac and T. Lui, "Bureaucratic Corruption and Endogenous Economic Growth," *Journal of Political Economy*, 107 (1999): S270–93.

Freedom House, *Freedom in the World: The Annual Survey of Political Rights and Civil Liberties, 1996–97*, New Brunswick, NJ: Transaction Publishers (1997).

Goetzmann, William, "Democracy Before Debt," The New York Times, 22 October (1999): A18.

Gray, Cheryl W. and Daniel Kaufmann, "Corruption and Development," *Finance and Development* (1998): 7–10.

Grossman, Gene M. and Elhanan Helpman, *Innovation and Growth in the Global Economy*, Cambridge, MA: MIT Press (1991a).

———, "Growth and Welfare in a Small Open Economy," in E. Helpman and A. Razin (eds.), *International Trade and Trade Policy*, Cambridge, MA: MIT Press (1991b): 141–66.

Hall, Robert E. and Charles I. Jones, "Why Do Some Countries Produce so Much More Output per Worker Than Others?" *Quarterly Journal of Economics*, 114 (1999): 83–116.

Helliwell, John, "Empirical Linkages between Democracy and Economic Growth," British *Journal of Political Science*, 24 (1994): 225–48.

Jacobs, Jane, *The Economy of Cities*, New York: Random House (1969).

Kaufmann, Daniel, Aart Kraay, and Pablo Zoido-Lobaton, "Governance Matters: From Measurement to Action," *Finance and Development*, 37 (2000): 10–13.

Kormendi, Roger and Philip Meguire, "Macroeconomic Determinants of Growth," *Journal of Monetary Economics*, 16 (1985): 141–63.

Krauss, Clifford, "Autocrat? Democrat? Well, Both," The New York Times, 4 June (2001): D-4.

Krueger, Alan B. and Mikael Lindahl, "Education for Growth: Why and for Whom?" *Journal of Economic Literature*, 39 (2001): 1101–1136.

La Porta, Rafael, Florencio Lopez-de-Silanes, Andrei Shleifer, and Robert Vishny, "The Quality of Government," *Journal of Law, Economics and Organization*, 15 (1999): 222–279.

Levine, Ross, "International Financial Liberalization and Economic Growth," *Review of International Economics*, 9 (2001): 688–702.

Mauro, Paolo, "Corruption and Growth," *Quarterly Journal of Economics* 110 (1995): 681–712.

North, Douglass, *Institutions, Institutional Change and Economic Performance*, Cambridge: Cambridge University Press (1990).

Paldam, M., "The Big Pattern of Corruption, Economics, Culture and the Seesaw Dynamics," unpublished manuscript, Aarthus University, Copenhagen (1999).

Przeworski, Adam and Fernando Limongi, "Political Regimes and Economic Growth," *Journal of Economic Perspectives*, 7 (1993): 51–69.

Pritchett, Lant, "Where Has All the Education Gone?," World Bank Policy Research Working Paper 1581 (1997).

Radelet, Steven and Jeffrey Sachs, "The East Asian Financial Crisis: Diagnosis, Remedies and Prospects," *Brookings Papers on Economic Activity*, 1 (1998): 1–74.

Ray, Jayant and Francisco L. Rivera-Batiz, "An Analysis of Sample Selection Bias in Cross-Country Growth Regressions," New York: Columbia University Department of Economics Discussion Paper No. 0102–10 (2002).

Rivera-Batiz, Francisco L., "Increasing Returns, Monopolistic Competition, and Agglomeration Economies in Consumption and Production," *Regional Science and Urban Economics*, 18 (1988): 125–53.

———, "The Economics of Technological Progress and Endogenous Growth in Open Economies," in Hans-Eckart Scharrer (ed.), *The Economics of High Technology Competition and Cooperation in Global Markets*, Hamburg: Institut für Wirtschaftsforschung (1996): 31–62.

———, "Trade Liberalization and the International Distribution of the Gains from Growth," in Satya Dev Gupta and Nanda K. Choudhry (eds.), *Globalization and Development: Growth, Equity and Sustainability*, Boston: Kluwer Academic (1997): 135–58.

———, "International Financial Liberalization, Corruption, and Economic Growth," *Review of International Economics*, 9 (2001a): 723–33.

———, "Is Education an Engine of Economic Growth? Theory and Evidence," New York: Columbia University, Program in Economic Policy Management (2001b).

Rivera-Batiz, Luis A. and Paul M. Romer, "Economic Integration and Endogenous Growth," *Quarterly Journal of Economics*, 106 (1991): 531–55.

Rodrik, Dani, "Democracy and Economic Performance," mimeo, John F. Kennedy School of Government, Cambridge, MA (1997).

———, "Who Needs Capital Account Convertibility?," Essays in International Finance, No. 207, Princeton University, Department of Economics, International Finance Section (1998).

Romer, Paul M., "Endogenous Technological Change," *Journal of Political Economy*, 90 (1990a): S71–102.

———, "Trade, Politics and Growth in a Small, Less Developed Economy," mimeo, Department of Economics, University of Chicago (1990b).

Sachs, Jeffrey D. and Andrew Warner, "Economic Reform and the Process of Global Integration," *Brookings Papers on Economic Activity* 1 (1995): 1–95.

Scully, Gerald W., "The Institutional Framework and Economic Development," *Journal of Political Economy*, 96 (1988): 652–62.

Sen, Amartya, *Development as Freedom*, New York: Alfred A. Knopf (2000).

Shleifer, Andrei and Robert Vishny, "Corruption," *Quarterly Journal of Economics*, 108 (1993): 599–617.

Solow, Robert M., "A Contribution to the Theory of Economic Growth," *Quarterly Journal of Economics*, 70 (1956): 65–95.

Tavares, Jose and Romain Wacziarg, "How Democracy Affects Growth," *European Economic Review*, 45 (2001): 1341–78.

Treisman, D., "The Causes of Corruption: A Cross-National Study," unpublished manuscript, UCLA (1999).

World Bank, The State in a Changing World: World Development Report 1997, Oxford, Oxford University Press (1997).

Chapter 9

Political Institutions, Capital Flows, and Developing Country Growth: An Empirical Investigation*

9.1 Introduction

Over the past decades some developing countries have been winners while others have experienced slow growth as well as steep turnarounds in growth rates, most often accompanied by dramatic changes in the level and composition of capital flows. It is important to determine which factors lead to faster growth and facilitate attracting greater amounts of sustainable capital inflows. Empirical studies by Borner *et al.* (1995), Barro (1997) and others have examined the development impact of political and legal institutions. The linkages between growth, institutions, and capital flows have not escaped analyst attention. However, the role of political institution quality and the rule of law in attracting capital flows and in creating a productive environment for them has not been systematically studied. The question of which types of capital flows are more

*This chapter was co-authored by Maria-Angels Oliva and Luis A. Rivera-Batiz and was originally published in *Review of Development Economics*, Vol. 6, No. 2 (June 2002), pp. 248–262. ©2002 Blackwell Publishers Ltd.

Oliva is grateful to ESCP-EAP for facilitating the work on this project. Rivera-Batiz gratefully acknowledges financing by a McGill University research grant. We wish to thank Francisco L. Rivera-Batiz, Kris Jacobs and two anonymous referees for insightful comments.

productive and which institutional factors attract productive capital flows is crucial in an evolving environment of declining regulation, greater financial integration, and keen competition for funds. In this new setting, there is little room for macroeconomic and financial growth policies targeting particular variables but there is a potentially pivotal role for institutions that impinge on the economic and financial environment.

This paper examines the growth effects of the degree of democratic development, the rule of law, and alternative forms of capital flows. Moreover, the analysis provides estimates of whether better institutional variables actually help to attract productive capital flows toward developing countries. The empirical analysis is based on a bare-bones benchmark growth model applicable to developing countries. Conducting regressions with variables defined as a 5-year average attenuates business cycle effects. The estimates of the benchmark growth framework confirm previous findings indicating that the growth rate increases with schooling, domestic fixed investment, and favorable terms of trade. The growth rate is found to fall with the level of initial income and with government consumption as a percentage of GDP. The direct growth effects of democracy are found to be positive and often statistically significant. The rule of law stimulates growth but the estimated coefficients are not statistically significant.

Policies toward capital flows hinge on the answer to several questions revolving around the empirical evidence contrasting the growth effects of domestic fixed investment, foreign direct investment (FDI), and other capital flows. While the estimated growth effects of FDI and domestic fixed investment are positive, the growth effect of FDI is found to be several times higher than the growth effect of domestic fixed investment. This striking finding confirms with a far larger sample the findings of De Gregorio (1992) for a group of 12 Latin American countries.

The rise of foreign investment as a major form of capital inflow in the late 1990s, and the fall of portfolio flows, raise the question of how to compare the effects of alternative forms of capital flows. One assessment criterion is to examine the evidence on the comparative growth effects of foreign investment and other types of capital flows. FDI has statistically significant growth effects and the inclusion of FDI substantially improves the explanatory power of the growth regressions. By contrast, we do not find support for the notion that non-FDI capital flows exert significant positive growth effects or improve the explanatory power of growth regressions. This general finding applies not only to reported results but also to a large number of trials and methods applied to a large sample of developing countries, as well as to various subsamples including those encompassing African and Latin American countries.

Do a greater degree of democracy and an improved rule of law exert indirect growth effects through other variables? We take a stab at this question by estimating a system of growth, FDI, and schooling equations. The estimates derived from a three-stage least-squares (3SLS) regression offer evidence that democracy has indirect growth effects that work by encouraging schooling. Moreover, these estimates also offer evidence that the rule of law influences growth indirectly by encouraging FDI. Overall, our results support the notion that institutional variables work both directly and through multiple channels.

The eminently reasonable findings have strong policy implications. The empirical evidence is consistent with the view that developing countries might do well to promote foreign direct investment. Institutional improvements, such as establishing a better-functioning democracy and securing attachment to the rule of law, help to create conditions for sustained growth both directly and through their effects of schooling (democracy) and FDI (the rule of law). The findings are also useful for the assessment of the controversy concerning the growth consequences of capital flows and capital account liberalization. On one side, the major international institutions and economic growth research conducted by Levine (2001) and others suggest that capital account liberalization has strong positive growth effects. On the other side, Rodrik (1998), Radelet and Sachs (1998), and other skeptics claim that the growth effects of capital flows and their liberalization can be positive or even negative. A proposed reconciliation of these conflicting views is that empirical evidence shows that the strength of the growth effect of capital flows depends on the type of flow considered. FDI works but the evidence suggesting that non-FDI capital flows are associated to faster growth is at best weak. Further work should examine decompositions of non-FDI capital flows to test whether some items can be determined to exert a positive growth effect.

The next section describes the data and the preliminary causality tests conducted. Section 9.3 focuses on the growth effects of quality of government as measured by indicators of democracy and the rule of law. Section 9.4 contrasts the growth effects of domestic investment, foreign direct investment, and other capital flows. Section 9.5 presents the results from a regression system consisting of growth, FDI, and schooling equations. Section 9.6 discusses the findings' policy and further research implications.

9.2   Data and Exploratory Causality Tests

9.2.1   *The Data*

The sample consists of 119 developing countries for which data were available between 1970 and 1994 (the countries are listed by region in the Appendix). However, many variables are missing for several countries so that the number of observations varies with the number of variables included. The reported equations exclude those countries with GDP less than \$5,000 million as measured in real terms in year 1987. Variables are transformed by computing 5-year averages in order to attenuate business cycle effects.

The growth rate is defined as the real per-capita annual growth rate expressed as a decimal. Capital inflows are measured in 1987 purchasing power parity (PPP) current dollars and are expressed as a percentage of GDP. This means that the translation into current 1987 US dollars is realized using purchasing power parity (PPP) calculations rather than currency exchange rates. Foreign direct investment (*FDI*) is defined as gross FDI inflows. Capital inflows (*KF*) are defined as total commercial capital inflows, and include foreign direct investment liabilities, portfolio flow liabilities, as well as other investment flow liabilities. The foreign direct investment and capital flow variables were constructed from the IMF database. Schooling, H, is measured as the average years of secondary schooling of the male population aged 25 years and above constructed by Barro and Lee (1996). This variable varies every five years. Government consumption (GC) is general government consumption (defined as a percentage of GDP) and was obtained from the World Bank's World Development Indicators. Domestic investment is gross domestic fixed investment in current US dollars measured as a percentage of GDP, and was again obtained from the World Bank's Development Indicators. External shocks, which represent an important variable impacting developing countries, are measured using the terms of trade. This variable is defined using as base 1987 US dollars and was obtained from the World Bank database.

Democracy, D, is measured by the Polity IV index, which refers to institutionalized democracy. The value of the Polity IV index is higher the greater the degree of democracy. It ranges between 0 and 10, where a value of 0 represents low levels of democracy while a value of 10 represents high levels of democracy. This indicator accounts for the presence of institutions and procedures allowing political participation, openness, and competitiveness of executive recruitment as well as the degree to which the executive is constrained. The index is the product of a project developed at the Center for International Development and Conflict Management (CIDCM) at the University of Maryland. The Polity IV index is highly correlated with the Polity IV index of Autocracy and with the widely used Gastil index of political rights. The Gastil democracy indexes (1987, 1990) quantify a country's degree of democracy measured in terms of political rights and civil liberties.

The Kaufmann index of the rule of law (ROL) is higher the better the implementation of the rule of law in a country. This index accounts for enforceability of public and private contracts, the extent of crime and insecurity, and intellectual rights protection (Kaufmann *et al.*, 1999a, b). It is highly correlated with the Kaufmann index measuring the absence of graft (which is not included in the analysis).

9.2.2   *Exploratory Causality Tests*

We conducted exploratory tests (available on request) to help us determine whether the direction of causation goes from domestic investment to growth, from growth to domestic investment, or both. In an attempt to abstract from business cycle effects, all variables were measured as 5-year averages. Exploratory tests suggest that growth might drive investment to a greater extent than investment drives growth, which is consistent with earlier work by Blomstrom *et al.* (1996) utilizing a smaller dataset. For that reason, estimated growth equations are reported with and without domestic investment as explanatory variable.

Causality tests were also conducted to explore whether growth drives FDI or vice versa, and whether growth drives other types of capital flows or vice versa. The tests were inconclusive. When 5-year averages are used to attenuate the business cycle effect, the association between growth and FDI becomes contemporaneous and the tests do not help to clarify Granger causality. Reichert and Weinhold (2000) conducted causality tests using a mixed fixed and random coefficient method to allow for heterogeneous behavior in the FDI-growth relation. They reported considerable heterogeneity in a panel of 24 developing countries from 1971 to 1995. They find that there is a causal relationship from FDI to growth that seems to be stronger in more open economies. In order to account for the endogeneity of FDI, we report estimates based on 3SLS growth equations.

9.3   Democracy, the Rule of Law, and Growth

The appealing notion that better democratic institutions encourage growth has not received strong support in empirical analyses. Brunetti's (1997) survey reviews 17 papers examining the relationship between democracy and growth. He finds that nine of them reported no relationship, four reported a positive relationship, and four reported a negative relationship. Similar ambiguous results are reported by Borner *et al.* (1995). Barro (1997) finds that the democracy–growth relationship is nonlinear and that a square term captures a positive relationship at low levels of the democracy index and a negative relationship at higher quality levels. He points out that the rule of law works better than other variables measuring the quality of political institutions in his growth regressions. Barro (1996) also found that the effects of democracy tend to disappear once other variables such as human capital and investment rates are included in the equations.

Tables 9.1 and 9.2 report the results from OLS growth equations incorporating the democracy (D) and rule of law (ROL) variables. The correlation between the democracy index used and the rule of law is low in this sample. The data are pooled cross-sectional time-series so that there is a growth equation for each country. The exploratory analysis strongly suggests that factors encouraging growth might result in faster investment in the future rather than domestic investment causing growth. For this reason, growth equations are reported with (Table 9.1) and without (Table 9.2) the fixed investment variable.

The growth rate of per-capita income (g) is related to initial gross domestic product (Y), schooling (H), the government consumption to GDP ratio, the terms of trade (TOT), the fixed investment to GDP ratio (in Table 9.1), the FDI to GDP ratio, and a vector X representing additional variables such as the total capital flow ratio (KF/GDP), the other foreign capital flows ratio (OKF/GDP), and dummies. Formally,

$$g_t = a_0 + a_1 \ln Y + a_2 H_t + a_3 GC_t/GDP_t + a_4 TOT_t + a_5 D_t$$
$$+ a_6 ROL + a_7 FDI_t/GDP_t + a_8 X + u_t,$$

where u represents the regression error.

The estimates for the whole sample are consistent with the notion that a better democratic regime and greater enforcement of the rule of law encourage growth, even after controlling for the investment rate and schooling. However, these results are not always statistically significant.

Tables 9.3 and 9.4 show results at the regional level for Africa and Latin America. The democracy variable does not have a statistically significant growth effect in Latin America but appears significant

Table 9.1. Growth Equation with Domestic Investment, 120 Developing Countries, 1970–94.

Growth	(1)	(2)	(3)	(4)	(5)	(6)	(7)	(8)
Log (initial GDP)	-0.0007	-0.0002	-0.0007	-0.0002	-0.0007	-0.0005	-0.00007	-0.00002
	(-1.6)	(-0.4)	(-1.5)	(-0.4)	(-1.5)	(-1.2)	(-0.15)	(-0.06)
Schooling	0.004	0.005	0.004	0.006	0.006	0.002	0.004	0.001
	(1.24)	(1.6)	(1.0)	(1.5)	(1.5)	(0.6)	(0.9)	(0.3)
Government consumption	-0.001*	-0.001*	-0.001*	-0.001*	-0.001*	-0.001*	0.001*	0.001*
	(-3.8)	(-3.2)	(-3.8)	(-3.2)	(-3.6)	(-4.3)	(-3.4)	(-3.5)
Investment	0.001*	0.001*	0.001*	0.001*	0.001*	0.001*	0.0012*	0.0012*
	(5.3)	(4.8)	(4.8)	(4.7)	(4.8)	(5.4)	(4.9)	(4.7)
TOT-TOT(-1)	6.0e-12*	4.4e-12*	6.3e-12*	4.4e-12*	7.3e-12*	6.7e-12*	5.5e-12*	5.3e-12*
	(3.5)	(2.5)	(3.6)	(2.5)	(3.6)	(3.9)	(3.1)	(3.0)
FDI		0.004*		0.003***			0.003*	0.003
		(2.5)		(1.7)			(2.0)	(1.5)
KF			0.0008	0.0007				
			(1.5)	(1.2)				
OKF					0.001			
					(0.7)			
Democracy						0.002*	0.001*	0.001**
						(3.5)	(2.4)	(2.0)
Rule of law								0.005
								(1.3)

Latin American dummy	-0.013*	-0.014*	-0.014*	-0.014*	-0.013*	-0.014*	-0.013*	-0.012**
	(-2.8)	(-2.6)	(-2.8)	(-2.5)	(-2.4)	(-2.7)	(-2.3)	(-2.0)
Africa dummy	-0.01***	-0.01	-0.01***	-0.01	-0.006	-0.005	-0.006	-0.007
	(-1.7)	(-1.5)	(-1.7)	(-1.5)	(-1.0)	(-1.0)	(-1.0)	(-1.1)
East Asia dummy	0.0009	-0.004	-0.002	-0.004	0.004	0.002	-0.002	-0.003
	(0.01)	(-0.5)	(-0.2)	(-0.5)	(0.4)	(0.3)	(-0.2)	(-0.4)
1975–79 dummy	-0.019*	0.02**	0.02*	0.02**	-0.02*	0.019*	-0.02***	0.04*
	(-3.0)	(2.0)	(3.5)	(2.1)	(-3.1)	(3.0)	(-1.8)	(3.3)
1980–84 dummy	-0.04*	-0.02*	-0.02*	-0.02*	-0.04*	-0.017*	-0.04*	-0.02*
	(-6.2)	(-3.6)	(-3.4)	(-3.7)	(-6.0)	(-3.0)	(-3.4)	(-3.0)
1985–89 dummy	-0.024*	-0.006	-0.005	-0.005	-0.026*	-0.005	-0.027*	-0.001
	(-4.1)	(-1.1)	(-1.0)	(-1.0)	(-4.1)	(-1.0)	(-2.4)	(0.2)
1990–94 dummy	-0.034*	-0.02*	-0.016*	-0.02*	-0.038*	-0.018*	0.04*	0.01*
	(-5.5)	(-3.3)	(-2.9)	(-3.3)	(-6.0)	(-3.2)	(3.6)	(2.6)
Observations	316	244	303	244	281	304	172	229
R^2	0.35	0.4	0.37	0.4	0.37	0.37	0.4	0.4
Adj. R^2	0.33	0.37	0.34	0.37	0.34	0.34	0.36	0.36

*Coefficient is statistically significant at the 99% confidence level. **Coefficient is statistically significant at the 95% confidence level. ***Coefficient is statistically significant at the 90% confidence level.

Table 9.2. Growth Equation with Domestic Investment Excluded, 119 Developing Countries, 1970–94.

Growth	(1)	(2)	(3)	(4)	(5)	(6)	(7)	(8)
Log (initial GDP)	-0.0009***	-0.0004	-0.0009***	-0.0004	-0.0008	-0.0007	-0.0002	-0.0001
	(-1.9)	(-0.7)	(-1.8)	(-0.8)	(-1.7)	(-1.6)	(-0.04)	(-0.3)
Schooling	0.005	0.006	0.004	0.006	0.008	0.004	0.003	0.0001
	(1.6)	(1.4)	(1.1)	(1.4)	(1.8)	(0.9)	(0.6)	(0.03)
Government consumption	-0.0006**	-0.0006***	-0.006**	-0.0006**	-0.0007*	-0.0008*	-0.0007*	-0.0007*
	(-2.0)	(-1.8)	(-2.1)	(-1.9)	(-1.8)	(-2.5)	(-2.1)	(-2.2)
TOT·TOT(-1)	8.0e-12*	5.75e-12*	8.05e-12*	5.7e-12*	9.36e-12*	8.7e-12*	6.9e-12*	6.8e-12*
	(4.5)	(3.1)	(4.4)	(3.1)	(4.4)	(4.9)	(3.7)	(1.6)
FDI		0.006*		0.005*			0.005*	0.004*
		(3.4)		(2.3)			(2.8)	(2.1)
KF			0.001***	0.0008				
			(1.5)	(1.3)				
OKF					0.0007			
					(0.5)			
Democracy						0.001*	0.001*	0.001***
						(3.2)	(2.4)	(1.8)
Rule of law								0.006
								(1.6)

	(1)	(2)	(3)	(4)	(5)	(6)	(7)	(8)
Latin American dummy	-0.015*	-0.018*	-0.015*	-0.018*	-0.014*	-0.015*	-0.001*	-0.016*
	(-3.0)	(-3.2)	(-2.9)	(-3.1)	(-2.6)	(-2.9)	(-2.1)	(-2.6)
Africa dummy	-0.01*	-0.014*	-0.012*	-0.014*	-0.01	-0.01	-0.01***	-0.012***
	(-2.1)	(-2.5)	(-2.2)	(-2.2)	(-1.5)	(-1.4)	(-1.7)	(-1.8)
East Asia dummy	0.009	-0.003	0.005	-0.0006	0.009	0.01	0.002	0.02
	(1.1)	(-0.04)	(0.7)	(-0.1)	(1.2)	(1.3)	(0.8)	(2.1)
1975–79 dummy	-0.007	0.02*	0.03*	0.03*	0.03*	-0.007	0.0007	0.021*
	(-1.2)	(2.6)	(5.1)	(2.8)	(5.0)	(-1.2)	(0.08)	(2.1)
1980–84 dummy	-0.03*	0.023*	0.02*	0.024*	0.23*	-0.03*	-0.02**	0.023*
	(-5.0)	(4.1)	(3.6)	(4.1)	(3.8)	(-4.6)	(-2.0)	(3.7)
1985–89 dummy	-0.021	0.0001	-0.002	0.012*	0.0001	-0.02*	-0.01	0.002
	(-3.4)	(0.01)	(-0.3)	(2.1)	(0.01)	(-3.4)	(-1.2)	(0.4)
1990–94 dummy	-0.03*	0.01**	0.009***	0.0009	0.009**	-0.03*	-0.02**	0.01*
	(-4.5)	(1.96)	(1.7)	(0.17)	(1.7)	(-4.9)	(-2.5)	(2.0)
Observations	334	255	321	255	299	322	244	240
R^2	0.26	0.32	0.28	0.32	0.28	0.28	0.32	0.32
Adj. R^2	0.24	0.28	0.26	0.29	0.25	0.25	0.28	0.28

*Coefficient is statistically significant at the 99% confidence level. **Coefficient is statistically significant at the 95% confidence level. ***Coefficient is statistically significant at the 90% confidence level.

Table 9.3.   Growth Equation, 23 Latin American Countries, 1970–94.

Growth	(1)	(2)	(3)	(4)	(5)	(6)	(7)
Log (initial GDP)	−0.0002	0.0001	−0.0003	0.0001	−0.0003	−0.0002	0.0001
	(−0.5)	(0.3)	(−0.6)	(0.3)	(−0.7)	(−0.5)	(0.3)
Schooling	0.01	0.006	0.01	0.007	0.01***	0.008	0.005
	(1.5)	(1.0)	(1.6)	(1.0)	(−1.8)	(1.0)	(0.6)
Government consumption	−0.001*	−0.001***	−0.001*	−0.001***	−0.002*	−0.001*	−0.001*
	(−2.8)	(−1.9)	(−2.8)	(−1.8)	(−2.5)	(−2.8)	(−2.0)
TOT-TOT(-1)	8.3e-12*	9.4e-11*	8.0e-12	9.4e-12***	8.0e-12	8.8e-12	1.0e-11**
	(1.6)	(−1.9)	(1.6)	(1.9)	(1.5)	(1.5)	(2.0)
FDI		0.01*		0.008*			0.008*
		(2.9)		(2.4)			(2.8)
KF			0.001***	0.0006			
			(1.7)	(1.1)			
OKF					0.002		
					(0.7)		
Democracy						0.0007	0.001
						(0.9)	(1.5)
1975–79 dummy	−0.02*	0.03*	−0.02*	−0.02	−0.02***	0.03*	0.04*
	(−2.7)	(2.2)	(−2.1)	(−1.5)	(−1.9)	(2.8)	(2.6)
1980–84 dummy	0.009	0.01	−0.05*	−0.05*	−0.05*	0.009	0.01
	(1.0)	(1.4)	(−5.8)	(−3.9)	(−5.4)	(1.0)	(1.6)
1985–89 dummy	−0.02*	−0.023*	−0.03*	0.03*	−0.04*	−0.02*	−0.02*
	(−3.0)	(−2.9)	(−3.9)	(−2.2)	(−4.0)	(−2.5)	(−2.1)
1990–94 dummy	−0.1	−0.002	−0.027*	−0.03*	−0.03*	−0.01	−0.001
	(−1.3)	(−0.3)	(−3.0)	(−2.2)	(−2.8)	(−1.2)	(−0.1)
Observations	103	86	103	86	102	97	80
R^2	0.39	0.39	0.4	0.4	0.38	0.38	0.40
Adj. R^2	0.34	0.32	0.34	0.32	0.33	0.32	0.31

*Coefficient is statistically significant at the 99% confidence level. **Coefficient is statistically significant at the 95% confidence level. ***Coefficient is statistically significant at the 90% confidence level.

for Africa. The evidence is generally consistent with the ambiguity deriving from previous work on the direct growth effect of democracy. Indirect growth effects are explored below.

Why is it that there is only weak evidence consistent with the notion that both democracy and the rule of law can stimulate growth? The result reminds us of the point that democracy has not always worked well, particularly in Latin America, and has not necessarily been associated with better institutions. The results are consistent with the results of Tavarés and Wacziarg (2001), who find that democracy stimulates growth by improving human capital

Table 9.4. Growth Equation, 47 Latin American Countries, 1970–94.

Growth	(1)	(2)	(3)	(4)	(5)	(6)	(7)
Log (initial	−0.004	−0.002	−0.005*	−0.003***	−0.004*	−0.003**	−0.001
GDP)	(−2.4)	(−1.3)	(−2.7)	(−1.7)	(−2.2)	(−2.0)	(−0.7)
Schooling	0.01	0.006	0.01	0.006	0.01***	0.006	−0.002
	(1.4)	(0.7)	(1.3)	(0.6)	(1.7)	(0.8)	(−0.17)
Government	−0.001	−0.001	−0.001***	−0.001***	−0.0008	−0.0008	−0.001***
consumption	(−1.2)	(−1.5)	(−1.7)	(−1.8)	(−1.2)	(−1.2)	(−1.7)
TOT-	2.8e-11	4.9e-11*	4.8e-11*	4.7e-11*	1.2e-10*	2.05e-11*	4.4e-11*
TOT(-1)	(1.5)	(2.1)	(2.2)	(2.1)	(4.0)	(1.4)	(2.0)
FDI		0.01*		0.007			0.13*
		(2.4)		(1.5)			(2.9)
KF			0.003***	0.003***			
			(1.9)	(1.7)			
OKF					0.003		
					(1.2)		
Democracy						0.002*	0.003*
						(2.3)	(2.8)
1975–79	−0.0005	−0.016	0.02**	−0.002	−0.01	0.0007	−0.01
dummy	(−0.05)	(−1.0)	(2.0)	(−0.1)	(−0.1)	(0.07)	(−0.8)
1980–84	−0.012	−0.008	0.015	−0.008	−0.02***	−0.013	−0.008
dummy	(−1.2)	(−0.8)	(1.5)	(−0.8)	(−1.8)	(−1.3)	(−0.3)
1985–89	−0.006	−0.006	0.01	0.008	−0.009	−0.004	−0.003
dummy	(−0.6)	(−0.5)	(1.0)	(0.8)	(−0.9)	(−0.5)	(−0.3)
1990–94	−0.3*	−0.03*	−0.017***	−0.016	−0.036*	−0.32*	−0.03*
dummy	(−3.1)	(−2.8)	(−1.7)	(−1.6)	(−3.5)	(−3.3)	(−3.0)
Observations	114	94	113	94	110	114	94
R^2	0.18	0.24	0.22	0.26	0.29	0.22	0.31
Adj. R^2	0.12	0.16	0.16	0.18	0.22	0.16	0.22

*Coefficient is statistically significant at the 99% confidence level. **Coefficient is statistically significant at the 95% confidence level. ***Coefficient is statistically significant at the 90% confidence level.

accumulation but hinders growth by reducing the rate of physical capital accumulation and increasing government consumption. The overall effect is found to be slightly negative in their sample.

9.4 Which Type of Capital Flow Has the Greater Growth Impact?

A large literature has focused on the determinants and effects of FDI. However, this literature has rarely focused on a comparison of alternative forms of capital flows and has usually excluded institutional variables. Our analysis makes a contribution by examining the growth effects of different types of capital flows and political institutions. The datasets used in many earlier studies usually extend only to the late 1980s or early 1990s, thus missing the boom period for capital flows toward emerging markets. Our capital flow dataset extends to 1994 and thus includes the capital flow boom of the nineties as well as institutional variables for over a hundred countries.

A most cited result in the foreign direct investment literature is that the productivity of FDI in Latin America is three times that of domestic investment (De Gregorio, 1992). This result was obtained by comparing the growth effects of domestic investment and FDI in a sample of 12 Latin American countries, after controlling for economic and institutional variables that have been found to have an effect on growth rates. Other studies using the growth regression methodology also find that FDI has significant growth effects, although the superiority of FDI over domestic investment is not always confirmed. Borenszstein *et al.* (1994, 1998) found a positive growth effect of FDI but only if the host country had surpassed a threshold schooling level. This result was derived from a sample of 69 developing countries during the decades 1970–79 and 1980–89. The study performed cross-country regressions of the growth rate of per-capita income g on human capital H, FDI from OECD countries as a proportion of GDP, the interaction between the FDI ratio and human capital H, and a vector X representing additional variables such as the regression constant, initial income, domestic investment, and others. Formally, the authors estimated the following equation:

$$g_t = a_0 + a_1 H_t + a_2 FDI_t/GDP_t + a_3 FDI_t H_t/GDP_t + a_4 X_t + U_t,$$

using pooled cross-sectional time-series data. The authors obtained a negative coefficient from FDI and a positive coefficient from the interaction between FDI and schooling. Putting these estimates together means that the effect of FDI becomes positive only if the schooling level is high enough.

The findings suggesting that FDI has a positive growth effect, at least for countries surpassing a threshold schooling level, and that this growth effect is greater than that of domestic investment, are often cited to argue for the superiority of FDI over other forms of capital flows in developing countries. It is also argued that FDI brings managerial talent, generates technological spillovers, features more advanced technologies than those available to local firms, and can serve as a catalyst for development (Markusen and Venables, 1999). The evidence from case studies, though, is mixed. Rhee and Belot (1989) offered evidence of technology transfer to domestic textile firms in Bangladesh, and Blomstrom (1989) found that Mexican sectors featuring greater foreign ownership experienced faster productivity growth and faster convergence to US productivity levels. However, Mansfield and Romeo (1980) failed to find evidence of local technology spillovers. Aitken and Harrison (1999) reported that the technology gains from foreign investment in Venezuela were captured by joint ventures and that foreign investment negatively affected the productivity of domestically owned plants with no foreign investment.

If FDI does not generate strong technological spillovers, then other types of capital flows might have a similar or larger growth effect than FDI. Moreover, if we take a long-term growth perspective, there is no presumption that FDI must produce greater growth effects than other forms of foreign financing. The growth effects of non-FDI flows can take place by financing new investment projects and the purchase of technologically advanced equipment. If FDI does not create any miracle in relation to other forms of capital flows, the introduction of a capital flow variable will capture the effects of FDI. According to this view, why is it that FDI produces special growth effects when using standard methodologies? The reason is that FDI is a component of capital flows and is thus correlated with total capital flows. The implication is that in the type of regression conducted by Borensztein *et al.* (1998), if the capital flows to GDP ratio is included instead of FDI over GDP alone, the positive effects of FDI would disappear or shrink.

Tables 9.1 and 9.2 report the results from OLS growth regressions incorporating domestic fixed investment, FDI, and other types of capital flows. The regressions re-examine the growth effects of FDI in developing countries using a longer and broader dataset than in previous studies. This also allows us to contrast the effects of FDI and other types of capital flows. The analysis uses pooled cross-section time-series regressions to examine whether foreign investment and other types of capital flows help to explain growth in developing countries during 1970–94. The growth regressions for developing countries using standard methodologies confirm the results that foreign investment has significant growth effects.

The findings are consistent with the hypothesis that FDI has contributed positively to economic growth but that other types of capital flows do not contribute significantly to explain growth. FDI is found to have stronger growth effects over and above those implicit in the fact that FDI flows are a component of capital flows. The results are robust to the econometric specification tried (OLS, 3SLS, SURE, and other specifications).

A comparison of the estimated coefficients for the domestic fixed investment rate and the FDI variable yields an estimate of the growth impact of FDI relative to that of domestic investment. We find that FDI has a stronger impact than domestic investment for the whole sample of developing countries. The coefficient of foreign direct investment is several times larger than that of domestic investment, confirming earlier results for Latin America. The greater growth effect of foreign investment relative to domestic investment is confirmed in several other econometric trials, but we could not detect a statistically significant effect from the interaction between foreign direct investment and human capital. Specifically, we were not able to find consistent evidence suggesting that FDI works through the interaction with human capital as measured by initial schooling. We surmise that large fluctuations in growth rates and the FDI to GDP ratio from period to period, which are often accentuated when the boom period of the 1990s is included in the sample, obscure the relationship with the schooling variable.

9.5   Do Better Democracies Attract More Capital Flows?

The ambiguity concerning the growth consequences of democracy might arise because the effect of democracy takes place through other channels. For instance, Mobarak (2001) does not find a clear statistical relationship between democracy and growth but finds a negative relationship between democracy and growth *volatility*, a variable that is in turn found to be negatively related to growth. Using a sample of 108 countries during 1974–89, Quinn and Wolley (1999) also find that democracies exhibit more stable growth rates.

Can a better democracy work to attract capital flows? We examine this question by estimating a system of growth, FDI, and schooling equations. Table 9.5 reports the three-stage least-squares (3SLS) simultaneous-equation estimation. The results using OLS and the 3SLS estimation of the structural form of the regression model are roughly consistent. Growth is estimated as a function of variables treated as endogenous (FDI and schooling) and other variables that are treated as exogenous. The three-equation system is then estimated simultaneously assuming that the errors from the three equations are dependent. The FDI equation was kept simple and admits additional explanatory variables such as lagged FDI (this actually worked very well), trade, indexes of openness, and others. The variables capital growth and bank assets are 5-year averages (taken from the World Bank database and defined as decimals) and affect FDI positively, although the coefficient of bank assets is not significant. Private credit (also taken from the World Bank database) significantly affects schooling, indicating the role of finance in education. The widely used institutional variables in La Porta *et al.* (1997) are not used as they would substantially reduce the sample size.

The estimates from the 3SLS regression system offer evidence that democracy has indirect growth effects that work by encouraging schooling, and that a greater index of the rule of law is associated with a higher FDI to GDP ratio. Overall, our results support the notion that institutional variables work both directly and indirectly through multiple channels.

Table 9.5. Growth, FDI, and Schooling Equations, 120 Developing Countries, 1970–94.

3SLS	Growth	FDI	Schooling
Log (initial GDP)	−0.0009		0.017*
	(−1.3)		(2.5)
Schooling	0.01		
	(1.5)		
Government consumption	−0.0002		−0.03*
	(−0.2)		(−4.2)
TOT-TOT(-1)	−0.02	2.3***	
	(−0.4)	(1.8)	
Log (black market premium)	−0.01**		
	(−2.0)		
FDI	0.018***		
	(1.6)		
KF	0.0015		
	(0.6)		
Log (inflation)	−0.02		
	(−0.9)		
Rule of law		0.23***	0.46*
		(1.9)	(7.2)
Democracy	0.002*		0.33*
	(2.5)		(2.8)
Investment	0.13*	−1.7	
	(2.5)	(−1.5)	
Capital growth (av)		5.99*	
		(3.2)	
Bank assets (av)		0.83	
		(1.3)	
Private credit (av)			0.92*
			(3.8)
Latin American dummy	−0.005	0.55***	−0.33*
	(−0.5)	(1.85)	(−2.5)
Africa dummy	−0.02*	0.14	−0.67*
	(−2.4)	(−1.6)	(−5.4)
East Asia dummy	−0.01	0.64*	−0.85*
	(−0.72)	(−2.3)	(−5.6)
1975–79 dummy	0.009		
	(0.7)		
1980–84 dummy	−0.02		
	(−1.2)		
1985–89 dummy	−0.009		
	(−0.7)		
1990–94 dummy	−0.007		
	(−0.5)		
Observations	121	121	121
χ^2	120.7	49.4	257.3
P-value	0.00	0.00	0.00
R^2	0.39	0.29	0.68

9.6 Conclusions

At the onset of the new millennium, creditors, investors, and developing countries recipient of funds and investment are at a crossroads. With developing countries featuring slow growth and all sources of capital flows drying up, the question of what comes or should come next looms large. This situation calls for a re-examination of the roles of different forms of external financing and a search for nontraditional policies for stimulating growth and attracting capital flows.

Let us go back to the original questions. Does FDI promote growth to a greater extent than other types of capital flows and domestic investment? The evidence presented, as well as other regressions performed, produce evidence consistent with the notion that FDI has a greater growth impact than does domestic investment. The evidence on the relative effects of FDI and other forms of capital flows uncovers positive growth effects associated with FDI but does not detect significant effects from other types of capital flows. These results are, we think, reasonable. On the one hand, rapid growth and a strong economy increase the likelihood of loan repayment and expectations that portfolio assets will yield an adequate rate of return for given risk levels. Therefore, rapid growth and expectations of rapid growth often attract capital flows seeking high returns. On the other hand, the repeated experience of capital flow booms ending up in turbulence, reversals, and crises does not lend support to the notion that capital flows have led to faster recipient country growth in recent decades. One would thus have good reason to be skeptical of empirical findings using developing country data for recent decades and suggesting that capital flows have led to faster growth rates after controlling for business cycle and other effects.

What is the effect of political institution quality and its interaction with FDI? The analysis yields positive but not always significant effects from the rule of law. Similarly, the democracy variable does not always yield statistically significant effects in growth equations. This finding can be explained if democracy works indirectly though other variables that might or might not be positively related to growth (Tavarés and Wacziarg, 2001). Also, the evidence presented by Mobarak (2001) and Quinn and Wolley (1999) indicates that a better democracy index is related to more stable growth. This evidence might suggest that voters demand growth stability to a greater extent than they demand high growth rates.

Our analysis has clear and strong policy implications. Improving democracy, securing the rule of law, and stimulating foreign direct investment encourage growth. These conclusions have important implications for current policy discussions about capital flows to developing countries and are consistent with a development role for FDI. The positive effects of institutional variables suggest that the concepts of growth policies and foreign investment promotion should be expanded to include the quality of government, as expressed in the quality of the democratic regime and the rule of law.

Should investors and countries look toward the continuation of foreign direct investment flows rather than toward portfolio flows? The deeper question that remains to be answered is what mechanisms can be utilized to establish an unambiguously positive role for non-FDI capital flows in developing countries. Further research will determine the extent to which better institutional quality, and policies establishing greater macroeconomic stability, can bring about a productive role for non-FDI capital inflows.

Data Appendix

Total number of countries included in the sample: 119.

- *Latin America* (23): Argentina, Belize, Bolivia, Brazil, Chile, Colombia, Costa Rica, Dominican Republic, Ecuador, El Salvador, Guatemala, Guyana, Haiti, Honduras, Jamaica, Mexico, Nicaragua, Paraguay, Peru, Suriname, Trinidad/Tobago, Uruguay, Venezuela.
- *Africa* (47): Angola, Benin, Botswana, Burkina Faso, Burundi, Cameroon, Cape Verde, Central Africa Republic, Chad, Comoros, Democratic Republic of Congo, Republic of Congo, Côte d'Ivoire, Equatorial Guinea, Ethiopia, Gabon, Gambia, Ghana, Guinea, Guinea-Bissau, Kenya, Lesotho, Liberia, Madagascar, Malawi, Mali, Mauritania, Mauritius, Morocco, Mozambique, Namibia,

Niger, Nigeria, Rwanda, Sao Tome & Principe, Senegal, Seychelles, Sierra Leone, Somalia, South Africa, Swaziland, Tanzania, Togo, Tunisia, Uganda, Zambia, Zimbabwe.

- *East Asia* (5): Indonesia, Kiribati, Malaysia, Philippines, Thailand.
- *Asia, others* (4): China, Nepal, Papua New Guinea, Sri Lanka.
- *Eastern Europe* (26): Albania, Armenia, Azerbaijan, Belarus, Bulgaria, Croatia, Cyprus, Czech Republic, Czechoslovakia, Estonia, Georgia, Hungary, Kazakhstan, Kyrgyz Republic, Latvia, Lithuania, Macedonia, Malta, Poland, Romania, Russia, Slovak Republic, Slovenia, Turkey, Turkmenistan, Ukraine.
- *Middle East* (14): Algeria, Bahrain, Djibouti, Egypt, Iran, Iraq, Jordan, Kuwait, Libya, Oman, Saudi Arabia, Sudan, Syria Arab Republic, Turkey.

References

Aitken, Brian J. and Ann E. Harrison, "Do Domestic Firms Benefit from Direct Foreign Investment? Evidence from Venezuela," *American Economic Review*, 89 (1999): 605–18.

Barro, Robert J., "Democracy and Growth," *Journal of Economic Growth*, 1 (1996): 1–27.

———, *Determinants of Economic Growth: A Cross-Country Empirical Study*, Cambridge, MA: MIT Press (1997).

Barro, Robert J. and Jong-Wha Lee, "International Measures of Schooling Years and Schooling Quality," *American Economic Review*, 86 (1996): 218–23.

Blomstrom, Magnus, *Foreign Investment and Spillovers*, London: Routledge (1989).

Blomstrom, Magnus, Robert E. Lipsey, and Mario Zejan, "What Explains Developing Country Growth?" NBER Working Paper 4132 (1992).

———, "Is Fixed Investment the Key to Economic Growth?" *Quarterly Journal of Economics*, 111 (1996): 268–76.

Borensztein, Eduardo, José De Gregorio, and Jong-Wha Lee, "How Does Foreign Direct Investment Affect Economic Growth?" International Monetary Fund working paper WP/94/110 (1994).

———, "How Does Foreign Direct Investment Affect Economic Growth?" *Journal of International Economics*, 45 (1998): 115–35.

Borner, Silvio, Aymo Brunetti, and Beatrice Weder, *Political Credibility and Economic Development*, New York: Macmillan Press (1995).

Brunetti, Aymo, "Political Variables in Cross-Country Growth Analysis," *Journal of Economic Surveys*, 11 (1997):163–90.

De Gregorio, José, "Economic Growth in Latin America," *Journal of Development Economics*, 39 (1992): 54–84.

Gastil, Raymond D., *Freedom in the World: Political Rights and Civil Liberties 1986–87*, Westport, CT: Greenwood (1987).

———, "The Comparative Survey of Freedom: Experiences and Suggestions," *Studies in Comparative International Development*, 25 (1990): 25–50.

Kaufmann, Daniel, Aart Kraay, and Pablo Zoido-Lobaton, "Aggregating Governance Indicators," World Bank Policy Research Working Paper 2195 (1999a).

———, "Governance Matters," World Bank Policy Research Working Paper 2196 (1999b).

La Porta, Rafael, Florencio López de Silanes, Andrei Shleifer, and Robert Vishny, "Legal Determinants of External Finance," *Journal of Finance*, 52 (1997): 1131–50.

Levine, Ross, "International Financial Liberalization and Economic Growth," *Review of International Economics*, 9 (2001): 688–702.

Mansfield, Edwin and Anthony Romeo, "Technology Transfer to Overseas Subsidiaries by US-Based Firms," *Quarterly Journal of Economics*, 95 (1980): 737–50.

Markusen, James R. and Anthony J. Venables, "Foreign Direct investment as a Catalyst for Industrial Development," *European Economic Review*, 43 (1999): 341–56.

Mobarak, Ahmed Mushfiq, "The Causes of Volatility and Implications for Economic Development," mimeo, University of Maryland, April (2001).

Quinn, Dennis P. and John T. Wolley, "Democracy and National Economic Performance: The Search for Stability," mimeo, Georgetown University (1999).

Radelet, Steven and Jeffrey Sachs, "The East Asian Financial Crisis: Diagnosis, Remedies and Prospects," *Brookings Papers on Economic Activity*, 1 (1998): 1–74.

Reichert, Usa-Nair and Diana Weinhold, "Causality Tests for Cross-Country Panels: A New Look at FDI and Economic Growth in Developing Countries," *Oxford Bulletin of Economics and Statistics*, 63 (2000): 153–67.

Rhee, Jong Wong and Therese Belot, "Export Catalysts in Low-Income Countries," World Bank Industry and Energy Department, Industry Series paper 5 (1989).

Rodrik, Dani, "Who Needs Capital Account Convertibility?" *Essays in International Finance*, no. 207, Princeton University, Department of Economics, International Finance Section (1998).

Tavarés, Jose and Romain Wacziarg, "How Democracy Affects Growth," *European Economic Review*, 45 (2001): 1341–78.

Chapter 10

International Financial Liberalization, Corruption, and Economic Growth*

10.1 Introduction

The globalization of capital markets in recent years has led to a historical degree of financial integration in the world. As Obstfeld (1998, p. 11) remarks: "the worldwide trend of financial opening in the 1990s has restored a degree of international capital mobility not seen since this century's beginning." Associated with this globalization has been a worldwide process of capital account liberalization. In industrialized countries, the elimination of restrictions on capital flows accelerated in the 1980s and 1990s, beginning with Margaret Thatcher's reforms in the United Kingdom, continuing with Japan's liberalization of capital inflows and outflows in the early 1980s, and ending with the European Community's elimination of intra-community barriers to capital flows in the 1990s. Among developing countries, liberalization efforts accelerated in the 1990s, with countries from Mexico to South Korea eliminating major barriers to international trade in assets.[1]

*This chapter was authored by Francisco L. Rivera-Batiz and was originally published in *Review of International Economics*, Vol. 9, No. 4 (November 2001), pp. 727–737. ©2001 Blackwell Publishers Ltd.

The author is grateful to two anonymous referees for useful comments.

The increased global financial integration has resulted in substantial capital inflows in emerging markets. But despite this overall expansion, many developing nations have not shared in the increased capital influx. For example, in 1998, the Latin America and Caribbean region together with the Europe and Central Asia region received $87 billion in net private capital inflows, excluding foreign direct investment (FDI). But in sub-Saharan Africa, this balance was negative that year, with the region suffering a net private capital *outflow* of $1 billion. In fact, aside from FDI, private capital flows to sub-Saharan Africa were either negative or negligible during the 1980s and 1990. As a result, massive amounts of the wealth owned by African residents lies invested elsewhere in the world. Collier *et al.* (1999) estimate that as much as 39% of the private wealth of the sub-Saharan Africa region in 1990 was held abroad. In recent years, African countries from Cameroon and Nigeria to South Africa have experienced sustained capital outflows (see Ajayi and Khan, 2000).

The experience of capital flight is not restricted to countries in sub-Saharan Africa. The situation applies also to a number of countries in Latin America and the Caribbean as well as in transition economies.[2] For example, when both officially recorded and unrecorded capital flows are taken into account, capital flight from some former Soviet Republics was extensive in the 1990s. Some studies estimate Russian private capital flight to have totaled $150 billion between 1992 and 1999 (Cooper and Hardt, 2000; Abalkin and Whalley, 1999). These capital outflows acted as substitutes for the massive capital inflows associated with international organizations, such as the IMF and the World Bank.

This paper provides a theoretical framework to examine how capital flight may be stimulated by the liberalization of a developing country's international financial transactions. It then studies the effects of the capital outflows on the long-run growth of the economy. A general-equilibrium, endogenous growth model is constructed in which corruption forms a part of the country's economic environment. Corruption is assumed to act as a tax on the firms and entrepreneurs innovating, designing, and producing new goods in the economy. This reduces the economy's rate of technological change and lowers the domestic rate of return to capital. In this context, the paper shows that the impact of international financial liberalization on long-run growth can be either positive or negative. A drop in growth is obtained when the level of corruption is high enough to cause domestic rates of return to capital before liberalization to drop below those in the rest of the world. Opening the capital account in this case generates capital flight, which causes the economy's innovation sector to contract, reducing the rate of technological change and causing output growth to decline. On the other hand, if the level of corruption in the economy is sufficiently low, the capital account liberalization will act to boost the country's technological change and growth.

The next section of the paper presents the endogenous growth model in the presence of corruption. Initially, the economy is assumed to be closed to international financial transactions. Section 10.3 examines the growth effects of opening the country to international trade in assets. The last section discusses the conclusions and policy implications of the analysis.

10.2   A Model of a Small Open Economy in the Presence of Corruption

A substantial literature has developed over the past few years examining the sources and consequences of corruption. A wide array of variables have been linked to corruption, including the (low) salaries received by civil servants, the availability of economic rents from which bribes can be extracted, and the under-development of the country's legal system, among many other variables.[3] In addition, empirical work has emerged presenting cross-country data on the level of corruption and examining the impact of corruption on development. Most of these studies show a significant negative relationship between corruption and various measures of economic welfare, including per capita income, income equality, and GDP growth.[4]

The model constructed in this paper seeks to capture the situation of a developing country where corruption forms an integral part of the economic system. Corruption acts as a tax on the firms and entrepreneurs innovating, designing and producing new goods in the economy. We assume that for each new good to be produced and sold, a license must be obtained and a government official must approve it. Although this may technically be costless, paperwork activity, officials are assumed to ask applicants for bribes in order to grant their approval. Government officials receive civil service income that is negligible compared with the bribes; for simplicity, this legitimate source of income is assumed to be zero.

The corrupt officials seek to maximize their expected income by setting a kickback or bribery tax rate, t, expressed as a proportion of the revenues received by producers of new goods in the country. They are free to set this rate, subject to two constraints: the size of the tax base, which depends on the revenues made by producers of new goods, R, and a probability that the bribery scheme will be dismantled, θ. Both the revenue base and the probability of the corruption scheme breaking-down are assumed to depend on the bribery tax rate. The revenues made by producers are assumed to decline with higher bribery tax rates. The probability of the corrupt regime being dismantled rises with the rate, t. As the bribery tax rates rise, those being taxed are more likely to find it in their interest to obtain the political capital to change the governance system in the country so as to eradicate corruption.

Under the assumptions, corrupt officials will seek to maximize their expected gain from bribes, G, which is equal to

$$G = (1 - \theta)tR(t), \tag{1}$$

with all symbols as defined before (note that the expected gain to the officials if the system is dismantled is zero). The first-order condition for the maximization of G results in the following expression for the equilibrium bribe tax rate in the economy:

$$t^* = \frac{(1 - \theta)(1 - \varepsilon)}{\theta'}, \tag{2}$$

where $\varepsilon = -(\frac{t}{R})(\frac{\partial R}{\partial t})$ is the elasticity of producers' revenues to the bribery tax rate $(0 < \varepsilon < 1)$, and $\theta' = d\theta/dt > 0$ is the derivative of the probability of the corruption regime been dismantled with respect to the tax rate.

Equation (2) suggests that the bribery tax rate which maximizes the corrupt officials' gain, G, will increase when: (1) the producers' revenue function is relatively more inelastic with respect to the bribery tax rate, (2) the probability that the corrupt regime will be dismantled drops, and (3) a rise of the bribery tax rates has a smaller impact on the probability that the corrupt regime will be dismantled.

The corruption module just discussed is now introduced into a general-equilibrium, endogenous growth model. Consider an open economy trading in final goods with the rest of the world.[5] Initially, the country is assumed to be closed to international financial transactions. The next section examines the case when financial liberalization allows international trade in assets to occur.

The economy produces two final goods, X and Y, whose prices are determined exogenously (P_x and P_y are exogenous). Sector X utilizes both physical and human capital, and is assumed to be a human-capital intensive sector whose production function is of the Cobb–Douglas type, given by

$$X = I_x^\beta H_x^{1-\beta}, \tag{3}$$

where X is the output of good X, H_x is the input of human capital, β is a positive fraction, and I_x is a sub-production function given by

$$I_x = \left(\sum_{i=1}^{n} Z_{ix}^\alpha \right)^{1/\alpha}, \tag{4}$$

where α is a positive fraction and Z_{ix} represents the use of physical capital good i in sector X, where each Z_{ix} is assumed to be slightly differentiated from other capital goods, the total number of which is n at any given moment in time.

Note that each capital good enters symmetrically the sub-production function in equation (4). On the assumption that all Z_{ix} are identical, then

$$I_x = n^{(1-\alpha)/\alpha} Z_x, \tag{5}$$

where $Z_x = nZ_{ix}$, representing the total quantity demanded of capital goods by sector X.

Substituting equation (5) into (3) yields

$$X = n^\gamma Z_x^\beta H_x^{1-\beta}, \tag{6}$$

where $\gamma = \beta(1-\alpha)/\alpha$. This shows that production of good X is a function of the quantities of physical and human capital used in production, Z_x and H_x, and the number of capital goods available in the economy, n. This type of production relationship, where the parameter $A = n^\gamma$ represents a technology parameter that increases with the number of capital goods available for production, is derived from Romer (1990a) and endogenizes technological change by connecting it to the number of capital goods, n.

Sector Y produces a commodity that is intensive in unskilled labor, and its production function is given by

$$Y = I_y^\beta L_y^{1-\beta}, \tag{7}$$

where Y is output, L_y is the input of unskilled labor, β is as defined earlier, and I_y is a sub-production function given by

$$I_y = \left(\sum_{i=1}^n Z_{iy}^\alpha \right)^{1/\alpha}, \tag{8}$$

with α as defined earlier, and with Z_{iy} representing the use of physical capital good i in sector Y. Following the same assumptions made in relation to equation (5), we can combine equations (7) and (8) into

$$Y = n^\gamma Z_y^\beta L_y^{1-\beta}, \tag{9}$$

where $Z_y = nZ_{iy}$ is the total demand for capital in sector Y.

Both final goods sectors are assumed to function in perfectly competitive markets. Firms minimizing costs of production in these sectors will set price equal to unit costs, as given by

$$P_x = n^{-\gamma} C_x(W_H, P_z), \tag{10}$$

$$P_y = n^{-\gamma} C_y(W_L, P_z), \tag{11}$$

where C_x and C_y are the unit cost functions in sectors X and Y, respectively, W_H is the wage rate of skilled labor or human capital,

W_L is the wage rate of unskilled labor, and P_Z is the price of each capital good (all capital goods will have the same price, as determined from the symmetry of the demand for, and supply of, each capital good, to be established next).

The production function for each capital good is given by

$$Z_i = H_{zi}^a L_{zi}^{1-a}, \tag{12}$$

where H_{zi} is the demand for human capital in the firm producing capital good i, L_{zi} is the demand for unskilled labor used by each firm, and the exponent "a" is a positive fraction.

The profit of each capital goods producer is

$$\pi_1 = P_z Z_i (1 - t^*) - W_L L_{zi} + W_H H_{zi}. \tag{13}$$

Assuming that each firm maximizes profits, the following first-order conditions are obtained:

$$a\alpha(1 - t^*)P_z Z_i = W_H H_{zi}, \tag{14}$$

$$(1 - a)\alpha(1 - t^*)P_z Z_i = W_L L_{zi}. \tag{15}$$

From these two equations, one can derive that

$$\alpha P_z(1 - t^*) = C_Z(W_L W_H), \tag{16}$$

where C_Z is the unit cost of production for each firm in the capital goods sector. Note that corruption acts as a tax on capital goods producers, reducing the effective price, P_z, that they receive per unit of the good sold. The greater the level of corruption, as represented symbolically by an increase in t, the greater the tax.

In a small open economy trading in final goods (but not capital goods, which remain nontraded), then P_x and P_y are both fixed by world markets. Given the number of capital goods, n, and the prices of final goods, P_x and P_y, then equations (2), (10), (11), and (16) constitute a system of four equations in four variables, W_L, W_H, P_z, and t^*.

In a dynamic economy, n will rise. I will discuss shortly the forces generating increases in n. But if we denote the steady-state growth rate of the number of capital goods by g, then equations (10), (11), and (16) imply that the wages of skilled and unskilled labor, as well as the prices of capital goods, will all rise at the rate γg. In addition, since in a steady state the usage of inputs will not be shifting across sectors X and Y, then X and Y will also grow at the steady-state rate γg. Consequently, the economy's aggregate output growth rate will also equal γg.

The increase in the number of capital goods, n, determines the long-run growth rate. How are new capital goods created? Following the literature (Romer, 1990a; Grossman and Helpman, 1991a, b), we assume that new capital goods are created by a research or technology sector that uses human capital and has the following production function:

$$dn/dt = \dot{n} = nH_n/a_n, \tag{17}$$

where H_n is the input of human capital in the technology sector, and a_n is an exogenous parameter that reflects the productivity of human capital in generating new capital goods, with lower values of a_n representing greater productivity. Given this productivity parameter, equation (17) suggests that the creation of new capital goods is positively related to the quantity of human capital used by the technology/research sector and to the existing number of capital goods, n. The latter represents the fact that, as n rises, the existing ideas available for innovators to generate new products increases, stimulating innovation and, as a result, the number of capital goods created (for more details, see Romer, 1990a).

Note that, from equation (17):

$$g = (\dot{n}/n) = (H_n/a_n). \tag{18}$$

This means that the rate of growth of new capital goods, which is directly related to the rate of growth of the economy, is determined by the amount of human capital allocated to the research/technology sector. The next step is to specify the equilibrium value of H_n.

The rate of return on producing a new capital good, r, is composed of the capital gain on the value of the capital good plus the dividend rate:

$$r = \dot{V}/V + \pi/V, \tag{19}$$

where V is the value of a new capital good, $\dot{V} = dV/dt$ and π denotes the profit obtained from the production of a capital good, so that π/V is the dividend rate.

The value of a new capital good is equal to the cost of producing the new capital good, which is given by

$$V = (W_H H_n/\dot{n}) = (W_H a_n/n). \tag{20}$$

From this one derives that the capital gain — the gain in the value of a new capital good — is given by

$$\frac{\dot{V}}{V} = \frac{\dot{W}_H}{W_H} - \frac{\dot{n}}{n}. \tag{21}$$

Substituting equation (21) into (19) yields

$$\frac{\dot{V}}{V} = \frac{\dot{W}_H}{W_H} - \frac{\dot{n}}{n} + \frac{\pi}{V}. \tag{22}$$

But the profits in the production of each capital good are

$$\pi = P_Z Z_i - C_z Z_i = [1 - \alpha(1 - t^*)]P_Z Z_i, \tag{23}$$

where we have made use of equation (16). Utilizing equations (14), (20) and (23), we can then modify equation (22) into

$$\begin{aligned} r &= \frac{\dot{W}_H}{W_H} - \frac{\dot{n}}{n} + [1 - \alpha(1 - t^*)]H_Z/a\alpha(1 - t^*)a_n \\ &= (\gamma - 1)g + [1 - \alpha(1 - t^*)]H_Z/[a\alpha(1 - t^*)]a_n, \end{aligned} \tag{24}$$

where $H_Z = nH_{iz}$. Use has been made of the fact that, at the steady state, skilled labor wages rise at the rate γg and the number of capital goods at the rate g.

Equation (24) determines the rate of return on new capital goods. But this relationship includes as a variable the total amount of human capital used in the capital goods sector, H_Z. To solve the model we thus need to introduce the human capital endowment constraint

$$H_n + H_x + H_Z = H. \tag{25}$$

Using equations (14), (15), and (18) and some derivations, we can transform equation (25) into

$$ga_H + bH_Z = H, \tag{26}$$

where $b = [(1 - \beta) + \beta a\alpha(1 + \lambda)(1 - t^*)]/\beta a\alpha(1 + \lambda)(1 - t^*)$, with $\lambda = Z_y/Z_x$, which is a fixed parameter under a steady state.

On combining equations (24) and (26), and with some manipulation, this yields an expression for the steady-state rate of growth of the economy:

$$g = \left\{ \frac{[1 - \alpha](1 - t^*)}{\delta a_n} \right\} H - \left[\frac{ba\alpha(1 - t^*)}{\delta} \right] r, \tag{27}$$

where $\delta = \alpha(1 - t^*) + b(1 - \gamma)a\alpha(1 - t*)$, which is assumed to be positive in order to ensure a stable steadystate equilibrium.[6]

Equation (27) provides a positive connection between the growth rate and the rate of return to capital, as established by the supply side of the economy. In a nation that does not trade in assets with the rest of the world, domestic consumers determine a second relationship between the rate of return to capital and growth.

From the consumption side, the rate of return can be determined from the consumer maximization problem which involves maximizing utility, U, given by:

$$U = \int_t^\infty \exp[-\rho(\tau - t)] \log U[D_x(\tau), D_y(\tau)] d\tau \tag{28}$$

where D_x and D_y represent quantities consumed of goods X and Y at any given time τ, and ρ is a rate of time preference. Equation (28) is maximized subject to a budget constraint stating the equality of income and expenditure at any given time. This optimization yields the following condition:

$$r = (\dot{E}/E) + \rho, \tag{29}$$

where E is aggregate consumption expenditure. But in the economy's steady state, as noted earlier, consumption expenditure will grow at γg, and therefore

$$r = \gamma g + \rho. \tag{29'}$$

Equations (27) and (29') constitute a system of two equations in two variables, g and r_o. Solving for the steady state growth rate results in

$$g = \left[\frac{[1 - \alpha(1 - t^*)]}{a_n[1 - \alpha(1 - t^*) + ba\alpha(1 - t^*)]H} \right.$$

$$\left. - \rho[a\alpha(1 - t^*)b]/[1 - \alpha(1 - t^*) + ba\alpha(1 - t^*)]. \tag{30}$$

The rate of growth of the economy is thus determined by the endowment of human capital (first term) and the rate of time preference (second term). Note that, the greater the endowment of human capital, H, the higher the growth rate, holding other things constant. In addition, the greater the degree of corruption, t^*, the lower the rate of growth, other things constant.

10.3 The Impact of Capital Account Liberalization on Economic Growth

Consider now the situation when the economy described in section 10.2 is opened to international trade in assets. In this case, domestic firms and households can both borrow and lend at the world interest rate, r^*. Under the assumption of perfect capital mobility, the domestic rate of return to capital must equal the exogenously-given world interest rate, or

$$r = r^*. \tag{31}$$

This condition replaces equation (29'), which no longer becomes relevant because the economy's steady-state equilibrium does not require that expenditure be equal to income at every moment (only an intertemporal budget constraint must be satisfied).

Using equation (27), the steady-state growth rate after capital account liberalization becomes

$$g = \{[1 - \alpha(1 - t^*)]/\delta a_n\}H - [ba\alpha(1 - t^*)/\delta]r^*, \qquad (32)$$

with all the variables as defined earlier. Under the assumption that δ is positive, equation (32) shows that the economy's growth rate is positively affected by increased human capital (rising H) but negatively affected by an increase in the world interest rate, r^*.

How does opening the capital account affect the economy's growth rate? If the equilibrium rate of return on capital before the liberalization, r, lies below r^*, then equation (32) suggests that the growth rate will decline. The explanation is that, when the capital account is liberalized and $r < r^*$, then capital flight will occur, as domestic residents can find higher rates of return in the rest of the world. As households shift their investments from domestic to foreign assets, which yield a higher rate of return, domestic innovation collapses and the output growth rate (the number of new capital goods created) drops. As the economy reaches a steady state after liberalization, domestic rates of return will align with world rates of return, but at a lower output growth rate.

Note that the higher the rate of corruption, the greater the tax rate t^*. This reduces the economy's rate of return to capital before the liberalization and makes it more likely that there will be capital flight from the economy after the liberalization, causing a drop in growth. On the other hand, the lower the level of corruption in the economy, the less likely that this event will occur and, instead, opening the capital account will result in capital inflows that will stimulate innovation, technological change, and growth.

International financial liberalization has distributional effects as well. Consider, for example, the case where the opening leads to capital outflows. In this event, even though the country's output growth rate declines, asset holders will benefit from the higher interest rate. But the increased income received by asset holders is matched by a fall both in the level and the rate of increase of the earnings of both skilled and unskilled workers. The drop in the real income of skilled and unskilled labor is associated with the reduction

in the amount of physical capital invested in the country as a result
of capital flight. The reduction in the growth rate of labor earnings is
directly related to the drop in the rate of growth of output since both
are equal. Note that if the skilled and unskilled workers were not asset
holders, their economic welfare would decline after the liberalization
because their labor income shrinks. If they are asset holders; however,
their welfare may increase, depending on the share of the country's
assets that they own.[7]

10.4 Conclusions

The impact of the liberalization of the capital account on emerging
markets has generated heated controversy in recent years. The
empirical work of Beck *et al.* (2000), Levine (2001), Errunza (2001)
and others suggests that international financial liberalization fosters
economic development not only by allowing developing nations to
accumulate physical capital but also by improving the domestic
financial system and stimulating productivity growth. Others, such
as Krugman (1993) and Rodrik (1998), find no evidence of a
connection between increased financial liberalization and economic
development. In fact, some have blamed the increased globalization
of capital flows for the rash of emerging market crises in the 1990s,
including the Mexican peso crisis and its Tequila effect, the East
Asian crisis, and the Russian financial crisis and its severe contagion
effects (see Radelet and Sachs, 1998; Eatwell and Taylor, 2000).

This paper shows that international financial liberalization has
ambiguous effects on the rate of growth of a developing economy.
Whether gains or losses in growth are realized depends on whether
the economy benefits from an influx of capital or suffers from a
capital flight after the liberalization. If the rate of return to capital
before liberalization is comparatively low compared with world rates
of return, then an opening of the capital account will result in capital
flight and a reduction of domestic growth. On the other hand, if the
domestic rate of return is high, capital inflows will result that increase
growth.[8]

The paper establishes a negative connection between domestic
corruption and the rate of return to capital. As a result, countries

where corruption is rampant will suffer from low rates of return to capital before the liberalization of international financial transactions. When liberalization does occur, capital flight erupts and the economy's growth rate declines. In low-corruption countries, on the other hand, capital account liberalization generates positive growth effects.

Capital flight has induced policymakers in many poor countries to introduce capital and exchange controls, to block the outflows that would result if liberalization were to occur. This paper shows, however, that this is not the first-best policy. Insofar as corruption is behind the relatively low domestic rates of return to capital, the first-best policy in this context is to intervene to reduce or eliminate corruption. Indeed, improved governance would result in a burst of growth since it would allow domestic entrepreneurs and innovators to be unbound from the chattels imposed by a corrupt regime, even in a closed economy. As bribe requests are eliminated or controlled, the returns to research and development will boom, fostering technological change. But, even more importantly, a drop in corruption allows an opening of the capital account to further benefit the domestic economy. With a drop in corruption, the developing economy's natural shortage of capital will reveal itself in high rates of return to capital, which would result in capital inflows as a result of international financial liberalization. On the other hand, introducing capital account liberalization without the appropriate domestic policies in place to improve governance and control corruption may result in a magnification of domestic distortions and a decline of economic growth.

Notes:

[1] A broad discussion of capital account liberalization in developing countries is presented in Lukauskas and Rivera-Batiz (2001), Ito and Krueger (1996), Edwards (1995), and Caprio *et al.* (1994).

[2] Theoretical and empirical models of capital flight are presented in Collier *et al.* (1999), Schineller (1997), Dooley and Kletzer (1994), Lessard and Williamson (1987), Rivera-Batiz (1987), and Cuddington (1986).

[3]See Gray and Kaufmann (1998), Adam and O'Connell (1997), and Shleifer and Vishny (1998).

[4]See Kaufmann *et al.* (1999), Ehrlich and Lui (1999), and Mauro (1995).

[5]The model is based on endogenous growth models of the open economy, such as Grossman and Helpman (1991a, b); see also Rivera-Batiz and Romer (1991) and Rivera-Batiz (1996, 1997).

[6]This requires that the exponent γ be small enough — or the parameter α in the capital goods sub-production function be large enough — to sustain a positive δ. This means that the increasing returns in the production of capital goods, which are directly related to α, are bounded.

[7]See Romer (1990b) for a discussion of this case.

[8]In different models, the dangers of international financial liberalization in the presence of domestic distortions have been examined by Detragiache (2001) and Agenor and Aizenman (1999).

References

Abalkin, Leonid and John Whalley, "The Problem of Capital Flight from Russia," mimeo, Center for the Study of International Economic Relations, University of Western Ontario (1999).

Adam, Christopher S. and Stephen A. O'Connell, "Aid, Taxation and Development: Analytical Perspectives on Aid Effectiveness in Sub-Saharan Africa," mimeo, Center for Study of African Economies, Oxford University (1997).

Agenor, Pierre-Richard and Joshua Aizenman, "Volatility and the Welfare Costs of Financial Market Integration," in P. R. Agenor, M. Miller, A. Weber, and D. Vines (eds.), *The Asian Financial Crisis: Causes, Contagion, and Consequences*, Cambridge: Cambridge University Press (1999): 195–229.

Ajayi, S. Ibi and Mohsin S. Khan (eds.), *External Debt and Capital Flight in Sub-Saharan Africa*, Washington, D.C.: International Monetary Fund (2000).

Beck, Thorsten, Ross Levine, and Norman Loayza, "Finance and the Sources of Growth," *Journal of Financial Economics* 58 (2000): 261–300.

Caprio, Gerard, Izak Atiyas, and James A. Hanson (eds.), *Financial Reform: Theory and Practice*, Cambridge: Cambridge University Press (1994).

Collier, Paul, Anke Hoeffler, and Catherine Pattillo, "Flight Capital as a Portfolio Choice," World Bank Policy Research Working Paper 2066 (1999).

Cooper, William H. and John P. Hardt, "Russian Capital Flight, Economic Reforms and US Interests: An Analysis," Report for Congress, Congressional Research Service (2000).

Cuddington, John T., "Capital Flight: Issues, Estimates and Explanations," *Princeton Studies in International Finance*, 58 (1986).

Detragiache, Enrica, "Bank Fragility and International Capital Mobility," *Review of International Economics*, 9 (4), 673–687.

Dooley, Michael P. and Kenneth M. Kletzer, "Capital Flight, External Debt and Domestic Policies," *Economic Review of the Federal Reserve Bank of San Francisco* (1994): 29–37.

Eatwell, John and Lance Taylor, *Global Finance at Risk: The Case for International Regulation*, New York: New Press (2000).

Edwards, Sebastian, *Crisis and Reform in Latin America: From Despair to Hope*, Oxford: Oxford University Press (1995).

Ehrlich, Isaac and T. Lui, "Bureaucratic Corruption and Endogenous Economic Growth," *Journal of Political Economy* 107 (1999): S270–93.

Errunza, Vihang, "Foreign Portfolio Equity Investments, Financial Liberalization, and Economic Development, *Review of International Economics*, 9 (4), 703–726.

Gray, Cheryl W. and Daniel Kaufmann, "Corruption and Development," *Finance and Development* (1998): 7–10.

Grossman, Gene M. and Elhanan Helpman, *Innovation and Growth in the Global Economy*, Cambridge, MA: MIT Press (1991a).

———, "Growth and Welfare in a Small Open Economy," in E. Helpman and A. Razin (eds.), *International Trade and Trade Policy*, Cambridge, MA: MIT Press (1991b): 141–66.

Ito, T. and Anne Krueger (eds.), *Financial Deregulation and Integration in East Asia*, Chicago: University of Chicago Press (1996): 220–45.

Kaufmann, Daniel, Aart Kraay, and Pablo Zoido-Lobaton, "Governance Matters," World Bank Policy Research Working Paper 2196 (1999).

Krugman, Paul, "International Finance and Economic Development," in A. Giovannini (ed.), *Finance and Development: Issues and Experience*, Cambridge: Cambridge University Press (1993): 11–28.

Lessard, Donald R. and John Williamson, *Capital Flight and Third World Debt*, Washington, DC: Institute for International Economics (1987).

Levine, Ross, "International Financial Liberalization and Economic Growth," *Review of International Economics*, 9 (4), 688–702.

Lucas, Robert E., "Why Capital Doesn't Flow from Rich to Poor Countries," *American Economic Review* 80 (1990):92–6.

Lukauskas, Arvid and Francisco L. Rivera-Batiz (eds.), *The Political Economy of the East Asian Crisis and Its Aftermath: Tigers in Distress*, Cheltenham: Edward Elgar (2001).

Mauro, Paolo, "Corruption and Growth," *Quarterly Journal of Economics*, 110 (1995): 681–712.

Obstfeld, Maurice, "The Global Capital Market: Benefactor or Menace?," *Journal of Economic Perspectives*, 12 (1998): 9–30.

Radelet, Steven and Jeffrey Sachs, "The East Asian Financial Crisis: Diagnosis, Remedies and Prospects," *Brookings Papers on Economic Activity*, (1998): 1–74.

Rivera-Batiz, Francisco L., "Modeling Capital Flight from Latin America: A Portfolio Balance Approach," *Modeling and Simulation* 14 (1987): 153–9.

———, "The Economics of Technological Progress and Endogenous Growth in Open Economies," in Hans-Eckart Scharrer (ed.), *The Economics of High Technology Competition and Cooperation in Global Markets*, Hamburg: Institut für Wirtschaftsforschung (1996): 31–62.

———, "Trade Liberalization and the International Distribution of the Gains from Growth," in Satya Dev Gupta and Nanda K. Choudhry (eds.), *Globalization and Development: Growth, Equity and Sustainability*, Boston: Kluwer Academic (1997): 135–78.

Rivera-Batiz, Luis A. and Paul M. Romer, "Economic Integration and Endogenous Growth," *Quarterly Journal of Economics*, 106 (1991): 531–55.

Rodrik, Dani, "Who Needs Capital Account Convertibility?" in *Essays in International Finance*, vol. 207, Princeton University, Department of Economics, International Finance Section (1998).

Romer, Paul M., "Endogenous Technological Change," *Journal of Political Economy* 90 (1990a): S71–102.

———, "Trade, Politics and Growth in a Small, Less Developed Economy," mimeo, Department of Economics, University of Chicago (1990b).

Schineller, Lisa, "An Econometric Model of Capital Flight from Developing Countries," IFDP Paper 579, International Finance Division, Board of Governors, Federal Reserve Board (1997).

Shleifer, Andrei and Robert Vishny, *The Grabbing Hand: Government Pathologies and Their Cures*, Cambridge: Harvard University Press (1998).

Chapter 11

The East Asian Crisis
and the Anatomy of
Emerging Market Disease[*]

11.1 Introduction

In 1997, after what had been a decade of remarkable growth, the economics of Thailand, the Philippines, Malaysia, Indonesia and Korea all came to a sudden and grinding halt, suffering a severe crisis from which it has taken them years to recover. What became known as the East Asian crisis was not foreseen by most observers. On the contrary, these countries had been characterized in previous years as 'miracle economies' and their economic policies as exemplary. In 1993, for example, the World Bank gave the region glowing marks, noting that, in these countries, 'fundamentally sound development policy was a major ingredient in achieving rapid growth. Macroeconomic management was unusually stable, providing the essential framework for private investment' (World Bank 1993, p. 5).

[*]This paper was authored by Francisco L. Rivera-Batiz and was originally published in Arvid J. Lukauskas and Francisco L. Rivera-Batiz, eds., *The Political Economy of the East Asian Crisis: Tigers in Distress*, Edward Elgar Publishers, Cheltenham, U.K., 2001, pp. 31–73. ©2001 Edward Elgar Publishing.

This paper was written while the author was director of the Program in Economic Policy Management and associate professor in the Economics department at Columbia University. The author gratefully acknowledges the comments of discussants and participants at a conference held at Columbia University on March 14–15, 1999.

What went wrong in East Asia? What turned-around the situation of countries that, just a few months earlier, had been hailed as examples of economic stability and as showcases of the way economic policies should be handled? It is the purpose of this chapter to discuss the background behind the crisis, its unfolding in 1997 and 1998, and its consequences.

The East Asian crisis emerged in the form of a sequence of severe currency crises. First was Thailand, on 2 July 1997, when its central bank abandoned frantic efforts to keep the baht from depreciating in value and decided to let the exchange rate float. This was followed by the Philippine peso on 11 July 1997, when the central bank of the Philippines also decided to let the peso float after losing close to $1 billion in foreign currency reserves a day in the previous week as a result of capital flight. Then, on Monday, 14 July 1997, Malaysia's central bank stopped intervening in foreign exchange markets, letting the ringgit float after a loss of over $10 billion in reserves in just two weeks. In Indonesia, the central bank first widened, on July 11 1997, the trading band around which it was permitting exchange rate changes, from 8 per cent to 12 per cent. However, by 13 August 1997, Bank Indonesia — facing massive capital flight could not prevent the rupiah from reaching its new band limit. The following day, the central bank decided to let the currency float.

Although the Thai baht, the Philippine peso, the Malaysian ringgit and the Indonesian rupiah fell sharply in value during July, August and September, the Korean won had remained relatively stable. The Korean central bank actively intervened to prevent the currency from depreciating. By October and November, the pressures from capital outflows were unsustainable and the Bank of Korea, facing dwindling foreign exchange reserves and a breakdown of its external payments system, allowed the won to depreciate against the dollar.

The tide of capital outflows encountered by the five East Asian economies was the proximate cause of their currency crises. It was a sharp turnaround compared to the situation in the previous ten years. During the early and mid 1990s, financial analysts all over the world encouraged investors to plunge into 'emerging markets,' the most dynamic of which were found indeed in East Asia. An example of this, one of a multitude of voices in a self-propelling chorus of encouragement, is the following statement published in a 1994 article in the *Columbia Journal of World Business*: 'The Asian stock markets have been hot and there are no signs of cooling off. Attracted by solid economies, credible reform and a trend of liberalization, global investors continue investing on a grand scale in these countries... the rates of economic growth in East Asia will continue at the highest in the world during the next decade' (Clemente 1994, p. 92).

The experts at international organizations did not fare much better in predicting at all what was happening in East Asia. In its annual *World Economic Outlook* in May 1996, the International Monetary Fund forcefully stated: 'it is likely that the emerging Asian economies will continue to boom during the next 12 months, although growth could slow down in some of them.... In the Philippines, economic recovery is expected to continue on a firm basis during the next 12 months' (International Monetary Fund 1996, p. 10). And the World Bank, in its annual outlook, was still stating in September of 1997 that: 'even though growth [in East Asia] is likely to slow down, a severe crisis like that of Mexico is unlikely' (World Bank, 1997).

What caused the East Asian crisis? Previous research has considered the role of a wide array of forces, including currency overvaluation, moral hazard and excessive risk-taking among financial institutions, the growth of short-term foreign-currency debt, domestic bank fragility, speculative lending bubbles, financial panic, herd effects and contagion.[1] Although these forces are important, this chapter argues that a focus on them has missed the fundamental, underlying economic phenomenon behind the crisis. We suggest that the crisis is a reflection of a more basic problem facing emerging markets in general, not just East Asia. The fact is that the investment and economic boom in these countries, which puts them in the category of emerging markets, also plants the seeds of an eventual slowdown, or a bust, that reverses some, if not all, of the economic progress. In some countries, such as Mexico, this process of boom and bust has continued for decades.

We refer to this economic phenomenon as 'emerging market disease'. The term disease, rather than virus or flu (which has been used by some experts in the case of the East Asian crisis) is utilized because the forces involved are not short-term in nature but are rather long-term and endemic to the development strategy followed in the countries involved. In essence, emerging markets seek to achieve high rates of economic growth through the rapid and substantial expansion of domestic investment accompanied by macroeconomic stabilization and a major liberalization of international financial transactions. The flood of capital inflows associated with this strategy allow the economies to boom, providing an aura of everlasting prosperity. However, the seeds of a future slowdown or bust are being planted at the same time, through the impact of the capital influx on the exchange rate. Capital inflows exert upward pressure on the value of the domestic currency. A persistent real currency appreciation eventually slows down export growth, increases imports and worsens the current account balance. This has serious consequences. A sluggish export sector will reduce output growth and undermine the confidence of investors on the future of the economy. Furthermore, a widening current account balance deficit, even if initially financed enthusiastically by foreign capital, leads to an accumulation of external debt that, at some point, raises the risk of default, whether in the public or private sector. The sustained real appreciation of the currency also means that expectations of devaluation will inevitably materialize, sooner or later. All of these developments eventually precipitate a withdrawal of funds from the country and a credit crunch that plunges the economy into recession. If the domestic banking system is fragile, and if the capital flight is aggravated by policymakers who tenaciously refuse to devalue, the result is a crisis.

The economic forces behind emerging market disease have been known for a long time. In Latin America, the 'capital inflows problem' has been studied for decades (Diaz-Alejandro 1985; Dornbusch 1986). The best-known cases of the disease in this region have been in Chile (1978–82) and Mexico (1980–84 and 1990–95), but there are other examples in Argentina, Brazil and Uruguay.[2] Some of the symptoms of emerging market disease are akin to what has been called 'Dutch disease'.[3] The latter describes the case of countries where a boom based on the exploitation of natural resources leads to a disastrous de-industrialization in the rest of the economy. Dutch disease erupts as a repercussion of the massive capital that flows into an economy stimulated by the discovery and exploitation of natural resources. These inflows increase the value of domestic currency, hurting the international competitiveness of local exports and shrinking the industrial base of the economy. Countries that were expected to grow rapidly due to their natural wealth end up instead with a sluggish expansion. In emerging market disease, the influx of capital is not necessarily linked to the exploitation of natural resources but is instead associated with rising domestic investment rates, financial liberalization and an opening of the capital account.

This chapter shows how the five East Asian crisis countries: Indonesia, the Republic of Korea, Malaysia, the Philippines, and Thailand, have displayed the main symptoms of emerging market disease. The next section begins with a discussion of the key long-run growth trends in East Asia. Later sections document the period before the crisis, its unfolding and its consequences. The last section outlines the policy implications of the analysis.

11.2 Patterns of Long-Run Growth in East Asia

A glance at some fundamental indicators of economic development shows why the East Asian economies involved in the crisis were generally considered 'miracle economies' in the years preceding the debacle. Table 11.1 displays the changes in real per-capita Gross Domestic Product (GDP) in these countries as well as in the United States between 1960 and 1995. The country with the highest growth rate was the Republic of Korea, which grew at an average rate of 6.5 per cent per year, making it one of the fastest-growing countries in the world during this time period. In 1960, Korea had per-capita income below that of Angola, Madagascar, Mozambique, Senegal, the Dominican Republic, Bolivia, Ecuador and Honduras, among many other developing nations. Yet, by 1996, Korea was catalogued as a high-income country by the World Bank (this rank was lost after the

Table 11.1.   Growth of Real GDP per Capita in East Asia, 1960–95.

	Per-capita GDP, 1960 (in 1995 $)	Per-capita GDP, 1995 (in 1995 $)	Rate of growth 1960–95 (%)
Indonesia	621	2,602	4.1
Rep. of Korea	883	8,505	6.5
Malaysia	1,381	6,613	4.5
The Philippines	1,112	1,756	1.3
Thailand	923	5,034	4.8
United States	9,774	19,621	2.0

Source: Barro and Lee 1994 and World Bank 1998. The data are expressed in constant 1995 dollars and have been adjusted for differences in purchasing power among the various countries.

1997–98 crisis). Thailand, Malaysia and Indonesia also exhibited a rapid expansion of per-capita income, each growing an average of over 4 per cent per year. This earned them the rating of 'high-performing economies' by the World Bank in 1993. The country with the slowest growth was the Philippines, whose GDP per-capita increased at an average rate of 1.3 per cent per year. But even the Philippines was showing a rising growth rate in the 1990s, leading Michael Taylor, an economist with Morgan Stanley, to describe the situation of that economy in 1995 as 'a truly unexpected Asian economic miracle' (as quoted in the *New York Times*, 7 May 1995, p. A6).

Table 11.1 shows that, except for the Philippines, the East Asian economies surpassed the US average rate of growth of per-capita income between 1960 and 1995. They also outperformed the industrialized world in general, diverging from the experience of most other developing countries, which grew slower than the industrialized economies in the period of 1960 to 1995 (see Barro and Sala-i-Martin 1995).

Associated with this economic growth was a substantial expansion of these countries' human and physical capital. Consider first the human component by looking at demographics. Table 11.2 shows the population levels in the East Asian countries in 1998 as well as the total fertility rates in 1960 and 1990. Indonesia is the most populous of the East Asian countries, with a population of

Table 11.2. Demographic Transition in East Asia, 1960–90.

	Population 1998 (millions)	Total fertility rate*	
		1960	1990
Indonesia	204	5.43	2.80
Rep. of Korea	46	5.64	1.70
Malaysia	22	6.81	3.50
The Philippines	75	6.97	3.90
Thailand	61	6.44	2.10

*The total fertility rate is defined as the number of children that would be born to a woman if she were to live to the end of her child-bearing years and bear children at each age according to the prevailing age specific birth-rates in the country.

204 million in 1998. It is followed, in order of decreasing population, by the Philippines, Thailand, Korea and Malaysia. All five countries showed sharp drops in total fertility rates between 1960 and 1990. In Korea, there was a 120 per cent drop in the fertility rate between 1960 and 1990 while for Thailand the reduction was 112 per cent, in Indonesia and Malaysia it was 66 per cent, and in the Philippines 58 per cent.

The demographic transition in East-Asian lowered both birth and death rates. However, death rates dropped before birth rates did. The result was a temporary 'bulge' in the age structure that, over time, made its way into an increased working-age population relative to the non-working, or 'dependent' population. As a recent Asian Development Bank publication has emphasized: 'part of East Asia's rapid growth in income per person between 1965 and 1990 is due to the rising share of the working-age population relative to the total population. During these years, the working-age population grew almost 1 percentage point faster than the total population in East Asia' (Asian Development Bank, 1997b, p. 76). This increased working-age population allowed a greater flow of resources into savings and investment, spurring the growth of GDP per capita (Bloom and Williamson, 1997).

Although the labor force grew rapidly, not all the educational and occupational categories increased at the same pace. The labor

Table 11.3.   Rising Schooling in East Asia, 1960–90.

	Proportion of the population over 25 years of age with no schooling	
	1960 (%)	**1990 (%)**
Indonesia	75.5	32.0
Rep. of Korea	56.9	11.0
Malaysia	58.5	25.6
The Philippines	33.5	9.1
Thailand	48.1	22.0

Source: Barro and Lee 1994.

force growth in the East Asian economies was accompanied by an unprecedented increase in educational attainment. This means, that, although the labor force was rising, the unskilled labor force, that is, the number of workers with no educational attainment, was actually *declining*. Table 11.3 presents the sharp drop in the adult population with no schooling at all. In Indonesia, the proportion of the population 25 years of age or older with no schooling was equal to 75.5 per cent in 1960. By 1990, only 32 per cent of the Indonesian population had no formal education. In the Republic of Korea, the corresponding drop was from close to 57 per cent to just 11 per cent over the thirty-year period. Similar patterns are exhibited by Malaysia, the Philippines and Thailand.

The expansion of schooling is reflected in a sharp decline of adult illiteracy rates. While in developing countries overall, the adult illiteracy rate was 25 per cent in 1998, in Korea it was 2 per cent, in Thailand and the Philippines it was 5 per cent, in Indonesia 10 per cent, and in Malaysia 13 per cent.

The comparative success of East Asian in raising the human capital of their labor force has been linked to a specific set of policies. First, the resources allocated by the government to education were generally greater than those in other developing economies. In 1960, developing countries allocated an average of 1.3 per cent of their GNP to public educational expenditures; in Malaysia, however, the corresponding proportion was 2.9 per cent, in Indonesia it was 2.5 per cent, in Thailand it was 2.3 per cent, and in Korea

2.0 per cent. Second, the proportion of public spending dedicated to primary and secondary education was much higher than in other developing economies in Africa and Latin America. This allowed both the quantity and quality of public primary and secondary education to increase quickly. Indeed, the high-growth East Asian countries all have performed at the highest levels in international assessments of educational progress in secondary schools, exceeding the scores in most countries, including high-income economies (Hanushek and Kim, 1995). Third, public spending was complemented with substantial private investment in education, especially at the secondary and higher education levels. Fourth, the expansion in the supply of skilled labor was accompanied by a sharp increase of the demand for such labor, associated in turn with colossal capital accumulation, as is discussed next. This allowed the human capital to gain employment in a growing economy, instead of becoming unemployed or underemployed. As a result, human capital accumulation explains a substantial portion of the income growth in the region. In Korea, as much as 43 per cent of the growth in per-capita GDP between 1960 and 1990 can be accounted for by the expansion of the skilled labor force (Rivera-Batiz 1999b).

The high-growth East Asian economies have displayed rapid rates of physical capital accumulation. Table 11.4 shows gross investment spending as a fraction of GDP. With the exception of the Philippines, investment rates more than doubled from the 1960s to the 1990s. This expansion was gradual but it was sustained all the way up to the period before the crisis. In Indonesia, investment spending

Table 11.4.   Investment Rates in East Asia, 1960–96.

	Investment as a percentage of Gross Domestic Product			
	1960–69 (%)	1970–79 (%)	1980–89 (%)	1990–96 (%)
Indonesia	9.8	21.8	29.1	34.8
Rep. of Korea	18.4	27.3	30.0	36.9
Malaysia	19.2	25.5	30.3	39.8
The Philippines	19.6	25.6	22.1	22.5
Thailand	20.5	25.8	27.6	42.1

Source: World Bank 1995, Asian Development Bank 1997a.

rose from an average of about 10 per cent of GDP in the 1960s
to about 35 per cent in the 1990s. For the Republic of Korea, the
increase was from 18.4 per cent to 36.9 per cent; for Malaysia it
was from 19.2 per cent to 39.8 per cent, and for Thailand from 20.5
per cent to 42.1 per cent. These investment rates sharply exceed
global investment rates, which have averaged between 20 and 25 per
cent over the last twenty years. Only the Philippines has had lower
investment rages, but even these have been around the worldwide
average.

One of the most popular explanations for East Asian growth
has focused on the export sector. It is argued that, by focusing on
production for export markets, developing economies can in principle
generate substantial short-term gains in efficiency, forced upon them
by the pressures of international competition.[4] It is also pointed out
that long-term gains in economic growth are often the result of the
introduction of new technologies and products, obtained through
greater international trade, as fostered by an externally-oriented
development strategy (see Romer 1990; Rivera-Batiz and Romer
1991).

There is no question that exports have boomed in East Asia.
Table 11.5 displays the increase in exports as a fraction of GDP
between 1960 and 1998. In Korea, for instance, the ratio of exports
to GDP rose from 9 per cent in 1960 to 41 per cent in 1998. In
Thailand, the ratio of exports to GDP expanded from 5.6 per cent in
1960 to 47.4 per cent in 1998. This positive and significant correlation
of increased exports with output growth has led many to conclude

Table 11.5.   Export Growth in East Asia, 1960–98.

	Exports/GDP (%)	
	1960	**1998**
Indonesia	3.0	53.4
Rep. of Korea	9.0	41.3
Malaysia	22.9	99.3
The Philippines	7.0	45.3
Thailand	5.6	47.4

Source: Barro and Lee 1994 and World Bank 2000d.

that export promotion was the key to economic expansion in the high-growth East Asian countries, suggesting that these policies would produce similar results in the rest of the developing world. As the World Bank concludes: 'The export-push strategy appears to hold great promise for other developing countries. Creating a free trade environment for exporters, providing finance and support services for small and medium-sized exporters, improving trade-related aspects of the civil service, aggressively courting export-oriented direct foreign investment, and focusing infrastructure on areas that encourage exports are all attainable goals' (World Bank, 1993, p. 25).

The view that export promotion has been the key force behind the accelerated growth in high-performing East Asian countries has been questioned in recent years. Some experts have reversed the direction of causality between export growth and output growth, indicating that export growth may have been caused by other forces which simultaneously stimulated output growth. As Dani Rodrik puts it, in his analysis of Korea and Taiwan: "The standard story is incomplete and quite misleading on the importance it attaches to the role of export orientation in growth performance ... The increase in the relative profitability of exports around the mid-1960s was modest in both countries, and can account fully neither for the initial jump in the export-GDP ratio at that time nor for the subsequent steady increase in the ratio" (Rodrik 1995, p. 56).

Instead of export promotion, Rodrik finds that it was the expansion of investment that led to sharp growth, at least in Taiwan and South Korea. He argues that, by removing impediments to investment and establishing a sound investment climate, the Korean and Taiwanese governments were able to engineer a sharp rise in private investment, which then led to the growth of both output and exports. The policy implication, as Rodrik puts it, is that 'the South Korean and Taiwanese "miracles" can best be understood by taking seriously what the two governments thought and said they were doing: namely, coordinating and encouraging private (and public) investments with a high degree of linkages with the modern sector' (Rodrik 1995, p. 97).

This section has presented some of the major indicators of long-run economic performance in East Asia since 1960. There appears to be little doubt that, except for the Philippines, the East Asian countries under consideration displayed remarkable long-run growth of physical and human capital and substantial increases in income per-capita between 1960 and 1995. No clues to the crisis could be found in this area. Ironically, on 21 May 1997, a few weeks before the crisis began to develop, the World Economic Forum, a business-financed research organization in Geneva, released its ranking of the most competitive economies and those with the biggest growth potential. Malaysia was ranked as the ninth most competitive economy in the world; Indonesia was ranked as the fifth in terms of biggest growth potential and Thailand was ranked tenth, out of the 53 countries, which included industrialized nations as well as many emerging markets and economies in transition.

One of the few voices of caution regarding the future of East Asia's economic growth in the mid 1990s was that of Paul Krugman, who argued that East Asia was due for a slowdown. Based on studies that found East Asia's growth to be due mostly to accumulation of human capital and physical capital, instead of technological change, he suggested that diminishing returns inevitably implied a slowdown of growth. Krugman, however, did not predict the growth collapse in the late 1990s, concluding that 'growth in East Asia would continue to outpace growth in the West' (Krugman 1994, p. 78).

11.3   Before the Typhoon: A Look at Some Key Macroeconomic Fundamentals

A look at some of the key macroeconomic indicators in East Asia during the period leading up to the crisis does not easily uncover any compelling signs of distress or potential trouble.

Overall, economic growth in the five economies was still going strong and did not appear to be threatened by any major forces. Table 11.6 shows that, for the five East Asian economies, the average rate of growth of real GDP in 1996 was 7.1 per cent, slightly higher than the average growth rate in the period of 1990 to 1995, which

Table 11.6. Growth of Real GDP before the Crisis: East Asia vs. the World, 1980–96.

	Average annual rate of growth of real GDP (%)		
	1980–89	**1990–95**	**1996**
East Asia*	5.6	6.9	7.1
Indonesia	5.3	8.0	8.0
Rep. of Korea	7.8	7.8	7.1
Malaysia	5.8	8.8	8.6
The Philippines	1.9	2.3	5.7
Thailand	9.0	7.3	5.5
Industrialized countries	2.7	1.8	2.5
Developing countries	4.3	5.8	6.6
Latin America	1.0	2.9	3.5

*The average for East Asia is a weighted average of the growth rates of the five East Asian countries considered.

Source: International Monetary Fund 1998.

was 6.9 per cent, and significantly greater than growth in the 1980s, which averaged 5.6 per cent per year. In Malaysia and Indonesia, real GDP had been growing at 8 per cent or higher per year since 1990. In South Korea, growth had hovered over 7 per cent since 1980. For the Philippines, growth was rising sharply, from less than 2 per cent per year in the 1980s, to 2.3 per cent in 1995 and 5.7 per cent in 1996. And although growth in Thailand had slowed-down in 1996, it was still a respectable 5.5 per cent, higher than for most other countries in the world. Indeed, the 7.1 per cent average real GDP growth rate characterizing the East Asian economies in 1996 exceeded the 6.6 per cent achieved by developing countries in general and the 2.5 per cent growth rate in industrialized nations.

The growth spurt displayed by the East Asian countries from the early 1990s to mid-1997 led most observers to predict strong growth for these economies in the future. For instance, the Asian Development Bank in its annual economic outlook completed in mid-1997 predicted that the growth of real GDP in Indonesia would be a strong 8.0 and 7.9 per cent in 1997 and 1998, respectively. For Korea, the estimate was that real GDP would rise between 6.3 and 6.9 per cent a year. The forecast for Malaysia was for 8.5 per cent growth in

1997 and 1998. For the Philippines, the outlook stated that 'growth prospects over the next two years are bright: GDP is expected to grow at an annual rate of 6–6.5 per cent' (Asian Development Bank 1997a, p. 96). Real GDP growth for Thailand was expected to be 6.3 per cent in each year, 1997 and 1998. These figures suggest that, on the eve of the crisis, most experts saw no dark clouds in the sustained expansion of East Asia in the 1990s.

Price instability was not a major concern either. Inflation rates were high by the standard of industrialized countries, but they were significantly lower than in most other developing countries and they were declining. Table 11.7 shows that, in the 1980s, the average inflation rate in East Asia was 9.1 per cent per year. This dropped to 7.9 per cent for 1990–95. By 1996, the average inflation rate had gone down further to 7 per cent. The Philippines had the highest inflation rate in 1996: 8.4 per cent, while Malaysia had the lowest, at 3.5 per cent. These figures lie substantially below the inflation rate among developing countries overall, which was 13.7 per cent in 1996, 43.6 per cent per year in 1990–95, and 36 per cent per year in the 1980s. In fact, compared to Latin America, where annual inflation

Table 11.7.   Inflation before the Crisis: East Asia vs. the Rest of the World, 1980–96.

	Average annual increase of Consumer Price Index (%)		
	1980–89	**1990–95**	**1996**
East Asia*	9.1	7.9	7.0
Indonesia	9.6	8.7	7.9
Rep. of Korea	6.4	6.2	5.0
Malaysia	3.6	3.5	3.5
The Philippines	14.1	10.8	8.4
Thailand	5.7	5.0	5.9
Industrialized countries	5.5	3.3	2.2
Developing countries	36.0	43.6	13.7
Latin America	116.7	195.6	22.3

*The average for East Asia is a weighted average of the growth rates of the five East Asian countries considered.

Source: International Monetary Fund 1998.

was as high as 195.6 per cent per year in the early 1990s, East Asia represented a region of remarkable price stability.

Underlying the low inflation rates in East Asian economies were government budgets that were close to balance. Any budget deficits had been comparatively small or had been severely curtailed in the years before the crisis. The Philippines, for example, had a budget deficit equal to 5.4 per cent of GDP in 1990. By 1996, this deficit had shrunk to half of one per cent. Indonesia, Malaysia and Thailand had all sustained budget surpluses during the 1990s; in 1996, Malaysia had a budget surplus of 3.9 per cent of GDP, Thailand's was 1.5 per cent, and Indonesia's was 1.0 per cent. The Republic of Korea had the greatest budget deficit in 1996 and it was equal to just 1 per cent of GDP and it followed a budget surplus in 1995.

Currency values in the five East Asian economies had been remarkably stable for many years. This is no surprise as government authorities intervened heavily in currency markets to avoid any substantial fluctuations. The International Monetary Fund (IMF) catalogued the exchange rate arrangements in Malaysia and Thailand during the early and mid-1990s as pegged exchange rate regimes. Those in Indonesia, Korea and the Philippines were catalogued as floating regimes. In reality, however, all five countries intervened heavily in foreign exchange markets during the 1990s, seeking to sustain currency values within a narrow range. In Thailand, the central bank, every morning at 8:30 a.m., fixed the baht exchange rage against a basket of currencies dominated by the dollar, agreeing to exchange baht for foreign currencies within a close range of the established rate. In Indonesia's 'managed floating' regime, the exchange rate was in reality 'administratively set, and in no sense was a genuine float in which market forces determined day-to-day movements' (Hill 1996, p. 75). In the Philippines, the central bank often clarified that the exchange rate was market-determined, not fixed by the central bank. But although the peso was the most volatile of the five East Asian currencies, foreign exchange intervention by the Bangko Sentral ng Pilipinas was frequent, and sometimes heavy, seeking to keep currency fluctuations within a very narrow range. Malaysian and Korean monetary authorities also exercised considerable control of exchange rate movements.

Figure 11.1 displays the behavior of nominal exchange rates between the currencies of the five East Asian nations and the dollar,

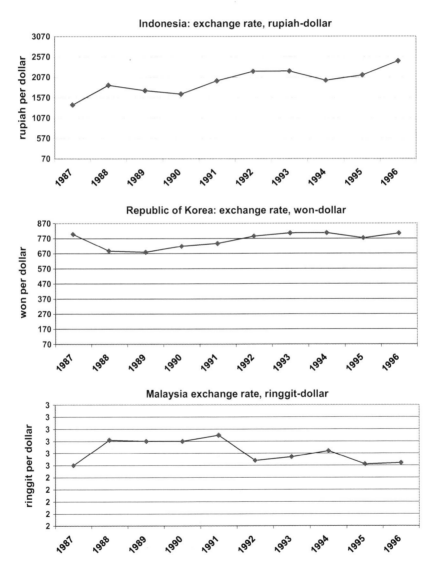

Figure 11.1.   Exchange Rates in East Asia, December 1988–December 1996.
Source: International Monetary Fund 1998.

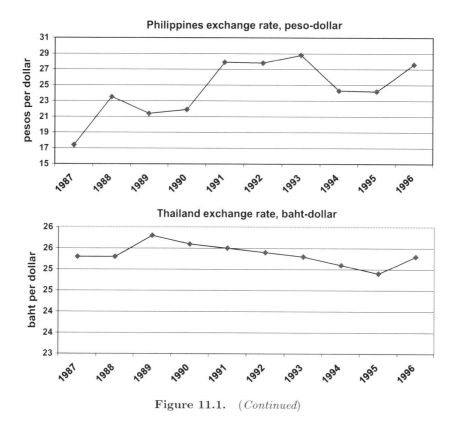

Figure 11.1. (*Continued*)

for the period of December 1987 to December 1996, before the crisis exploded. As can be seen, Thailand's baht had been fluctuating close to 25 baht per dollar since 1987. In the Philippines, the peso–dollar exchange rate remained stable around 25 to 27 pesos per dollar after 1990. There was also a narrow range of fluctuation for the Indonesian rupiah — between 1,900 and 2,100 rupiah per dollar. And for the Malaysian ringgit, the exchange rate remained close to 2.6 ringgit per dollar in the 1990s. Finally, in South Korea, the value of the won remained between 700 and 800 per dollar.

This exchange rate stability operated within the context of rapidly growing capital inflows. All five East Asian economies introduced major policy initiatives that acted to liberalize their financial markets in the 1980s and 1990s.[5] For some, this was a consolidation of earlier movements of liberalization. For instance,

Indonesia had an open capital account since the 1960s, but kept tight controls on the domestic banking system, maintaining a regime of financial repression that was liberalized significantly only in the 1980s and 1990s. Lending and deposit interest rates were lifted in 1983, bank entry requirements were liberalized in 1988, and the regulatory and supervisory structure of stock markets was revamped in the late 1980s. In Thailand, on the other hand, both domestic and international financial transactions were tightly controlled until the late 1980s and early 1990s. Controls on deposit rates were lifted in 1989–90, restrictions on lending rates were eliminated in 1992, most controls on capital outflows were removed in 1991, and in 1993 the Bangkok International Banking Facility was established, allowing domestic and foreign businesses to borrow locally in foreign currency. In the Philippines, the Foreign Investment Act of 1991 for the first time allowed foreign investors to own 100 per cent of business enterprises in the Philippines in most sectors of the economy, supplanting restrictions which limited foreign equity participation to 40 per cent. In the Republic of Korea, financial markets were liberalized in the early 1990s, eliminating controls on interest rates, and allowing foreign capital to increase their access to domestic institutions.

Close to $263 billion in capital flowed to the five East Asian countries on a net basis in the period of 1990 to 1996. The capital influx accelerated in the mid-1990s, rising from $15 billion in 1990 to $67.3 billion in 1996. Table 11.8 shows the decomposition of the capital flows by country and by type of inflow. The Republic of Korea was the country with the greatest resource influx, equal to $70.9 billion from 1990 to 1996. The Philippines, on the other hand, was the country with the smallest inflow of capital, equal to $23.5 billion.

There was great diversity in the type of foreign capital entering East Asia. The largest category was Foreign Direct Investment (FDI), which constituted $78.5 billion on a net basis during the 1990 to 1996 period. However, the importance of FDI varied by country. In Malaysia, Indonesia, the Philippines and Thailand, FDI accounted for a substantial portion of net capital flows. But for Korea, net FDI inflows were not as important. For the latter, sales of private

Table 11.8.   Capital Flows to East Asia, 1990–1996.

Country	Net capital inflows (billions of U.S. dollars)				
	1990	1992	1994	1996	1990–96
Indonesia	**5.9**	**8.0**	**9.6**	**15.6**	**62.6**
FDI	1.1	1.8	2.1	6.2	19.0
Portfolio equity	0.3	0.1	3.7	3.1	14.5
Bank lending	2.4	2.7	0.6	2.8	7.1
Private bonds	0.0	0.2	0.5	3.7	7.1
Other flows	2.1	3.2	2.7	−0.2	14.9
Republic of Korea	**1.4**	**7.8**	**17.0**	**20.4**	**70.9**
FDI	0.8	0.7	0.8	2.3	8.2
Portfolio equity	0.5	3.0	2.5	3.7	19.7
Bank lending	−1.2	1.5	5.8	7.7	17.7
Private bonds	0.2	2.6	8.5	6.7	27.1
Other flows	1.1	1.4	−0.6	0.0	1.8
Malaysia	**1.2**	**6.1**	**8.7**	**12.0**	**53.8**
FDI	2.3	5.2	4.3	5.1	30.0
Portfolio equity	0.3	0.4	1.3	4.4	12.4
Bank lending	−0.2	1.4	1.7	1.2	9.1
Private bonds	−1.2	−0.4	1.2	2.1	4.3
Other flows	0.0	−0.5	0.2	−0.8	2.0
Philippines	**1.9**	**0.9**	**4.3**	**5.2**	**23.5**
FDI	0.5	0.2	1.6	1.5	7.2
Portfolio equity	0.0	0.3	1.4	1.3	6.5
Bank lending	−0.3	−1.4	0.0	−0.2	2.5
Private bonds	0.4	0.0	1.0	2.5	5.7
Other flows	1.3	1.8	0.3	0.1	6.6
Thailand	**4.7**	**4.2**	**4.9**	**14.1**	**52.0**
FDI	2.4	2.1	1.4	2.3	14.1
Portfolio equity	0.4	0.0	−0.5	1.6	6.8
Bank lending	1.5	1.5	0.1	6.0	16.9
Private bonds	−0.1	0.5	3.8	3.8	11.9
Other flows	0.5	0.1	0.1	0.4	2.3

Source: World Bank 1999.

equities and bonds represented the most significant source of foreign capital. The commercial banking industry was another major source of funding. In 1990, only $2.2 billion entered East Asia on a net basis through commercial bank loans; by 1996 the corresponding figure was $48.3 billion. The magnitude of the lending boom varied by country.

In the Philippines, the period of 1990 to 1996 was associated with a reduction of commercial bank loans. But in Thailand and Korea, commercial bank lending accounted for a significant fraction of net capital inflows, with a total of over $34 billion in loans flowing into these countries alone between 1990 and 1996. Japanese, US, British, German and French banks were heavily involved in what literally became a frenzy of loan pushing. As Dennis Phillips, a spokesman for Commerzbank, a major German bank involved in the lending spree, puts it: 'There was a huge euphoria about Asia and Southeast Asia. It was the place to be' (O'Brien *et al.* 1998, p. D1).

As Table 11.8 presents, portfolio equity flows also exploded. While in 1990 there were only $1.5 billion in net flows of portfolio equity into the five East Asian countries, by 1996 this had increased to $14.1 billion. The growth of stock markets in the region reflected these figures. Stock market capitalization was minimal in the East Asian countries in the early 1980s, but by the early 1990s, these emerging stock markets were the darling of investors and the fastest-growing markets in the world. Table 11.9 shows that the country with the highest rate of growth in stock market capitalization was Indonesia, whose market capitalization increased, in real terms, by an astounding 2,952 per cent per year during the period of December 1988 to June 1997, just before the crisis erupted. In Thailand, market capitalization rose by 655.8 per cent during the same time period, in Malaysia it was 336 per cent, in the Philippines the annual growth was 66.4 per cent, and in Korea, where stock markets had started to boom a few years earlier, the annual increase was 18.4 per cent. Although these high growth rates reflected the expansion of markets that had developed from very small sizes in the 1980s, their dynamism was unparalleled in the rest of the world.

Having examined a broad set of macroeconomic indicators for the East Asian economies in the period before the crisis emerged, we have failed to find evidence of the macroeconomic policy malaise that often surrounded economic crises in the past. These signs include acute public budget deficits, high rates of money supply creation, chronic inflation, capital flight and currency instability, among others. In seeking to understand the crisis, the next section describes its unfolding and the aftermath.

Table 11.9. The Stock Market in East Asia before the Crisis, 1988–97.

	Market capitalization*		Real growth per year** Dec. 1988–
	Dec. 1988	June 1997	June 1997 (%)
Indonesia	434 178	259 561 000	2 952
Rep. of Korea	64 543 684	136 229 883	18.4
Malaysia	63 193	714 170	336.3
The Philippines	88 592	1 961 893	66.4
Thailand	221 958	1 614 920	655.8

*Nominal value, in millions of local currency.
**The increase in real capitalization is equal to the percentage increase in nominal capitalization adjusted by a stock market price index.

11.4   The Development of the Crisis

Most accounts of the crisis place its start on 2 July 1997, when the Thai central bank let the baht float, after spending close to $23 billion to sustain its value in the face of massive capital outflows and frenzied devaluation expectations. Almost immediately, the other East Asian countries became the subject of intense capital flight. Central banks desperately intervened in foreign exchange markets, selling billions of dollars and other reserve currencies in order to buy their own currencies and avoid depreciation, but they failed in this attempt. The Philippine peso was the first one to follow the baht: the central bank of the Philippines decided to let the peso float on 11 July. And on 14 July, Malaysia's central bank also let the ringgit float. Indonesia was next, on 14 August, when the rupiah was allowed to freely float. The last country to be affected was the Republic of Korea, which finally let the won depreciate in value in November 1997 after months of capital outflows and failed foreign exchange market intervention.

What happened to currency values after the July–November debacle? The data presented in Table 11.10 shows that by December 1997 all five currencies had sharply depreciated in value. The Thai baht had depreciated by close to 80 per cent relative to its value at the end of May, from 24.8 to 44.8 baht per dollar. The Malaysian ringgit lost 52 per cent of its value between May and December 1997;

Table 11.10. Currency Depreciation in Five East Asian Economies: 1997–2001.

	Value of currency in dollars				
	30 May 1997	19 Dec. 1997	11 May 1998	3 March 1996	31 Jan. 2001
Indonesia (rupiah)	2 432	5 100	9 400	8 885	9 450
Republic of Korea (won)	891	1 550	1 395	1 229	1 265
Malaysia (ringgit)	2.51	3.82	3.86	3.80	3.80
The Philippines (peso)	26.4	39.6	39.3	39.1	49.5
Thailand (baht)	24.8	44.8	38.6	37.7	42.8

Source: Wall Street Journal, various issues.

the Indonesian rupiah depreciated by 110 per cent in the same time period, the Philippine peso dropped by 50 per cent, and the Korean won by 74 per cent. The rupiah went on to depreciate even more in the first half of 1998, going from a value of 2,432 rupiah per dollar in May 1997 to 9,400 in May 1998, a devaluation of 287 per cent in one year!

By the spring of 2001, some currencies had rebounded relative to their lowest values after the crisis, but as Table 11.10 displays all remained sharply devalued relative to May 1997. Some, such as the rupiah and the peso, had not increased in value at all since the worst moment of the crisis.

In the aftermath of the crisis, all five East Asian countries faced higher interest rates, stock market collapses, banking debacles, and a deepening recession. In the case of Indonesia, the interest rate (measured by the money market rate) increased from 13 per cent in January of 1997 to over 40 per cent by late December. In Korea, the interest rate (on overnight call money) rose from 13 per cent in early 1997 to 25 per cent by the end of December. In Thailand, the interest rate hike (of the one-month inter-bank rate) was from 9.2 per cent to 27 per cent in the same time period, and in the Philippines the 90-day Treasury bill rate jumped from 11.7 per cent to 19.3 per cent. Only in Malaysia did the interest rate fail to increase substantially, with the three-month inter-bank rate rising from 7.4 per cent in January 1997 to 10.1 per cent by the end of the year.

The stock market crashes that occurred in parallel to the currency crises not only dried up sources of capital for domestic investments but also acted to severely shrink the wealth of local investors. In Indonesia, the Jakarta Stock Exchange Composite Index dropped from a value of 696 at the end of May 1997 to 402 at the end of December 1997. For Korea, the Korea Stock Exchange KOSPI Index went down by 50 per cent, from 757 in May 1997 to 376 in December 1997. In Malaysia, the Kuala Lumpur Stock Exchange Composite Index declined from 1,105 at the end of May 1997 to 595 by the end of December 1997. The stock market crash in the Philippines, as measured by the Philippine Stock Exchange Composite Index, was from a value of 2,809 in May 1997 to 1,891 in December of that year. And in Thailand, the Stock Exchange of Thailand Index went from 566 in May to 373 in December. The International Finance Corporation, which assesses world stock market performance, catalogued the five East Asian countries among the worst ten performers in 1997. The bourses have recovered since the end of 1997, but prices remain substantially below the levels before the crisis, except for Korea, whose stock market price index in mid-2000 substantially exceeded its value before the crisis in 1997.

With declining growth in the second half of 1997 and a full-blast recession in 1998, all five countries suffered from lower standards of living. This is reflected in the data presented in Table 11.11, showing the growth rate of real GDP for the period of 1996 through 1999 as well as forecasts for 2000. Strong growth in early 1997, before the collapse, allowed the countries to avoid sharply negative annual growth rates for 1997, but all of them had a drop of real GDP in 1998. The sharpest recessions occurred in Indonesia, where real GDP fell by 13.2 per cent in 1998, and in Thailand, where it fell by 10.4 per cent. The situation improved in 1999, with Korea leading the region with a strong 10 per cent growth, and with the Philippines, Malaysia and Thailand also displaying respectable growth. Only Indonesia showed

Table 11.11. Growth of Real GDP in East Asia: Before and after the Crisis.

	Annual rate of growth of real GDP (%)				
	1996	**1997**	**1998**	**1999**	**2000***
Indonesia	8.0	4.7	−13.2	0.2	4.0
Rep. of Korea	9.1	5.0	−6.7	10.7	7.5
Malaysia	5.8	7.5	−7.5	5.4	6.0
The Philippines	5.7	5.2	−0.5	3.2	3.8
Thailand	9.0	−1.8	−10.4	4.1	4.5

*Forecast by Asian Development Bank.

Sources: International Monetary Fund 1998; Asian Development Bank 2000.

no growth in 1999. All economies were expected to sustain at least moderate growth in the year 2000.

The recessions resulted in sudden increases of unemployment. In Korea, urban unemployment had been between 2 and 3 per cent before the crisis. This went up to 7.4 per cent in 1998 and peaked at 8.7 per cent in February 1999. For Indonesia, the crisis displaced approximately 3 per cent of the labor force between July 1997 and July 1998, with unemployment ranging from 10 to 14.8 per cent in early 1999 (Krongkaew 2000). In Thailand, the labor market condition before the crisis was very tight, with less than 2 per cent of the labor force unemployed. The crisis increased unemployment by 2.5 percentage points between early 1997 and early 1999. In Malaysia, open unemployment rose from close to 2 per cent in the period before the crisis to 4.5 per cent in early 1999. Unemployment in the Philippines had been substantially higher than in the other East Asian countries, reflecting its slower growth. In 1996, the average unemployment rate was 8.5 per cent, slightly below the average for 1993–95, which was 9.5 per cent. The crisis made the unemployment rate jump to 13.3 per cent by April 1998.

In some of the countries, the official unemployment figures do not show the full impact of the crisis because they do not reflect underemployment. In the Philippines, for instance, in addition to an unemployment rate of over 10 per cent, it is estimated that about one-third of the labor force is underemployed. In Indonesia, the informal labor market may comprise as much as 65 per cent of total employment. The social impact of the crisis was devastating. Low-income households bore the brunt of the crisis and social safety nets to deal with their worsening situation were not in place. Emergency public works program, in the Philippines and Korea, helped to alleviate the crisis for some unemployed workers, but these programs reached only a small portion of the poor (World Bank 1998, 2000b). As Khun Bunjan, a community leader from the slums of Khon Kaen, in Thailand, bitterly commented: 'It was the rich who benefited from the boom... but we, the poor, pay the price of the crisis. Even our limited access to schools and health is now beginning to disappear' (World Bank 1998, p. 73).

In Indonesia, where the crisis lingered compared to other countries, daily survival became the norm for between 40 and 100 million people in 1998. Food prices, in particular, spiraled upwards and a large segment of the population could no longer afford more than one meal a day. The price hikes were partly linked to an El Nino-related drought, but they were fueled by the elimination of price supports by the government, and the sharp inflation associated with the crisis. By early February 1998, inflation was running at a rate of over 200 per cent a year. And by October of that year the country was facing a major famine. It was estimated that more than 45 million Indonesian could no longer buy enough rice to meet their daily nutritional requirements. Despite emergency government programs, which gave vouchers to women to buy rice at a quarter of the market price, a large segment of the population struggled to avoid malnourishment or famine during this time period. The personal anguish over the situation was captured by the following *Wall Street Journal* report: 'We can no longer eat rice every day,' complains Mahfud, a 56 year-old teacher who, each day, earns less than the 30 cents now needed to buy a kilogram of the grain. In this village on the outskirts of Jember, most residents work all day for the government. But they speed countless hours in nearby fields trying to coax along vegetables they can trade for their staple food: rice' (Brauchli 1998, p. A1).

The financial and economic collapse of the five East Asian economies led them to seek the emergency assistance of the International Monetary Fund. Following its approach to the 1994–95 Mexican crisis, the IMF pulled together a $17.2 billion bailout package for Thailand in August 1997. The package included loans from the IMF, the World Bank, the Ex-Im Bank, the Asian Development Bank, a number of countries including Japan, Australia and China and, ironically as it turned out, Malaysia, Indonesia and the Republic of Korea. A second assistance package of $38 billion was put together for Indonesia in late October. In December, Korea reached an agreement with the IMF for a third massive bailout plan; this loan package was equal to $57 billion, the largest ever, surpassing the 1994–95 Mexico rescue package.

The role of the IMF in the aftermath of the crisis has been sharply questioned, not only in terms of the specific policy menu adopted by the IMF, but also in terms of the role of that institution in assisting economies in distress. For one, the IMF requested that the governments reduce government spending in order to raise the funds required to restructure financial institutions. But by shrinking government spending in a recession situation, the policy further aggravated the crisis. This reproduced the often-quoted mistake made by the United States in the 1930s, when President Hoover tried to balance the budget in the midst of the Great Depression. The IMF, in its quest for immediate public sector austerity, also acted to reduce subsidies and safety nets that adversely impacted on the poor. And IMF requests for the speedy closing and restructuring of ailing financial institutions may have worsened the situation by encouraging bank runs on healthy institutions. Federal Reserve Chairman Alan Greenspan, in a Congressional testimony, noted that the IMF 'misread the depth of the really fundamental problems that were involved in the crisis that evolved . . . . I think their actions were somewhat misguided in the early stages' (as quoted in Wessel and Davis 1998). The IMF itself reversed course, after heavy criticism. For instance, in early 1998, it allowed Thailand to post a budget deficit, instead of a budget surplus, as had been in the original terms of agreement that led to the bailout. Similar leniency was also observed later with respect to Indonesia, after the social impact of the crisis reached enormous proportions.

The moral hazard attached to IMF bailouts has been raised as a major question surrounding IMF intervention in East Asia. By allowing creditors to be paid in full, the IMF:

> encourages those lenders and others to take excessive future risks. Banks that expect loans to be guaranteed by governments do not as carefully as they should look at the underlying commercial credit risks. And when banks believe that the availability of dollars to meet foreign exchange obligations will be guaranteed by the IMF, they will not look carefully at the foreign exchange risk of the debtor countries. (Feldstein 1998, p. 30; see also Calomiris 1998).

There is, however, a lack of empirical evidence on this issue.

The events of 1997 and 1998 constituted for many a surprising and unexpected development. Until the crisis, the five East Asian economies had been displayed, by both the private sector and international organizations, as showcases for the rest of the developing world. Given the strength of key fundamental variables displayed earlier, the question emerges: What went wrong?

11.5   The Anatomy of an Emerging Market Crisis: Capital Inflows and the Exchange Rate

Although the East Asían crisis was unanticipated in most circles, there were danger signs long before it exploded in July 1997.

Investors in stock markets in the five countries had been nervous about the economic situation in these nations for quite some time. This preoccupation was reflected in the stagnation of prices in the East Asian bourses in the years before the crisis. Table 11.12 presents the International Finance Corporation (IFC) Stock Market Price Index (in local currency) for the five East Asian countries during the period of December 1988 to June 1997. There is a clear split in the behavior of stock market prices before and after 1994. While there was a sharp increase of the IFC price index in the period from 1988 to the end of 1993 (for ail countries except Korea), for the period of January 1994 to June 1997 the increase of the index sharply slowed down or even turned around, displaying price reductions.

Table 11.12.   Stock Market Prices before the Crisis, December 1988–June 1997.

	IFC Stock Market Price Index*			Annual real change (%)	
	Dec. 1988	Dec. 1993	June 1997	88–93	93–97
Indonesia	305	588	724	18.5%	6.6%
Korea	907	866	745	−1.0	−4.0
Malaysia	357	1,275	1,077	51.4	−4.4
Philippines	842	3,196	2,809	55.9	−3.5
Thailand	387	1,682	527	66.9	−19.6

*In local currency.
Index base year: Philippines (1984=100), Indonesia (1982=100), South Korea (1980=100), Malaysia (1977=100), and Thailand (1984=100).

Source: International Finance Corporation 1998.

In Thailand, for example, the index dropped by 19.6 per cent a year in real terms between January 1994 and June 1997. For South Korea, the drop was equal to 4 per cent, and for Malaysia the reduction was 4.4 per cent. In Indonesia, stock market prices went up, but at a slower pace compared to earlier years. Although market capitalization continued to rise in the five East Asian economies until the crisis erupted (both domestic and foreign investors continued to plunge into the markets), the boom in prices had ended much earlier.

What explains the deflated stock market prices? There are a number of economic and political factors involved, the importance of which varies by country, but there is one major force that is common to all the economies involved: There was a growing perception that the East Asian currencies would be sharply devalued in the near future and that associated with this devaluation would be economic distress. Eventually, these expectations of devaluation would lead to massive capital flight in all five countries.

In Thailand, the capital outflows had started in 1996 and early 1997, long before the currency markets collapsed in July 1997. Speculation based on an expected devaluation of the baht aggravated considerably in May 1997. Hedge funds, which move billions of liquid dollars across the globe to speculate on future exchange rate adjustments, had entered the scene in a major way (Eichengreen and Mathieson 1999, pp. 8–9). A few years before, in 1992 and 1993, hedge funds had been a critical part of the speculative attack on, and collapse of, the exchange rate mechanism of the European Monetary System.[6] The Bank of Thailand, though, was intent on preventing a devaluation. During the 1990s, throughout a period that included major domestic political events (including a short-lived military coup), the central bank had tightly controlled the value of the baht, keeping it around 25 baht per dollar. The May speculative outburst put powerful upward pressure on the exchange rate, moving it close to 27 baht per dollar. The Bank of Thailand, in cooperation with other central banks in the region, intervened in foreign exchange markets to support the value of the baht. Short-term interest rates were raised and, in a surprise move, the Bank of Thailand ordered local commercial banks to stop lending baht to foreign residents, unless they could show that the transactions would not be used to speculate, thus effectively creating a two-tier foreign exchange market. Having millions of dollars tied-up in open baht positions, many speculators suddenly found themselves unable to borrow dollars except from the Bank of Thailand, whose short-term lending rate skyrocketed. As a result, hedge funds lost what is estimated to be $450 million in May 1997. Stanley Druckenmiller, chief investment officer at the Soros Fund Management, which handles one of the major global hedge funds, stated at the time: 'They [the Bank of Thailand] have taken a lot of profit we might have had. They did a masterful job of squeezing us out' (Henderson 1998, p. 105).

Unfortunately for the Bank of Thailand, the victory over hedge funds was only temporary. It was temporary because hedge funds and short-term currency speculators were not the only ones who were anticipating a baht devaluation. As other local and foreign investors acted on their own devaluation expectations, massive capital flight resumed shortly after this event. Embattled by the sustained attack on the currency, on Tuesday, 1 July, Thailand's Prime Minister Chavalit Yongchaiyudh came on television to restate that the baht would never be devalued. This echoed another momentous television statement made 15 years earlier by President José López Portillo of Mexico in 1982 when he declared that the peso would not be devalued and that he would defend its value 'like a mad dog.' Just as the peso was devalued shortly after López Portillo's statement, so did the baht, the next day.

What stimulated the expectations of devaluation of the baht and the other East Asian currencies as well? As was noted earlier, the value of these currencies had remained remarkably stable in the 1990s. Yet, as we also saw earlier, prices had been rising in the region, albeit at a moderate rate. Inflation was declining, but it was still about 8 per cent per year between 1990 and 1996. With exchange rates fixed and domestic prices rising, the prices of goods produced in East Asia increased relative to the prices of goods produced in other countries, implying a loss of price competitiveness in world markets. This loss of competitiveness is reflected in the changes of the *real exchange rate* in the East Asian economies during the 1990s. The real exchange rate of any given country is defined as the price of foreign goods relative to the price of domestic goods, both measured in local currency. A rise of the real exchange rate is linked to an increase of domestic competitiveness as it shows foreign goods becoming relatively more expensive. On the other hand, a reduction of the real exchange rate is linked to a decrease of domestic competitiveness, with domestic goods becoming relatively more expensive.[7]

Real exchange rates had been declining among all East Asian countries in the 1990s. Consider the case of Korea, which because of its strong fundamentals few had anticipated it could fall into the abyss it did in 1997 and 1998. The data show that the real exchange rate of the won relative to the dollar had persistently and sharply declined over a period lasting a decade.[8] Between 1985 and 1996, the won had appreciated in real terms by close to 30 per cent of its original value. In fact, the won also appreciated in *nominal* terms between 1985 and 1996, from 881 won per dollar in 1985 to 771 in 1995. The depreciation associated with the East Asian crisis moved the real value of the won in 1998 and 1999 back down to levels prevailing in 1984 and 1985.

Real exchange rates decreased in all five East Asian crisis countries during the period preceding the crisis, to a greater or lesser extent.[9] For Malaysia, the currency appreciated in real terms by approximately 15 per cent in the relatively short period between 1991 and 1996. In Indonesia, the rupiah appreciated by close to 11 per cent in the same time period. In the Philippines, the peso's *real* exchange rate declined by close to 30 per cent in the period of 1989 to 1996. Finally, in Thailand, the baht gradually but continuously appreciated by close to 15 per cent in the period of 1985 to 1996.

The persistent real exchange rate reductions (and the resulting loss of competitiveness of East Asian products in world markets) caused a fall in the exports of goods and services relative to imports in all of the five countries. As a result, trade and current account balance deficits grew. Table 11.13 presents the behavior of the current account balance in East Asia from 1985 to 1997, measured relative to GDP. In all five countries, the current account balance deteriorated during this time period and, in some, it moved from surplus to deficit. The country with the largest current account balance deficit before the crisis was Thailand, which had a deficit of 6.8 per cent of GDP during the 1990–95 period and 8.3 per cent in 1996.

The growing current account balance deficits displayed by the East Asian countries began to attract attention in some circles. In its annual outlook, completed before the crisis erupted, the Asian Development Bank expressed some concern over the situation: 'In 1996, most Asian countries experienced a sharp slowdown in

Table 11.13. East Asian Countries: Current Account of the Balance of Payments as a Percentage of GNP.

	1985–89 (%)	1990–95 (%)	1996 (%)	1997 (%)	1998 (%)	1999 (%)
Indonesia	−2.5	−2.4	−3.5	−2.3	4.2	2.9
Rep. of Korea	4.3	−1.3	−4.8	−1.9	12.6	6.0
Malaysia	2.4	−5.6	−4.9	−5.1	6.6	16.3
The Philippines	−0.5	−3.7	−4.6	−5.0	2.0	8.6
Thailand	−2.0	−6.8	−8.3	−2.0	12.8	11.0

Source: World Bank 1995, 2000a.

export growth. This decline in export growth rates has generated yet another economic debate, with apprehensions being expressed regarding the ability of the Asian economies to continue their high performance because their competitiveness in the international markets is slipping.'[10] Similarly, in a conference on the major macroeconomic issues facing the member countries of the Association of South East Nations (ASEAN), held in Jakarta, Indonesia, on 5–7 November 1996, Michael Camdessus, then the Managing Director of the IMF, examined the challenges facing East Asian economies. He observed:

> large net private capital inflows have tended to raise aggregate expenditures, increase inflationary pressures, and widen current account deficits in all major recipient countries. Yet, part of these inflows — especially those of a short-term nature — can be suddenly reversed, because of either changes in market sentiment about the recipient country, contagion effects, or changing financial conditions in other countries. Countries in such situations must thus pay particular attention to the sustainability of their external position. (Camdessus 1997, p. 20).

The growing current account balance deficits raised serious fears regarding the financial soundness of the economies, as they implied growing indebtedness. A current account balance deficit, that is, an excess of payments over receipts on current account, must be financed. There are basically two ways to finance it: a loss of international reserves on the part of the central bank or through external borrowing (see Rivera-Batiz and Rivera-Batiz 1994, ch. 9). How did the East Asian economies finance their current account balance deficits? In 1996, for example, the combined current account deficit for the five economies was $53.9 billion. How was this deficit paid for? As it turns out, it was financed entirely through external financing. In fact, throughout the early 1990s, the central banks of the five countries *accumulated* foreign exchange reserves, thus augmenting the amount of external borrowing the economies undertook during these years. In 1996, the external borrowing of the five countries amounted to $74.4 billion.

The accumulation of current account deficits in the 1990s and their financing through private capital flows made the East Asian

Table 11.14.   Biggest Debtors in the Developing World, 1996.

	External debt (millions US$)	External debt/GNP (%)
Brazil	194 046	25.0
Mexico	167 469	50.6
China	150 541	18.3
Korea	142 070	29.3
Indonesia	132 816	58.3
Russia	123 186	27.9
Argentina	105 388	35.4
Thailand	98 368	53.0
India	97 491	27.7
Turkey	79 747	44.0
Greece	55 299	44.7
The Philippines	50 120	59.5
Malaysia	41 967	42.4
Poland	41 628	31.1

Source: World Bank 1998.

economies the biggest debtors in the world by the end of 1996. The data presented in Table 11.14 show that all five countries were among the developing world's largest debtors. Furthermore, when the debt is calculated relative to the size of the economy, by dividing the external debt by GDP, one finds that three of the East Asian economies — the Philippines, Indonesia and Thailand — were at the top of the list of the world's most indebted countries at the end of 1996. Indeed, the Philippines had the highest debt-to-GDP ratio among developing countries (59.5 per cent), followed by Indonesia (58.3 per cent) and Thailand (53 per cent).

Although the five East Asian countries became more heavily indebted in the 1990s, they were already highly-indebted countries to begin with. The developing country debt crisis of the 1980s had left all five countries among the top 20 debtors in the world in 1990. For some of them, the debt increased faster than GDP as the 1990s unfolded, while for others debt increased slower than GDP. For Thailand, the debt-to-GDP ratio jumped from 33.4 per cent in 1990 to 53 per cent in 1996. Similarly, in Korea, the debt-to-GDP ratio rose from 18.7 per cent in 1990 to 29.3 per cent in 1996. In the other three countries, however, debt-to-GDP ratios did not rise significantly in the 1990s and, for Indonesia and the Philippines, the ratio actually declined. In Indonesia, the debt-to-GDP ratio went down from 64 to 58.3 per cent in the period from 1990 to 1996 while for the Philippines it dropped from 69.4 per cent to 59.5 per cent. In Malaysia, the ratio slightly rose from 37.5 per cent in 1990 to 42.4 per cent in 1996.

Because indebtedness had been comparatively high in East Asia for some time, the massive borrowing undertaken in the 1990s gave rise to major concerns regarding the servicing of this debt, despite the miraculous economic growth. In addition, there were some major changes regarding the composition of the debt in the 1990s. First of all, the external debt was increasingly private debt, not public sector debt, as was the situation in the 1980s. Furthermore, an increasing share of the private debt was not being guaranteed by the government. In Indonesia, private, non-guaranteed debt rose from 17.4 to 37.9 per cent of all long-term external indebtedness between 1990 and 1996. In Korea, the increase was from 22.3 to 36 per cent, and in Malaysia from 11.9 to 32.5 per cent. For Thailand, which already had a substantial portion of long-term private debt in 1990 (36.8 per cent), the share increased to 68.3 per cent in 1996. Finally, in the Philippines, private, non-guaranteed debt rose from less than 5 per cent of all long-term external debt in 1990 to 15.4 per cent in 1996.

With the growing role of private debt, the significance of current public sector budgets on the financing of external debt payments declined sharply. What became more important was the health of the economy and, in particular, its financial system. Both of these were critical to the transformation of the external debt into productive investments. An economic downturn and/or a major mismanagement of investment funds into projects with low expected returns or high risks, could trigger a loss of investor confidence, leading to capital flight and a possible crisis. Worries about the future fiscal costs of such bailouts and the revenues they require, say in the form of inflationary taxes, become the topic of concern (see Burnside *et al.* 1998). These worries were magnified by two additional trends regarding external debt in the 1990s: the rise of short-term debt (in foreign currency) and commercial bank lending.

The experience of Latin American economies, from Mexico to Brazil, suggests that mismanagement of the maturity structure of debt lies at the core of financial crises. Growth of short-term debt has been a major common factor in many financial crises. In East Asia, short-term debt expanded substantially in the 1990s. In Thailand, the share of short-term debt on the country's stock of debt increased from 21.3 per cent in 1986 to 68.3 per cent in 1996. In Korea, the share of short-term debt rose from 19.8 per cent in 1986 to 50 per cent in 1996. In Indonesia, the increase was from 9.1 per cent in 1986 to 25 per cent in 1996. And in Malaysia, it was from 12.1 per cent in 1986 to 28 per cent in 1996. Only in the Philippines did short-term debt remain constrained, equal to 19 per cent of all debt in 1986 and 20 per cent in 1996.

The growth of short-term debt constituted a major warning sign of potential troubles ahead. The absence of this type of debt had helped East Asian economies to survive relatively unscathed through the developing country debt crisis in the 1980s. This is the conclusion, for example, of Woo and Nasution in their analysis of Indonesia:

> there is a trade-off in external debt management between generally lower interest payments and predictability of debt-service payments. Short-term liabilities pay lower interest rates most of the time, but it is risky to rely on a strategy which rolls over a large amount of short-term debt every period. An unforeseen credit crunch would force the country to increase borrowing in order to cover its interest payments. If this credit squeeze were to persist ... the extra borrowing would be difficult to sustain as the situation increasingly smacked of a Ponzi game. (Woo and Nasution 1989, p. 115).

A second major issue regarding the external indebtedness of East Asian countries in the 1990s was the growing portion of the debt accounted for by commercial banks. In all five economies, bank lending became more significant. In the Philippines, the proportion of long-term debt accounted for by commercial bank loans skyrocketed from 6 per cent in 1990 to 31 per cent in 1996. In Korea, the increase was from 32.4 per cent in 1990 to close to 50 per cent in 1996. In Malaysia, bank lending rose from 30.6 per cent to 50 per cent of the stock of long-term debt. In Thailand, commercial bank debt increased from 47 to 55 per cent of all debt between 1990 and 1996, and in Indonesia, the corresponding change was from 32.2 to 37.2 per cent.

The rapid expansion of bank lending as a component of external debt was potentially troublesome because of the weak and imperfect state of the banking systems of these economies. Despite the squeaky-clean image of East Asia in the early 1990s, the reality was that all of the five East Asian countries had underdeveloped, imperfect financial systems and a history of banking crises, leading up to the period right before the crisis.[11]

The Philippines suffered from a series of crises in the period of 1981 to 1987. In 1986, 19 per cent of bank loans were non-performing. Three commercial banks, 128 rural banks, and 32 thrift institutions failed, and two other private banks were under intervention. Furthermore, the biggest commercial bank, the Philippines National Bank, and the Development Bank of the Philippines, both government-owned, became de facto insolvent and had to be bailed out. Although this crisis was partly caused by external factors (rising world interest rates and a global recession), by macroeconomic mismanagement (including substantial budget deficits), and by political uncertainty, the state of the banking industry itself was a major issue. The presence of bank-holding-company groups created dangerous, incestuous interrelations between lending institutions. When combined with bank supervisory weaknesses, excessive risk-taking, fraud and mismanagement, it was a prescription for trouble.[12]

Korea also had significant banking problems in the mid-1980s. The government had to provide emergency loans to troubled banks accounting for 24 per cent of commercial bank assets. Indonesia had its own difficulties in the 1990s; non-performing loans, which were concentrated in state-owned banks, were over 25 per cent of total lending in 1993. Malaysia had undergone a major banking crisis from 1985 to 1988, with non-performing loans estimated at 32 per cent of all loans in 1988. And Thailand had suffered a severe banking collapse from 1983 to 1987 in which more than 25 per cent of the country's financial assets were affected. Fifteen finance companies failed after a number of bank panics and runs developed (Lindgren *et al.* 1996, p. 33).

The weaknesses of the financial systems in the East Asian countries had been repeatedly noted by a wide array of analysts. In the case of Thailand, as early as 1991, Barry Johnston had observed:

> the emergence of distressed financial institutions in Thailand had its origins mainly in weak managerial practices and in inadequate legal, regulatory and supervisory frameworks for financial institutions. The indigenous private sector financial institutions were established by trading families and other powerful economic groupings and had a high concentration of ownership and, in several cases, of loan exposure to inter-related entities. Such institutions were not 'self-regulatory' in the sense that there was a lack of normal checks and balances between shareholders, directors and management, and this resulted in inherent management weakness. (Johnston 1991, p. 274).

Despite this assessment, it was a series of developments five years later that made clear that the Thai situation had not substantially changed since that time, giving fuel to the capital flight that led to the financial crisis.

In May 1996, Thailand was stunned to hear the revelation that the Bangkok Bank of Commerce, the nation's ninth largest bank, had close to 50 per cent of its assets (about $3 billion) in the form of non-performing bank loans, many of them made to acquaintances of the bank's president. Opposition parties in the country alleged that it was laxity and political partisanship on the part of the Bank of Thailand that explained this disaster. This was followed, in August, by allegations of government corruption in the granting of licenses to new banks, with bribes of $90 million involved. Both the governor of the central bank and the prime minister resigned, with Chavalit Yongchaiyudh, head of the New Aspiration party, becoming the new Prime Minister in elections held in November. More bad news surfaced in January 1997, when Thailand's largest finance company, Finance One, collapsed. It was apparent at this time that the Thai financial system was under serious stress, giving rise to the speculative capital outflows that would eventually lead to the currency crisis of May 1997.

The problems of the banking system in East Asia have been summarized by the World Bank, with the benefits of hindsight: 'The East Asian countries had some weaknesses in their banking systems including: low capital-adequacy ratios of banks; inadequately designed and weakly-enforced legal lending limits on single borrowers or group of related borrowers; asset classification systems and provisioning rules for possible losses, which fell short of international standards; poor disclosure and transparency of bank operations; lack of provisions for an exit policy of troubled financial institutions; and weak supervision.' (World Bank 2000d, p. 35)

One might add that inadequate project evaluation and risk-assessment techniques were also serious problems. In part, the public sector bailouts of financial institutions in the earlier episodes of financial distress in the 1980s and early 1990s (noted above), acted to create a moral hazard incentives problem, as private institutions took excessive risks or mismanaged their portfolios on the assumption that they would be bailed out by the government in case of financial difficulties. The result of these problems was the expansion of lending to questionable projects that had small or negative short-term returns and relied on rosy assessments of risky long-term returns. Massive investments in infrastructure and in real estate were not carefully assessed in terms of their risk. For instance, at the time the crisis occurred, Malaysia was involved in seeking finance for a $4.55 billion dam/hydroelectric project in Bakun, a northern regional airport in Kedah, the Linear City in Kuala Lumpur, and a road linking three islands in the central range of the country's peninsula. In Kuala Lumpur stands the tallest building in the world, a 1,483-foot high tower completed just before the crisis began. In Thailand, the abandoned beginnings of a $1 billion elevated light-rail project on the outskirts of Bangkok is called Stonehenge by local residents and the skyline is dotted with the skeletons of unfinished buildings. Indonesia was at the verge of completing financing packages for a 60-mile long bridge between Indonesia and Malaysia. A syndicated loan was also being arranged to build the Jakarta Tower, which would have become the tallest building in the world. All these investments were made within the context of a real estate sector that was plagued by overcapacity and at the verge of a collapsing bubble.

Each of the forces discussed in this section may not have had the power to generate a crisis by itself, but all of them together were potentially explosive. A slowdown in domestic economic activity or a worsening current account balance, for example, could turn around the confidence of lenders and investors. Local commercial banks and financial institutions, which had borrowed abroad substantially, were then subject to the risk that nervous foreign lenders would not roll-over their short-term loans. With a large portion of bank assets tied-up in the form of long-term loans, the banks would encounter a liquidity crisis. The possibility of a bank run made the situation worse. And even though an expansion of central bank credit could temporarily avert a crisis, the fact that the short-term external debt was denominated in foreign currency meant that the central bank would lose international reserves in the process. This could eventually force a balance of payments crisis.[13]

11.6   The Aftermath of the Crisis: Where Are We Now?

The current situation of East Asia provides ground for optimism, but the financial system remains fragile. Growth of GDP has picked-up in all five countries and current forecasts are for continued growth. Korea, in particular, has had a remarkable recovery, growing over 10 per cent in real terms during 1999 and with similarly high forecasts for 2000. The current account balance in all five countries is in surplus and exports have rebounded. The real currency depreciations in all five currencies are likely to provide an even stronger impetus to exports.

Despite these positive signs, the recovery continues to be delicate. Banks remain under-capitalized, even after a wide array of government policies seeking to inject capital into the financial system have been implemented. The exit of many financial institutions has left the sector much more concentrated than before. Many banks remain under state control and the public sector debt associated with the crisis keeps rising. Although Korea and Malaysia have been more aggressive in the restructuring of banks, other financial institutions in those countries remain in weak condition. Thailand has dealt more aggressively with finance companies, proceeding to deal with the banking system on a more gradual basis. Indonesia has made the least progress and most financial institutions remain under state control and insolvent (see Claessens *et al.* 1999 and Asian Development Bank 2000).

Non-performing loans continue to be a major difficulty, far over that encountered by Mexico and other Latin American countries in 1995 and 1996. Korea has been the most successful country in restructuring the financial sector. The Korean state agency in charge of taking over financial institutions and transferring, consolidating or liquidating claims on non-performing loans had been able to reduce the percentage of these loans in the financial system to about 10 per cent of all loans by the beginning of 2000. In Malaysia, the corresponding figure was 25 per cent. For Thailand, the ratio of non-performing loans to total loans was still 39 per cent at the start of 2000. In Indonesia, where the financial crisis has been particularly severe, non-performing loans constituted over 60 per cent of all loans in early 2000.

The impact of the East Asian crisis on capital inflows has been long-lasting. Net capital flows to the five East Asian countries are still negative and are expected to remain so during 2000 and 2001. The exorbitant fiscal cost of the financial and corporate restructuring has created a huge debt overhang. At the beginning of the year 2000, the external debt of the five countries, as a fraction of GDP, remained above the levels before the crisis. As a percentage of GDP, the external debt of Indonesia grew from 58.3 per cent at the end of 1996 to 149.4 per cent at the end of 1998 and 95.5 per cent at the end of 1999. In Malaysia, the corresponding percentage grew from 42.4 per cent at the end of 1996 to close to 60 per cent in 1998 and 55.3 per cent in 1999. In Thailand, the percentage of the debt relative to GDP increased from 53 per cent at the end of 1996 to 76.8 per cent by the end of 1998 and 61.5 per cent in 1999. In the Philippines, the percentage rose from 59.5 per cent in 1996 to 73.3 per cent in

Table 11.15. East Asian Countries: The Budget Balance in the Aftermath of the Crisis.

	General budget balance/GDP (%)		
	1997	**1998**	**1999**
Indonesia	−0.7	−1.9	−2.3
Rep. of Korea	−0.9	−4.0	−2.9
Malaysia	4.0	−1.0	−4.1
The Philippines	−0.8	−2.7	−4.4
Thailand	−0.9	−2.5	−3.0

Source: International Monetary Fund 2000.

1998 and 68 per cent in 1999. In Korea, the debt-to-GDP ratio rose from 29.3 per cent at the end of 1996 to 46.9 per cent in 1998 and 33 per cent at the end of 1999.

The danger in the coming years, however, lies in the growing budget deficits that have emerged after the crisis. They are linked to rising public indebtedness. Table 11.15 shows the general budget balance as a fraction of GDP for East Asia, from 1997 to 1999. Note that, as we discussed earlier, all five countries had either surpluses or negligible deficits in 1996. However, by 1999, Indonesia had a budget deficit of 2.3 per cent of GDP, Korea's was 2.9 per cent, Malaysia's was 4.1 per cent, the Philippines 4.4 per cent and Thailand's deficit was 3 per cent of GDP. These budget deficits are likely to widen, as a result of the additional resources needed to complete bank capitalization plus the interest on the existing public debt (International Monetary Fund 2000).

11.7 Policy Implications: The Political Economy of Emerging Market Disease

The analysis of the East Asian crisis developed in this chapter suggests the presence of a vicious cycle facing policymakers in emerging markets. Countries that have increased their domestic investment while liberalizing their capital accounts encounter a surge of capital inflows. These capital inflows allow increased investment rates and the rapid growth of national income. Yet, they also plant the seeds of a future downturn and, possibly, a crisis. The reason is that capital inflows generate upward pressures on the value of domestic currency. In countries with floating exchange rates, the value of the domestic currency would immediately rise, directly causing a real currency appreciation. Under fixed or managed exchange rates a real currency appreciation also occurs, through the inflationary impact of the capital inflows.[14] The result is an economic pattern that was seen in all East Asian countries in the first half of the 1990s: an economic boom (especially in non-traded goods sectors), moderate or low inflation, stable exchange rates, a real currency appreciation, and rising international reserves.

The seeds of the bust, however, have been planted in the boom period. As the value of the currency rises in real terms, the growth of domestic exports eventually slows down and the current account balance deteriorates. External debt accumulates and at some point investors will revise their local risk assessments in the upward direction. This then leads to capital flight and currency depreciation. If the central bank stubbornly defends prevailing currency values, and its foreign exchange reserves are not enough to withstand the massive capital exodus, the country will eventually face a balance of payments crisis and the currency will have to be allowed to float.

The crisis is accelerated, and its impact greater, if domestic financial institutions are fragile and do not have the ability to handle the credit crunch and the higher interest rates linked to the capital outflows. The situation is also worsened if price bubbles (in real estate or in domestic capital markets in general) have existed, which burst and generate even greater capital flight. Financial panics and bank runs linked to liquidity crises can also worsen the crisis and its aftermath (Radelet and Sachs 1998b; Chang and Velasco 1998, 1999). And if there has been over-investment, in the form of excessive lending to risky projects with low short-term returns, the crisis can freeze economic activity on a grand scale (McKinnon and Pil 1996). Finally, the presence of contagion effects can assist in transmitting the crisis to countries in the same region or suffering from similar economic circumstances (Eichengreen *et al.* 1996; Eichengreen and Rose 1998).

We have characterized this type of phenomenon as emerging market disease. Understanding it leads to a set of policy prescriptions, which we now examine in the context of the East Asian crisis. The sharp, real appreciation of all five currencies in East Asia, and the growing current account balance deficits, suggest that the currencies were overvalued by mid-1997. This was already the conclusion that the firm Goldman-Sachs had obtained in October 1996 from their model of real exchange rates, which indicated that the real exchange rate was overvalued in Indonesia, Thailand and the Philippines. Later, in 1997, before the crisis erupted, Goldman-Sachs added Korea and Malaysia to the list of countries with overvalued real exchange rates. More recently, Chinn (1998) used a purchasing power parity model of equilibrium exchange rates to determine that 'as of May 1997, the baht, ringgit and peso were overvalued.'

The fact that central banks delayed currency devaluations, which was a central factor in the crisis, is well-known. What has not been noted in the literature, though, and what the analysis of emerging market disease helps us understand, is that central banks face a disturbing trade off regarding currency values. Under the influence of capital inflows, emerging markets' equilibrium real exchange rates decline over time. In this situation, central banks would be ill-advised to devalue the currency, as it would only stimulate expectations of a revaluation. A devaluation would be called for only after the negative effects of a sustained real currency appreciation on the current account balance are imminent. At that time, capital flows may begin to reverse their direction and this is the moment when policy action is required. Clearly, in the East Asian economies, as in the case of Mexico in 1994, the exchange rate adjustments carne too late. But in a situation where policymakers may be anticipating (perhaps unrealistically so) an improvement of the current account balance, the exact timing of the switch of the equilibrium exchange rate from currency appreciation to depreciation is uncertain.

What remains true, though, is that once capital outflows begin in earnest, and expectations of devaluation become widespread, the devaluations cannot be delayed. As Radelet and Sachs conclude:

> had Thailand responded ... in early 1997 by floating the baht and moderately tightening monetary and fiscal policies, the Asian financial crisis could have been largely avoided. Thailand and Korea, of course, made the paramount mistake of trying to defend their exchange rate peg until they had effectively exhausted a substantial proportion of their foreign exchange reserves. (Radelet and Sachs 1998a, p. 37).

Since capital flows are at the center of the economic phenomena that are linked to emerging market disease, capital controls have surfaced in many policy discussions in the aftermath of the crisis. Most experts agree, however, that the introduction of widespread restrictions on capital flows has its own problems and can be counterproductive. The ample historical experience on the imposition of capital and exchange controls indicates that they are troublesome because they (1) lead to the formation of black markets, widespread evasion and corruption, and (2) delay the implementation of short-term policy reforms required to dissipate the symptoms behind the capital flight, such as a currency devaluation, budget deficit reduction and anti-inflation policies (Rivera-Batiz and Rivera-Batiz 1994, ch. 3). The existing research also suggests that controls on capital outflows have been unable to effectively stop massive capital flight and balance of payments crises (see Edwards 1989; Kaminsky and Reinhart 1999).

Despite the skepticism with controls on capital flows in general, many economists agree that emerging markets should consider adopting policies intended to reduce the volatility of short-term capital flows, particularly capital inflows. Even the IMF, which at one point considered amending the institution's charter to make the free flow of capital one of its major goals, has been more flexible on this issue in recent years. Michael Camdessus, as Managing Director of the IMF in 1996, encouraged East Asian countries to consider temporary controls on capital inflows, stating: 'because the greatest threat to instability is posed by more

volatile short-term inflows... the adoption of prudential requirements *vis-a-vis* short-term inflows... has... played a useful role.
However, in our experience, direct quantitative controls on capital inflows rarely work for any sustained period' (Camdessus
1997, p. 23).

The imposition of direct taxes on short-term capital inflows,
and indirect taxes, such as reserve requirements on short-term
bank deposits, have been among the policies proposed by various
economists (Calvo *et al.* 1995, p. 380). Chile represents the most
visible case where this type of policy was implemented. Various high-
profile economists have endorsed it. For example, in 1998, Joseph
Stiglitz, then Chief Economist at the World Bank, in response to a
question about what policies can be developed to deal with financial
crises, stated: 'You want to look for policies that discourage hot
money but facilitate the flow of long-term loans, and there is evidence
that the Chilean approach or some version of it, does this' (*New York
Times*, 1 February 1998; see also Eichengreen 2000).

Established in 1991 in the face of a surge of capital inflows,
Chile imposed a minimum one-year requirement for the stay of
foreign direct investment in the country. It also required that all
other foreign funds flowing into the country include a deposit of
30 per cent in the form of no-interest accounts at the central bank
for one year. The policy was phased-out by May 2000, when a
long period of sustained capital outflows led policymakers to seek
incentives (rather than disincentives) for capital inflows. Evidence
on the effectiveness of the controls suggests that the policy was
highly successful in switching capital inflows away from short-term
flows (see Hernandez and Schmidt-Hebel 1999; Calvo and Reinhart
1999). On the other hand, a number of studies show that the controls
only changed the composition, not the level, of capital inflows. They
also do not appear to have controlled one of the key symptoms
of emerging market disease: the real exchange rate appreciation
linked to massive capital inflows. Finally, it should be realized that
this type of policy is not without costs since it raises the cost of
capital and, over time, may give rise to various tax-evasion schemes
(Edwards 1999).

The final set of policy prescriptions we discuss here relates to financial fragility and the speed at which emerging markets liberalize the capital account. The severe impact of financial liberalization and massive capital inflows into imperfect, weak financial systems was a crucial factor behind the East Asian crisis.[15] Adequate regulatory and supervision systems, which define and monitor appropriate capital-adequacy ratios of banks; enforce legal lending limits on single borrowers or groups of related borrowers; require banks to hold an adequate fraction of liquid reserves; establish standards to follow in case of losses, provide for mechanisms to insure depositors and deal with possible bankruptcy of financial institutions; engage in strict audits of institutions and impose severe corporate and managerial penalties for the violation of rules, procedures and regulations; and assure greater disclosure and transparency of bank operations, are sorely needed in place before the capital account is opened to cross-border banking transactions (Caprio and Honohan 1999; Caprio and Klingebiel 1996). A sequencing of financial liberalization, where foreign direct investment (FDI) is opened-up before short-term capital flows and commercial bank lending transactions, may allow both policymakers and the private sector enough time for the institution-building required to intermediate effectively large inflows of capital.[16]

At this time, the five East Asian countries are embarked in a major restructuring process that will take time to be fully resolved. The external debt overhang and wide public sector deficits constitute serious public policy concerns. However, the basic fundamentals regarding physical and human capital accumulation in East Asia (as we discussed them in Section 11.2 above) have not essentially changed. This suggests that economic growth will rebound in the region (as it is already doing). As confidence on this growth gathers momentum, capital inflows will return. Note, however, that the basic phenomena associated with emerging market disease have not disappeared. They are just dormant. Once capital inflows return, the disease will reawaken. Careful policy management, along the lines discussed in this concluding section, will need to be implemented to prevent a recurrence of the events in the past few years.

Notes:

[1] See, for example, Chang and Velasco 1999; Corsetti *et al.* 1999a, 1999b; Goldstein 1998; Kaminsky and Reinhart 1998; Krugman 1998, 1999; Radelet and Sachs 1998a, 1998b; Rivera-Batiz 1999a; and Stiglitz 1998.

[2] See Blejer and del Castillo 1998, Dombusch 1997, and Edwards and Edwards 1987.

[3] An analytical presentation of Dutch disease appears in Rivera-Batiz and Rivera-Batiz 1994, pp. 355–7.

[4] The view that the so-called East Asian miracle was fueled by export-led growth, is presented in World Bank 1993. For a theoretical analysis of the links between trade and growth, see Rivera-Batiz 1996.

[5] For an analysis of financial liberalization in the five East Asian countries, see Alba, Hernandez and Klingebiel (this volume), Callen and Reynolds 1997, Claessens and Glaessner 1997, Collins and Park 1989, Dekle and Pradhan 1997, Dohner and Intal 1989, Johnston 1991, Lindgren *et al.* 1996, Montgomery 1997, Montiel 1997, Nascimento 1991, and Woo and Nasution 1989.

[6] For a discussion of the 1992–93 crisis of the European Monetary System, see Buiter *et al.* 1998.

[7] Symbolically, the real exchange rate is represented by q, where $q = eP*/P$, with e representing the nominal exchange rate (say, baht per dollar), $P*$ the price of foreign goods (measured say in dollars), and P the price of domestic goods (measured in baht). The real exchange rate q then depicts how expensive foreign goods are compared to domestic goods. An increase in q means foreign goods are relatively more expensive while a drop in q suggests that domestic goods are becoming more expensive.

[8] In the Korean case, we use the symbol e to represent the dollar–won exchange rate (in dollars per won), $P*$ is the price level in the United States (we use the consumer price index), and P is the price level in Korea (measured by the Korean consumer price index).

[9] We measure the real exchange rate of the currencies relative to the US dollar, so that the foreign price level $P*$ is the US price level (the US consumer price index).

[10] Asian Development Bank 1997a, p. 10. The Bank, however, ends up dismissing the significance of the deficits.

[11] For a comprehensive description of the banking and financial fragility in East Asia, see Delhaise 1998.

[12] Nascimento 1991 and Dohner and Intal 1989 provide an analysis of the Philippine crisis in the 1980s.

[13]See Chang and Velasco 1998, 1999 for an analysis of the role of international illiquidity on financial crises.

[14]Although central bankers often seek to minimize this impact by sterilizing their purchases of foreign exchange through sales of bonds.

[15]See, for example, the comprehensive analysis of Thailand by Alba *et al.*, Chapter 5 in this volume.

[16]See Rivera-Batiz 2000 for a discussion of the costs and benefits of FDI.

References

Asian Development Bank (1995), *Asian Development Outlook, 1995 and 1996*, Oxford: Oxford University Press.

Asian Development Bank (1997a), *Asian Development Outlook, 1997 and 1998*, Oxford: Oxford University Press.

Asian Development Bank (1997b), *Emerging Asia: Changes and Challenges*, Manila: Asian Development Bank.

Asian Development Bank (2000), *Asia Recovery Report 2000*, Manila: Asian Development Bank, May.

Barro, Robert J. and Jong-Wha Lee (1994), "Data Set for a Panel of 138 Countries," mimeo, Department of Economics, Harvard University.

Barro, Robert J. and Xavier Sala-i-Martin (1995), *Economic Growth*, New York: McGraw-Hill.

Birdsall, Nancy and F. Jaspersen (1997), *Pathways to Growth: Comparing East Asia and Latin America*, Washington, DC: Inter-American Development Bank.

Blejer, Mario and Graciana del Castillo (1998), "Déja vu All Over Again? The Mexican Crisis and the Stabilization of Uruguay in the 1970s," *World Development*, 26: 449–64.

Bloom, David E. and John Williamson (1997), "Demographic Transitions and Economic Miracles in Emerging Asia," mimeo, Harvard Institute for International Development.

Brauchli, Marcus W. (1998), "Indonesia's Struggles Become Elemental: A Shortage of Rice," *Wall Street Journal*, October 20: Al, A8.

Buiter, Willem, Giancarlo Corsetti and Paolo Pesenti (eds) (1998), *Financial Markets and European Monetary Cooperation: The Lessons of the 1992–93 Exchange Rate Mechanism Crisis*, Cambridge: Cambridge University Press.

Burnside, Craig, Martin Eichenbaum and Sergio Rebelo (1998), "Prospective Deficits and the Asian Crisis," Washington, DC: Development Research Group, World Bank.

Callen, Tim and Patricia Reynolds (1997), "Capital Market Development and the Monetary Transmission Mechanism in Malaysia and Thailand," in John Hicklin, David Robinson and Anoop Singh (eds), *Macroeconomic Issues Facing ASEAN Countries*, Washington, DC: International Monetary Fund, pp. 184–230.

Calomiris, Charles (1998), "The IMF's Imprudent Role as Lender of Last Resort," *Cato Journal*, 17: pp. 275–94.

Calvo, Guillermo and Carmen Reinhart (1999), "When Capital Inflows Come to a Sudden Stop: Consequences and Policy Options," mimeo, University of Maryland.

Calvo, Guillermo, Leonardo Leiderman and Carmen Reinhart (1995), "Capital Inflows to Latin America with Reference to the Asian Experience," in S. Edwards (ed.), *Capital Controls, Exchange Rates and Monetary Policy in the World Economy*, Cambridge: Cambridge University Press, pp. 339–82.

Camdessus, Michel (1997), "Sustaining Macroeconomic Performance in the ASEAN Countries," in John Hicklin, David Robinson and Anoop Singh (eds), *Macroeconomic Issues Facing ASEAN Countries*, Washington, DC: International Monetary Fund, pp. 19–28.

Caprio, Gerard and Daniela Klingebiel (1996), "Bank Insolvency: Bad Luck, Bad Policy or Bad Banking?," in M. Bruno and B. Pleskovic (eds), *World Bank Annual Conference on Development Economics*, Washington, DC: World Bank, pp. 32–44.

Caprio, Gerard and Patrick Honohan (1999), "Restoring Banking Stability: Beyond Supervised Capital Requirements," *Journal of Economic Perspectives*, 13: pp. 43–64.

Chang, Roberto and Andres Velasco (1998), "The Asian Liquidity Crisis," National Bureau of Economic Research Working Paper, No. 6796.

Chang, Roberto and Andres Velasco (1999), "Liquidity Crises in Emerging Markets: Theory and Policy," in Ben S. Bernanke and Julio J. Rotemberg (eds), *NBER Macroeconomics Annual 1999*, Cambridge, MA: MIT Press, pp. 11–57.

Chinn, Menzie D. (1998), "Before the Fall: Were East Asian Currencies Overvalued?," National Bureau of Economic Research Working Paper, No. 6491.

Claessens, Stijn and Thomas Glaessner (1997), *Are Financial Sector Weaknesses Undermining the East Asian Miracle?*, Washington, DC: World Bank.

Claessens, Stijn, S. Djankov and D. Klingebiel (1999), "Financial Restructuring in East Asia: Halfway There?," Financial Sector Discussion Paper No. 3, World Bank.

Clemente, Lilia (1994), "Investing in Asia's Emerging Equity Market," *Columbia Journal of World Business*, 29: pp. 92–111.

Collins, Susan M. and Won-Am Park (1989), "External Debt and Macroeconomic Performance in South Korea," in J.D. Sachs (ed.), *Developing Country Debt and the World Economy*, Chicago: University of Chicago Press, pp. 121–40.

Corsetti, Giancarlo, Paolo Pesenti and Nouriel Roubini (1999a), "What Caused the Asian Currency and Financial Crisis?," *Japan and the World Economy*, 11: 305–73.

Corsetti, Giancarlo, Paolo Pesenti and Nouriel Roubini (1999b), "Paper Tigers? A Model of the Asian Crisis," *European Economic Review*, 43: 42–63.

Dekle, Robert and Mahmood Pradhan (1997), "Financial Liberalization and Money Demand in ASEAN Countries: Implications for Monetary Policy," in John Hicklin, David Robinson and Anoop Singh (eds), *Macroeconomic Issues Facing ASEAN Countries*, Washington, DC: International Monetary Fund, pp. 153–83.

Delhaise, Philippe (1998), *Asia in Crisis: The Implosion of the Banking and Finance Systems*, Singapore: Wiley & Sons.

Demirguk-Kunt, Asli and Enrica Detragiache (1998), "The Determinants of Banking Crises in Developing and Developed Countries," *IMF Staff Papers*, 45: 81–109.

Diaz-Alejandro, Carlos (1985), "Good-Bye Financial Repression, Hello Financial Crash," *Journal of Development Economics*, 19: 64–93.

Dohner, Robert S. and P. Intal (1989), "Debt Crisis and Adjustment in the Philippines," in J.D. Sachs (ed.), *Developing Country Debt and the World Economy*, Chicago: University of Chicago Press, pp. 169–91.

Dornbusch, Rudiger (1986), "Stabilization Policies in Developing Countries: What Have We Learned?," in R. Dornbusch (ed.), *Dollars, Debts and Deficits*, Cambridge, MA: MIT Press, pp. 151–65.

Dornbusch, Rudiger (1997), "The Folly, the Crash and Beyond: Economic Policies and the Crisis," in S. Edwards and M. Naim (eds), *Mexico 1994: Anatomy of an Emerging-Market Crash*, Washington, DC: Carnegie Endowment for International Peace, pp. 125–40.

Edwards, Sebastian (1989), *Real Exchange Rates, Devaluation and Adjustment*, Cambridge, MA: MIT Press.

Edwards, Sebastian (1998), "Capital Controls are not the Reason for Chile's Success," *Wall Street Journal*, April 3: A19.

Edwards, Sebastian (1999), "How Effective are Capital Controls?," *Journal of Economic Perspectives*, 13: 65–84.

Edwards, Sebastian and Alejandra Cox Edwards (1987), *Monetarism and Liberalization: The Chilean Experiment*, Cambridge, MA: Ballinger.

Eichengreen, Barry (2000), "Taming Capital Flows," *World Development*, 28(6): 1105–1116.

Eichengreen, Barry and Andrew Rose (1998), "Staying Afloat When the Wind Shifts: External Factors and Emerging-Market Banking Crises," National Bureau of Economic Research Working Paper, No. 6370.

Eichengreen, Barry and Donald Mathieson (1999), "Hedge Funds: What Do We Really Know?," *IMF Economic Issues*, No. 19, September.

Eichengreen, Barry, Andrew Rose and Charles Wyplosz (1996), "Contagious Currency Crises: First Tests," in T.M. Andersen and K. Moene (eds), *Financial Liberalization and Macroeconomic Stability*, Oxford: Blackwell Publishers, pp. 1–23.

Feldstein, Martin (1998), "Refocusing the IMF," *Foreign Affairs*, 77: 20–33.

Fischer, Stanley (1998), "The Asian Crisis and the Changing Role of the IMF," *Finance and Development*, 35: 2–5.

Goldstein, Morris (1998), *The Asian Financial Crisis: Causes, Cures and Systemic Implications*, Washington, DC: Institute for International Economics.

Hanushek, E. and O. Kim (1995), "Schooling, Labor Force Quality and Economic Growth," National Bureau of Economic Research Working Paper, No. 5399.

Henderson, Callum (1998), *Asia Falling*, New York: McGraw Hill.

Hernandez, Leonardo and Klaus Schmidt-Hebel (1999), "Capital Controls in Chile: Effective? Efficient? Endurable?," Central Bank of Chile Working Paper, Santiago, Chile.

Hill, Hal (1996), *The Indonesian Economy Since 1996*, Cambridge: Cambridge University Press.

International Finance Corporation (1998), *Emerging Stock Markets Factbook 1998*, Washington, DC: International Finance Corporation.

International Finance Corporation (1999), *Emerging Stock Markets Factbook 1999*, Washington, DC: International Finance Corporation.

International Monetary Fund (1996), *World Economic Outlook*, Washington, DC: International Monetary Fund.

International Monetary Fund (1998), *World Economic Outlook*, Washington, DC: International Monetary Fund.

International Monetary Fund (1999), *International Financial Statistics Yearbook*, Washington, DC: international Monetary Fund.

International Monetary Fund (2000), *World Economic Outlook*, Washington, DC: International Monetary Fund, April.

Johnston, R. Barry (1991), "Distressed Financial Institutions in Thailand: Structural Weaknesses, Support Operations, and Economic Consequences," in V. Sundararajan and Tomas Balino (eds), *Banking Crises: Cases and Issues*, Washington, DC: International Monetary Fund, pp. 234–75.

Kaminsky, Graciela L. and Carmen M. Reinhart (1998), "Financial Crises in Asia and Latin America: Then and Now," *American Economic Review*, 88: 444–48.

Kaminsky, Graciela L. and Carmen M. Reinhart (1999), "The Twin Crises: The Causes of Banking and Balance of Payments Problems," *American Economic Review*, 89: 473–500.

Krongkaew, Mehdi (2000), "Mitigating the Social Cost of Financial Crisis in East Asia: Experiences and Policy Lessons," paper presented at the Workshop on Managing Capital Flows in a Volatile Financial Environment, World Bank Institute, Bangkok, February 21–24.

Krugman, Paul (1979), "A Model of Balance of Payments Crises," *Journal of Money, Credit and Banking*, 11: 311–25.

Krugman, Paul (1994), "The Myth of Asia's Miracle," *Foreign Affairs*, 73: 62–78.

Krugman, Paul (1998), "What Happened to Asia?," mimeo, Department of Economics, Massachusetts Institute of Technology.

Krugman, Paul (1999), "Analytical Afterthoughts on the Asian Crisis," mimeo, Department of Economics, Massachusetts Institute of Technology.

Lindgren, Carl-Johan, Gillian Garcia and Matthew Saal (1996), *Bank Soundness and Macroeconomic Policy*, Washington, DC: International Monetary Fund.

McKinnon, Ronald and Huw Pil (1996), "Credible Liberalization and International Capital Flows: The Overborrowing Syndrome," in T. Ito and A. Krueger (eds), *Financial Deregulation and Integration in East Asia*, Chicago: University of Chicago Press, pp. 220–45.

Montgomery, John (1997), "Indonesian Financial System: Its Contribution to Economic Performance and Key Policy Issues," in John Hicklin, David Robinson and Anoop Singh (eds), *Macroeconomic Issues Facing ASEAN Countries*, Washington, DC: International Monetary Fund, pp. 23–52.

Montiel, Peter J. (1997), "Exchange Rate Policy and Macroeconomic Management in ASEAN Countries," in John Hicklin, David Robinson and Anoop

Singh (eds), *Macroeconomic Issues Facing ASEAN Countries*, Washington, DC: International Monetary Fund, pp. 253–98.

Nascimento, Jean-Claude (1991), "Crisis in the Financial Sector and the Authorities' Reaction: The Philippines," in V. Sundararajan and Tomas Balino (eds), *Banking Crises: Cases and Issues*, Washington, DC: International Monetary Fund, pp. 175–233.

O'Brien, Timothy, Edmund Andrews, and Sheryl WuDunn (1998), "Covering Asia with Cash: Banks Poured Money into Region Despite Warning Signs," *New York Times*, 28 January.

Radelet, Steven and Jeffrey Sachs (1998a), "The East Asian Financial Crisis: Diagnosis, Remedies and Prospects," *Brookings Papers on Economic Activity*, No. 1, 1–74.

Radelet, Steven and Jeffrey Sachs (1998b), "The Onset of the East Asian Financial Crisis," National Bureau of Economic Research Working Paper, No. 6680, August.

Rivera-Batiz, Francisco L. (1996), "The Economics of Technological Progress and Endogenous Growth in Open Economies," in G. Koopmann and H.E. Scharrer (eds), *The Economics of High-Technology Competition and Cooperation in Global Markets*, Baden: Nomos Verlagsgesellschaft, pp. 31–62.

Rivera-Batiz, Francisco L. (1999a), "The East Asian Financial Crisis: What Went Wrong?," in Lin Guijun and C. Jayachandran (eds), *China in the Globalization of the World Economy*, Beijing: University of International Business and Economics Press, pp. 20–30.

Rivera-Batiz, Francisco L. (1999b), "Education and Economic Development: The Case of East Asia," Working Paper, Program in Economic Policy Management, Columbia University.

Rivera-Batiz, Francisco L. (2000), "Foreign Direct Investment in Latin America: Current Trends and Future Prospects," in United Nations, *Interregional Cooperation in Trade and Investment: Asia-Latin America*, Bangkok: United Nations Economic and Social Commission for Asia and the Pacific, pp. 161–91.

Rivera-Batiz, Francisco L. and Luis A. Rivera-Batiz (1994), *International Finance and Open Economy Macroeconomics*, Englewood Cliffs, NJ: Prentice-Hall.

Rivera-Batiz, Luis A. and Paul Romer (1991), "Economic Integration and Endogenous Growth," *Quarterly Journal of Economics*, 10: 531–56.

Rodrik, Dani (1995), "Getting Interventions Right: How South Korea and Taiwan Grew Rich," *Economic Policy*, 21: 53–107.

Romer, Paul M. (1990), "Endogenous Technological Change," *Journal of Political Economy*, 98: S71–S102.

Stiglitz, Joseph (1998), "Bad Private-Sector Decisions," *Wall Street Journal*, February 4.

Sundararajan, V. and T. Balino (1990), "Issues in Recent Banking Crises in Developing Countries," IMF Working Paper, WP-90-19, Washington, DC, March.

Wessel, David and Bon Davis (1998), "Limits of Power: How Global Crisis Grew Despite Efforts of a Crack U.S. Team," *Wall Street Journal*, September 24: Al, A10.

Woo, Wing Thye and Anwar Nasution (1989), "The Conduct of Economic Policies in Indonesia and Its Impact on External Debt," in Jeffrey D. Sachs (ed.), *Developing Country Debt and the World Economy*, Chicago: University of Chicago Press, pp. 101–20.

World Bank (1993), *The East Asian Miracle: Economic Growth and Public Policy*, Oxford: Oxford University Press.

World Bank (1995), *World Tables*, Baltimore, MD: Johns Hopkins University Press.

World Bank (1996), *Managing Capital Flows in East Asia*, Washington, DC: World Bank.

World Bank (1997), *Global Economic Prospects and the Developing Countries*, Washington, DC: World Bank.

World Bank (1998), *East Asia: The Road 10 Recovery*, Washington, DC: World Bank.

World Bank (1999), *Global Development Finance*, Washington, DC: World Bank.

World Bank (2000a), *Global Development Finance*, Washington, DC: World Bank.

World Bank (2000b), *Global Economic Prospects and the Developing Countries*, Washington, DC: World Bank.

World Bank (2000c), *World Development Report 1999–2000*, Oxford: Oxford University Press.

World Bank (2000d), *World Development Indicators 2000*, Washington, DC: World Bank.

Part 4

The Effects of Foreign Direct Investment

Chapter 12

Foreign Ownership, Non-Traded Goods and the Effects of Terms of Trade Changes on National Welfare*

12.1 Introduction

Recent developments in international trade theory have shown the key role that the presence of foreign-owned factors of production has on the welfare impact of external disturbances [see Brecher and Bhagwati (1981), Brecher and Choudhri (1982), and Brecher and Findlay (1983)]. It has been noted, for instance, that a deterioration in a country's terms of trade could raise national welfare if there is a differential trade pattern phenomenon, defined as a situation where the national and aggregate trade specialization patterns differ due to the foreign presence in the economy. As Bhagwati and Brecher (1980, p. 114) state: 'The paradoxical behavior of national welfare arises simply because the aggregate pattern of trade masks a contrary pattern of trade for the domestically-owned, national factors of

*This chapter was authored by Francisco L. Rivera-Batiz and was originally published in *Economics Letters*, Vol. 20, No. 4 (July 1986), pp. 367–371. ©1986 Elsevier Science Publishers.

This paper was written while the author was a Visiting Post-Doctoral Fellow at the Department of Economics of the University of Chicago. The support of a grant from the National Research Council of the National Academy of Sciences is gratefully acknowledged.

production.' This literature has exclusively considered the case where only internationally-traded goods are produced. This paper extends the analysis to incorporate internationally non-traded goods. It is shown that, in the presence of non-traded goods, national welfare might increase in response to a deterioration in the economy's external terms of trade even when there is no differential trade pattern phenomenon.

12.2   The Effects of Changes in Terms of Trade on National and Aggregate Welfare

We assume three types of commodities are produced and consumed: exportables, importables and non-traded goods, indexed by the subscripts $j = 1, 2, 3$, respectively. We consider only cases of incomplete specialization at both the aggregate and national levels [for details of the analysis when there is complete specialization, see Rivera-Batiz (1985)]. Aggregate and national welfare are given by

$$W^k = U^k(C_1^k, C_2^k, C_3^k), \tag{1}$$

where $k = $ A, N indexes aggregate and national welfare, respectively, U^k is a twice-differentiable utility function — with positive but diminishing marginal utilities, denoted by $U_j^k = \partial U^k / \partial C_j^k$ — and C_j^k depicts consumption of the jth commodity by the kth group in the economy, with C_j^A equal to the consumption of nationals-cum-foreign factors. For simplicity — and following the literature — we assume foreign income is consumed in the host country rather than being remitted [see Rivera-Batiz (1985) for a discussion of the effect of remittances].

The utility function in (1) is maximized subject to the budget constraint

$$Y^k = C_1^k + PC_2^k + qC_3^k = X_1^k + PX_2^k + qX_3^k, \tag{2}$$

with Y^A, Y^N denoting the real value of aggregate and national income, respectively, in terms of the first commodity, $P = P_2/P_1$ is the reciprocal of the terms of trade, and $q = P_3/P_1$ is the relative price of non-traded goods in terms of commodity 1. It is assumed that the country is a small, open economy facing exogenously-given terms of trade.

The impact of a deterioration in the terms of trade — an increase of P — on aggregate and national welfare can be determined by differentiating eqs. (1) and (2) with respect to P. The result is

$$\mathrm{d}W^k = P(X_2^k - C_2^k)\hat{P} + q(X_3^k - C_3^k)\hat{q}, \tag{3}$$

where we are using the first-order conditions for maximization of utility and profits: $U_2^k/U_1^k = P, U_3^k/U_1^k = q$ and $\mathrm{d}X_1 + P\mathrm{d}X_2 + q\mathrm{d}X_3 = 0$. Without loss of generality, it is also assumed that, initially, $U_1^k = 1$. Notice that we utilize a circumflex, ^, to denote percentage changes, so that $\hat{P} = \mathrm{d}P/P$ and $\hat{q} = \mathrm{d}q/q$.

Due to the local nature of non-traded goods production and consumption, the demand for and supply of non-traded goods must equalize at the aggregate level, or: $C_3^A = X_3^A$. At the same time, in the presence of foreign-owned factors, the demand for and supply of non-traded goods on the part of nationals do not have to equalize. That is, in general: $C_3^N \neq X_3^N$. The explanation is that, with foreign factors in the local economy, the nationals can engage in internal trade in (internationally) non-traded goods with the foreign-owned factors. Therefore, even though at the economy-wide level, demand for and supply of non-traded goods are equal, this fact can hide significant internal imbalances. Nationals, for instance, might be showing an excess supply of non-traded goods ($X_3^N - C_3^A > 0$), exporting them to foreigners in the economy in exchange for a net import of traded goods — of commodities 1 and/or 2 — from them. The foreigners, in turn, would show an excess demand for non-traded goods (a net import of non-traded goods from nationals), which they would pay for by means of a net export of traded goods to nationals.

With these observations, eq. (3) can be transformed to yield

$$\mathrm{d}W^A = P(X_2^A - C_2^A)\hat{P} \tag{4}$$

and

$$\mathrm{d}W^N = P(X_2^N - C_2^N)\hat{P} + q(X_3^N - C_3^N)\hat{q}. \tag{5}$$

The existing literature on the theory of trade in the presence of foreign-owned factors has abstracted from examining the effects of exogenous disturbances on the nontraded goods sector. In terms of eqs. (4) and (5), it is usually assumed that $X_3^N = C_3^N = 0$, implying that a deterioration of the economy's terms of trade ($\hat{P} > 0$) alters aggregate and national welfare in different directions only when the national and aggregate international trade specialization patterns differ. That is, only when $\text{sign}(X_2^N - C_2^N) = -\text{sign}(X_2^A - C_2^A) < 0$, will $\text{sign}(dW^A/dP) = -\text{sign}(dW^N/dP) < 0$. In this case, a deterioration of the terms of trade will lower aggregate welfare but raise national welfare. If, on the other hand, the national and aggregate international trade specialization patterns coincide — if $\text{sign}(X_2^N - C_2^N) = \text{sign}(X_2^A - C_2^A) < 0$ — then national welfare would move in the same direction as aggregate welfare in response to an exogenous disturbance in the terms of trade. This assumes, though, the absence of a non-traded goods sector.

In the presence of non-traded goods, a terms of trade deterioration for the economy might raise national welfare even if the national and aggregate international trade specialization patterns coincide. The explanation lies in that, with non-traded goods, changes in national welfare are related not only to the external trade specialization pattern of nationals but also to their internal pattern of specialization on trade in non-traded goods. Therefore, whether national welfare rises or declines depends on the internal trade pattern in non-traded goods between nationals and foreigners and on the impact of the terms of trade disturbance on the prices of non-traded goods. As is clear from eqs. (4) and (5), even if sign $(X_2^A - C_2^A) = \text{sign}(X_2^N - C_2^N) < 0, \text{sign}(\frac{dW_2^N}{dP}) = \text{sign}(dW^A/dP) > 0$ if $q(X_3^N - C_3^N)\hat{q}$ is positive and larger than the first term in the right-hand side of eq. (5). This might arise if nationals are exporting non-traded goods to the foreigners inside the economy ($X_3^N - C_3^N > 0$) and the terms of trade deterioration raises non-traded goods prices substantially (q is positive and large). Of course, the key question involves how changes in the terms of trade influence the prices of non-traded goods.

12.3 Terms of Trade Changes, Non-Traded Goods Prices and Welfare

We assume that the output of each commodity, X_j, is produced through the use of labor, L_j, and capital, K_j. Full employment implies

$$a_{L1}X_1 + a_{L2}X_2 + a_{L3}X_3 = \bar{L}, \qquad (6)$$

$$a_{K1}X_1 + a_{K2}X_2 + a_{K3}X_3 = \bar{K}, \qquad (7)$$

with the a_{ij}'s representing the quantity of input i required per unit of $X_j (i = K, L$ and $j = 1, 2, 3)$, $\bar{L}$ is the economy's aggregate endowment of labor and $\bar{K}$ is its aggregate capital endowment. Note that $\bar{L}$ and $\bar{K}$ include both national and foreign-owned factors and that the a_{ij}'s are a function of relative factor prices on the assumption of constant returns to scale,

$$a_{ij} = a_{ij}(w/r), \qquad (8)$$

where w is the economy's wage rate and r is the rental rate on capital.

On the assumptions made, of perfect competition and constant returns to scale, producers will set price equal to unit costs, or

$$wa_{L1} + ra_{K1} = P_1, \qquad (9)$$

$$wa_{L2} + ra_{K2} = P_2, \qquad (10)$$

$$wa_{L3} + ra_{K3} = P_3, \qquad (11)$$

where P_j is the price of the jth commodity, with P_1 and P_2 exogenous and P_3 determined by

$$D_3^A(P, q, Y^A) = X_3^A, \qquad (12)$$

with Y^A denoting aggregate real income, as defined in eq. (2). This completes the basic model utilized to examine the effects of terms of trade changes. The impact of an exogenous change in the terms of trade, $\hat{P} = \hat{P}_2 - \hat{P}_1 > 0$, on the relative price of non-traded goods, $\hat{q} = \hat{P}_3 - \hat{P}_1$, can be determined by differentiating this system of equations with respect to a change in the terms of trade and solving.

This is fairly standard [see Batra (1973, ch. 12), Komiya (1967)), and the result is

$$\hat{q} = \frac{Pa_{L3}(k_3 - k_1)}{qa_{L2}(k_2 - k_1)}\hat{P}, \tag{13}$$

where $k_j = K_j/L_j$ is the capital-labor ratio in sector j. Suppose, for the sake of the argument, that the production of importables is relatively labor-intensive compared to that of exportables. Given the widely-observed relative labor-intensity of non-traded goods production relative to that of traded goods [see Kravis, Heston and Summers (1983)], then $k_3 < k_2 < k_1$. Under these assumptions, the implication of eq. (13) is that a deterioration of the terms of trade will be associated with an increase in the relative price of non-traded goods: the relative increase in the price of labor-intensive importable goods raises their output and, therefore, the demand for labor in the economy, pushing wage rates upwards; the relatively labor-intensive non-traded goods sector is particularly affected by this increase in relative labor costs and, at the initial relative price, it would result in a reduction of their supply. The consequent excess demand for non-traded goods at the aggregate level is then eliminated through an upwards readjustment of the relative price of non-traded goods.

Substitution of eq. (13) into (5) yields

$$dW^N = \left[P(X_2^N - C_2^N)\hat{P} + q(X_3^N - C_3^N)\frac{Pa_{L3}(k_3 - k_1)}{qa_{L2}(k_2 - k_1)}\right]\hat{P}. \tag{14}$$

Therefore, even if $\text{sign}(X_2^N - C_2^N) = \text{sign}(X_2^A - C_2^A) < 0$, $dW^N/dP > 0$ if

$$(X_3^N - C_3^N)\frac{a_{L3}(k_3 - k_1)}{a_{L2}(k_2 - k_1)} > -(X_2^N - C_2^N). \tag{15}$$

Once this condition is satisfied, changes in the terms of trade will move national and aggregate welfare in different directions, even when national and aggregate international trade specialization patterns are the same. There is, of course, the reduction in real national income associated with the terms of trade deterioration, represented by the first term in eq. (14). But this negative impact is more than compensated by the improvement in the internal terms of trade that nationals obtain through the rise in the relative price of non-traded goods. As net exporters of non-traded goods within the economy, nationals receive a gain in real income when the relative price of their internal exports rise.

Of course, if the nationals were importers of non-traded goods and the national and aggregate international trade specialization patterns were the same, the real income of nationals would unambiguously decline with the terms of trade deterioration. In this case, $X_3^N - C_3^N < 0$ and, with everything else held constant, the rise in the price of non-traded goods would augment the reduction in national welfare associated with the terms of trade deterioration. Nationals would thus lose real income not only through the decline in the price of the commodity which they export at the international level, but also from the increase in the relative price of the commodity (non-traded goods) they import in their internal trade with foreign-owned factors. Furthermore, even if nationals were net exporters of non-traded goods within the economy, if importables were relatively capital-intensive compared to exportables (with $k_3 < k_2 < k_1$), then a deterioration of the terms of trade would lower the relative prices of non-traded goods and enlarge the welfare deterioration associated with the terms of trade disturbance.

References

Batra, R.N., 1973, *Studies in the pure theory of international trade* (St. Martin's, New York).

Bhagwati, Jagdish N. and Richard A. Brecher, 1980, "National welfare in an open economy in the presence of foreign-owned factors of production," *Journal of International Economics*, 10, 103–115.

Brecher, Richard A. and Jagdish N. Bhagwati, 1981, "Foreign ownership and the theory of trade and welfare," *Journal of Political Economy*, 89, 497–511.

Brecher, Richard A. and Ehsan U. Choudhri, 1982, "Immiserizing investment from abroad: The Singer–Prebisch thesis reconsidered," *Quarterly Journal of Economics*, 97, 181–190.

Brecher, Richard A. and Ronald Findlay, 1983, "Tariffs, foreign capital and national welfare with sector-specific factors," *Journal of International Economics*, 14, 277–288.

Komiya. R., 1967, "Nontraded goods and the pure theory of international trade," *International Economic Review*, 8, 132–152.

Kravis, Irving, Alan Weston and Robert Summers, 1983, The share of services in economic growth, in: F. Gerard Adams and Bert Hickman, eds., *Global econometrics: Essays in honor of Lawrence R. Klein* (MIT Press, Cambridge, MA).

Rivera-Batiz, Francisco, 1985, "Foreign ownership, nontraded goods and the theory of trade and welfare." Mimeo. (University of Pennsylvania, Philadelphia, PA).

Chapter 13

Foreign Capital
and the Contractionary Impact
of Currency Devaluation,
with an Application to Jamaica*

13.1   Introduction

Despite the considerable amount of literature examining the effects
of currency devaluation in developing countries, surprisingly little
attention has been devoted to the role played by the presence of
foreign capital. Though micro studies have looked at the interaction
between exchange rate changes and the profits of multinational
corporations,[1] the macroeconomic aspects of devaluation in this
context do not appear to have been explored. It is the purpose
of this paper to examine the effects of currency devaluation in

*This chapter was co-authored by Luca Barbone and Francisco L. Rivera-Batiz
and was originally published in *Journal of Development Economics*, Vol. 26, No.
1 (June 1987), pp. 1–15. ©1987 Elsevier Science Publishers.

The authors wish to thank Richard Eckaus, Paul Krugman, Ruben Lamdany,
Lance Taylor and the members of seminars at the Federal Reserve Bank of New
York and the University of the West Indies in Jamaica for helpful comments
on previous versions of this paper. A portion of the manuscript formed part of
Barbone's Ph.D. dissertation and was completed when he was consultant with the
Planning Institute of Jamaica at Kingston, Jamaica. Neither this organization nor
the Organization for Economic Co-operation and Development necessarily shares
the views expressed here.

a small open economy host to foreign capital. We show that the presence of foreign capital provides devaluation with an additional contractionary mechanism, besides those that have already been identified — and popularized — in the literature, generating the possibility that exchange rate increases could reduce both Gross Domestic Product (GDP) and Gross National Product (GNP), immiserizing domestic residents.

The fact that currency devaluation can have a short-run negative impact on GDP has been known for many years[2] and has received some recent theoretical attention. In their influential paper, Krugman and Taylor (1978) utilize a simple Keynesian model of the open economy to show that the impact effect of a devaluation is to be contractionary if the economy is initially in a trade deficit, if there are export or import tax revenues which are affected by devaluation, or if the exchange rate change redistributes income from labor to capital, which results in a reduction of aggregate demand when the marginal propensity to consume out of wages exceeds the marginal propensity to consume out of profits.

This paper re-examines this analysis by showing that, even if these effects do not operate, devaluation can still be contractionary when the economy is host to a substantial amount of private direct foreign investment. That is, even if the devaluation is made from a situation of balanced trade, with no export and import taxes and the marginal propensities to consume out of wages and profits are the same, output will decline if the share of domestic capital owned by foreigners is large enough. The explanation lies in that a fraction of the profits received by foreign capital is remitted abroad and cannot, therefore, be spent on home goods. Within a short-run framework, with rigid nominal wages, a devaluation raises the prices of home goods and redistributes income from wages to profits. Some of the increased profits, however, are repatriated, and thus leak out of domestic consumption. If the leakage is large enough, the amount of home goods consumed out of the remaining profits will not be sufficient to compensate for the contraction in demand associated with lower domestic real wages. The consequence is a decline in aggregate demand and, in a short-run Keynesian context, a contractionary effect on output. Furthermore, the impact on national product (versus its impact on domestic product) will be even more negative since the claims of foreign capital on domestic output (the foreign profits) rise with devaluation. In other words, GNP will decline by more than GDP.

That policy measures can have unexpectedly negative effects on national welfare in the presence of foreign ownership is a well-known phenomenon in the trade theoretic literature. Beginning with the work of Brecher and Diaz-Alejandro (1977), Bhagwati and Tironi (1980), and others, the possibility that policy measures such as tariff changes or trade liberalization might be immiserizing (reduce national welfare) in the presence of foreign capital is well-established.[3] Our discussion can be visualized as extending this literature's concerns to the open economy macroeconomics arena.

In section 13.2 we develop a simple short-run macroeconomic model of a small open economy playing host to foreign investment. Section 13.3 examines the basic mechanism generating the contractionary and immiserizing effects of devaluation in the presence of foreign capital, emphasizing how the results obtained by Krugman and Taylor (1978) are modified. Section 13.4 extends the discussion to consider alternative cases involving the current account and to examine the impact of export taxes. Finally, section 13.5 provides estimates of the relevant effects for Jamaica, country where the bauxite industry provides the bulk of foreign exchange earnings, and is substantially foreign-owned.

13.2   The Model

The economy is assumed to consist of an export sector whose output is sold in foreign markets and a non-traded goods sector whose output is sold only in the home market. We decompose the export sector into a foreign-owned component producing a traditional export good, B, and a domestically-owned component producing non-traditional exports, E. Output of traditional exports, B, is assumed to be given by fixed capacity and their price determined by $P_B = eP_B^*$, where e is the exchange rate (in units of domestic currency per unit of foreign currency) and P_B^* is the price of non-traditional exports in world markets (in foreign currency). It is assumed that the economy is small in the sense that it faces an exogenously-determined price, P_B^*.

The short-run supply elasticity of non-foreign-owned exports with respect to the real exchange rate is assumed to be positive. Non-traditional export volumes are, therefore, a positive function of the real exchange rate, defined here as the domestic currency price of exports relative to the price of non-traded goods, as in the standard dependent-economy model. That is,

$$E = E(eP_E^*/P_H), \tag{1}$$

where P_E^* denotes the foreign-currency price of non-traditional exports — exogenously determined under the small-country assumption — and P_H is the price of non-traded goods.

Both traditional and non-traditional export owners use labor and imported intermediate goods as inputs in production. Unit input coefficients are fixed and given by a_{ij}, where $i = L, M$ and $j = E, B, L$ is labor and M is the symbol used to denote imported intermediate inputs.

Output of non-traded goods is determined in Keynesian fashion by demand for non-traded goods, with the underlying assumption that the economy is subject to unemployment at a given, rigid wage, W, denominated in domestic currency. Demand for non-traded goods, H, is given by

$$H = C(Y_N/P_H) + I + G, \tag{2}$$

where I and G denote investment demand and government spending, respectively, both assumed to be fixed for analytical convenience, and C represents consumption as a function of real national income, where Y_N denotes nominal national income. The consumption function used implies that the marginal propensities to consume out of profits and wages are the same, though incorporating differences in these propensities would not alter our basic conclusions.[4] We also assume, for simplicity, that no foreign profits are spent on home goods in the host country.

Non-traded goods are assumed to be produced under conditions of imperfect competition, with price, P_H equal to a markup Z above average variable costs, or

$$P_H = (a_{LH}W + a_{MH}P_M)(1 + Z), \tag{3}$$

where a_{LH} and a_{MH} are fixed unit input coefficients for the use of labor and imported intermediate goods into the production of non-traded goods; P_M is the price of imports in domestic currency and is equal to $P_M = eP_M^*$, where P_M^* is the price in foreign currency.

We turn now to examine the impact of an exchange rate increase. Though we do not discuss the expectational underpinnings of our model, which shall remain in the background, it should be clear that it is implicitly assumed that the devaluation is unanticipated.

13.3 Foreign Ownership and Exchange Rate Management

We start by looking at the effects of currency devaluation on GDP. GDP is equal to the value of output produced domestically, Y, and is given by

$$Y = P_H H + eP_E^* E + eP_B^* B - eP_M^* a_{MH} H - eP_M^* a_{MB} B - eP_M^* a_{ME} E, \tag{4}$$

which represents the equality of GDP, Y, with the sum of domestic absorption, $P_H H$, and the trade balance,

$$T = eP_E^* E + eP_B^* B - eP_M^* a_{MH} H - eP_M^* a_{MB} B - eP_M^* a_{ME} E. \tag{5}$$

Observe that the trade balance is equal to the value of the exports of goods E and B minus the value of the intermediate inputs used in domestic production. For expositional convenience we ignore imports of final goods, stressing instead the major role played by intermediate imports in the balance of payments of developing countries.

Real GDP in terms of home goods is given by

$$Y/P_H = [C(Y_N/P_H) + I + G][1 - qa_{MH}] + qE(1 - a_{ME})$$
$$+ Wa_{LB}B/P_H + Y_{RE}/P_H, \tag{6}$$

where Y_{RE} denotes the profits received by foreign capital, $q = e/P_H$ and the foreign currency prices, P_E^*, P_B^*, and P_M^*, have all been equated to one for notational convenience by choice of units. Note also that in deriving (6) we have used the following decomposition of the value of output in the B industry:

$$eP_B^* B = Wa_{LB}B + eP_M^* a_{MB}B + Y_{RE}. \tag{7}$$

Equation (6) can be differentiated with respect to the exchange rate, e, yielding (through some manipulation)

$$d(Y/P_H) = \delta(1-\alpha)(T/P_H)\hat{e} + \delta qE(1 - a_{ME})\eta_E(1-\alpha)\hat{e}$$
$$+ (1-\delta)d(Y_{RE}/P_H), \tag{8}$$

where $\delta = 1/[s + (1 - qa_{MH})(1 - s)]$ is the open-economy income multiplier, with the marginal propensity to save equal to $s = 1 - dC/d(Y/P_H)$; $\eta_E = (dE/dq)(q/E)$ is the elasticity of supply of exports with respect to the real exchange rate; the parameter $\alpha = MP_M/(WL_H + P_M M)$ is the proportion of imported inputs in variable costs of production in the non-traded goods sector; and caps, $\wedge$, are used to represent proportional changes (so that $\hat{q} = dq/q$, etcetera). Note that $\hat{q} = \hat{e} - \hat{P}_H = (1-\alpha)\hat{e}$, that is, within the present short-run framework, a nominal currency devaluation increases the real exchange rate. In addition, in deriving eq. (8) we have made use of the definition of GNP,

$$Y_N = Y - Y_{RE}. \tag{9}$$

GNP differs from GDP by the amount of profits received by foreign capital, Y_{RE}. These profits are obtained from production of commodity B and are implicitly defined by eq. (7).

Equation (8) shows that the impact of devaluation on GDP is influenced by (a) the initial state of the trade balance, T, as Krugman and Taylor have previously emphasized, (b) the elasticity of supply of non-traditional exports, η_E, an effect traditionally stressed by the elasticities approach to the balance of payments, and by, finally, (c) the impact of the devaluation on the profits earned by foreign capital, dY_{RE}.

To highlight the particular role that foreign ownership plays in the impact of currency devaluation, let us momentarily assume that the economy is initially in balanced trade (so that the current account is in deficit) and that the elasticity of supply of non-traditional exports is zero. In this case, the first two terms of eq. (8) vanish, leaving us only with the final term involving foreign profits. To specify the impact of devaluation on the profits of foreign-owned capital, dY_{RE}, differentiate (7) with respect to the exchange rate, and solve, to obtain:

$$d(Y_{RE}/P_H) = [(1-\alpha)Y_{RE}/P_H + Wa_{LB}B/P_H]\hat{e}. \qquad (10)$$

Equation (10) shows that devaluation raises the profits earned by foreign capital through two mechanisms: by augmenting the real value of the existing profit remittances, and by increasing remittances through the reduction of real wages ensuing in response to the induced home goods inflation in the presence of rigid nominal wages.[5] Substitution of eq. (10) into (8), with $T = 0$ and $\eta_E = 0$, results in

$$\hat{Y} - \hat{P}_H = (1-\delta)(Y_{RE}/Y)[(1-\alpha)Y_{RE}/P_H + Wa_{LB}B/P_H]\hat{e}. \qquad (11)$$

The expression on the right-hand side of (11) is negative, implying that foreign capital provides devaluation with an additional contractionary impact on output. Even when the conditions established by Krugman and Taylor as preventing a negative impact on output hold, that is, when the economy is initially under balanced trade, with identical marginal propensities to consume out of wages and profits, and in the absence of export or import taxes, devaluation will still have a short-run negative effect on domestic product. The explanation is the following. By reducing real wages, devaluation tends to lower real labor income and, therefore, the demand for home goods. At the same time, profits in the export and non-traded goods sectors increase, raising the real income of capital owners and, consequently, the demand for non-traded goods. In the absence of foreign capital — with $Y_{RE} = 0$ — the decline in wage income would be exactly offset by the increase in the profits of domestic capital, leaving domestic output unchanged. In the presence of foreign ownership, however, some of the increased profits associated with devaluation leak out of domestic absorption, inducing an output contraction. The absolute magnitude of the contraction depends on the share of domestic income accruing to foreigners in the form of profits, Y_{RE}/Y.

We have now established how the presence of foreign capital affects the impact of devaluation within a standard Krugman–Taylor framework, showing that foreign ownership adds an additional contractionary mechanism on GDP.

13.4   The Current Account, Export Taxes and the Effects of Devaluation on GDP

This section extends our previous discussion to examine (1) the effects of exchange rate changes on GNP, and (2) the impact of export taxes. These considerations serve as a basis for the empirical analysis carried out in Section 13.5.

From eq. (9), real GNP is equal to real GDP minus the real value of remittances. Therefore, using (6), real GNP is given by

$$Y_N/P_H = H(1 - qa_{MH}) + qE(1 - a_{ME}) + Wa_{LB}B/P_H. \qquad (12)$$

Equation (12) shows the key impact of the presence of foreign ownership on GNP in the present context; the only component of value added in the foreign-owned sector contributing to real national income is the wage bill [the last term in (12)]. Differentiating (12) with respect to the exchange rate, and simplifying, one obtains

$$\hat{Y}_N - \hat{P}_H = [(1 - \alpha)CA - Wa_{LB}B/P_H$$
$$+ qE(1 - a_{ME})\eta_E(1 - \alpha)]\omega\hat{e}, \qquad (13)$$

where $\omega = \delta/(Y_N/P_H)$, and CA represents the current account in real terms,

$$CA = -Hqa_{MH} + qE(1 - a_{ME}) + Wa_{LB}B/P_H. \qquad (14)$$

Equation (13) shows that the impact of currency devaluation on GNP is influenced by three main factors. First, the initial state of the current account balance, CA, depicted by the first term in (13). This represents the national income gain or loss due to the initial current account position of the country. Its role is thus analogous to that played by the trade balance position in models with no remittances (such as Krugman–Taylor), or — within our framework — to the function played by the trade balance on GDP [note the analogy between T and CA in eqs. (8) and (13)].

The second effect of devaluation on national income is related to the presence of foreign ownership and is contractionary in nature. An increase in the nominal exchange rate, e causes, as noted earlier, an increase in the prices of non-traded goods, reducing real wages and yielding an increase in the real profits of sector B, the foreign-owned sector. This redistribution of income from domestic to foreign residents tends to reduce real GNP, as in the second term of eq. (13). Note that, in the presence of foreign capital, the contractionary effects of currency devaluation are stronger on GNP than on GDP. Since GNP is equal to GDP minus the profits of foreign capital, and since devaluation raises foreign profits, any contractionary impact on GDP is magnified on GNP. Whatever the effect on domestic output, the share accruing to nationals out of that output declines with an exchange rate increase.

The real wage reduction induced by devaluation in the short-run serves to increase domestic competitiveness and provides an incentive for exports to increase. This effect is reflected in the third term of eq. (13), which is positive if the elasticity of supply of exports with respect to the real exchange rate, η_E, is positive. The implication is that currency devaluation can be expansionary, but only if the elasticity effect in the non-traditional export sector is large enough to dominate the foreign-ownership effect in the traditional export sector and the impact of any initial current account deficit. For instance, if the current account balance is in an initial position of equilibrium, so that $CA = 0$, then a devaluation will be expansionary if

$$\eta_E > (W a_{LB} B/P_H)/[(1-\alpha)qE(1-a_{MH})], \qquad (15)$$

which is easily derived from eq. (13).

The introduction of a tax on the foreign-owned export sector modifies somewhat our previous results and offers an interesting addendum to the contractionary effects of export taxes examined by Krugman and Taylor (1978).

Suppose that an ad valorem tax is levied on the foreign currency value of the foreign-owned export good at the rate of t. Eq. (12), showing GNP, is then modified in the following way to incorporate tax revenues:

$$Y_N/P_H = H(1 - qa_{MH}) + qE(1 - a_{ME}) + (Wa_{LB}/P_H + qt)B.$$
$$(16)$$

Observe that the tax revenues make a direct positive contribution to real GNP since part of what was previously exiting the system in the form of profit remittances now remains within it. The last term of eq. (16) shows this effect: whereas the contribution of the foreign-owned export sector to real national income previously consisted only of the wage bill [see eq. (12)], it now also includes the real tax revenues.

The impact of devaluation is altered by the presence of export taxes since the exchange rate increase will raise the value of exports — that is, the tax base — and, therefore, tax revenues. Though this represents a direct transfer to nationals and, thus, a direct gain in national welfare, the impact of the devaluation will also depend on whether (and how) the government spends its tax revenues. In the analysis of Krugman and Taylor (1978), tax revenues are not spent and the assumption is that they represent government savings. In that case, export taxes generate a wedge between what the private sector earns from its exports and the cost of imports. In other words, the export tax reduces the private sector's export earnings relative to the value of imports. As Krugman and Taylor show, this situation is similar to a trade deficit: the devaluation will raise the value of imports proportionally more than the private export earnings, with a consequently negative impact on domestic product. At the same time, if there is foreign ownership, some of that loss is recouped by nationals through the increment in tax revenues, which augments the share of domestic product accruing to nationals by means of an increase in government savings.

Algebraically, the effect of a currency devaluation is modified by the presence of export taxes in the following way:

$$\hat{Y}_N - \hat{P}_H = \omega\{(1-\alpha)[CA + qE\eta_E(1-a_{ME})]$$
$$- [Wa_{LB}/P_H - (1-\alpha)qt]B\}\hat{e}$$
$$+ [qt(1-\alpha)B/(Y_N/P_H)]\hat{e}. \tag{17}$$

Eq. (17) shows that a tax on the foreign-owned export sector adds two additional mechanisms on how devaluation affects GNP. On the one hand, the term inside the square brackets in the first term, $-(1-\alpha)qtB$, represents the contractionary mechanism emphasized by Krugman and Taylor. On the other hand, the last term shows that the export tax also exerts a positive effect on real GNP since it reduces at the margin the amount of profits remitted abroad. It can be seen, though, that the overall effect of the export tax is negative, as in Krugman and Taylor, though it is minimized by it being imposed on the foreign-owned sector.

Finally, the presence of export taxes, with a non-zero current account, transforms condition (15) into

$$\eta_E > -CA/qE(1-a_{ME}) + Wa_{LB}B/qE(1-a_{ME})P_H(1-\alpha)$$
$$- [(1-\delta)/\delta]qtB/qE(1-a_{ME}). \tag{15'}$$

13.5 An Application to Jamaica and the Bauxite Industry

The conclusions reached in the preceding analysis can be applied for illustrative purposes to the economy of Jamaica. Table 13.1 shows some key macroeconomic indicators for this country. As it can be appreciated, Jamaica is a small country with a remarkably open economic system (exports have been in the order of 40 to 60 percent of GNP for the relevant period). Its main exports have been, since the mid-fifties, bauxite and alumina, the intermediate step in the production of aluminum. The importance of the traditional mineral export sector has indeed been substantial; it has provided over two-thirds of visible export earnings for the country and over half of total exports of goods and services. Of particular importance for our

Table 13.1. Jamaica, Main Indicators.

J$ Million	1973	1974	1975	1976	1977	1978	1979	1980	1981	1982
GDP	1717.9	2153.1	2594.1	2694.3	2951.5	3732.1	4273.6	4727.9	5298.1	5806.9
in 1974 prices	2240.6	2153.1	2143.8	2009.5	1961.8	1968.5	1941.2	1837.5	1897.7	1900.9
GNP	1692.5	2004.8	2613.8	2625.1	2853.6	3580.6	4016.7	4409.7	5005.4	5512.4
Consumption	1342.9	1848.8	2193.1	2439.3	2629.9	3119.2	3521.7	4072.8	4731.8	5270.8
Investment	448.2	478.2	609.6	450.8	349.5	498.9	748.1	690.1	953.8	1172.7
Ch. in stocks	93.6	47.0	60.5	43.6	15.6	64.0	71.3	64.0	159.8	111.2
Imports	707.4	991.2	1186.1	1021.6	971.8	1525.2	2132.6	2524.8	3057.6	2959.7
Exports	542.6	770.3	917.0	783.2	928.3	1575.2	2065.0	2425.8	2510.3	2211.9
Bauxite sector										
Value added	139.0	187.3	213.5	228.5	301.5	503.7	614.9	671.1	535.9	331.1
Empl. comp.	47.7	55.4	57.1	56.3	65.6	85.8	92.4	108.3	120.4	138.7
Imports (cif, US$)						136.1	148.8	264.5	336.7	202.3
Profit remittances (mill. J$)	20.0	25.2	29.7	14.1	7.7	75.2	147.4	143.2	28.1	25.8
Exports (J$)	227.3	501.2	487.3	354.8	480.4	825.1	1027.7	1310.7	1353.4	862.3
Bauxite	79.5	118.3	97.5	170.4	186.6	335.2	376.7	353.5	306.3	230.7
Alumina	147.8	382.9	389.8	184.4	293.8	489.9	651.0	957.2	1047.1	631.6
Bauxite levy (US$)	24.5	168.7	139.4	118.6	172.3	195.2	194.2	205.7	192.9	103.0

Source: Planning Institute of Jamaica, Economic and Social Report, and STATIN (1983a).

purposes is the fact that the bauxite-alumina industry in Jamaica is substantially owned by a small group of foreign, vertically-integrated companies, notably ALCAN of Canada, Keyser, Reynolds Mines Ltd., ALCOA (which, however, terminated operations in 1984 and 1985) and ALPART, all U.S. or Canadian companies.

Foreign exchange bottlenecks have been felt rather painfully, particularly during the seventies, and, since 1978, the exchange rate has been used on several occasions as a means to attempt a restoration of a viable balance of payments deficit.[6] In addition, since the mid-seventies, Jamaica has enforced a taxation system in the bauxite sector based on a tax rate linked to the volume of exports of the mineral (in U.S. dollar terms). This makes the discussion carried out at the end of the previous section of particular relevance for Jamaica.

Table 13.1 provides additional indicators showing the performance of the bauxite industry. As can be seen, the wage bill has been, in the relevant period, around one-fifth, or less, of value added in the industry. At the same time, the available data indicate a fairly high import content in the production of bauxite and alumina and, until 1981 (the beginning of the crisis in the international bauxite and aluminum markets), a fairly steady flow of imputed profit remittances, a characteristic in accord with the main interest of this paper.

By using input-output and national income accounts for 1980 [see STATIN (1983a, b)], we can proceed to evaluate the effects of a real exchange rate increase. One key parameter is missing, however, i.e., the elasticity of non-bauxite exports with respect to the real exchange rate. As a result, rather than estimating directly the effect of devaluation on GNP, we calculate the value of the export elasticity necessary to obtain a positive impact. In other words, we use eq. (15′) to compute the cut-off value of η_E that guarantees a positive impact of devaluation on GNP. We then specify the relative numerical importance of the contractionary impact connected to foreign ownership in determining that value. The year chosen for our computations is 1980. This choice is based on two considerations: the fact that the bauxite market was still in a relatively healthy state in

1980 — before the beginning of world recession and the slump in world bauxite prices — and the availability of input-output data.

Some clarifications are in order before presenting numerical estimates of eq. (15′). Firstly, given the importance of foreign ownership in the bauxite and alumina industries (bauxite from now on), we concentrate our attention on the impact of devaluation on that sector. The presence of foreign ownership in other sectors is not ignored, though, being embodied in the initial level of net factor payments from abroad. Secondly, we assume that the intermediate input coefficients are the same across all non-bauxite sectors, and we note that the multiplier δ is adjusted for taxation (at a rate of 0.176, as derived from input-output tables). Finally, the relevant figure for CA in our calculations is not the actual current account balance since it must be adjusted to: (1) eliminate unrequited transfers, which contribute to disposable income but not to GNP, (2) subtract the imports of consumer and capital goods, which are assumed to be fixed and whose impact on real GNP is not specified in our analysis.[7]

Table 13.2 shows the cut-off value of the non-bauxite export supply elasticity required for an expansionary outcome on GNP of a devaluation of the Jamaican dollar. The total value of the elasticity is 0.6784. Of this, 0.58 (i.e., 85 percent) is needed to compensate for the foreign ownership effect. Thus, the structure of ownership of the bauxite sector accounts for a very high proportion of the effort required on the part of the rest of the export sector to obtain a positive outcome on GNP.

The influence of foreign capital on the impact of devaluation is also related to the presence of export duties. As noted in the previous discussion, if the duties are imposed on foreign-owned exports, the effect will be less contractionary than if they are imposed on the export of locally-owned capital. The 0.1786 effect of export taxes shown in Table 13.2 is in fact decomposed into a 0.3588 subcomponent representing the 'Krugman–Taylor' effect, and a –0.1802 subcomponent due to the imposition of the export tax on foreign owners.

Finally, even though the initial, adjusted current account balance is in surplus and lowers the cut-off elasticity required for an

Table 13.2. Effects of Currency Devaluation in Jamaica; 1980 Data.[a]

Components of cut-off elasticity[b]		
(1) Current account effect		−0.0802
(2) Wage bill (foreign ownership) effect		0.5800
(3) Bauxite levy		0.1786
Krugman–Taylor effect	0.3588	
Foreign ownership effect	−0.1802	
Total		0.6784

[a]*Source*: STATIN (1983b) and Planning Institute of Jamaica. 'Total' is the cut-off value of the non-bauxite export elasticity required for a positive effect on GNP of a devaluation of the Jamaican dollar. (1) is the contribution to the cut-off value due to the original surplus in the adjusted current account, (2) represents the effects of the reduction in the real wage bill and in purchases of domestic inputs by the foreign-owned bauxite industry, (3) shows the effect of the levy on bauxite exports, decomposed into the contractionary Krugman–Taylor effect, and the expansionary foreign ownership effect.
[b]Based on data from Table 13.1 and the following:

CA, actual balance (J$ million)		−296.2
(a) imports of consumer goods	235.0	
(b) imports of capital goods	353.5	
(c) unrequited transfers	−161.8	
CA, adjusted [actual minus (a) + (b) + (c)]		130.2
Intermediate imported inputs coefficient, $qa_{MH} = qa_{ME}$		0.2541
$\alpha = MP_M/(MP_M + WL_H)$		0.4875

expansionary effect of devaluation (by 0.0802), the component of foreign ownership on this number raises the cut-off elasticity: foreign-owned profit remittances constitute a major debit in the adjusted current account balance and a real currency devaluation raises their initial, real value, exerting a strong negative impact on GNP.

13.6 Conclusions

This paper has shown that the presence of foreign ownership provides currency devaluation with an additional potential contractionary effect on GNP and GDP. The explanation lies in that devaluation redistributes income from domestic residents to foreign capital, which tends to reduce GNP and GDP. The redistribution effect has its origins in the short-run redistribution of income from wages to profits connected to unanticipated devaluation. A fraction of the increased profits accrues to the owners of the foreign capital in the economy, while the fall in real wages is completely borne by domestic residents. The net effect can therefore be negative on both domestic output and national income. It can be concluded that foreign capital makes more problematic the use of the exchange rate as a tool of short-run macroeconomic adjustment.

Data for Jamaica indicates that our concerns regarding the contractionary mechanisms of currency devaluation in the presence of foreign capital (and the ameliorating effects of taxes on foreign-owned production) are well-founded. For this country, using data for 1980, the foreign ownership effect provides the largest negative impact on GNP following a devaluation, accounting for close to 85 percent of the 'burden' placed on non-traditional exports to yield an overall GNP expansion.

These results go a long way in explaining the reluctance of many developing countries (host to a large volume of direct foreign investment) to devalue. Indeed, the real wage repression effect of devaluation in the short run is well-documented for many cases in Latin America.[8] It is also frequently observed that the profits of foreign-owned firms are strongly increased by devaluation in the short run (this is the conclusion, for instance, obtained recently by Grunwald and Flamm[9] in their discussion of the earnings of foreign-owned assembly plants established in Mexico during the aftermath of the 1982 peso devaluation).

It should be stressed that our results are derived under the stringent assumptions of short-run, Keynesian macroeconomics. They are not meant to understate possible effects of devaluation on GNP in the long run or even medium run. Over periods of time longer than those allowed in our analysis, one can expect nominal wages to react to higher home goods prices, reversing the negative impact of devaluation on the income of labor. The higher profits received by foreign capital might also induce additional direct foreign investment, shifting aggregate supply upwards and counteracting the short-run contractionary impact discussed in this paper.

Notes:

[1] See Dufey (1972) and Kohlhagen (1977).

[2] See Diaz-Alejandro (1963) and Cooper (1971a, b).

[3] See Bhagwati and Brecher (1980).

[4] For a discussion of the case with different marginal propensities, see Rivera-Batiz (1985).

[5] The implicit assumption is made that the currency devaluation is unanticipated by agents in the economy and its inflationary effects are not embodied in the cost of living adjustments or wage provisions of labor contracts. See Rivera-Batiz and Rivera-Batiz (1985, pp. 383–393) for a discussion of the role of expectations on the impact of devaluation.

[6] For a description of recent developments in the Jamaican economy, see Barbone and Collins (1985).

[7] Incorporating the effects of devaluation on these imports should be the task of future work, though it introduces complications. For instance, during 1980, consumer goods imports were subject to binding quantitative restrictions in Jamaica. Analyzing the impact of exchange rate changes in this case must take into account the fact that domestic prices of importables will diverge from world prices (converted to the same currency) and look at the issue of the rents earned by the importers of the quota-restricted commodities; see Dornbusch (1980, pp. 68–69).

[8] See Foxley (1983, pp. 171–174), Weintraub (1981, pp. 289–290) and Cooper (1971a, b).

[9] Grunwald and Flamm (1985, pp. 157–158).

References

Barbone, Luca, 1985, "Essays on trade and macro policies in developing countries," Doctoral dissertation (Department of Economics, Massachusetts Institute of Technology, Cambridge, MA).

Barbone, Luca and Susan M. Collins, 1985, "Short-term stabilization and structural adjustment: The Jamaican economy in the eighties," Paper presented at the SELA Conference on The Fund, the Bank, and the Latin American Experience, Caracas, Venezuela, May 16–17, 1985.

Bhagwati, Jagdish N. and Richard A. Brecher, 1980, "National welfare in an open economy in the presence of foreign-owned factors of production," *Journal of International Economics*, 10, 103–115.

Bhagwati, Jagdish N. and Ernesto Tironi, 1980, "Tariff change, foreign capital and immiserization: A theoretical analysis," *Journal of Development Economics*, 7, 71–83.

Brecher, Richard and Carlos Diaz-Alejandro, 1977, "Tariffs, foreign capital and immiserizing growth," *Journal of International Economics*, 7, 317–322.

Cooper, Richard N., 1971a, "An assessment of currency devaluation in developing countries," in: G. Ranis, ed., *Government and economic development* (Yale University Press, New Haven, CT).

Cooper, Richard N., 1971b, "Devaluation and aggregate demand in aid-receiving countries," in: J.N. Bhagwati *et al.*, eds., *Trade, balance of payments and growth* (North-Holland, Amsterdam).

Diaz-Alejandro, Carlos, 1963, "A note on the impact of devaluation and the redistributive effect," *Journal of Political Economy*, 71, 577–580.

Dornbusch, Rudiger, 1980, *Open economy macroeconomics* (Basic Books, New York).

Dufey, Gunter, 1972, "Corporate finance and exchange rate variations," *Financial Management* 1, 51–57.

Foxley, Alejandro, 1983, "Latin American experiments in neo-conservative economics" (University of California Press, Berkeley, CA).

Grunwald, Joseph and Kenneth Flamm, 1985, *The global factory: Foreign assembly in international trade* (Brookings Institution, Washington, DC).

Kohlhagen, Steven W., 1977, "Exchange rate changes, profitability and direct foreign investment," *Southern Economic Journal*, 44, 43–52.

Krugman, Paul and Lance Taylor, 1978, "Contractionary effects of devaluation," *Journal of International Economics*, 8, 445–456.

Planning Institute of Jamaica, 1983, "National income and product accounts" (Government Publications, Kingston).

Rivera-Batiz, Francisco, 1985, "Devaluation, foreign capital and immiserization," Discussion paper (Department of Economics, Indiana University, Bloomington, IN).

Rivera-Batiz, Francisco and Luis Rivera-Batiz, 1985, *International finance and open economy macroeconomics* (Macmillan, New York).

Statistical Institute of Jamaica (STATIN), 1983a, "National income and product accounts," (Government Publications, Kingston).

Statistical Institute of Jamaica (STATIN), 1983b, "Input-output table for the Jamaican economy," 1980, Mimeo, (Kingston).

Taylor, Lance, 1979, *Macro models for developing countries* (McGraw-Hill, New York).

Weintraub, Sidney, 1981, "Case study of economic stabilization: Mexico," in: William R. Cline and Sidney Weintraub, eds., *Economic stabilization in developing countries* (Brookings Institution, Washington, DC), 271–296.

Chapter 14

The Effects of Direct Foreign Investment in the Presence of Increasing Returns due to Specialization*

14.1 Introduction

A sizeable volume of work now exists looking at the array of possible gains and losses that foreign capital inflows might exert on host countries [see, for instance, MacDougall (1960), Bhagwati (1979), Bhagwati and Srinivasan (1983, chapter 28) and Brecher and Diaz-Alejandro (1977)]. An aspect that has not received much attention in this literature, though, is the stimulative effects that capital inflows can have on the host country's producer or business services sector and the external economies that this can generate. This paper pursues this issue by means of a simple model that specifies explicitly the role played by specialized, differentiated producer services on manufacturing production. The model is used to

*This paper was co-authored by Francisco L. Rivera-Batiz and Luis A. Rivera-Batiz and was originally published in *Journal of Development Economics*, Vol. 34, No. 1 (November 1990), pp. 287–307. ©1990 Elsevier Science Publishers.

The authors are grateful to Howard Gruenspecht, Kaz Miyagiwa, the referees of this journal, and the participants of seminars at the University of Pennsylvania and the Spring 1988 Midwest International Economics Conference held at the University of Minnesota for useful comments. Mathematical derivations of the results in this paper are available from the authors.

establish the particular channels of influence that foreign investment has on domestic industry through its ability to increase the extent of the local market and induce greater specialization in services.

The producer or business services sector comprises the whole spectrum of intermediate input requirements that industry demands in the form of advertising, transportation, distribution and communications networks, engineering and legal support, accounting and financial services, etc. Although they are not often recognized as a significant force in production, the available evidence shows that producer services are a major source of employment and economic activity. As much as 22 percent of total Canadian employment, for example, and over 17 percent of British employment were accounted for by the producer services sector in the early 1980s [Wood (1987, p. 55)]. In the United States, the share of business services in Gross National Product has hovered above 20 percent over the last few years [see U.S. Congress (1988, p. 169)]. Although these numbers are lower for developing countries, this does not undermine the fact that the use of local services is one of the major linkages between foreign-owned firms and the host economy. This is especially so of assembly plants, whose link with the local economy — besides direct employment — is sometimes almost exclusively in the form of the purchase of local services. In the case of the Mexican assembly industry, for example, as much as 19 percent of value added has been accounted for by the use of local private and public services, such as transportation, repair and maintenance. By contrast, Mexican materials and supplies used by assembly plants have constituted only an average of 1.5 percent of value added [see Grunwald (1985, Table 4-8)].

There is very little in the trade and development literature regarding the producer services sector and its role in generating external economies of scale.[1] By contrast, this connection is well-known in urban economics. Indeed, it is one of the main arguments posited to explain agglomeration economies in industrial location.[2] As Henderson (1986, p. 271) states: 'In a larger city a manufacturing firm may be able to contract out various service and specialized production activities to firms specialized in those activities', an advantage that is not available to firms located in small towns. The increased productivity that this allows induces firms to agglomerate. Evidence from the United States and Brazil suggests that this kind of external economy substantially explains urban agglomeration [see Henderson (1988, chapter 8), Segal (1976), and Moomaw (1985)].

We visualize the producer services sector as supplying an array of specialized, differentiated inputs within a market structure of Chamberlinian monopolistic competition. We thus follow recent literature formalizing the role played by differentiated intermediate products in production [see Ethier (1982), Grossman and Helpman (1990), Rivera-Batiz and Romer (1989) and Romer (1987, 1990)], extending that approach to incorporate the specifics of the producer services sector. That this sector can be characterized by monopolistic competition is a result of the fact that service markets are generally highly competitive, facing relatively minor entry and exit barriers, while, at the same time, industrial requirements are highly specialized, making each supplier differentiated from others for manufacturing purposes.

Given the monopolistic competition nature of the market, and the existence of fixed costs in the development of new products, the equilibrium number of service firms is an endogenous variable in our model, partly determined by industrial demands. Although these demands can come from either domestically-owned or foreign industrial firms located in the economy, a large share of producer services is not traded geographically across borders and remains exclusively supplied by local firms that, because of high transport costs, governmental regulation, or the local nature of the service being sold, do not compete with firms situated in foreign markets.[3] As Kravis and Lipsey (1988, p. 2) emphasize: 'services are defined by the fact that production and consumption take place simultaneously ... in most cases either the producers have moved to the point of consumption or the consumers have moved to the location of production, but the transaction itself takes place within one country. There are some exceptions, in which a service, such as telecommunications, re-insurance, or some banking activities, is produced in one country and simultaneously consumed in another country, but these are not a large part of service production or trade'.[4] The degree of specialization in services is, therefore, limited by the extent of the local market, as determined by the demands of industry.

The purpose of this paper is to provide a model showing how foreign capital operates to increase the extent of the local market and generate more specialization among producer service firms, enhancing their productivity and, as a consequence, also that of the nationally-owned firms using them. There is, then, a direct positive externality generated by foreign capital inflows on national welfare. These external effects, in our framework, are not pure technological externalities à la Meade but are closely allied to Scitovsky's concept of pecuniary externalities [see Scitovsky (1954)]. The source of pecuniary externalities here is the divergence between price and marginal cost in the service sector and the corresponding undervaluation of capital. An inflow of an input whose private reward falls short of its marginal social value leads to a welfare gain for the receiving country.

In sections 14.2 and 14.3 we describe the host country model, stressing how we determine diversity and specialization among producer services endogenously and how these make manufacturing behave as if there were external economies of scale. Sections 14.4 and 14.5 then examine the allocative and welfare effects of a foreign capital inflow on the host country under full employment conditions. Finally, section 14.6 extends the analysis to the situation of an economy suffering from unemployment due to a rigid wage set above equilibrium.

14.2   Producer Services and Increasing Returns due to Specialization

For simplicity, we assume that the country is specialized in producing a manufactured good (or composite of goods) symbolized by the subscript m. Output of this product (or composite of products) is generated through the use of labor, L_m, capital, K_m and a set n of differentiated producer services sold within a market structure characterized by Chamberlinian monopolistic competition.

Product differentiation among service sector firms is a result of the wide range of different types of specialized activities demanded by the manufacturing sector. Thus any modern industrial complex generates a derived demand for transportation, distribution and communications networks as well as for maintenance and repair of all types of machinery and office equipment. At the same time, the organizational and marketing aspects of production depend critically on banking, insurance, legal counsel, advertising and design, and so on.

Each of the tasks required of these professions is highly specialized. Equipment maintenance, for instance, frequently requires adequate expertise in specific components and types of machinery. Similarly, legal counsel is often demanded on particular aspects of business law relating to the idiosyncrasies of the industry or client firm. Indeed, the degree of sophistication of the tasks demanded by industry is so large and diverse that there is always scope for further specialization. The degree of specialization, though, is limited by the extent of the market and the number of services actually supplied by the market is, therefore, always much smaller than their potential number. The presence of fixed costs that must be spread over a given level of demand constrains the degree of specialization. An increase in the industrial demand for services allows the extent of the market for specialized inputs to increase, inducing entry that results in a larger number of these firms. This augmented specialization, in turn, allows manufacturing producers to find more productive service suppliers, resulting in increased industrial efficiency that yields higher industrial output even when the amount of resources spent on inputs is unchanged. An increased variety of producer services thus shifts out industrial production for given amounts of capital, labor, and total spending on services.

Note that since the number of services is linked to the scale of the industry that demands them, the productivity gains involved here can be visualized as representing external economies of scale in manufacturing. In contrast to much of the literature on this subject, though, in this approach the external effects are modeled endogenously — being connected to the expansion of the service sector induced by an increase in the scale of industry.

On the basis of our discussion so far the technology used in the production of each industrial good m is assumed to be given by the following production function:[5]

$$X_m = L_m^a K_m^b V_m^c, \quad a + b + c = 1, \tag{1}$$

where X_m is the output of good m, K_m is the amount of capital used by industry, L_m, represents raw labor, the parameters a, b and c are a function of technology (and are associated with the factor shares and marginal products of labor, capital and services, respectively), and V_m is a sub-production function involving the array of producer services used by industry. The sub-production function V_m is assumed to be of the CES type, given by

$$V_m = \left(\sum_{i=1}^{n} S_i^\sigma \right)^{1/\sigma}, \quad 0 < \sigma < 1, \tag{2}$$

with S_i denoting the amount of each service demanded by manufacturing, σ is a parameter to be interpreted shortly, and n represents the number of services used by industry.

Given the symmetric way in which individual services enter the sub-production function, V_m, and the similarity of their cost, and therefore supply, functions — to be established below — the amount of each service purchased by industry is identical for all $i = 1, \ldots, n$. As a result, the aggregate quantity demanded of producer services is equal to

$$S_m = \sum_{i=1}^{n} S_i = n S_i.$$

Equation (2) can then be transformed into

$$V_m = S_m n^{(1-\sigma)/\sigma}. \tag{3}$$

Inserting this expression into eq. (1) yields a production function that incorporates input specialization:

$$X_m = n^{c(1-\sigma)/\sigma} L_m^a K_m^b S_m^c. \tag{4}$$

Equation (4) states that domestic output is related to the quantities of labor, capital and producer services demanded by industry *and* to the number of producer services used in production. Observe that the form of (4) is such that it can be interpreted as representing a standard Cobb–Douglas production function with inputs given by labor, capital and services and a shift parameter equal to $n^{c(1-\sigma)/\sigma}$. This shift parameter is suggestive of endogenous external economies of scale to the extent that an increase in industrial production due to, say, capital accumulation, is associated with greater specialization among services and, therefore, with enhanced industrial productivity. Indeed, we shall show that a foreign capital inflow, by increasing the number of producer services in equilibrium, raises overall industrial productivity and generates a positive externality on national welfare.

That the number of services used by industry, n, has an effect on output independent of that of their quantity demanded, S_m, is an outcome of the form of the sub-production function for services, V_m, and reflects the presence of specialization economies in the use of producer services. As mentioned earlier, a rise in the number of producer services available increases the output of industrial goods, even if the industry keeps their total quantity demanded the same. This is because the services used become more specialized and therefore yield higher marginal and average productivity, resulting in increased manufacturing output.

The parameter σ is positive, indicating that the sub-production function V_m is concave and that increased variety of services results in specialization economies $(\partial X_m / \partial n) > 0$. As the value of σ goes to 1, however, the exponent of the number of services, n, in eq. (4) approaches zero and the influence of n on X_m disappears. The reason is that, as σ goes to 1, the sub-production function, V_m, becomes the simple sum of the quantities of services used by the industrial sector. That is, in this case, services become perfect substitutes for each other. With services homogeneous there is no influence of the number of services on industrial production; only total quantity demanded, S_m, has an impact. On the other hand, as the value of σ declines towards zero, the exponent of n in eq. (4) increases, and the importance of diversity becomes more significant (the exponent of n rises).

Profits in the manufacturing sector, π, are given by:

$$\pi = P_m L_m^a K_m^b V_m^c - W L_m - r K_m - \sum_{i-1}^{n} P_i S_i,$$

where W is the wage rate in manufacturing or industry, r is the rental rate on capital, P_i is the price charged by a producer service firm i for its services, and P_m is the price of commodity m in world markets. It is assumed that the country is a small open economy so that the latter is exogenously given.

First-order conditions for profit maximization imply:

$$P_m a(X_m/L_m) = W, \tag{5}$$

$$S_i = [cP_m X_m/V_m^\sigma P_i]^{1/(1-\sigma)}, \tag{6}$$

$$cP_m X_m = \sum_{i=1}^{n} P_i S_i, \tag{7}$$

$$bP_m X_m/K_m = r. \tag{8}$$

Equation (5) shows the equality of the wage rate to the marginal value product of labor where the latter is equal to $aP_m X_m/L_m$. Equation (6), on the other hand, depicts the quantity demanded of each producer service, and eq. (7) shows that the total expenditure of the industrial sector on producer services is equal to a constant fraction of the total revenues made by the industry, a standard implication of the Cobb–Douglas production function. Finally, eq. (8) depicts the equality of the rental rate and the marginal value product of capital.

Substitution of the expression for X_m in eq. (4) into the left-hand side of eq. (5) results in the following expression for the wage rate:

$$W = n^{c(1-\sigma)/\sigma} a P_m L_m^{a-1} K_m^b S_m^c. \tag{9}$$

And using eqs. (5) and (8) implies that, or:

$$r = n^{c(1-\sigma)/\sigma} b P_m L_m^a K_m^{b-1} S_m^c. \tag{10}$$

Equations (9) and (10) indicate that the wage and rental rates are influenced by the price of the industrial good produced domestically, by the parameters a, b, c and σ, and by the variety and total quantity of producer services demanded. We now proceed to specify the determinants of the latter variables, which are endogenous.

14.3 The Producer Services Market: Pricing and Output Decisions

We assume producer services use both capital and labor in production. Capital is assumed to enter as a fixed input, with the given capital input requirement of each producer equal to γ. Labor is a variable input, with the labor demanded by each service firm given by $L_i = \beta S_i$, where β denotes the firm's unit labor requirement. The total costs faced by each service firm, TC_i, are then given by

$$TC_i = \gamma r + \beta S_i W. \tag{11}$$

Following the standard Chamberlinian framework, the technology used by all service firms is considered to be identical, implying that γ and β are the same for all firms i.

With the input requirements depicted by (11), average costs are then given by: $AC_i = \beta W + \gamma r / S_i$, reflecting the presence of decreasing average costs in the production of each service. Marginal costs are equal to $W\beta$, a constant for each single firm in the market. The equality of marginal cost to marginal revenue implied by profit maximization indicates that

$$W\beta = P_i \left(\varepsilon_i - 1 \right) / \varepsilon_i. \tag{12}$$

Since marginal revenue is related to the price elasticity of demand facing each firm, $\varepsilon_i = (P_i / S_i)(\partial S_i / \partial P_i)$, we must specify this variable in order to determine the profit-maximizing price and output of each service.

Equation (6) can be used to describe the demand curve facing a single service sector firm. By differentiating it with respect to P_i and some manipulation, the price elasticity of the demand for each service, ε_i, can be determined. However, calculating the elasticity of demand facing one firm in a market composed of firms supplying differentiated products can be quite complicated. The discussion is greatly simplified if the market structure within which services are

sold is assumed to be one of Chamberlinian monopolistic competition
à la Dixit and Stiglitz (1977). In this framework, each producer acts
in a Cournot–Nash fashion in conjecturing that other firms in the
sector will not change their output in response to changes in the
firm's own price. In addition, it is assumed that there is a large
enough number of firms in the market such that the influence of
each firm on the total output of the sector is insignificant.

Under the assumptions, it is easy to show that the price elasticity
of demand for a single service in this monopolistically competitive
market would be

$$\varepsilon_i = 1/(1 - \sigma). \tag{13}$$

Observe that since σ is a fixed parameter, the demand curve for each
service sector firm exhibits constant elasticity. However, as σ is exogenously increased toward 1, this elasticity tends to approach infinity.
The explanation is that, when σ rises, the services demanded by the
industrial sector become closer substitutes, raising the responsiveness
of quantity demanded to any particular firm's change in price. On the
other hand, when the parameter σ declines, the services demanded
by domestic manufacturing become more differentiated, allowing
each particular service firm to have more leeway in manipulating
its demand, lowering the value of the elasticity.

Substitution of the expression for the elasticity of demand shown
by eq. (13) into eq. (12), and some simplification, yields

$$P_i = \sigma^{-1}\beta W. \tag{14}$$

Equation (14) can be interpreted as stating that each service sector
firm sets its price at a mark-up above its marginal cost, βW. The
markup is inversely related to the parameter σ, reflecting the role
played by product differentiation in allowing firms to increase price
above marginal cost. As σ decreases toward 0, the services used by
the industrial sector become more strongly differentiated from each
other, allowing any given number of firms operating in the market
to increase their price markups.

Since all firms have identical cost and demand parameters — β
and σ are the same for all i — the profit-maximizing prices they

charge will all be the same. Note also that each service firm supplies only one service: in the Chamberlinian framework of monopolistic competition firms can differentiate their products costlessly, and since the demand available for each service is symmetric, it would not be profitable for a firm to share the demand for any given service with other firms.

Entry into the service sector guarantees that the industry's equilibrium is one with no unexploited profit opportunities. Zero profits exist when total revenue, $P_i S_i$, equals total cost, TC_i. Using eqs. (11) and (14), the zero profits equilibrium occurs at a level of output equal to

$$S_i = \sigma \gamma r / ((1 - \sigma) \beta W). \tag{15}$$

Since each firm has the same σ, γ, and β parameters, eq. (15) indicates that each service sector firm will produce the same equilibrium level of output. This output is positively related to the fixed capital requirement since γ augments fixed costs, shifting average costs upward and raising the break-even level of output. An increase in variable labor requirements, on the other hand, reduces output — everything else constant — since an increment in β raises the marginal cost of producing any given level of output. In addition, a higher degree of differentiation among services — a reduction in σ — tends to reduce the firm's level of output by decreasing the elasticity of demand for each service. Finally, an increase in the wage-rental ratio raises the variable cost-fixed cost ratio, reducing each service's production level.

An expression for the number of firms in the producer services sector is derived from eqs. (7) and (8), which imply: $n = (c/b)(r K_m / P_i S_i)$. Using eq. (14) for P_i and eq. (15) for S_i yields

$$n = \frac{c}{b} \frac{1 - \sigma}{\gamma} K_m. \tag{16}$$

This equation shows how the number of producer services is positively related to the capital stock used in manufacturing, an outcome of the increased industrial production associated with a greater capital stock, which raises the demand for services. In addition, the number of services will tend to increase if the fixed capital requirements of each firm, γ, decline, if the ratio c/b raises (which raises the marginal productivity of services relative to capital, augmenting the demand for services), and if the parameter σ declines, which increases the markup of prices over wages and, from eq. (15), lowers the output of each service firm, encouraging entry of new producers.

Note that to derive the aggregate supply of services, S_m, one only has to add up the identical quantities of each service, or

$$S_m = n \ S_i = (\sigma c/a\beta)L_m, \tag{17}$$

where we have used the relationship $(rK_m/b) = (WL_m/a)$ derived from (5) and (6).

The final building blocks of our model involve the endowment constraints

$$K_m + n\gamma = \bar{K} \tag{18}$$

and

$$L_m + n\beta S_i = \bar{L}, \tag{19}$$

where $n\gamma$ is the demand for capital by the service sector and $n\beta S_i$ is the demand for labor in that sector.

This completes the description of the model, which consists of eight equations [(9), (10) and (14)–(19)] in eight endogenous variables, $W, r, L_m, K_m, S_m, n, S_i$, and P_i, with exogenous variables and parameters given by $\bar{K}, \bar{L}, P_m, a, b, c, \sigma, \gamma$, and β. In the next section we examine the effects of an increase in the economy's capital stock, $\bar{K}$, forthcoming as a consequence of a foreign capital inflow.

14.4   Foreign Capital Inflows, External Economies of Scale and Industrial Growth

The effects of foreign capital inflows in our framework operate through two main channels. There is, first of all, a 'relative factor price' effect. As the stock of capital is augmented, with everything else held constant, the resulting increase in the economy's endowment of capital relative to labor tends to lower the rental rate on capital relative to the wage rate. As a consequence, the ratio of fixed costs to variable costs declines in the service sector, inducing entry of new firms and greater specialization. This increased specialization in business services raises industrial productivity, exerting a positive externality on national welfare.

A second channel through which foreign investment affects the economy involves a pure growth or 'extent of the market' effect. To specify this mechanism, note that, for a given wage–rental ratio, an expansion of the capital stock would raise industrial output, inducing in turn an increment in the (derived) demand for producer services. This elicits entry of new firms and greater specialization in services that pulls industrial productivity upwards. This phenomenon of growth-induced specialization and external economies is related to the notion that specialization is limited by the extent of the market, an idea that underlies Adam Smith's theory of the division of labor and growth [see Romer (1987)].

It should be noticed that, in contrast to capital accumulation, labor force growth creates opposite 'extent of the market' and 'relative factor price' effects. On the one hand, an increase in the labor force expands industrial output and raises the demand — and extent of the market — for services, which encourages entry and, therefore, greater specialization. On the other hand, an increased labor force lowers the economy's wage–rental ratio, augmenting the ratio of fixed costs to variable costs for service firms. The latter discourages entry into the sector and works to reduce specialization. In our model, this negative impact exactly offsets the 'extent of the market' effect, leaving no net increase in specialization as population grows. More generally, it can be concluded that, when taking into account both the extent of the market and relative price effects, specialization is not necessarily a monotonically increasing function of population size.[6]

These concepts are embodied in the following reduced-form expression [obtained by substituting eq. (16) into (18)] showing the link between the economy's capital stock and the equilibrium number of services

$$n = \frac{(1 - \sigma) c}{\gamma \left[(1 - \sigma) c + b \right]} \bar{K}. \tag{20}$$

The dependence of n on the economy's capital endowment means that when foreign investment effectively adds to the country's capital stock,[7] it engenders new local producer service enterprises and greater specialization. Observe that the economy's endowment of labor, $\bar{L}$, does not enter as a factor affecting the equilibrium number of service firms, as explained in the last paragraph.

Although foreign capital inflows increase specialization in the service sector, they also reduce the output of each service firm. The higher wage–rental ratio linked to the increased capital endowment tends to raise marginal costs and to lower fixed costs, reducing the break-even level of output for each service [see eq. (15) for S_i; above]. The consequence is that the total quantity of producer services supplied in the economy ($S_m = nS_i$) is pulled in two different directions by the capital inflow: the larger number of firms in the sector tends to raise it while the lower output of each firm tends to reduce it. These two effects compensate each other, leaving the total quantity of services unchanged in response to capital inflows. The exact reduced-form expression is[8]

$$S_m = nS_i = \left[c\sigma / \beta (a + c\sigma) \right] \bar{L}. \tag{21}$$

Equation (21) is independent of the capital stock, $\bar{K}$. It is, however, directly related to the labor force, $\bar{L}$. The explanation is that, in contrast to changes in the capital stock, an increase in the labor force tends to reduce the wage–rental ratio, raising the ratio of fixed costs to variable costs in service firms. This induces the service sector to respond to a demand expansion by increasing the quantity supplied of each existing firm. Since, as noted earlier, there is no net impact of the increased population on the degree of specialization itself (no net effect on n), total quantity supplied, S_m, expands.

Both the labor and capital used by service firms are derived from the demands of the manufacturing or industrial sector for services. One can therefore relate the employment of capital and labor in the service sector to the employment of labor and capital in manufacturing. This is reflected in the following relationships

$$L_m = [a/(a + c\sigma)]\,\bar{L}, \tag{22}$$

$$K_m = [b/(b + c\,(1 - \sigma))]\,\bar{K}. \tag{23}$$

Substituting eqs. (21)–(23) into eq. (4) yields

$$X_m = X_o n^{c(1-\sigma)/\sigma} \bar{K}^b \bar{L}^{1-b}, \tag{24}$$

where

$$X_0 = \left[\frac{a}{a + c\sigma}\right]^a \left[\frac{b}{b + c(1 - \sigma)}\right]^b \left[\frac{c\sigma}{\beta(a + c\sigma)}\right]^c.$$

Equation (24) relates industrial production in the economy to the endowments of capital and labor, and to the number of services n. Differentiating first (24) with respect to $\bar{K}$ and then also (20), one obtains

$$\hat{X}_m = c((1 - \sigma)\,/\sigma)\hat{n} + b\hat{K}$$

$$\hat{X}_m = [c((1 - \sigma)/\sigma) + b]\,\hat{K}, \tag{25}$$

where a circumflex is used to denote proportional changes $\hat{X}_m = \mathrm{d}X_m/X_m$, etc.). Equation (25) indicates that capital inflows have two effects on the growth of manufacturing production, one linked to the productivity of the capital used directly in industry (reflected by the b parameter) and the other related to the productivity of services [embodied by $c((1 - \sigma)/\sigma)$]. This follows from the fact that a foreign capital inflow gives rise to an increase in the capital used as an input directly in manufacturing and also to the capital utilized in the service sector, where it covers the fixed capital required in the formation and operation of new service firms. The latter affects the growth of manufacturing since it increases industrial productivity through specialization economies. Note that, as specialization loses its importance in industrial production, this last effect tends to vanish, reducing the growth of manufacturing in response to capital inflows [as the parameter σ approaches the value of one, the term $c((1 - \sigma)/\sigma)$ in eq. (25) goes to zero].

While foreign capital adds to domestic production, it also earns a return on its services. Consequently, the latter has to be substracted from domestic production in order to specify the net impact of capital inflows on national product and welfare. The next section examines this issue.

14.5   Foreign Capital and National Welfare

The conventional wisdom regarding the effects of foreign capital inflows under a framework of constant returns to scale is that: 'in the absence of distortions, a "small" inflow of foreign capital will neither harm nor benefit the recipient nation. For, the rental on such capital will then equal the value of its private marginal product which, in turn, will equal the social marginal product' [Bhagwati (1979, p. 76)]. That is, under the assumptions, foreign capital earns a return on its services precisely equal to what it contributes in terms of production. National income accruing to domestic factors thus remains unaltered by the capital inflow. Within the increasing returns framework developed in this paper, however, direct foreign investment can improve national welfare, even when the capital inflow is 'small'. This section formally proves this statement.

Since national income is given by $Y_N = W\bar{L} + r\bar{K}$ (assuming, for simplicity, that there is no foreign capital initially in the economy), the impact of direct foreign investment on national income is given — in proportional terms — by

$$\hat{Y}_N = \Theta_L \hat{W} + \Theta_k \hat{r}, \tag{26}$$

where $\Theta_L = W\bar{L}/Y_N$ and $\Theta_k = r\bar{K}/Y_N$. A foreign capital inflow raises the wage rate and lowers the rental rate on capital. It is not immediately clear, then, whether the expression in eq. (26) is positively or negatively related to capital inflows; the precise effects of the increase in $\bar{K}$ on W and r are required to specify $\hat{Y}_N$.

The reduced form expressions for the wage and rental rate in the present model are

$$W = W_0 \bar{L}^{-b} \bar{K}^{b+c(1-\sigma)/\sigma} \tag{27}$$

and

$$r = r_0 \bar{L}^{1-b} \bar{K}^{b-1+c(1-\sigma)/\sigma},\tag{28}$$

where W_0 and r_0 are functions of the parameters of the model.[9] Differentiating eqs. (27) and (28) with respect to $\bar{K}$ then yields

$$\hat{W} = [b + c(1-\sigma)/\sigma]\,\hat{K} > 0\tag{29}$$

and

$$\hat{r} = [b + c\,(1-\sigma)\,/\,(\sigma) - 1]\,\hat{K} < 0,\tag{30}$$

where we assume $[b + c(1-\sigma)/(\sigma) - 1]$ that to ensure stability of equilibrium in factor markets.

Substituting the expressions in eqs. (29) and (30) into eq. (26) and some manipulation results in

$$\hat{Y}_N = [c(1-\sigma)^2/\sigma]\bar{K}.\tag{31}$$

Even though the rental rate on capital declines, the increase in wages is large enough to leave a net positive balance on national income. To understand this result, observe that, were services to be perfect substitutes — so that specialization had no relevance in production — then a small capital inflow would have no impact on national income (when $\sigma = 1, \hat{Y}_N/\hat{K} = 0$). In the presence of increasing returns due to specialization, however, foreign capital generates a positive externality on nationals. By widening the extent of the market and inducing entry of new service firms, the increase in the capital stock leads to a proliferation of specialized service firms that results in increased industrial productivity. This improvement in productivity allows an increment in national income.

The welfare-enhancing impact of foreign capital inflows is linked to the fact that, in the present context, capital is undervalued, that is, the rental rate on capital is below the marginal contribution of capital services to final output. This is visualized by combining eqs. (24) and (20) to yield a reduced form production function expressing final goods output in terms of capital and labor inputs

$$X_m = X_0' \bar{K}^{c(1-\sigma)/\sigma+b} \bar{L}^{1-b}, \tag{24'}$$

where

$$X_0' = X_0 \left\{ (1-\sigma)\, c/\gamma\, [(1-\sigma)\, c + b] \right\}^{c(1-\sigma)/\sigma}.$$

Equation (24′) can be differentiated with respect to $\bar{K}$ to yield the marginal contribution of capital to final output, $P_m \partial X_m / \partial \bar{K}$

$$P_m \partial X_m / \partial \bar{K} = P_m\, (c(1-\sigma)/(\sigma) + b)\, X_0' \bar{K}^{b-1+c(1-\sigma)/\sigma} \bar{L}^{1-b}.$$

This expression for $P_m \partial X_m / X$ is greater than the rental rate on capital, r, as given by eq. (28). Indeed, dividing the two expressions by each other,

$$r/(P_m \partial X_m / \partial \bar{K}) = [b + c(1-\sigma)] \,/\, [b + c(1-\sigma)/\sigma] < 1.$$

This undervaluation of capital means that capital accumulation augments output by a greater amount than the payments to capital, which underlies our earlier conclusion to the effect that capital inflows are welfare-improving. By the same token, if capital accumulation were to arise from domestic savings instead of foreign investment, the social benefits of savings would exceed their private return.

Note that labor is also undervalued in our model since it is utilized in the producer services sector. in which price exceeds marginal cost and factors are paid less than their marginal value product. Comparing the wage rate in (27) with the value of the marginal contribution of labor to final output, $P_m \partial X_m / \partial \bar{L}$, derived from (24′), we obtain

$$W/(P_m \partial X_m / \partial \bar{L}) = (a + c\sigma)/(a + c) < 1.$$

This implies that labor force growth has welfare-enhancing effects, notwithstanding the fact established earlier that the aggregate quantity demanded of labor does not influence the extent of specialization; the welfare-improvement effects here are due to the undervaluation of the labor input in the intermediate services sector.

Finally, by using eqs. (27) and (28) jointly with footnote (9), it can be confirmed that factor rewards exhaust the value of output

$$r\bar{K} + W\bar{L} = P_m \left[b + c(1 - \sigma)X_m \right] + P_m \left(a + c\sigma \right) X_m = P_m X_m.$$

Factor undervaluation explains why, even though the reduced-form production function in eq. (24′) exhibits increasing returns, factor rewards still exhaust total product.

14.6   Foreign Investment, Specialization and Employment in LDCs

So far we have looked at the impact of direct foreign investment on specialization in services and national welfare in the context of a fully-employed economy. The question remains as to the effects of foreign capital inflows in the presence of unemployment or underemployment, the more likely situation in a developing economy. The role of capital inflows in inducing externalities and stimulating employment in the service sector in LDCs has scarcely been examined formally in the literature. Baer and Samuelson (1981), though, have explored empirically how industrial growth can elicit a secondary employment effect by stimulating an expansion of the service sector. The existence of these secondary effects suggests that foreign investments made in industries that are highly capital-intensive but use a large number of services could induce a greater overall employment effect than alternative labor-intensive projects that fail to generate significant secondary employment. The explicit consideration of secondary service employment effects is therefore an important qualification to discussions that focus only on the labor-intensity of multinational firm operations in LDCs and question the 'appropriateness' of the factor intensities adopted by these firms.

In order to address these issues, we examine an economy characterized by a rigid wage rate set above the equilibrium, full-employment level. Under these conditions, we replace the labor full-employment condition in eq. (19) with the following employment relationship

$$E = L_m + n\beta S_i = (aP_m X_m)/\bar{W} + \beta S_m, \tag{32}$$

where E represents the economy-wide employment level, $\bar{W}$ the rigid wage rate, and L_m and $L_s = n\beta S_i$ denote employment in the industrial and service sectors, respectively.

Solving for sectoral employment levels yields

$$L_m = a\bar{X}_0(P_m/\bar{W})^{1/b}\bar{K}^{1+c(1-\sigma)/b\sigma}, \tag{33}$$

$$L_s = c\sigma\bar{X}_0(P_m/\bar{W})^{1/b}\bar{K}^{1+c(1-\sigma)/b\sigma}, \tag{34}$$

where $\bar{X}_0$ is positive and a function of exogenous parameters in the model.[10] Finally, substituting (33) and (34) into (32), one obtains the reduced-form expression for total employment

$$E = (a + c\sigma)\,\bar{X}_0(P_m/\bar{W})^{1/b}\bar{K}^{1+c(1-\sigma)/b\sigma}. \tag{35}$$

Equation (35) shows that employment is positively related to the capital stock. A foreign capital inflow equal to K then creates employment growth given by

$$\hat{E} = [1 + c(1 - \sigma)/b\sigma]\,\hat{K}.$$

Job creation occurs both through a direct employment effect in manufacturing — given by eq. (33) — and a secondary employment impact in the service sector, shown by (34). Note that the employment generated by any given capital inflow is augmented by the degree to which specialization stimulates industrial production. That is, as the parameter σ goes to zero, indicating a growing importance of specialization in industrial production, the employment growth effect of a given capital inflow increases. In this case, as the variety of services rises, the marginal productivity of industrial labor shifts upwards by a larger proportion, augmenting the demand for labor, and employment, by a greater extent.

The impact of capital inflows on national welfare depends on its effect on employment and labor income as well as on its impact on the capital rental rate.[11] The reduced-form expression for the effect of direct foreign investment on national income is given by

$$\hat{Y}_N = \Theta_L \hat{E} + \Theta_k \hat{r}$$
$$\hat{Y}_N = [(1-\sigma)/b\sigma + \Theta_L]\hat{K}. \tag{36}$$

This indicates that capital inflows affect national income positively and that the impact is larger the greater the significance of increasing returns and specialization in production (the smaller the value of σ). Our earlier results within a full-employment context are thus robust with respect to the labor market specification change introduced in the present section.

14.7 Conclusions

In this paper we have utilized a simple yet rigorous model of endogenous specialization and external economies of scale to examine the effects of foreign capital inflows in a small open economy. The focus is on the role played by producer services as an engine for growth in the industrial sector. We find that capital inflows stimulate specialization in producer services and raise the productivity of the industry that uses them. The impact of foreign capital on the number or variety of producer services occurs through two mechanisms: a relative factor price effect and an extent of the market effect. The former relates to the fact that a capital inflow lowers the economy's rental rate, reducing the fixed costs of setting-up and operating new services and stimulating entry of new firms into that sector. The extent of the market effect, on the other hand, indicates that, at given relative factor prices, capital inflows induce entry into the service sector by augmenting industrial output and, therefore, shifting upwards the derived demand for services. Both of these mechanisms act to raise industrial productivity and, in fact, work to raise national welfare.

In the absence of distortions, a small foreign capital inflow in the presence of constant returns to scale does not affect national welfare in the recipient country.[12] In the present model, however, capital inflows generate positive effects on national welfare by means of their stimulus to entry and increased specialization in the producer services sector. The resulting increase in industrial productivity acts as an external effect on nationally-owned factors that benefit from the use of the more specialized services. The significance of these gains from capital inflows to the host country are directly related to the importance of services in production and the degree to which increased variety and specialization in services raises industrial productivity. If industry, for instance, were not to require specialized services in production, then the impact of foreign capital inflows on national welfare would vanish. If, on the other hand, the industrial sector can profit from the use of a wide array of very specialized services, the effect of capital inflows on welfare can be highly positive. As noted earlier, the evidence suggests that the latter may be the case in many developing countries [see also Chong-Yah (1988, ch. 9) and Rivera-Batiz and Rivera-Batiz (1991)].

The gains yielded by foreign capital inflows in the presence of increasing returns due to specialization operate whether the economy is at full-employment or suffers from unemployment. We have examined both cases, finding that, in the unemployment regime, direct foreign investment enhances national welfare through its direct and secondary effects on employment. As the industrial sector grows, employment is created directly in manufacturing and also in the service firms emerging in response to expanded industrial demands. The proliferation of more specialized service firms, in turn, raises productivity in manufacturing, shifting upwards the demand for industrial labor and raising further the employment growth in that sector. It can be concluded, then, that in evaluating the employment effects of direct foreign investment, one should consider not only the direct employment created but also the induced secondary employment generated in the service sector. Foreign investments in industries that, due to their high capital-labor ratios, generate meager direct employment effects may stimulate sufficient secondary employment in services to be more job-creating than investments in industries that use substantial amounts of direct labor but do not have extensive service linkages. As we have discussed in this paper, such calculations are critical in the evaluation of the impact of foreign capital inflows.

Although not explicitly modeled as such, the foreign capital inflows examined in this paper could be considered to be the result of the elimination of barriers to foreign investment in LDCs. Our analysis thus suggests that the liberalization of restrictions on direct foreign investment can generate positive direct and indirect effects on income and welfare in the developing countries.

Notes:

[1] Exceptions are the recent works of Jones and Kierzkowski (1990) and François (1990a, b).

[2] For formal urban models of agglomeration economies, see Kanemoto (1987) and Rivera-Batiz (1988).

[3] The emphasis on the role of non-traded producer services makes our model differ from those by Markusen (1989) and François (1990a, b), whose main concern is with trade in services.

[4] The exceptions noted by Kravis and Lipsey are becoming much more significant over time as technological advances in the information and communications industries allow geographical trade in these services to grow [See Bhagwati (1984)].

[5] In general, one could disaggregate the use of services in manufacturing by introducing arrays or bundles of different types of services into the industrial production function (several V_m functions instead of one). Although this makes the algebra more complicated, it does not alter the basic mechanisms and externalities discussed in the present model.

[6] Some models of product variety and increasing returns exhibit a positive relationship between population and variety [see Krugman (1979)]. What our model incorporates which reverses such a relationship is the impact of greater population on relative factor prices, which has a negative effect on entry (due to the increase in the ratio of fixed costs to variable costs facing each service firm).

[7] We are concerned with investment that effectively adds to the economy's stock of capital and not with mere purchases of domestic assets by foreigners. The acquisition of ownership and control over domestic assets is counted in official statistics as direct foreign investment but does not necessarily enlarge the economy's capital resources. There is a long-standing controversy in development economics as to the degree to which multinationals use local capital funds in LDCs to finance their investments there, how much they add to LDCs' capital stock, and the extent to which their activities entail technology transfer [see Hood and Young (1979, p. 184)].

[8] To derive eq. (21), use eqs. (15) and (20) as well as the full-employment conditions and the manufacturing labor and capital first-order conditions.

[9]The exact expressions for W_0 and r_0 are:

$$W_0 = aP_m \left[\frac{a}{a+c\sigma}\right]^{a-1} \left[\frac{c\sigma}{\beta(a+c\sigma)}\right]^c \left[\frac{b}{b+c(1-\sigma)}\right]^b$$

$$\times \left[\frac{c(1-\sigma)}{\gamma\left[b+c(1-\sigma)\right]}\right]^{c(1-\sigma)/\sigma} > 0,$$

and

$$r_0 = bP_m \left[\frac{a}{a+c\sigma}\right]^a \left[\frac{c\sigma}{\beta(a+c\sigma)}\right]^c \left[\frac{b}{b+c(1-\sigma)}\right]^{b-1}$$

$$\times \left[\frac{c(1-\sigma)}{\gamma\left[b+c(1-\sigma)\right]}\right]^{c(1-\sigma)/\sigma} > 0.$$

[10]The exact expression for $\bar{X}_0$ is

$$\bar{X}_0 = \left[\frac{c(1-\sigma)}{\gamma\left\{(1-\sigma)c+b\right\}}\right]^{c(1-\sigma)/\sigma b} \left[\frac{b}{b+c(1-\sigma)}\right] a^{a/b} \left(c\sigma/\beta\right)^{c/b}.$$

[11]In analyzing the effects on national welfare one should strictly speaking include, as a counterpart to the increased employment, some adjustment for the opportunity cost of labor — say, in the form of reduced leisure. Such a calculation diminishes — but does not eliminate the positive effects of increased employment on national welfare.

[12]Our analysis has proceeded at a fairly aggregate level, looking at the linkages between manufacturing or industry and producer services. Additional sectors could be added, in which case the mechanics of how foreign capital inflows affect variety in services could become more complex. If, for instance, the sectors using services are labor-intensive, a foreign capital inflow could — à la Rybcrinski — reduce the output of these labor-intensive sectors and shrink the demand for services. Direct foreign investment could thus lead to de-specialization in services. This is unlikely, however, as in most developing countries direct foreign investment is indeed concentrated in sectors that do use services intensively (manufacturing as opposed to, say, agriculture, a sector with relatively low use of producer services).

References

Baer, W. and L. Samuelson, "Toward a service-oriented growth strategy," *World Development*, 9 (1981): 499–514.

Bhagwati, J.N., "International factor movements and national advantage," *Indian Economic Review*, 14 (1979): 73–100.

Bhagwati, J.N., "Splintering and disembodiment of services and developing nations," *The World Economy*, 7 (1984): 133–143.

Bhagwati, J.N. and T.N. Srinivasan, *Lectures in international trade*, (MIT Press, Cambridge, MA 1983).

Brecher, R. and C. Diaz-Alejandro, "Tariffs, foreign capital and immiserizing growth," *Journal of International Economics*, 7 (1977): 317–322.

Chong-Yah, L., *Policy options for the Singapore economy*, (McGraw-Hill. Singapore 1988).

Dixit. A.K. and J. Stiglitz, "Monopolistic competition and optimum product diversity," *American Economic Review*, 67 (1977): 297–308.

Ethier, W., "National and international returns to scale in the modern theory of international trade," *American Economic Review*, 72 (1982): 389–405.

François, J.F., Producer services, scale and the division of labor, *Oxford Economic Papers*, 42 (1990a): 715–729.

François, J.F., "Trade in producer services and returns due to specialization under monopolistic competition," *Canadian Journal of Economics*, 23 (1990b): 109–124.

Grossman, G. and E. Helpman, "Comparative advantage and long-run growth," *American Economic Review*, 80(4) (1990): 796–815.

Grunwald, J., "The assembly industry in Mexico," in: J. Grunwald and K. Flamm, eds., *The global factory: Foreign assembly in international trade* (Brookings, Washington, DC) (1985): 137–179.

Helpman, E. and P. Krugman, *Market structure and foreign trade: Increasing returns, imperfect competition and the international economy* (The MIT Press, Cambridge, MA 1985).

Henderson, J.V., "Urbanization in a developing country: City size and population composition," *Journal of Development Economics*, 22 (1986): 269–293.

Henderson, J.V., *Urban development: Theory, fact and illusion* (Oxford University Press. New York 1988).

Hood, N. and S. Young, *The economics of multinational enterprise*, (Longman, London 1979).

Jones, R.W. and H. Kierzkowski, "The role of services in production and international trade: A theoretical framework," in: R.W. Jones and A.O. Krueger, eds., *The political economy of international trade: Essays in honor of Robert F. Baldwin* (Blackwell, Cambridge) (1990): 31–48.

Kanemoto, Y., 1987, "Externalities in space," in: T. Miyao and Y. Kanemoto, *Urban dynamics and urban externalities* (Harwood Academic Publishers, London).

Kravis, I., A.W. Heston and R. Summers, 1983, "The share of services in economic growth," in: F. Gerard Adams and B. Hickman, eds., *Global Econometrics: Essays in Honor of Lawrence Klein* (MIT Press, Cambridge, MA) 188–219.

Kravis, I. and R. Lipsey, 1988, "Production and trade in services by U.S. multinational firms," Working Paper No. 2615 (National Bureau of Economic Research, Cambridge, MA).

Krugman, P., 1979, "Increasing returns, monopolistic competition and international trade," *Journal of International Economics*, 9, 469–479.

MacDougall, G.D.A., 1960, "The benefits and costs of private investment from abroad: A theoretical approach," *Economic Record*, 36, 13–35.

Markusen, J., 1989, "Trade in producer services and in other specialized intermediate inputs," *American Economic Review* 79, 85–95.

Moomaw, R.L., 1985, "Firm location and city size: Reduced productivity advantages as a factor in the decline of manufacturing in urban areas," *Journal of Urban Economics*, 17, 73–89.

Rivera-Batiz, F.L., 1988, "Increasing returns, monopolistic competition, and agglomeration economies in consumption and production," *Regional Science and Urban Economics*, 18, 125–153.

Rivera-Batiz, F.L. and L.A. Rivera-Batiz, 1991, *The political economy of Mexico* (Working Paper, Regional Science Department, University of Pennsylvania).

Rivera-Batiz, L.A. and P.M. Romer, 1989, "International trade with endogenous technological change," Mimeo. (University of Chicago, Chicago, IL).

Romer, P.M., 1987, "Growth based on increasing returns due to specialization," *American Economic Review*, 7, 56–62.

Romer, P.M., 1990, "Endogenous technological change," *Journal of Political Economy*, 98, S71–S102.

Scitovsky, T., 1954, "Two concepts of external economies," *Journal of Political Economy*, 62, 143–151.

Segal, D., 1976, "Are there returns to scale in city size" *Review of Economics and Statistics*, 58, 339–350.

U.S. Congress, Office of Technology Assessment, 1988, "Technology and the American economic transition: Choices for the future" (U.S. Government Printing Office: Washington, DC).

Wood, P.A., 1987, "Producer services and economic change: Some Canadian evidence," in: K. Chapman and G. Humphrys, eds., *Technical change and industrial policy* (Blackwell, Oxford) 51–77.

Chapter 15

Europe 1992, and the Liberalization of Direct Investment Flows: Services versus Manufacturing*

15.1 Introduction

In spite of the great overall liberalization of direct foreign investment flows within the European Economic Community (EC) over the last twenty years, strict restrictions remain in certain sectors, notably services. The European economic integration project known as Europe 1992 pursues the creation of a single internal market among the member nations of the EC and it has targeted certain components of the service sector for liberalization. The financial services industry, in particular, has been the subject of directives to allow firms (commercial and investment banks, insurance companies, etc.) to establish activities and branches wherever they like within the EC.[1] This is likely to induce capital flows into those countries that have had high barriers to foreign investment. In Italy, for instance, direct foreign

*This paper was co-authored by Francisco L. Rivera-Batiz and Luis A. Rivera-Batiz and was originally published in *International Economic Journal*, Vol. 6, No. 1, Spring 1992, pp. 45–57. ©1992 Routledge–Taylor & Francis Group.

The authors are grateful to the comments offered by the participants of seminars at the Universidad Central de Venezuela in January 1991 and the North American Economics and Finance Annual Meetings in Washington, D.C. in December 29, 1990.

investment has been hampered by a variety of regulations involving taxes, equity ownership limitations, etc. As a result, foreign direct investment in Italy — including other European investments — have been among the lowest in the European Community. In 1984, only 2.9% of the Italian capital stock was owned by foreigners, compared to 12.6% in the U.K.[2]

It is purpose of this paper to examine the effects of eliminating restrictions on direct foreign investment in a small open economy. Our focus of attention is on the impact of foreign investment in the service sector and how this differs from capital that flows into manufacturing. A voluminous literature exists looking at the array of possible gains and losses that liberalization of foreign capital inflows might exert on host countries [see, for instance, MacDougall (1960), Bhagwati and Srinivasan (1983: chapter 28), and the papers in Choksi and Papageorgiou (1986)]. Much of this literature, however, has assumed, firstly, that foreign capital can freely flow into any sector of the recipient economy and, secondly, it has tended to ignore services.

We model sector-specific direct foreign investment in the host country's producer services sector and compare it with manufacturing investment. The framework used emphasizes the role played by specialized, differentiated services on manufacturing production; it is shown that there are major differences in the way foreign investment affects the economy, depending on the distortion or externality existing in the sector into which capital moves. This result is related to the literature on linkages in economic development (see Hirschman, 1958). This paper suggests that linkages do not necessarily imply that direct investment will have positive effect on welfare. Rather, there will be positive welfare effects only if there is a distortion or externality, and the welfare impact depends on the sector in which the distortion or externality exists.

Producer (or business) services are intermediate inputs utilized by industry, such as transportation, legal support, accounting and financial services. Although they are not often recognized in economic theory as a significant force in production,[3] the available evidence shows that producer services are a major source of employment and economic activity, and a dynamic sector in growing economies.

Indeed, financial services alone account for an estimated 7 percent of value added in the EC, (up to 20% of value added in the U.K.)[4] We visualize business services as specialized, differentiated inputs functioning within a market structure of monopolistic competition. In this sense, we follow the growing literature formalizing how differentiated intermediate goods enter production [Ethier (1982), Rivera-Batiz (1988), Grossman and Helpman (1989), Rivera-Batiz and Romer (1991), and Romer (1987, 1990)]. That the producer services sector can be described by monopolistic competition is linked to the fact that these inputs are generally competitive, facing relatively minor entry and exit barriers. In addition, industry requires highly-specialized services, making each supplier differentiated from others.[5]

A large component of the business services sector is not traded geographically across borders, that is, it consists of nontraded goods. These services are supplied by local firms that because of various reasons — such as high transport or transactions costs — do not compete with firms situated in foreign markets.[6] The degree of specialization in these services is, therefore, limited by local, domestic demand and supply.

This paper develops a model showing how foreign capital flowing into the service sector operates to generate greater specialization among business services, augmenting industrial productivity. There is, then, a direct positive externality of these capital flows on national welfare. These external effects originate here in the existence of a wedge between price and marginal cost in the service sector due to the presence of monopolistic competition. This wedge is linked to an undervaluation of capital in the service sector. But an inflow of an input whose private rate of return falls short of its marginal social value leads to a welfare gain for the receiving country. In this case, then, capital flowing into services will raise national host-country welfare. To emphasize this point, we consider a situation where foreign investment in the industrial sector does not generate the external effects just described. Capital in manufacturing is assumed to be sector-specific, homogenous and traded in a competitive market. As a consequence, there is no externality originating in industry. Capital in this sector is paid its marginal product; and a small capital inflow has no effects on national welfare: the foreigners take away from the economy (as a rate of return) as much as they contribute (through their marginal productivity).

The next section describes the host country environment and specifies the relationship between business services and external economies of scale in industry.

15.2   The Industrial Sector and Specialization Economies

The host country is assumed to be specialized in producing an industrial good (or composite of goods) symbolized by Y, through the use of labor, L_Y, industrial capital, K_Y, and a set n of differentiated producer services sold in a monopolistically competitive market. On the basis of our earlier discussion, industrial goods are assumed to be internationalized but services are considered to be nontraded goods.

The production function for industrial goods is:

$$Y = L_Y^a K_Y^b V^c, \quad a + b + c = 1 \tag{1}$$

where Y is industrial output, K_Y is capital used by industry (which is assumed to be exogenously-given), L_Y represents raw labor, the parameters a, b, c are a function of technology, and V is a sub-production of the services used by industry. For simplicity, the latter is assumed to be of the CES type:

$$V = \left(\sum_{i=1}^{n} X(i)^\alpha \right)^{1/a}, \quad 0 < \alpha < 1 \tag{2}$$

with $X(i)$ denoting the amount of each service i demanded by manufacturing, α is a positive parameter to be interpreted shortly, and n represents the number of producer services.

Under Chamberlinian monopolistic competition, the amount supplied of each service is identical for all $i = 1, \ldots, n$. Therefore, the aggregate quantity demanded of producer services is equal to $X_Y = nX(i)$. Equation (2) can then be transformed into: $V = X_Y n^{(1-\alpha)/\alpha}$.

And substituting this expression into the industrial production function in equation (1) yields:

$$Y = n^{c(1-\alpha)/\alpha} L_Y^a K_Y^b X_Y^c. \tag{3}$$

Equation (3) shows that domestic output is related to the quantities of labor, capital and producer services demanded by industry, and to the number of services used in production through the shift parameter $n^{c(1-\alpha)/\alpha}$. This shift parameter can be visualized as influencing the overall productivity of the industrial sector and is dependent on the number of services. We shall show that a foreign capital inflow into the service sector raises the number of producer services, in turn shifting upwards overall industrial productivity and generating a positive externality on national welfare. That the number of services used by industry, n, has an effect on output, holding constant the total quantity of services used by industry, X_Y, suggests the presence of specialization economies in the use of producer services: an increased number of specialized services (holding their total usage constant) shifts upwards the industrial sector's marginal and average productivity. The parameter α reflects these in equation (3) grows and diversity becomes more significant in production.

Firms in the manufacturing sector, π, maximize profits and the usual first order conditions imply:

$$\frac{a P_Y Y}{L_Y} = W, \tag{4}$$

$$\frac{b P_Y Y}{K_Y} = r_Y, \tag{5}$$

$$c P_Y Y = \sum_{i=1}^{n} P(i) X(i), \tag{6}$$

$$X(i) = [c P_Y Y / V^\alpha P(i)]^{1/(1-\alpha)}, \tag{7}$$

where W is the wage rate, r_Y is the rental rate on the sector-specific, industrial capital, $P(i)$ is the price charged by a service firm, and P_Y is the price of industrial goods (assuming a small country, P_Y is exogenously-given by world market prices). Equation (4) represents the equality of the wage rate to the marginal value product of labor; equation (5) states the equality of the rental rate and marginal value of product of capital in industry; equation (6) shows that the total expenditure of the industrial sector on services is a constant fraction of the revenues made by the industry; and equation (7) shows the quantity demanded of each producer service.

Substituting Y in equation (3) into the left-hand side of equation (4) results in the following expression for the wage rate:

$$W = n^{c(1-\alpha)/\alpha} a P_Y L_Y^{a-1} K_Y^b X_Y^c. \tag{8}$$

And using equations (4) and (5) implies that $r_Y = (bL_Y/aK_Y)W$, or:

$$r_Y = n^{c(1-\alpha)/\alpha} b P_Y L_Y^a K_Y^{b-1} X_Y^c. \tag{9}$$

The wage rate and industrial rental rate in equations (8) and (9) are influenced by the price of the industrial good produced domestically, by the parameters a, b, c, and α, and by the variety and total quantity of producer services demanded. To determine the latter we must take a closer look at the service sector.

15.3   The Producer Services Sector

Services use labor and capital as inputs. Capital, which is sector-specific, is in the form of a fixed capital input requirement equal to μ for each supplier. Labor usage is variable and the quantity demanded by each firm is represented by $L(i) = \beta X(i)$, where β is the firm's unit labor requirement. The total cost of each firm, $C(i)$, is then:

$$C(i) = \mu r_s + \beta X(i)W. \tag{10}$$

where r_s is the rental rate on capital in the service sector. Following the standard Chamberlinian framework, μ and β are the same for all firms.

With the input requirements depicted by (10), average costs are then given by: $\frac{C(i)}{X(i)} = \beta W + \mu r_s/X(i)$, which declines with X (a decreasing average cost curve). Marginal costs are equal to $W\beta$.

The equality of marginal cost to marginal revenue then implies:

$$W\beta = P(i)[1 - 1/\varepsilon(i)]. \tag{11}$$

Given the marginal revenue is related to the price elasticity of demand facing each firm, $\varepsilon(i) = -[P(i)/X(i)][\partial X(i)/\partial P(i)]$, we must specify this variable in order to determine the equilibrium price and output for each firm. By taking the partial derivative of equation (7) with respect to $P(i)$, and some manipulation, the price elasticity of demand, ε_i, can be determined. Under the standard assumptions of Chamberlinian monopolistic competition[7] a' la Dixit–Stiglitz (1977), the price elasticity of demand for a single service is $\varepsilon(i) = 1/(1 - \alpha)$. Since a is α fixed parameter, the demand curve for each service firm exhibits constant elasticity. As α is exogenously increased toward 1, this elasticity tends to approach infinity (intuitively, when α rises, the services demanded by the industrial sector become closer substitutes, raising the responsiveness of quantity demanded to any particular firm's change in price). Substituting the expression for the elasticity of demand into equation (11) results in:

$$P(i) = \alpha^{-1}\beta w. \tag{12}$$

Equation (12) states that each service firm sets its price at a mark-up above its marginal costs, βw. The markup is inversely related to the parameter α, reflecting the role played by product differentiation in allowing firms to increase price above marginal cost. Since all firms are assumed to have identical cost and demand functions, the profit-maximization prices they charge are also equal.

Free entry ensures a zero profit equilibrium, with total revenue, $P(i)X(i)$, equal to total cost, $C(i)$. Using equations (10) and (12), zero profits determine an equilibrium output level of:

$$X(i) = \alpha\mu r_s/(1 - \alpha)\beta W. \tag{13}$$

Given that all firms have identical technology parameters, they also have identical output levels. This output is positively related to the fixed capital requirements, μ, and the rental rate on capital, r_s, but negatively related to the variable labor requirement, β, and the wage rate, W.

An expression for the number of firms in the producer services sector is derived from the supply–demand relationship in the market for capital in that sector:

$$n = K_s/\mu. \tag{14}$$

This states that the equilibrium number of services will rise if the supply of capital to the sector increases and/or if the fixed capital requirement declines. The aggregate supply of services, X_Y, is then equal to:

$$X_Y = nX(i) = \frac{\alpha c}{\alpha \beta} L_Y, \tag{15}$$

To determine the rental rate on the capital used in the service sector, observe that equations (5) and (6) imply: $nP(i)X(i) = (\frac{c}{b})r_Y K_Y$. Using equation (12) for $P(i)$, equation (13) for $X(i)$, and equation (14) for n — with some manipulation yields:

$$r_s = \frac{c(1-\alpha)W}{aK_s} L_Y. \tag{16}$$

This equation shows how the rental rate in the producer services sector is negatively related to the supply of capital in the sector and positively related to the wage bill in manufacturing (WL_Y).

Perfect competition in the labor market assures full-employment:

$$L_Y + n\beta X(i) = L, \tag{17}$$

where L_Y is the industrial labor demand, $n\beta X(i)$ is the demand for labor in the service sector and L is the available labor force.

This completes our model, consisting of eight equations [(8), (9) and (12)–(17)] in eight endogenous $W, r_Y, L_Y, r_s, X(i), n, X_Y$ and $P(i)$, with exogenous variables and parameters given by $K_s, K_Y, L, P_Y, a, b, c, \alpha, \mu$, and β. We now analyze the effects of increases in the economy's capital stocks, K_m and K_s, forthcoming as a consequence of foreign capital inflows.

15.4   The Effects of Direct Foreign Investment

Under a framework of constant returns to scale: 'in the absence of distortions, a "small" inflow of foreign capital will neither harm nor benefit the recipient nation. For, the rental on such capital will then equal the value of its private marginal product which, in turn, will equal the social marginal product.' [Bhagwati (1979), p. 76]. Within the increasing returns framework used in this paper, however, direct foreign investment can improve national welfare, even when the capital inflow is 'small', as we proceed to show.

Consider first the effects of a foreign capital inflow into the service sector. As is shown by equation (14), this would raise the equilibrium number of producer services. This increased specialization in business services raises industrial productivity, exerting a positive externality on national welfare. At the same time, the increased capital tends to lower the rental rate on capital in services, which acts to reduce the optimum production of each service firm. Using equations (13) and (16) — and noting that $L_Y = [a/(a+c\alpha)]L$ — the reduced form the output of each service is:

$$X(i) = c\alpha\mu L/\beta(a + c\alpha)K_s. \qquad (18)$$

In the present model, although the number of services in the market rises with the foreign capital, the quantity of each service produced declines in the same proportion, leaving the total quantity of services used by industry unchanged. This is reflected by the reduced form for X_Y:

$$X_Y = c\alpha L/\beta(a + c\alpha) \qquad (19)$$

which depends on the labor force, L, but not on the capital stock in either sector of the economy.

National income is given by $I = WL + r_s K_s + r_Y K_Y$ (assuming, for simplicity, that there is no foreign capital initially in the economy). The impact of direct foreign investment on national income is then given — in proportional terms — by:

$$\hat{I} = \Theta_L \hat{W} + \Theta_{KS} \hat{r}_s + \Theta_{KY} \hat{r}_Y \qquad (20)$$

where $\Theta_L = WL/I$, $\Theta_{KS} = r_s K_s/I$, and $\Theta_{KY} = r_Y K_Y/I$ and '^' are used to denote proportional changes. How do foreign capital inflows affect the wage rate and the rental rates on capital? The reduced form expressions are:

$$W = W_o L^{-b} K_s^{c(1-\alpha)/\alpha} K_Y^b \tag{21}$$

$$r_Y = r_{oY} L^{1-b} K_s^{c(1-\alpha)/\alpha} K_Y^{b-1} \tag{22}$$

and

$$r_s = r_{os} L^{1-b} K_s^{\frac{c(1-\alpha)}{\alpha-1} - } K_Y^b \tag{23}$$

where W_o and r_{os} are functions of the parameters of the model.[8]

Differentiating equations (21), (22) and (23) with respect to K_s, yields:

$$\hat{W} = [c(1-\alpha)/\alpha]\hat{K}_s > 0 \tag{24}$$

$$\hat{r}_Y = [c(1-\alpha)/\alpha]\hat{K}_s < 0 \tag{25}$$

$$\hat{r}_s = \left[\frac{c(1-\alpha)}{\alpha} - 1 \right] \hat{K}_s < 0 \tag{26}$$

where we assume that $[\frac{c(1-\alpha)}{\alpha} - 1] < 0$ to ensure stability of equilibrium in factor markets.

An increase in the capital stock in the service sector, K_s, raises the wage rate and the rental rate in manufacturing since it enhances industrial productivity by augmenting the degree of specialization, shifting upwards marginal products in that sector. On the other hand, there is a drop in the rental rate on capital in services. It is not immediately clear, then, whether national income is positively or negatively related to direct foreign investment in services; the precise effects of the increase in K_s on W, r_s and r_Y must be weighted against each other to specify how I is affected. Substituting equations (24)–(26) into (20),

$$\hat{I} = \frac{c(1-\alpha)}{\alpha} \hat{K}_s. \tag{27}$$

Even though the equilibrium rental rate on capital in the service sector declines, the increase in wages and in the industrial rental rate are large enough to leave a net positive balance on national income. Note that, were services to be perfect substitutes — so that specialization had no relevance in production — then a small capital flow into the service sector would have no impact on national income (when $\alpha = 1, I$ is unaffected by K_s). In our model, though, α is generally positive, meaning that there are increasing returns due to specialization. In this case, direct foreign investment in the service sector acts to create a positive externality on nationals. By allowing new services to enter the market, the increased capital stock results in a greater number of specialized services that augments industrial productivity. It is this improvement in productivity that translates into an increment in the income of nationals.

It should be clear, though, that the market imperfection associated with monopolistic competition (the gap between price and marginal cost in the service sector) is behind the externality generated in the present model (without distortions, there would be no net welfare effects). Capital in the service sector is undervalued, that is, the rental rate on capital is below the marginal contribution of capital to final output. This undervaluation of capital means that direct investment augments output by a greater amount than it is paid, which underlies our earlier conclusion to the effect that capital inflows into the service sector are welfare-improving.

In contrast to the positive effect of foreign capital in services, direct foreign investment in industry has no impact on national income. That is:

$$\frac{\hat{I}}{\hat{K}_Y} = 0. \tag{28}$$

This can be obtained by differentiating equations (21), (22) and (23) and substituting into equation (20). The explanation for this result is that foreign capital inflows into manufacturing do not alter the number of services, which are determined by fixed capital requirements and the supply of capital to the service sector. As a result, there are no external effects and no net gain in national welfare.

15.5   Conclusions

The recent policy shifts in the European Community (EC) associated with the Europe 1992 project are leading to increased liberalization of direct foreign investment flows into the service sector of member countries. In this paper we have built a model of endogenous specialization and external economies of scale to examine the impact of foreign capital flowing into the producer services sector of a recipient economy. Traditionally, this issue has been examined within the context of the linkages existing between services and industry. We find that direct foreign investment in the business services sector stimulates specialization and raises the productivity of the industry that uses them. This effect, however, does not emerge in a perfectly-competitive environment even when there are significant linkages between services and manufacturing. The crucial factor is the existence of distortions or externalities that induce positive welfare effects. When the service sector is characterized by monopolistic competition, an inflow of capital specifically into that sector has positive impact on national welfare.

The traditional result in trade theory is that, in the absence of distortions, a small foreign capital inflow in the presence of constant returns to scale does not affect national welfare in the recipient country. In the present model, however, capital flows into the service sector generate positive effects on national welfare by means of their stimulus to entry and increased specialization in producer services. The resulting increase in industrial productivity acts as an external effect on nationals, who benefit from the use of the more specialized services. The magnitude of these gains depends on the importance of services in production and the degree to which increased specialization in services augments industrial productivity. Empirical evidence of increasing returns in manufacturing is growing and, therefore, the effects described in this paper may be quite real. Given that, historically, capital inflows into services have been severely restricted within the EC, one can expect the liberalization under 1992 to be highly significant.[9]

On the other hand, the gains yielded by foreign capital inflows in the presence of increasing returns due to specialization do not operate in the present model if the foreign capital flows into the industrial sector and none into services. So long as the supply of services remains constrained by the availability of capital in that sector, foreign investment in manufacturing will not augment domestic service-sector specialization and will lack the external effects which act to increase national welfare.

Notes:

[1] See Golembe and Holland (1990), and Walter and Smith (1990).

[2] See Giovannini and Mayer (1991).

[3] Exceptions are the recent works of Jones and Kierzkowski (1990) and Francois (1990a, 1990b).

[4] See Begg (1990).

[5] Our emphasis on the role of nontraded producer services makes our model differ from those by Markusen (1989) and Francois (1990a, 1990b), who are more interested in international trade in services.

[6] As Kravis and Lipsey (1988, p.2.) have noted: "services are defined by the fact that production and consumption take place simultaneously... in most cases either the producers have moved to the point of consumption or the consumers have moved to the location of production, but the transaction itself takes place within one country. There are some exceptions, in which a service, such as telecommunications, reinsurance, or some banking activities, is produced in one country and simultaneously consumed in another country, but these are not a large part of service production or trade."

[7] The assumptions made are that each producer acts in a Cournot–Nash fashion in conjecturing that other firms in the sector will not change their output in response to changes in the firm's own price. In addition, it is assumed that that there is a large enough number of firms in the market such that the influence of each firm on the total output of the sector is insignificant.

[8] The exact expressions for W_o, r_{os} and r_{oY} are:

$$W_o = aP_Y \left[\frac{a}{a+c\alpha}\right]^{a-1} \left[\frac{c\alpha}{\beta(a+c\alpha)}\right]^c [1/\mu]^{c(1-\alpha)/\alpha} > 0$$

$$r_{oY} = bP_Y \left[\frac{a}{a+c\alpha}\right]^{a} \left[\frac{c\alpha}{\beta(a+c\alpha)}\right]^c [1/\mu]^{c(1-\alpha)/\alpha} > 0$$

$$r_{oS} = a\left[\frac{c(1-\alpha)}{a+c\alpha}\right] P_Y \left[\frac{a}{a+c\alpha}\right]^{a-1} \left[\frac{c\alpha}{\beta(a+c\alpha)}\right]^c [1/\mu]^{c(1-\alpha)/\alpha} > 0$$

[9] See Caballero and Lyons (1990 and 1991).

References

Begg, I., "The Regional Consequences of Completion of the EC Internal Market for Financial Services: An Overview and a Case Study of Scotland," *International Economic Journal*, Spring 1992.

Bhagwati, J. N. and Srinivasan, T. N., *Lectures in International Trade*, Cambridge: MIT Press, 1983.

Caballero, R. J. and Lyons, R. K., "Internal Versus External Economies in European Manufacturing," *European Economic Review*, 34, 1990, 805–30.

———, "External Effects and Europe's Integration," in L. Alan Winters and A. Venables, eds. *European Integration: Trade and Industry*, Cambridge: Cambridge University Press, 1991, 34–51.

Choksi, A. and Papageorgiou, D. eds., *Economic Liberalization in Developing Countries*, Oxford: Basil Blackwell, 1986.

Dixit, A. K., and Stiglitz, J., "Monopolistic Competition and Optimum Product Diversity," *American Economic Review*, 67, 1977, 297–308.

Ethier, W. "National and International Returns to Scale in the Modern Theory of International Trade," *American Economic Review*, 72, 1982, 389–405.

Francois, J. F., "Producer Services, Scale and the Division of Labor," *Oxford Economic Papers*, 80, 1990, 715–29.

———, "Trade in Producer Services and Returns Due to Specialization under Monopolistic Competition," *Canadian Journal of Economics*, 23, 1990, 109–24.

Giovannini, A. and Hines, J., "Capital Flight and Tax Competition: Are There Viable Solutions to Both Problems?," in A. Giovannini and C. Mayer, eds., *European Financial Integration*, Cambridge: Cambridge University Press, 1991.

Golembe, C. and Holland, D. S., "Banking and Securities," in G. C. Hufbauer, ed., *Europe 1992: An American Perspective*, Washington, D.C.: The Brookings Institution, 1990, 65–118.

Grossman, G. and Helpman, E., "Comparative Advantage and Long-Run Growth," *American Economic Review*, 80, 1990, 796–815.

Helpman, E. and Krugman, P., *Market Structure and Foreign Trade: Increasing Returns, Imperfect Competition and the International Economy*, MIT Press, Cambridge, 1985.

Hirschman, Albert O., *The Strategy of Economic Development*, New Haven: Yale University Press, 1958.

Jones, R. W. and Kierzkowski, H. "The Role of Services in Production and International Trade: A Theoretical Framework," in R. W. Jones and A. O. Krueger, eds., *The Political Economy of International Trade: Essays in Honor of Robert E. Baldwin*, Cambridge: Blackwell, 1990, 31–48.

Kravis, I., Heston A. W., and Summers, R., "The Share of Services in Economic Growth," in F. Gerard Adams and B. Hickman, eds., *Global Econometrics: Essays in Honor of Lawrence Klein*, Cambridge: MIT Press, 1989, 188–219.

Kravis, I. and Lipsey, R., "Production and Trade in Services by U.S. Multinational Firms," National Bureau of Economic Research, Working Paper No. 2615, 1988.

MacDougall, G. D. A., "The Benefits and Costs of Private Investment from Abroad: A Theoretical Approach," *Economic Record*, 36, 1960, 13–35.

Markusen, J., "Trade in Producer Services and in Other Specialized Intermediate Inputs," *American Economic Review*, 79, 1989, 85–95.

Rivera-Batiz, F. L., "Increasing Returns, Monopolistic Competition, and Agglomeration Economies in Consumption and Production," *Regional Science and Urban Economics*, 18, 1988, 125–153.

_____ and Rivera-Batiz, L. A., "The Effects of Direct Foreign Investment in the Presence of Increasing Returns Due to Specialization," *Journal of Development Economics*, 34, 1990, 287–307.

_____ and Romer, P. M., "International Trade with Endogenous Technological Change," *European Economic Review*, 35, 1991, 531–548.

Romer, P. M., "Growth Based on Increasing Returns Due to Specialization," *American Economic Review*, 77, 1987, 56–62.

_____, "Endogenous Technological Change," *Journal of Political Economy*, 98, 1990, S71–S102.

Scitovsky, T., "Two Concepts of External Economies," *Journal of Political Economy*, 62, 1954, 143–151.

Walter, I. and Smith, R., *Investment Banking in Europe: Restructuring for the 1990s*, New York: Blackwell, 1954.

Printed in the United States
By Bookmasters